MW01629797

HANDBAGS

A Love Story

LEGENDARY DESIGNS FROM
AZZEDINE ALAÏA TO YVES SAINT LAURENT

HANDBAGS
A Love Story

MONICA BOTKIER

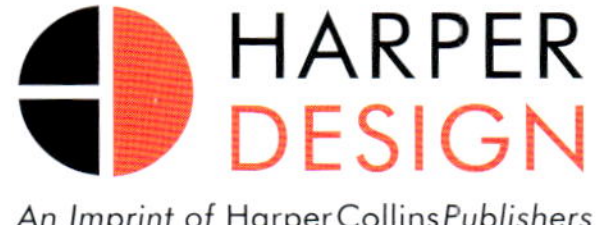

An Imprint of HarperCollinsPublishers

TO MISHA AND ROSA BOTKIER

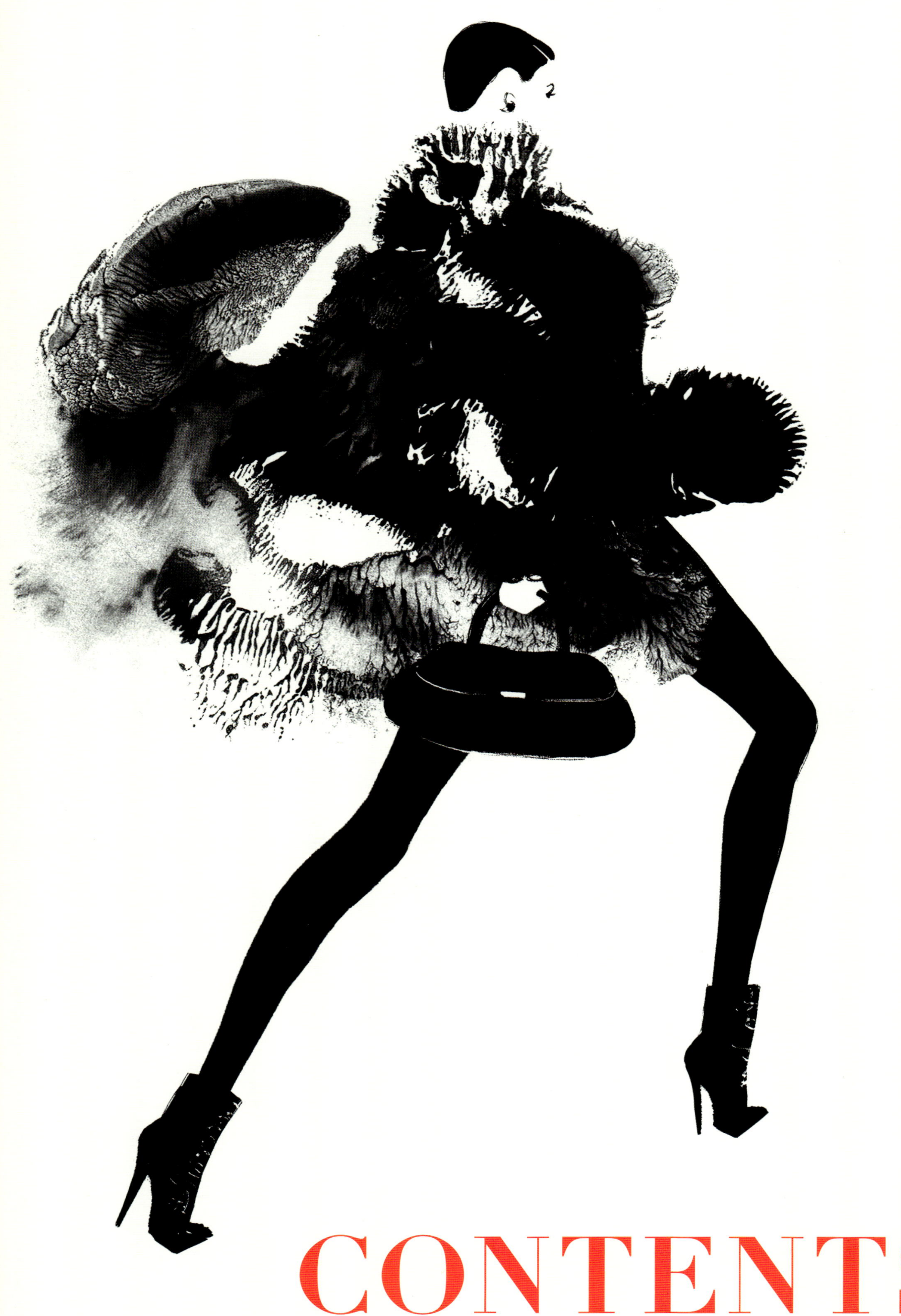

CONTENTS

INTRODUCTION 8

THE BAGS 14

ACKNOWLEDGMENTS 226

SELECT BIBLIOGRAPHY 228

PHOTOGRAPHY AND
ILLUSTRATION CREDITS 236

INTRODUCTION

I remember the first time I fell in love . . . with a bag. It was locked away inside a glass tower at Bergdorf Goodman on the main floor. I strolled through, as I usually do every time the seasons and the collections change, and noticed this buttery soft brown hobo with impeccable stitching, a confident slouch, and the most alluring antique-like horn handle attached by simple rings on each side. It was everything I wanted to be: sophisticated, well traveled, exotic. That bag represented all my dreams. I had to have it. The bag was Yves Saint Laurent's Mombasa, designed by the sexiest of designers, Tom Ford. I went to visit it every day for a week until I finally convinced myself that buying it was more important than paying the rent.

Once I was the proud owner of my first designer bag, I began to notice how many other women had one. I also started to see bags for their color, size, condition, and brand. Designer bags had become my addiction, and I was inducted into a secret society that came with its own silent language spoken between members in knowing nods and glances of approval—in the streets, on the subway, at restaurants.

Men have various trophies—cars, watches—and women have bags. It's true that bags are practical—they protect our belongings and carry us through the day—but they also reveal taste, power, and status. A gorgeous bag signals to other women what tribe we belong to. Handbags, whether pristine and pricey or worn with character, project who we are and, more often, who we want to be.

After my initial purchase, I wound up adding several more beauties to my stable. I was seduced and enticed by material, stitching, hardware, construction, and silhouette—even zipper teeth! The bags infused luxury into my daily routine, made my heart skip a beat every time I carried them. Often, a woman will catch my eye on the street because of her hair or her clothes or her beauty, but usually it's because of her handbag. "Where did she get it?" I wonder. Followed by: "I want it, I need it."

So, realizing that I had a problem—I couldn't afford to plunk down four figures for each bag I wanted—I decided to beat the system. As a fashion photographer who created her own portfolios, I had already begun experimenting with leathers and had a sizable collection of swatches. And in New York you can do anything if you are resourceful. So I designed my first bag, the Trigger, in 2003 and, using the Yellow Pages, found a local manufacturer to help make it.

Slouchy, with zipper accents and tasseled pulls, that bag embodied my downtown mood at the time. Priced at $595, it became a knockout. The formula seems so simple now, affordable luxury, but back then the handbag market was very clear-cut—mass on one side, pricey on the other, and nothing in the middle. Now "approachable luxury" is a term we hear all the time in fashion and never think about twice, but to this day women still come up to me to tell me that their gateway to designer bags was a Trigger.

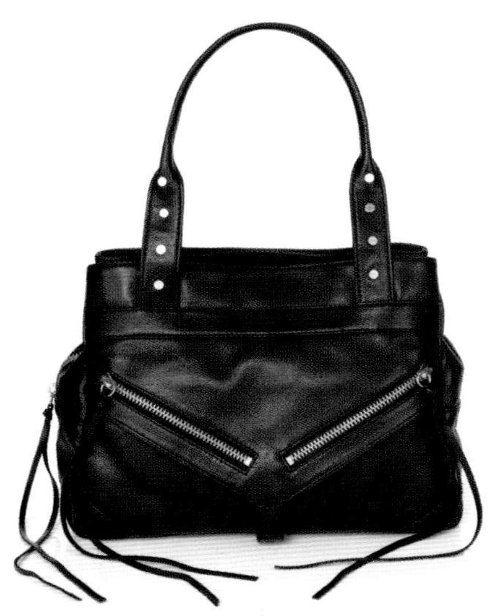

As a handbag designer, I'm always asked about the secret to making a hit bag. If only it were that simple. For starters, timing and being able to gauge the direction of the fashion current are important. In 2000, when Nicolas Ghesquière set about designing his first bag, the Lariat, for Balenciaga, he looked at what was out there and realized "that all the bags were with logos and were stiff, very heavy and kind of structured," according to *Women's Wear Daily* in 2005. "We thought, 'Why don't we do a very soft, supple and light bag that is kind of friendly and recognizable without a logo?'" Proenza Schouler's Jack McCollough and Lazaro Hernandez did the same for their PS1 satchel. "It was very much about an 'It Bag,'" explained McCollough to *Women's Wear Daily* in

THIS PAGE:
Trigger bag, Monica Botkier, Spring 2005.

2013. "Aesthetically those bags were very much covered in hardware and buckles and logos, and we kind of wanted to do something that was the antithesis . . . something more stripped down and incognito, easy wearing."

The celebrity factor is fashion's not-so-secret secret. Mary-Kate Olsen helped ignite Alexander Wang's Rocco, while the tales of Princess Diana and Lady Dior or Jane Birkin and the Hermès namesake have reached almost mythic status. The rise of tabloid culture, celebrity glossies, social media, blogs, and street-style photographers only amplifies the reach now. I'll confirm it for you here: designers do send the bags out early to editors and bold-faced names to add a little glamorous cachet early on.

Quality is a must, as is a distinguishing feature. Whether it's allover logos and decorative frippery you can spot a mile away, a quiet yet distinctive silhouette, or a particularly alluring leather, there has to be something recognizable, a calling card that announces, or even whispers, that you're part of a designer's inner circle.

There's a certain balance that hits the eye when a handbag is really well designed—it's no different than successful architecture or interior design. It captivates and draws you in. Of course, there's a certain mystery involved, too. "Trying to do an It Bag is like doing market research or studies," Marc Jacobs told *W* in 2005. "You can try, but I think you just have to do your own thing. Ultimately, it's the women who decide whether it's 'It' or it's not."

What matters is exclusivity and supply versus demand. It's simply human nature to want what you can't have. Brands will cap the number of bags they produce each season to avoid oversaturation and stoke the appetite. I remember being advised to retire the Trigger. There are waiting lists—some real, others manufactured—that stir up the urgency to buy. The Hermès wait list is legendary—up to six years, according to a 2015 *Fortune* report.

Handbags: A Love Story isn't a history of handbags—there are plenty of great reads out there that trace the lineage, dating back to the 1790s, when women began wearing gauzy Empire dresses and the drawstring purses they previously tied to their waist went solo in the hands. This book is about the handbag as a modern phenomenon that exists in the swirl of desire, style, and aspiration as well as celebrity, marketing, and social-media cachet. Every bag featured here is a fashion and cultural *happening*, winnowed down from the past twenty-five or so years. But before eagle-eyed observers start quibbling about dates, the earlier styles, such as Chanel's 2.55 from the 1950s, made the cut because they're still wholly relevant and ever present.

Handbags focuses on a more modern time frame because that's the era that begat the It Bag—that must-have, most-wanted fashion creation that can instantly confer and telegraph a certain status and discriminating taste. Sure, covetable high-priced bags go back to the 1950s, when the Hermès Kelly became the Kelly and Coco Chanel added gilt straps to a quilted bag, and the 1970s, when logomania had its first wave—socialite Nan Kempner's horrified response, as she told *Women's Wear Daily* in 1973: "I had all my Vuitton painted solid brown in Paris. They nearly died." But it wasn't until the 1990s, the era of luxury conglomerates, that the handbag became this intoxicating *thing* that proliferated from city to city and the It Bag notion and name were cemented. The Fendi Baguette, the Prada backpack, and the Kate Spade tote gave way to the monogram madness of Gucci, Dior, and Vuitton, which led to the Balenciaga Lariat, the Chloé Paddington, and the posse of Roxannes, Alexas, Sofias, and Zoes from Mulberry and Marc Jacobs. Between 2002 and 2007 handbag sales surged 139 percent. And that's what's *on* the record—the It Bag is a boon for counterfeiters. Meanwhile, some brands poked fun: Dooney & Bourke named its candy-colored logo bag—the one Vuitton took to court—the It Bag, while Spade, in collaboration with artist Hugo Guinness, created a canvas tote in 2006 with the word "it" scrawled in the corner.

It Bags eventually fell out of favor when "it" became a bit of a dirty word. Part of being It is the inevitable countdown to *not* being It, and countless designers began wordsmithing their way around, tossing out It for the PR-friendly "iconic" and other romanced alternatives. "I think the It Bag is the kiss of death," observed Cameron Silver, founder of the vintage store Decades, in *Harper's Bazaar* in 2008.

Yet after every article that rang the death knell for the It Bag—"Much like the popular pretty girl who always dies first in a horror film, the It Bag was a victim of its own ambition," reported the *Los Angeles Times* in 2008—another would pop up, introducing a new trend of discreet, restrained, relatively hardware- and logo-free bags that did the bumping off. And isn't that really just the same thing? As Tom Ford noted of Bottega Veneta in *The New Yorker* in 2011, "By not doing the It Bag, you do the It Bag."

The idea of It will always be there in some form or another. But nowadays, as handbags become an ever-increasing and ever-essential element of the fashion industry and as women become more educated about what's out there, there's a new freedom of choice. Anything goes, really. With the exception of a few houses, women aren't as brand-loyal anymore. You can have your allover embellishment and indulge your inner minimalist, too—all with a swap of a handbag. It's about individuality and embracing a woman's modern, multifaceted life and personality.

Handbags: A Love Story celebrates all those bags that have had the power to quicken our pulse and give us a pang of desire or jealousy when we ran our hands over the leather or slipped our fingers between the handles. Perhaps, for you, it wasn't the Mombasa but Céline's coolly minimal Trapeze. Or Valentino's Rockstud. Or one of Alexander McQueen's edgy and often bejeweled skull minaudières. Chances are, if you're reading this, you're thinking back to more than one—a 2016 report noted that women between eighteen and forty-five own an average of thirteen different bags from seven different brands.

Flip the page. It's your turn to decide. I've dug through research, polled industry friends, and interviewed experts to compile an illustrated anthology of the most influential and compelling handbags. I hope you fall in love like I did and perhaps even rediscover lost loves or learn something new about an old favorite.

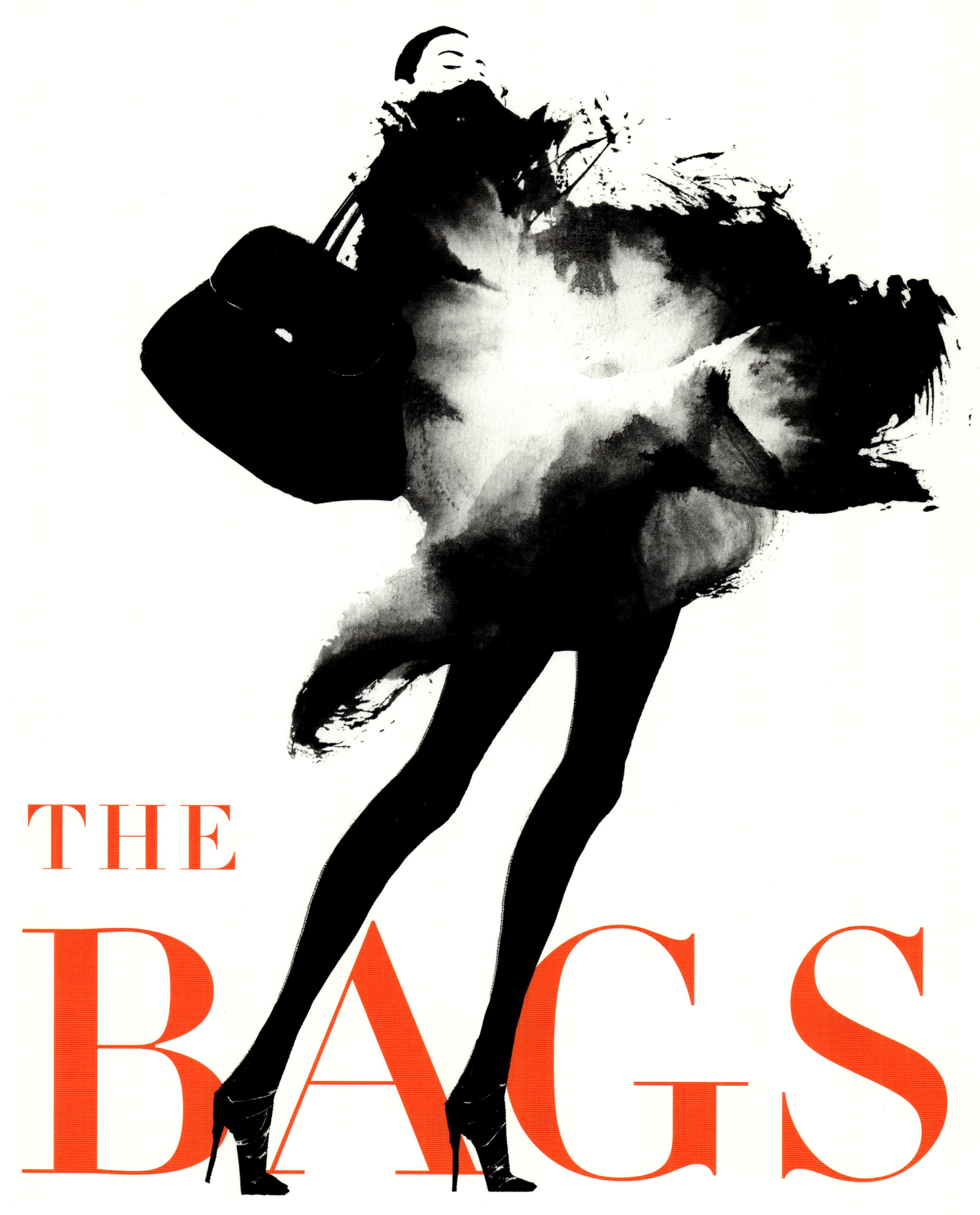
THE
BAGS

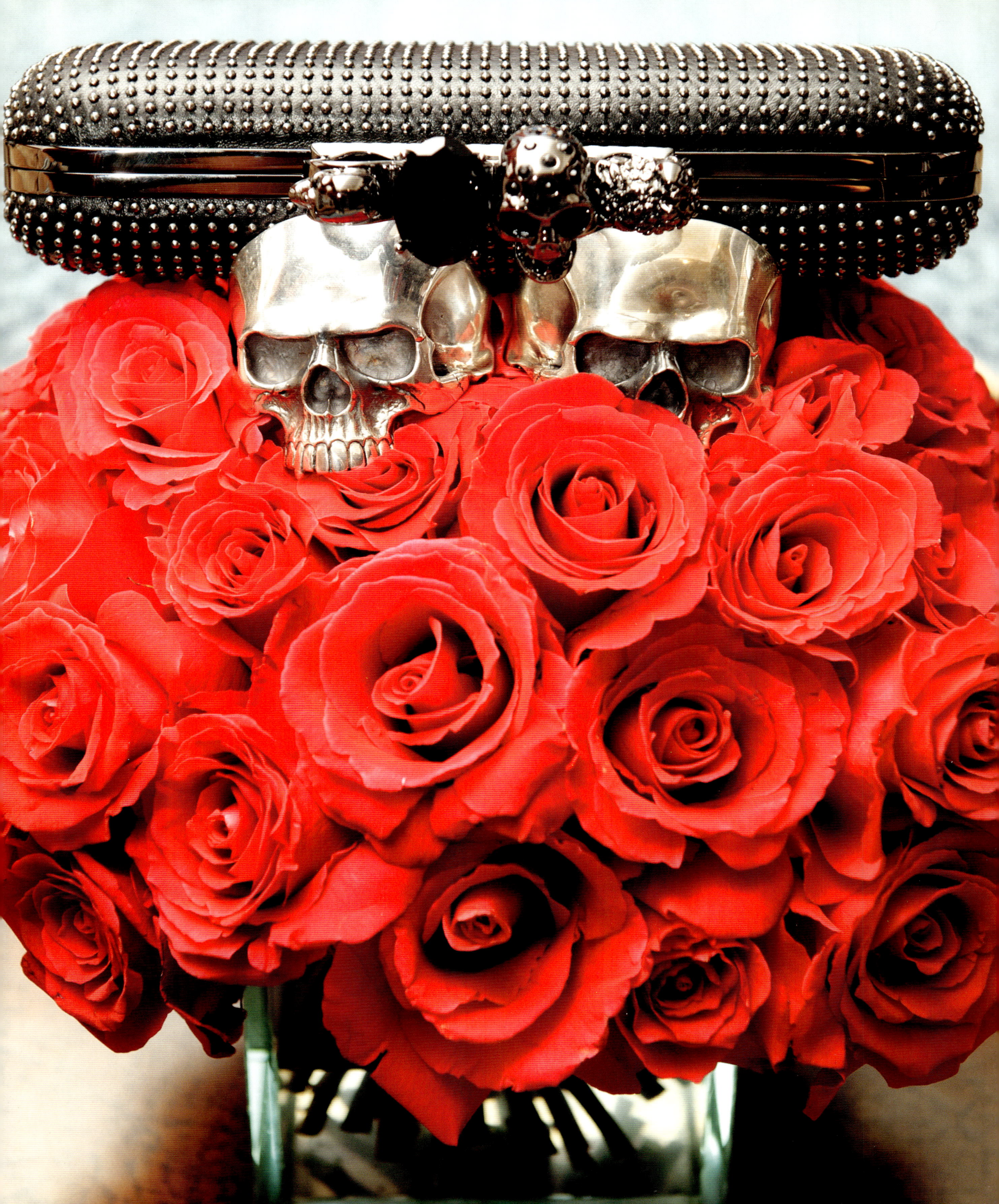

Alexander McQueen

NOVAK, 2005
SKULL CLUTCH, 2008

An Alexander McQueen runway show was a visceral experience. You were overcome by emotion, by *something*, before your mind could even register what you were seeing. Sarah Burton, who took over the label in 2010 after McQueen's death, told *ES Magazine* in 2015, "He wanted to move people. Whether you liked it or hated it, he really wanted you to feel something. That's what made those shows."

McQueen gave us some truly powerful moments—from "The Birds" (Spring 1995), his homage to Alfred Hitchcock; to his controversial "Highland Rape" collection (Fall 1995), with ripped lace dresses; to models re-creating the dance marathon, equal parts exhilaration and exhaustion, from "They Shoot Horses, Don't They?" (Spring 2004); to Kate Moss as a beautiful hologram emerging, smokelike, within a glass pyramid (Fall 2006). Even his more restrained shows hummed with a disturbing electricity. "Nicey nicey just doesn't do it for me," McQueen told the *Guardian* in 2005.

In the Fall 2005 collection, "The Man Who Knew Too Much," he resurrected Hitchcock's 1950s and 1960s ice queens Grace Kelly and Tippi Hedren with prim sheaths and hypercontrolled elegance. In another designer's hands, the collection would have been an exercise in sharp tailoring, hourglass silhouettes, and ladified sophistication. In McQueen's, there was a dark psychological undercurrent—not unlike in Hitchcock's films. In the accessories world, that collection was a milestone because it saw the introduction of his Novak handbag—named after *Vertigo*'s Kim Novak—a structured 1950s-style satchel that's a staple to this day. It also came in a limited-edition bejeweled version done with Boucheron. "I'm drawn to Kim Novak in the same way that Hitchcock was. She had an air of uptightness you wouldn't want to cross," McQueen told the *The Times* (London) in 2006.

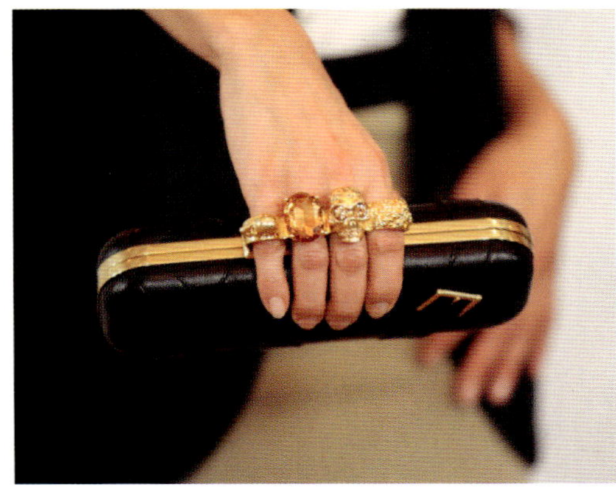

Ultimately, the sinister undertone of McQueen's take on 1950s dressing may not matter to a woman who just wants a great structured bag. But there's a reason a woman buys a bag from McQueen versus Chanel or Fendi. It telegraphs a certain edge and mysterious underpinnings; the embrace of the twisted and the macabre is part of the appeal.

OPPOSITE:
Skull knuckle box clutch, Alexander McQueen, March 2011.

RIGHT:
Skull knuckle box clutch, Alexander McQueen, August 2011.

"You've got to know the rules to break them. That's what I'm here for, to demolish the rules but to keep the tradition."

—ALEXANDER MCQUEEN, from *Alexander McQueen: Savage Beauty* by Andrew Bolton, 2011

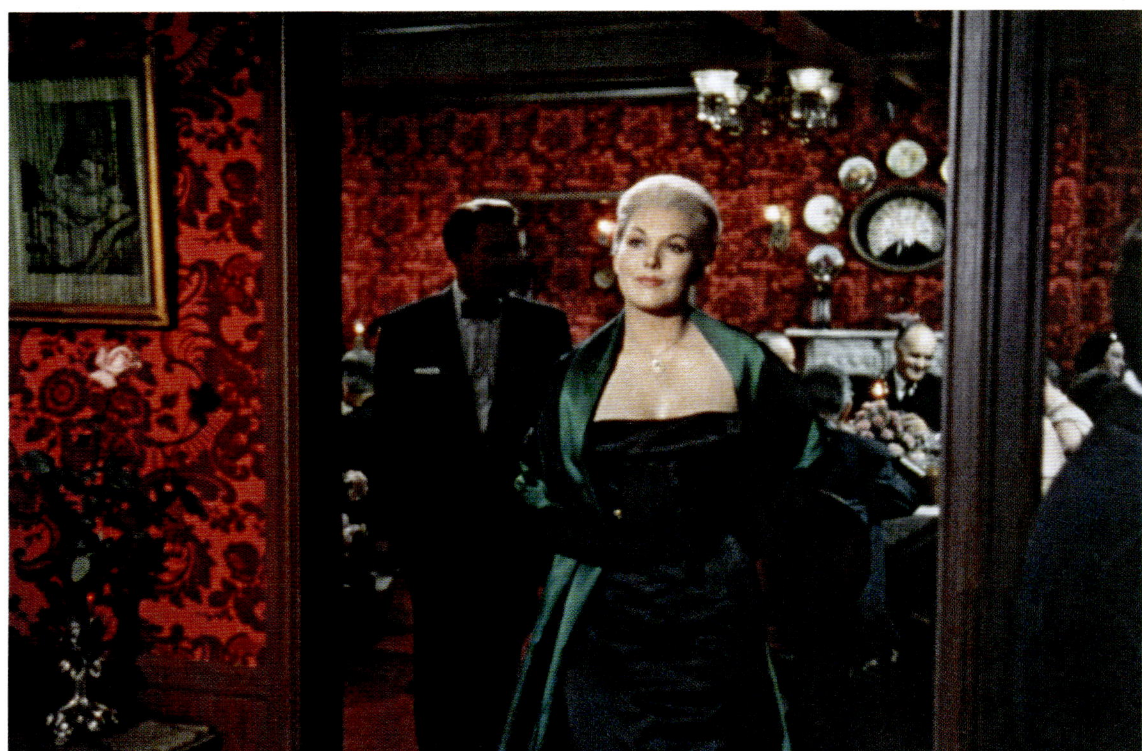

The same ethos applied to McQueen's signature skull minaudières. No other designer is as inextricably linked to that motif as he. He used that memento mori imagery as a foil to glamour, countering gorgeous lace or crystal-beaded evening bags with a skull-shaped clasp; some styles had knuckle-ring toppers. Talking about his own series of portraits of subjects holding skulls with *Women's Wear Daily* in 2011, photographer Sante D'Orazio explained, "It permits the conservative type to be a part of the fantasy of something dangerous." For McQueen, it was more than a fantasy. "I oscillate between happiness and sadness, life and death, good and evil," he told *Numéro* in December 2007.

Even when the designer was at his most romantic—and he had some gloriously romantic shows such as his Spring 2007 ready-to-wear collection, when the last model closed in a gown made from roses, petals trailing on the floor behind her—there was a tinge of darkness. "There's blood beneath every layer of skin," McQueen said in the *Observer Magazine* in 2001.

In 2011, a little more than a year after his death, New York's Metropolitan Museum of Art staged a retrospective that drew a massive crowd day after day: a record-breaking 660,000 visitors in three months. "Even if you never bother with fashion shows, go to this one," urged *The New Yorker*. The exhibition's title: *Savage Beauty*.

ABOVE:
Kim Novak in a still from *Vertigo*, 1958.

OPPOSITE:
Novak bag, Alexander McQueen, Fall/Winter 2005 ready-to-wear.

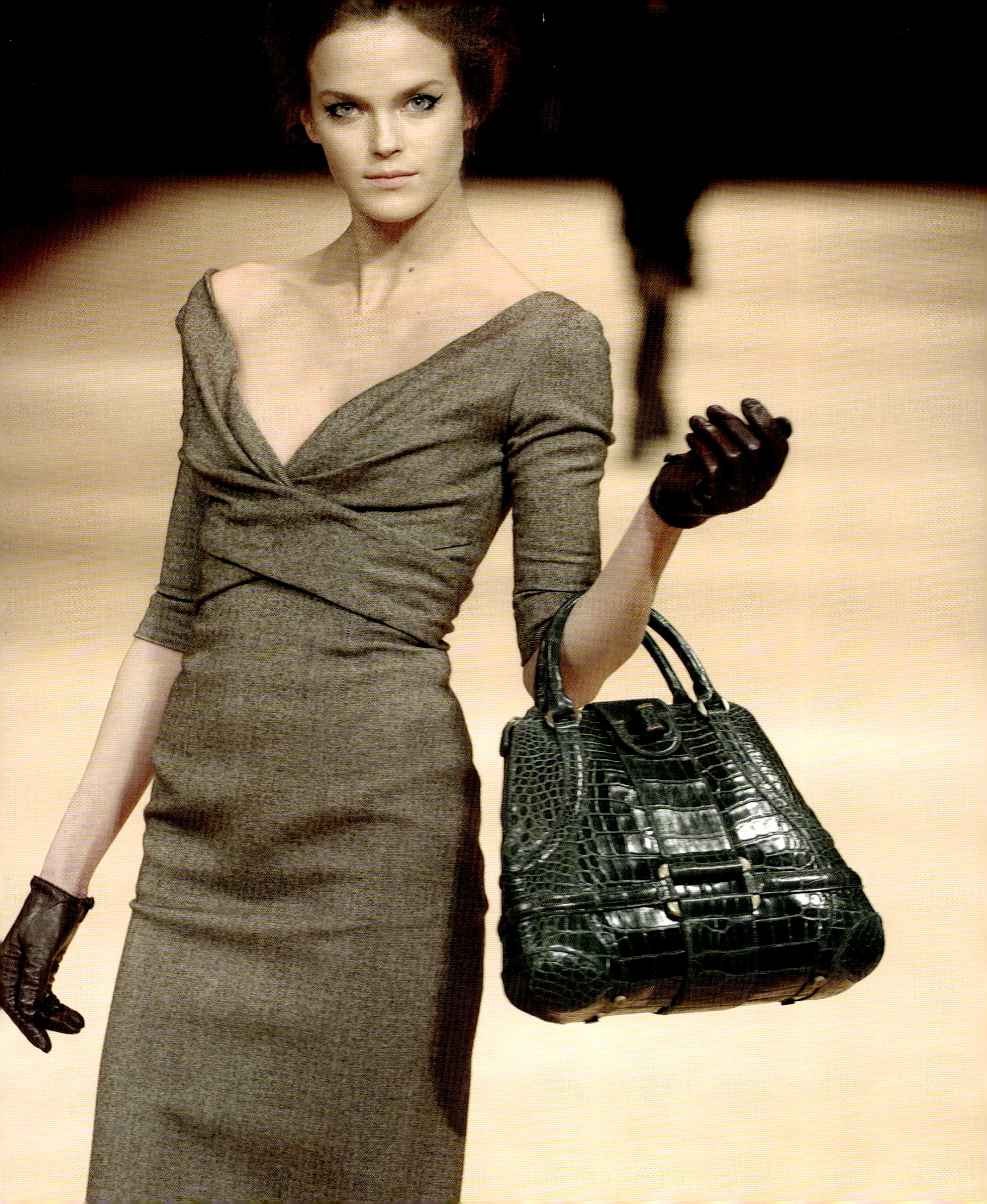

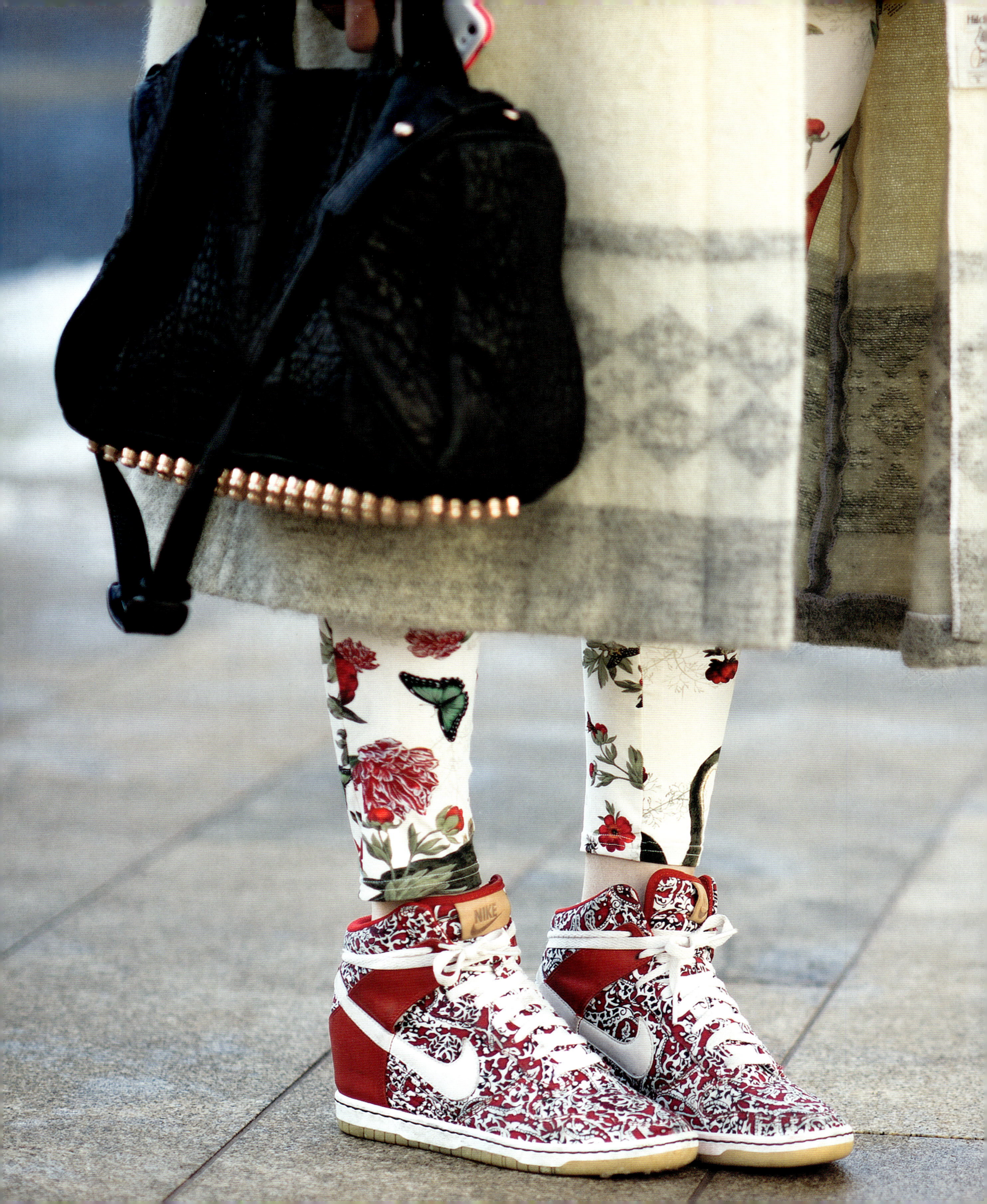
NIKE

Alexander Wang

BRENDA, 2008

ROCCO, 2009

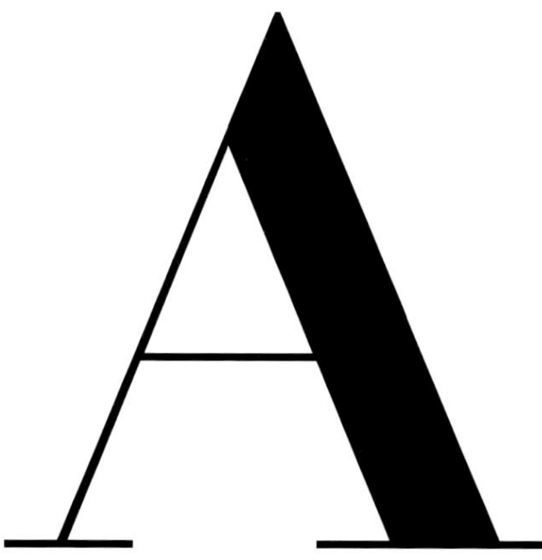

lexander Wang has been a master of subversion since he launched his line in 2004 with six oversized tomboy sweaters, including one with a colossal intarsia of a model smiling and smoking. Just shy of twenty-one when he landed on the fashion industry's radar, the kid from San Francisco, with his long, tousled hair and giddy smile, would go on to spark an entire fashion cycle in which downtown cool and street-smart savvy reigned supreme. He gave us deliberately wilted tees, sweat stains reinterpreted as lace patterns, and the model-off-duty look, like a disheveled Kate Moss just out of bed.

His accessories similarly strike just the right balance of edge and irreverence. In 2008, Wang modeled his first handbag after one of his old toiletry bags. It eventually evolved into the popular Brenda style, named for good-girl-gone-bad Brenda Walsh on the television show *90210*. Wang is eternally 1990s, with a penchant for pulling inspiration from where you least expect it, including bags modeled after *Miami Vice* and *Golden Girls* characters.

In 2009, he sent out the Rocco, a studded, slouchy leather duffel inspired by gym bags. Instead of using studs as a decorative factor, he placed them in a bag's oft-overlooked zone: the bottom. The designer once again upturned the expected, and the Rocco, with its brazenly studded underbelly, became the bag that every girl—uptown, downtown, East Coast, West Coast—had to have.

With a little help from fan Mary-Kate Olsen, the handbag managed to become an even greater cult classic than the Brenda. She was the first to be spotted carrying the Rocco and, eternally nestled in the crook of her arm with the bright gold studs on full view for the paparazzi to snap, the bag became a sensation before it even hit the stores. Since then, Wang has spun off a smaller version named, appropriately enough, Rockie.

OPPOSITE:
Rocco bag, Alexander Wang, New York City, January 2013.

PAGES 22–23:
Rocco bag *(left)*, Alexander Wang, Paris, 2014.

"What's beautiful and interesting to me is a scuffed shoe, a girl with her hair a little messed up."

—ALEXANDER WANG, *W*, July 2008

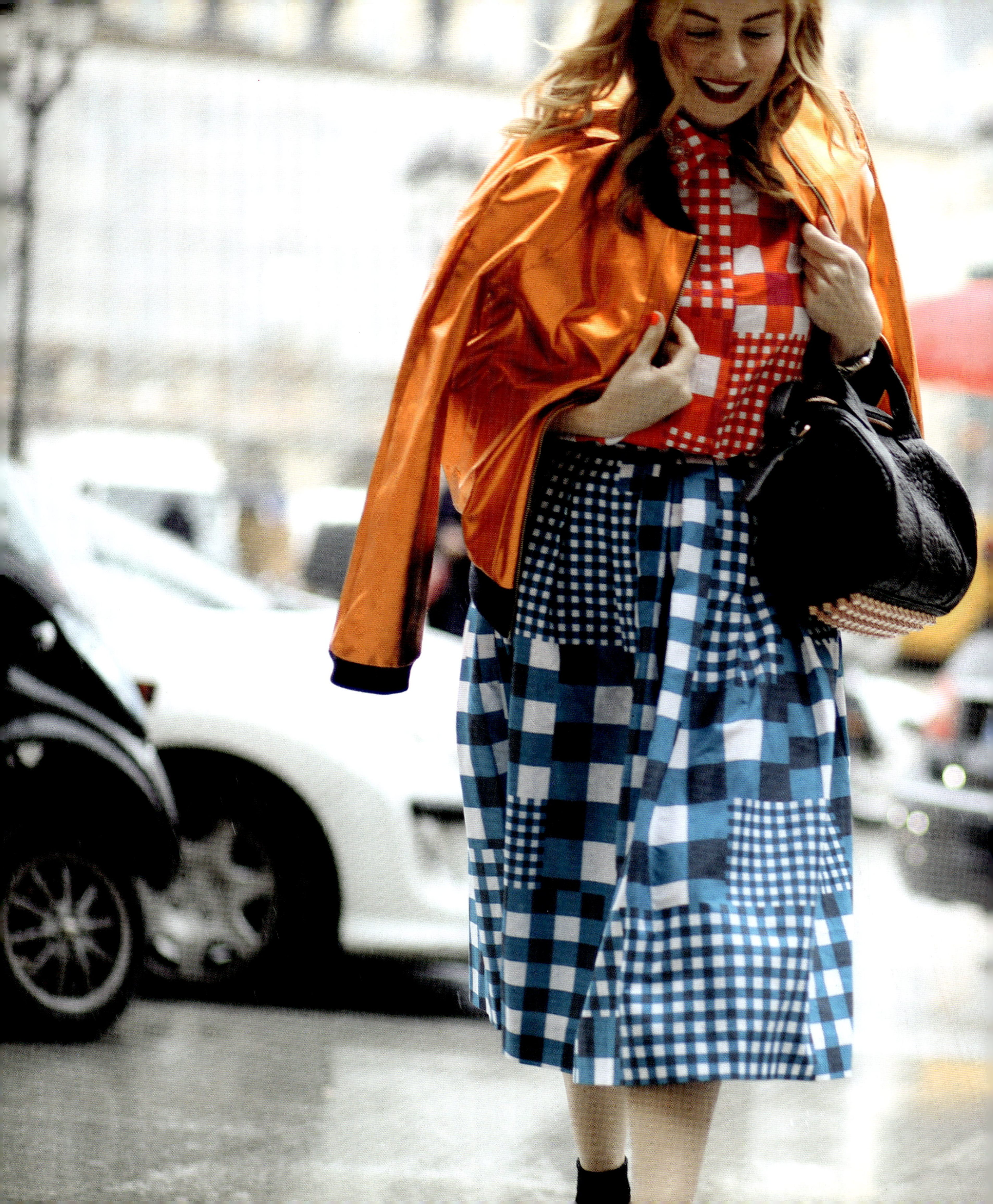

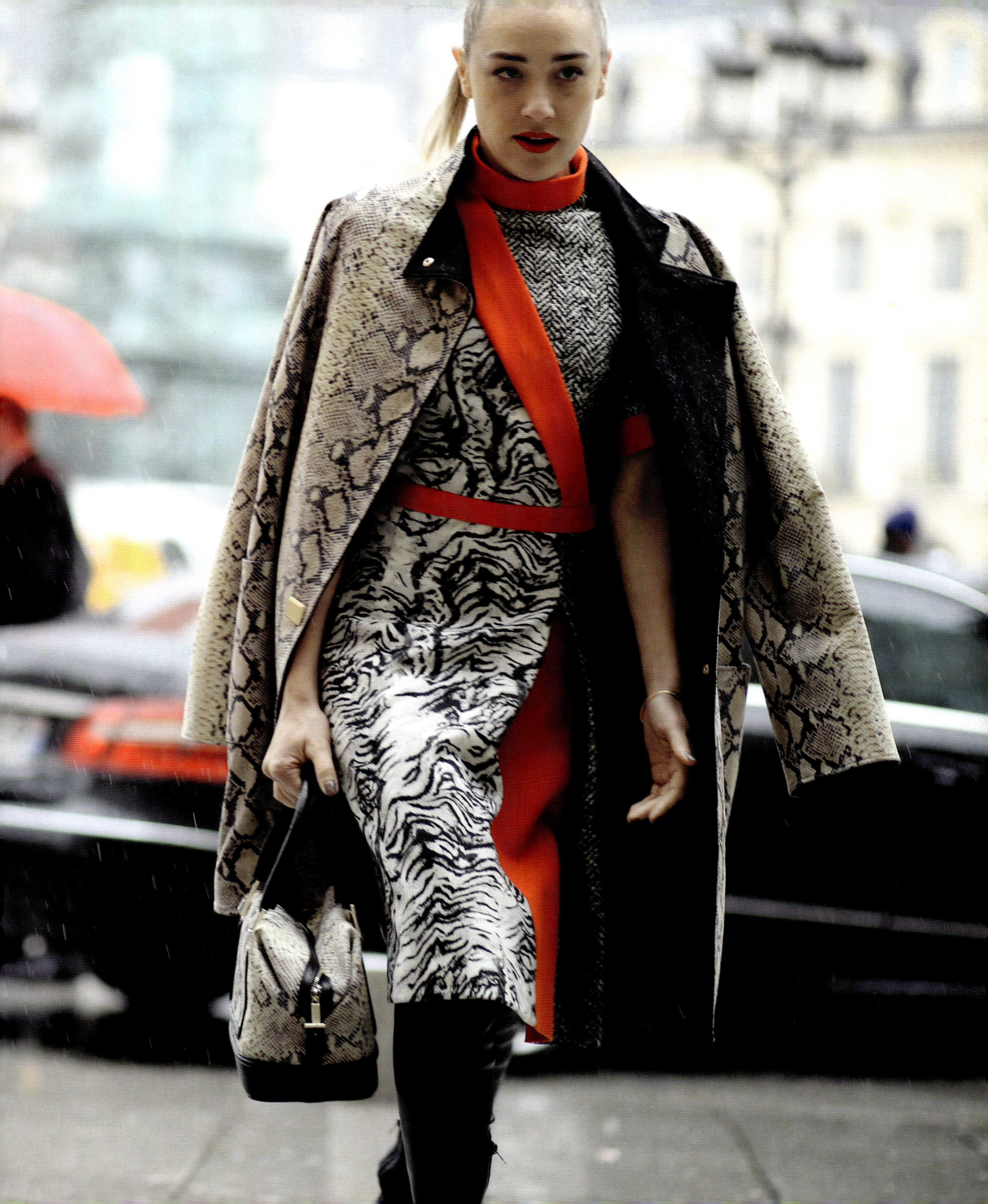

Altuzarra

GHIANDA, 2015

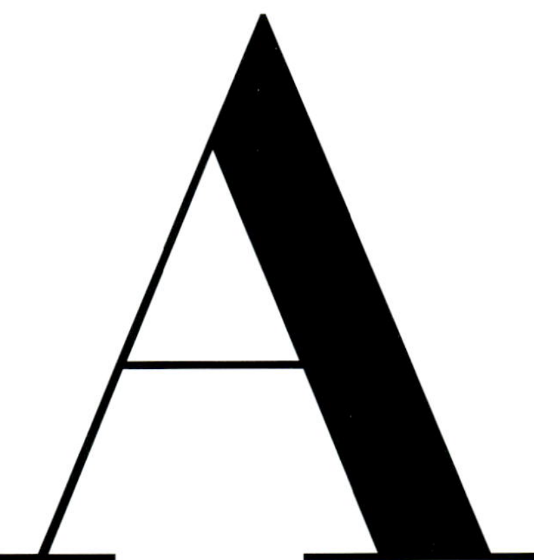

A lot of designers sell sex. Joseph Altuzarra sells sex appeal. In sartorial terms, that's an alluring skirt with a thigh-high slit—not an abbreviated mini. It's the difference between a woman, confident of her sexuality, and a girl. And, as Altuzarra has expressed again and again, he's not designing for the latter.

To understand his sensibility, you have to dig into his background—which is equal parts American (his mother) and French (his father). He's worked at companies on both sides of the Atlantic: the very American Marc Jacobs and Proenza Schouler and the distinctly French Givenchy. It's in that clash of cultures where Altuzarra, who was born in Paris, resides. The Stateside influence appears in his beautiful—and consummately wearable—sportswear, while his French side is readily apparent in his approach to women.

"I think women in France have this way of carrying themselves, this relationship with their bodies, which I find really inspiring; not necessarily wanting to correct your flaws, but wanting to highlight the things you like about yourself," Altuzarra told *Fashion Magazine* in 2013.

His debut Ghianda handbag collection from 2015, which features two styles—a smooth-leather hobo and a saddlebag, both elegantly spare and restrained in silhouette—reflects all of the above. It's a good example of a handbag that doesn't dominate a woman's personality. It's not overtly fun or rock star or even ladylike—there's a sophisticated sensuality to the design, one you can picture only a self-assured woman wearing.

The inspiration speaks to his dual heritage while playing with the idea of sexiness in a decidedly Altuzarra way. Those beautifully braided straps have their origins in the American cowboy culture, specifically bull-riding ropes and whips; the designer actually worked with a rodeo hand in New Mexico. The French half comes in the hardware, which resembles the bottom of a gold cigarette lighter. What could be more representative of *la vie Parisienne* than that?

As for the name, there's an acorn-like knot at the base of each strap that the craftspeople at the factories he uses in Italy casually dubbed *ghianda*—after the Italian word for "acorn"—during production. It stuck.

OPPOSITE: Ghianda bag, backstage at Altuzarra, Fall/Winter 2015 ready-to-wear.

PAGES 26–27: Ghianda bag, Altuzarra, New York City, September 2015.

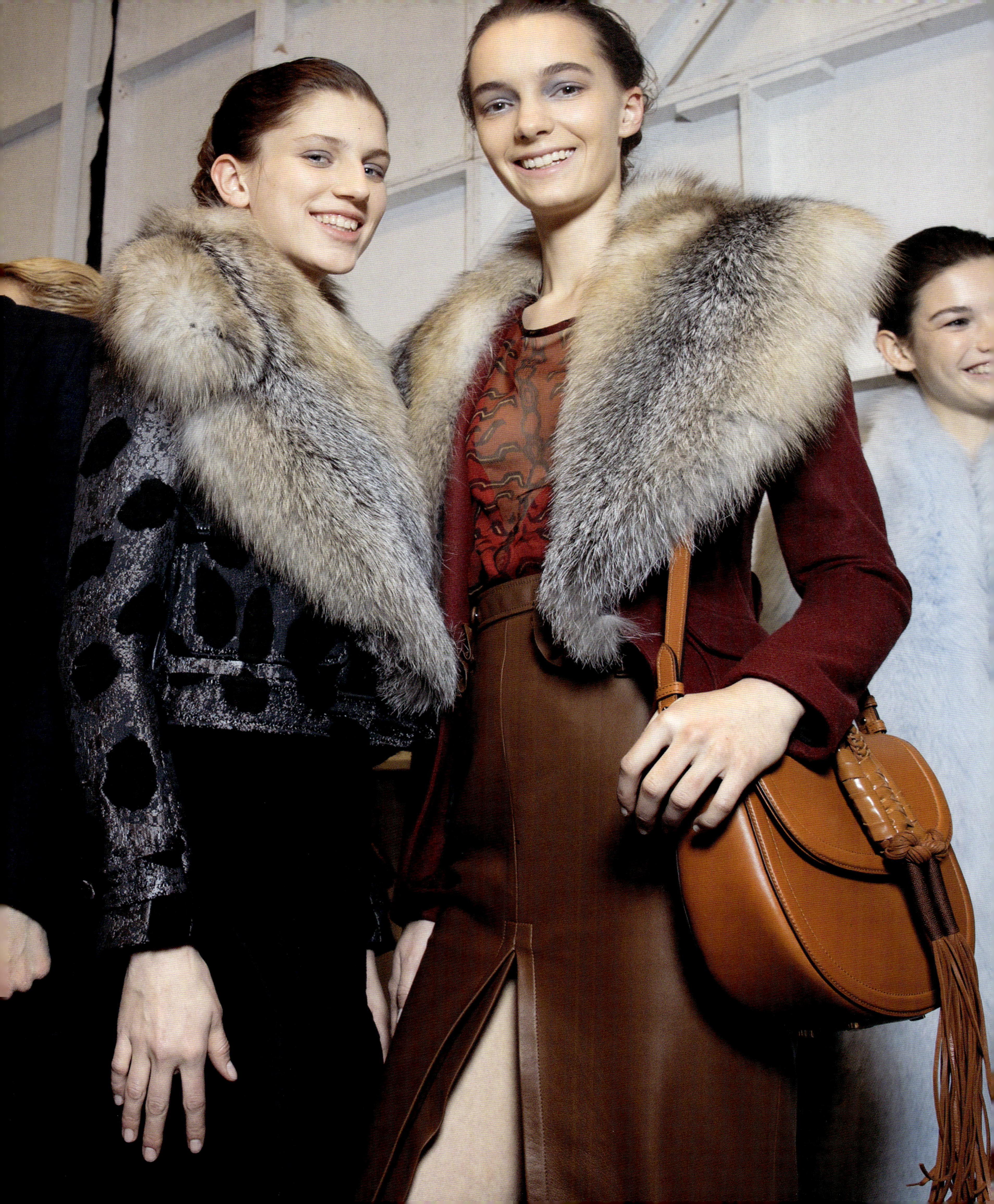

"It's the idea of tension between different elements—masculine and feminine, bourgeois and perverse—that I find interesting."

—JOSEPH ALTUZARRA, *W*, April 2013

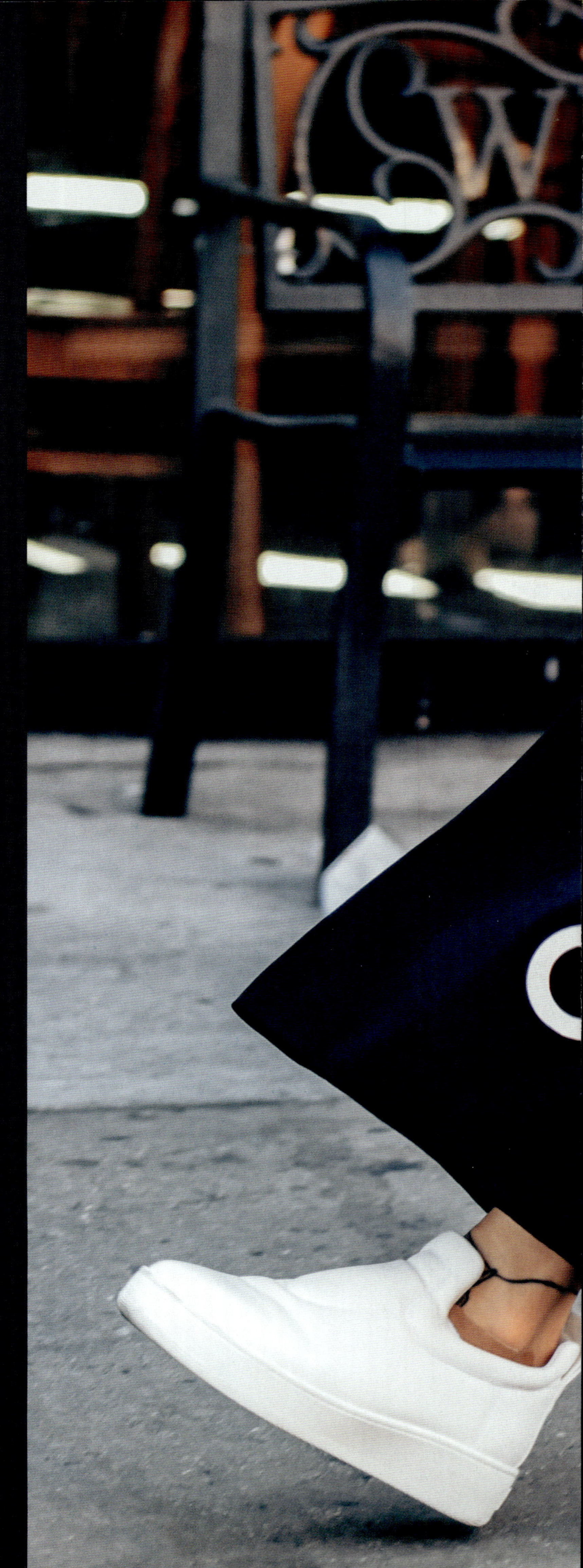

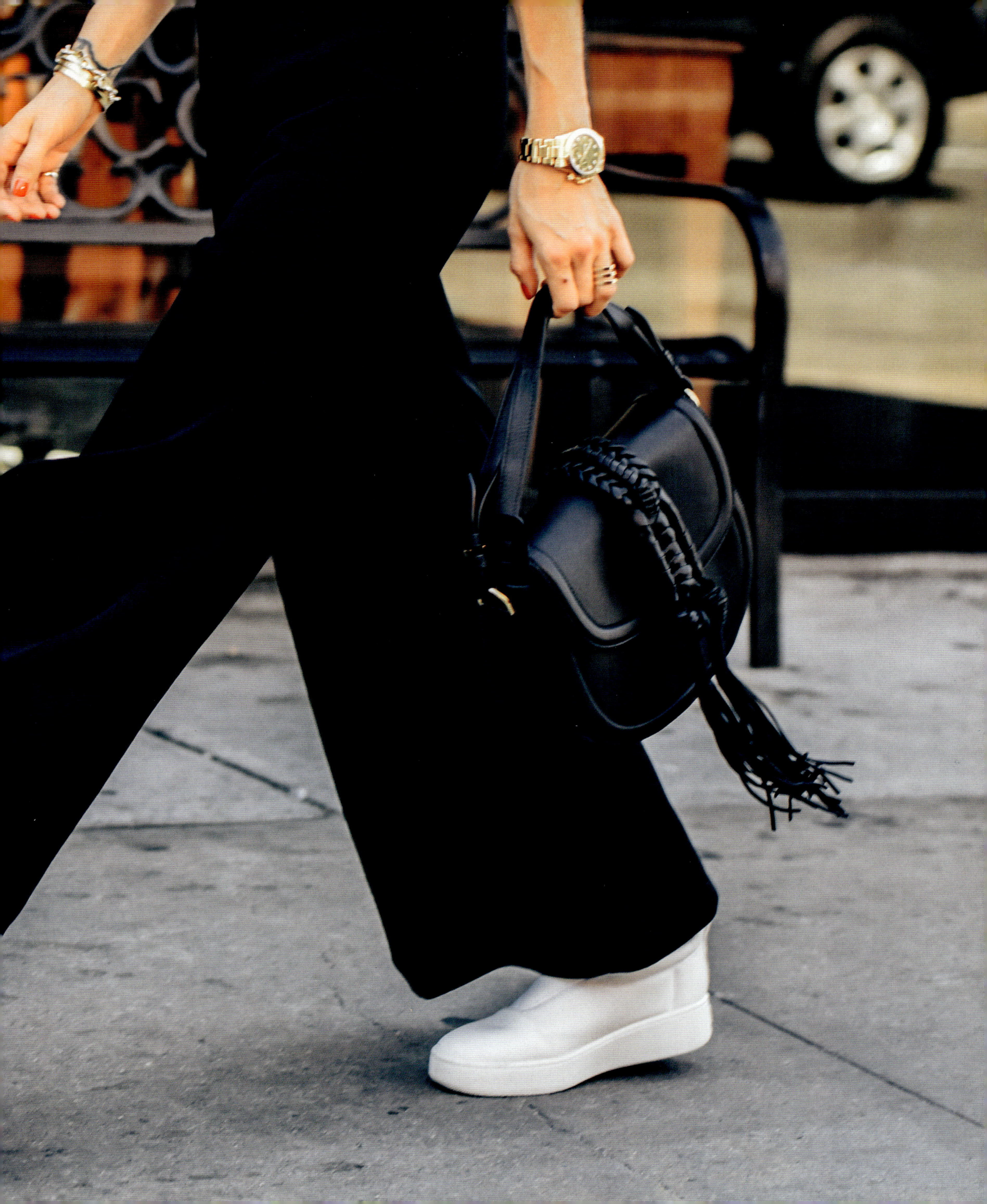

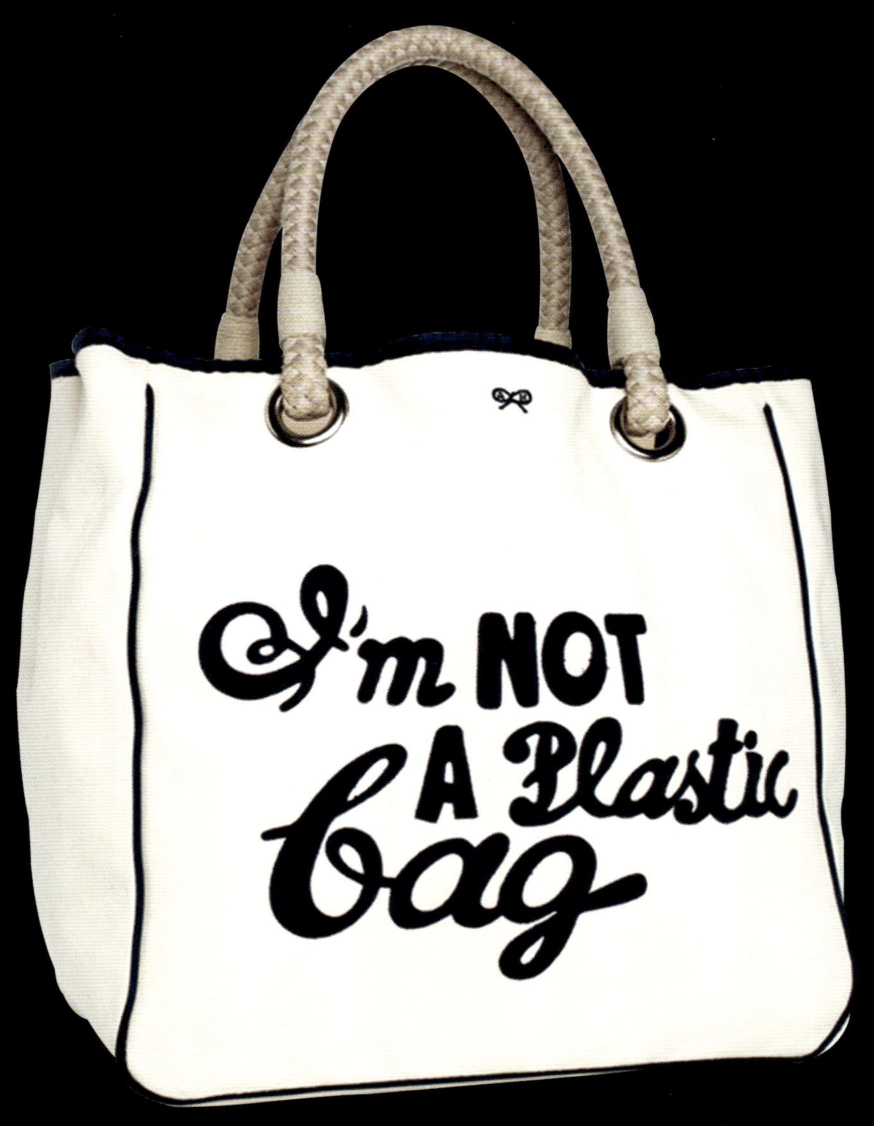

"A woman's relationship with her handbag is tribal. It's human nature."

—ANYA HINDMARCH, *Wall Street Journal*, February 7, 2013

Anya Hindmarch

I'M NOT A PLASTIC BAG, 2007

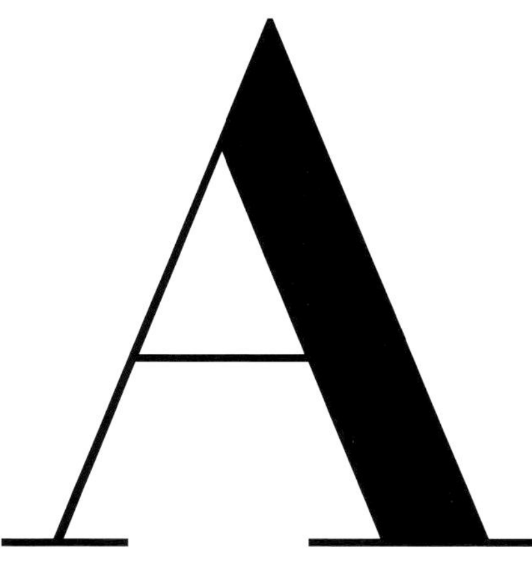

Anya Hindmarch has designed witty cereal-box clutches and minaudières shaped like a crinkled bag of crisps, and she began the trend of adding leather emoji and slogan stickers to her handbags. It's hard to believe that Hindmarch, born in Essex, England, in 1968, was inspired to begin her line because of Margaret Thatcher. "I started my business when I was 18, and I realized the difference it made having Thatcher in power," she told *Vanity Fair* in 2009. "It was the start of privatization—there was a feeling of 'Get out there, get going, be an entrepreneur.'"

Her first design was a drawstring duffel bag she discovered during a gap year in Florence that she knew she could sell back in England. Hindmarch brought it back and, with that start-up spirit, found a manufacturer and convinced *Harper's & Queen* to feature the style; she sold five hundred through the magazine.

While her company has grown, she's carved a niche with luxury leather with a jolt of humor. Her most famous design, "I'm Not a Plastic Bag," was an anomaly. Priced at a mere five pounds, the rather plain canvas tote was more about the message behind it than the design or craftsmanship. The day it debuted, eighty thousand people lined up at London's Sainsbury's supermarket to grab one, New Yorkers waited through the night outside Whole Foods before the doors opened at 8:00 A.M., and in Taiwan there was a stampede, sending thirty people to the hospital.

In its stance against wasteful consumption, the tote came to represent the environmental movement, appearing in countless articles alongside plastic bottles and climate change. This simple strap tote, done in collaboration with the nonprofit We Are What We Do and emblazoned with the words "I'm Not a Plastic Bag," became an object of pride for women who wanted to join in on the ecology battle cry or at least look the part.

There were, however, detractors. It didn't go unnoticed that this anti-plastic-bag symbol came wrapped in its own plastic bag when you bought it or that it was made in China and with non-sustainable materials. Hindmarch, whose father worked in plastics, gamely weathered the backlash. "I make no bones about the fact that I'm below par on the eco-front," she admitted to *Vogue* in 2007. "I drive, I have five kids and I fly. But I also go to the supermarket and see how plastic bags are so unnecessary, ugly and wasteful. You can tax bags, or work to make them more recyclable, but neither is the perfect solution. The other way is to change behavior. To make it cool to shop with your own bag. My project is a billboard for that."

OPPOSITE:
I'm Not a Plastic Bag, Anya Hindmarch, 2007.

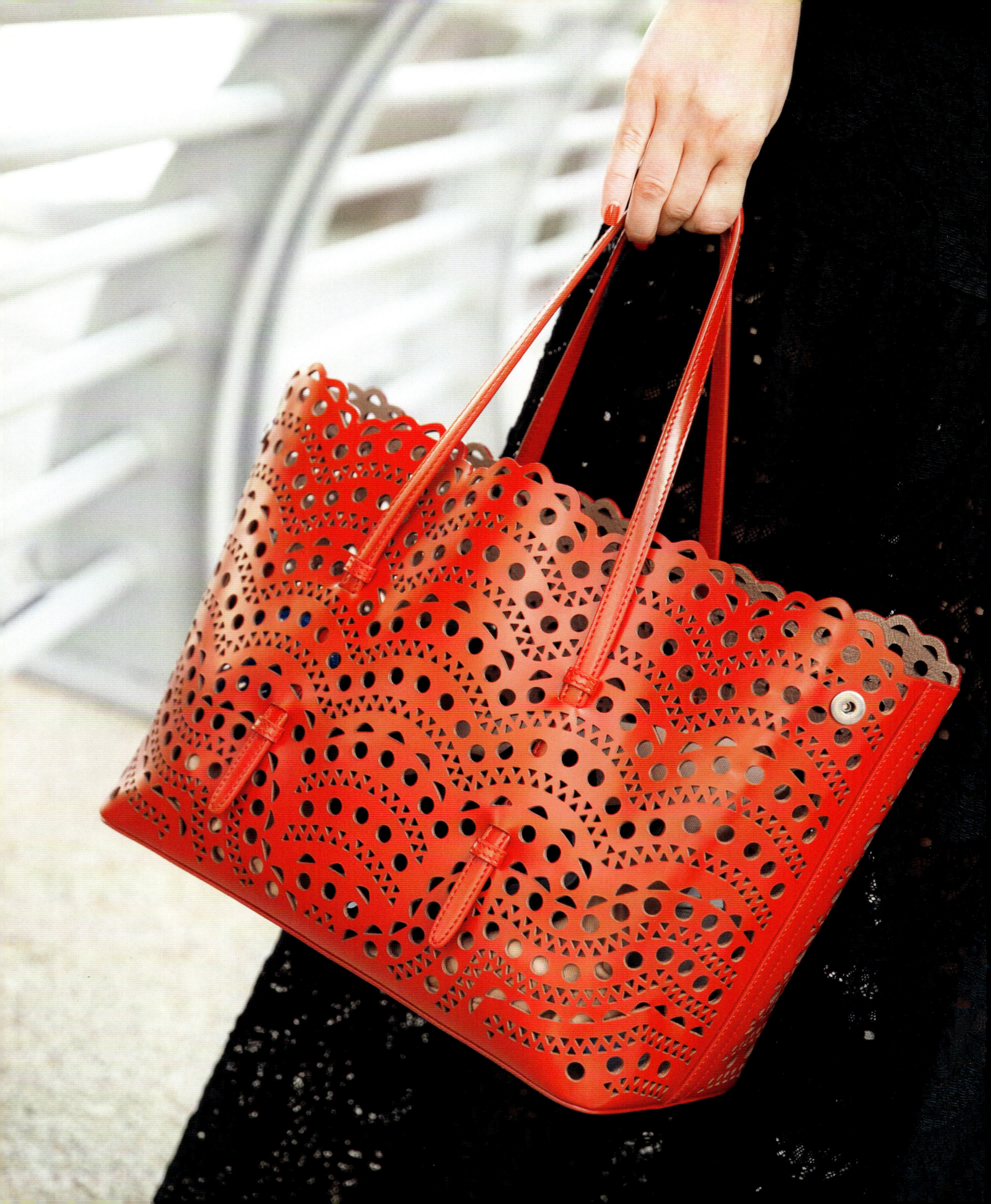

Azzedine Alaïa

VIENNE, 2000

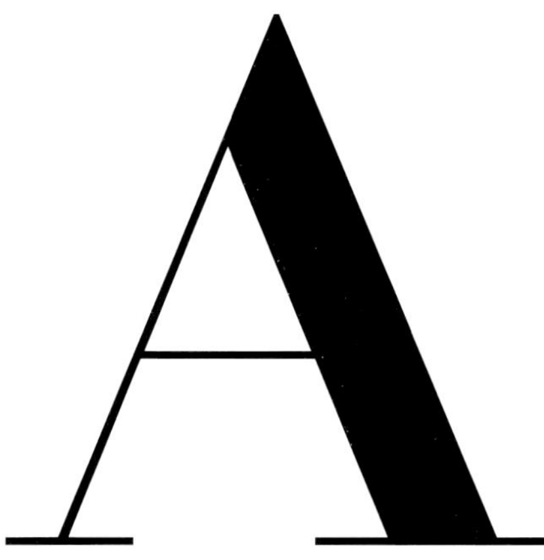

zzedine Alaïa, whose designs are known for skintight curves and invigorating sex appeal, is a curious figure in the annals of fashion. From the moment he arrived in Paris from his native Tunisia in 1957 until today, Alaïa has continued to fascinate. How many other designers still craft each and every garment by hand or refuse to play by the fashion calendar's rules, presenting when he wants, without fanfare, in his atelier? "He's so authentic in the way he works," designer Alber Elbaz told *Women's Wear Daily* in 2016. "He's not part of the system—he's created a system of his own." Few others, with the exception of Rei Kawakubo and Karl Lagerfeld, elicit the sort of obsessive reverence and superlatives that he does. "This man is the most unique designer . . . in . . . the . . . world," Naomi Campbell told *Harper's Bazaar* in 2013.

"Thanks to his dresses," trilled Mathilde de Rothschild to *Vanity Fair* in 2012, "a lady already has 50 percent of her work done for her, whether her aim is to do business or to seduce a man."

And Tina Turner raved to *Vogue* in 1990, "Azzedine sews for WOMAN! I'm not talking tits and ass, I mean he gives you the very best line you can get out of your body."

Like his clothes, Alaïa's bags possess a strong physical structure and project a bold femininity. They never slouch or sag. The designer studied sculpture at the local École des Beaux-Arts, in Tunis, and his designs reflect his interest in the field. The Vienne captures that love of precision and structure—a virtuoso display of craftsmanship, with meticulous allover laser cutting that harks back to his love of perforation, seen in his early leather corsetry and signature eyelet patterns. In fact, one of the earliest designs to gain him international recognition was a 1981 black leather tunic covered in silver grommets.

As far as luxury laser-cut bags go, there is nothing on a par with the Vienne. The lacelike markings are extraordinary in their detailed craftsmanship and are reminiscent of the intricate, ornamental, geometric patterns so prevalent in Tunisian tilework and decor. In order to emphasize its construction, the bag is not lined. Its interior is as exemplary as its exterior, reflecting the fine design for which Alaïa is renowned as well as his expert engineering that always has a handcrafted feel. For Alaïa, craftsmanship is about the touch.

OPPOSITE:
Vienne tote, Azzedine Alaïa, Dubai, April 2015.

PAGE 32:
Christy Turlington *(left)* and Naomi Campbell on the runway at Azzedine Alaïa, Fall 1991.

PAGE 33:
Azzedine Alaïa, *Madame Figaro*, September 2016.

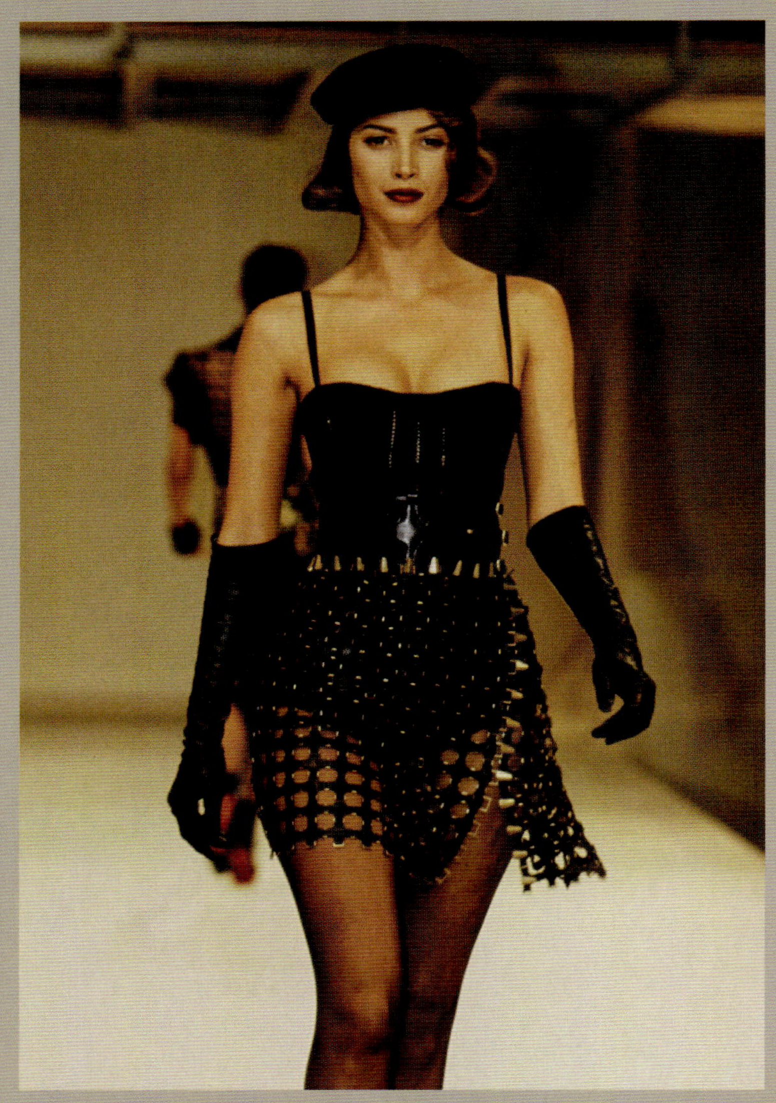

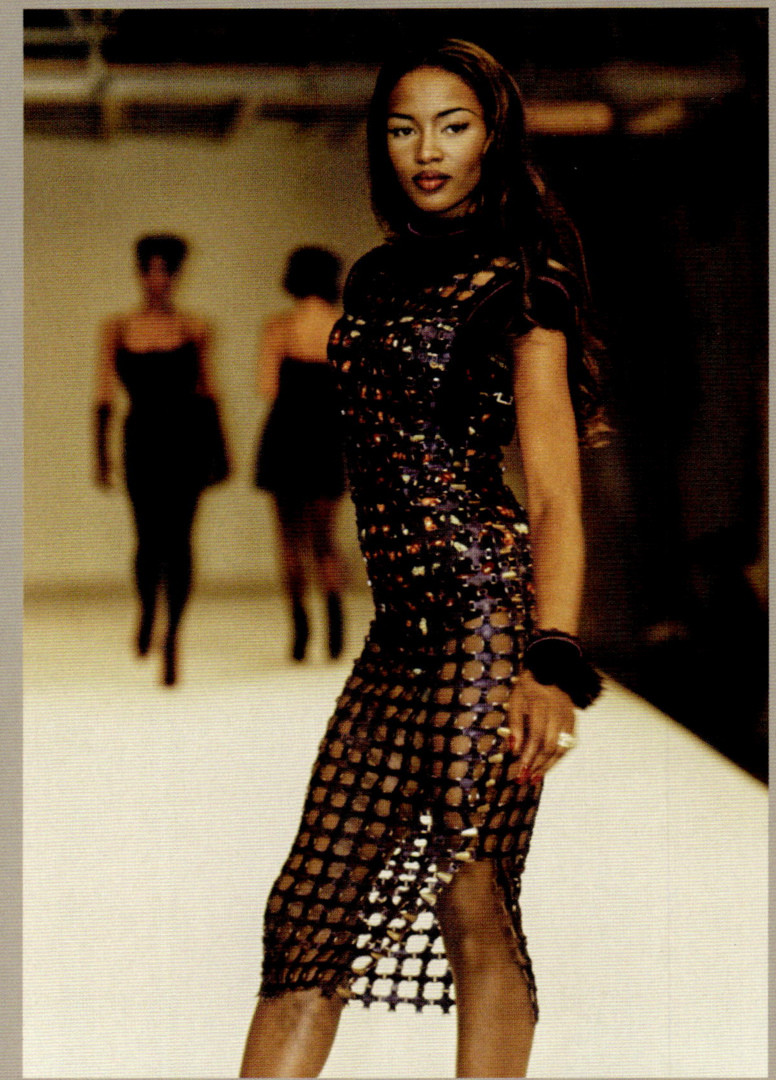

“I make cut-outs because a hand on the waist, the contact of skin is important.”

—AZZEDINE ALAÏA, *Vogue*, November 1985

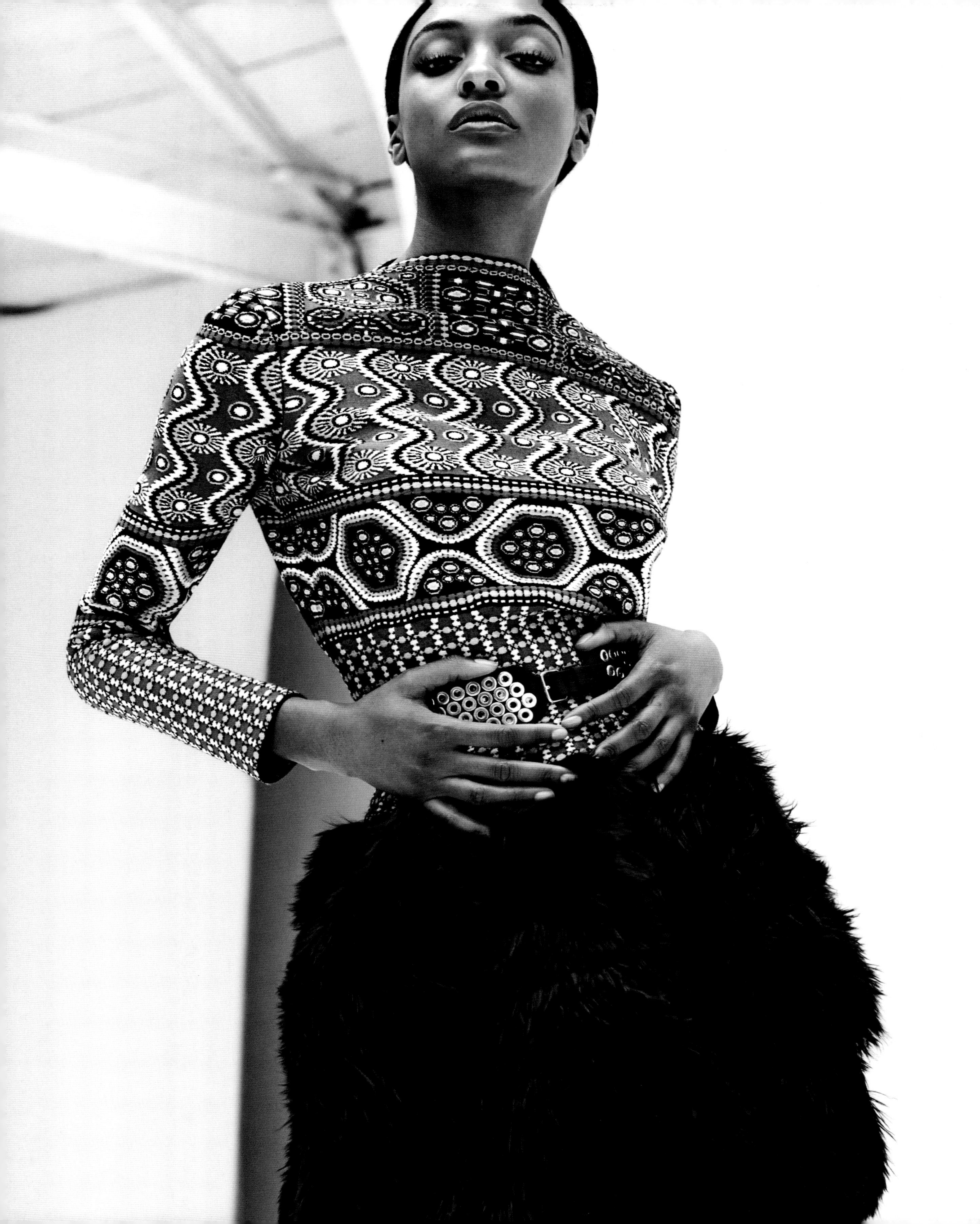

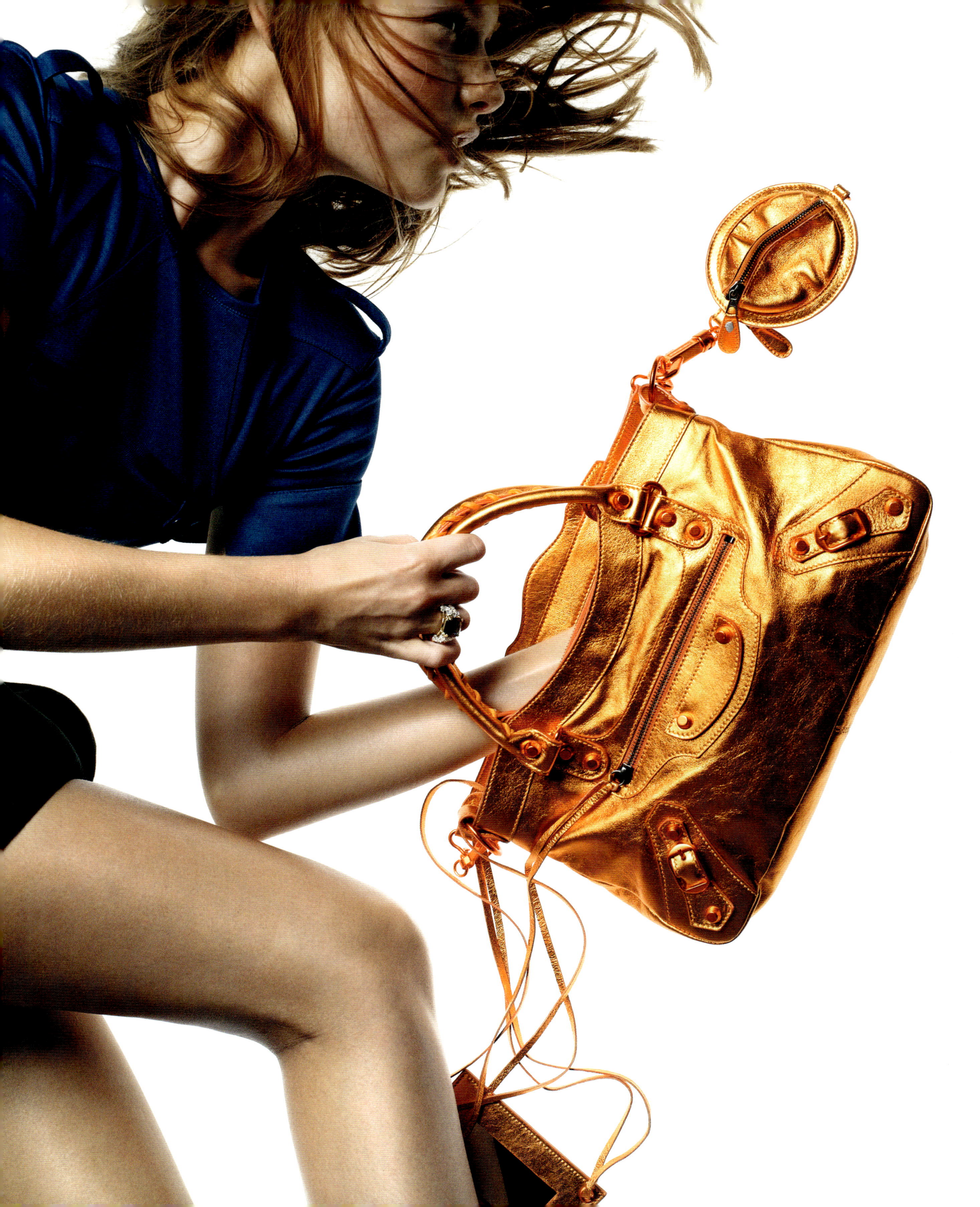

Nicolas Ghesquière for Balenciaga

LARIAT, 2000

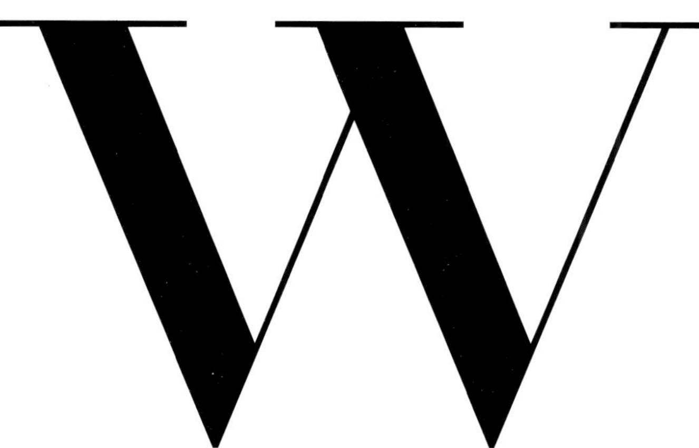

When designer Nicolas Ghesquière arrived at Balenciaga in 1995, he toiled in anonymity in the licensing department, designing event garments and funeral clothes for a mostly Japanese market. Then, in 1997, the director of ready-to-wear, Josephus Thimister, was let go and Ghesquière, at twenty-five, stepped in from the wings. He brought a shock wave of energy to the house virtually overnight, firing off one It item after another, such as skinny schoolboy blazers, motorcycle jackets, metallic leggings, and cargo pants.

Surprisingly, in 2000, when he designed the slouchy Lariat, with its beat-up leather, long zipper pulls, and hardware, the higher-ups rejected it and the prototype sat around the atelier for a year. "Accessories were rigid," Ghesquière told *Women's Wear Daily* in 2011. "Luxury leather, especially, was about rigidity. So they were not really happy, and they decided not to produce it." But in the weeks leading up to the runway show, it caught the eye of models who came by for fittings and of one model in particular, Kate Moss, who mistook it for a vintage design. Encouraged, Ghesquière whipped up twenty-five samples as gifts for the girls and then sent them to fashion editors to drum up interest. This was the era when street-style photography was just revving up, which meant the images went around the world, driving up demand and stirring an online craze for secondhand versions that caused the bag's price to skyrocket.

"It was a new fresh thing, but it looked like an old, good, friendly thing," Ghesquière recalled in *Women's Wear Daily*. "The brand also was becoming desirable. You could be a Balenciaga girl with that bag."

OPPOSITE:
Lariat bag, Nicholas Ghesquière for Balenciaga, *Vogue*, December 2014.

PAGES 36–37:
An array of Lariat bags, Nicholas Ghesquière for Balenciaga, June 2011.

> "Balenciaga handbags had a big success without advertising or promotions or logos. Suddenly, women wanted one because they saw another woman with it. It was like a tribe."
>
> —NICOLAS GHESQUIÈRE, Elle.com, February 26, 2010

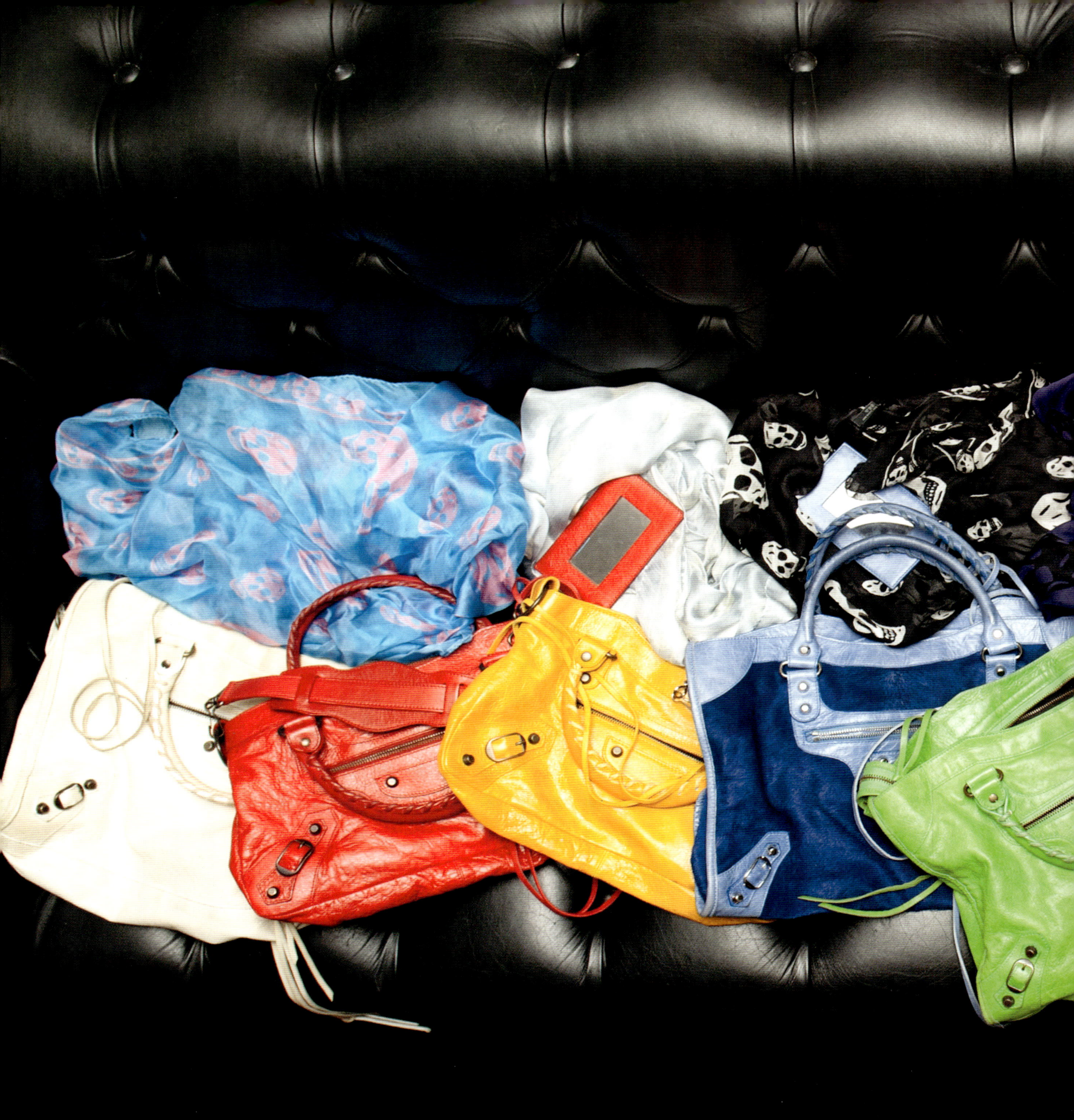

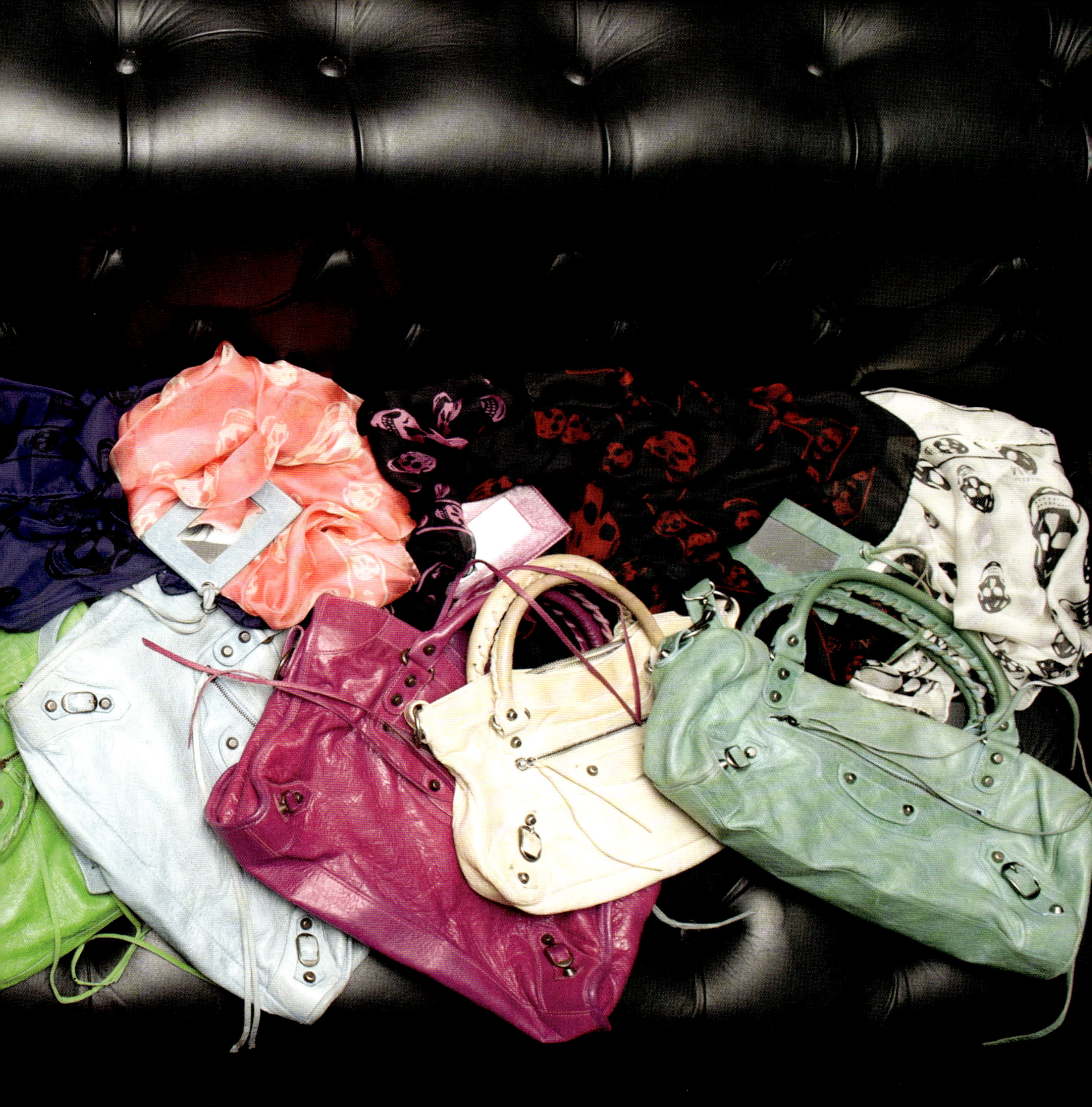

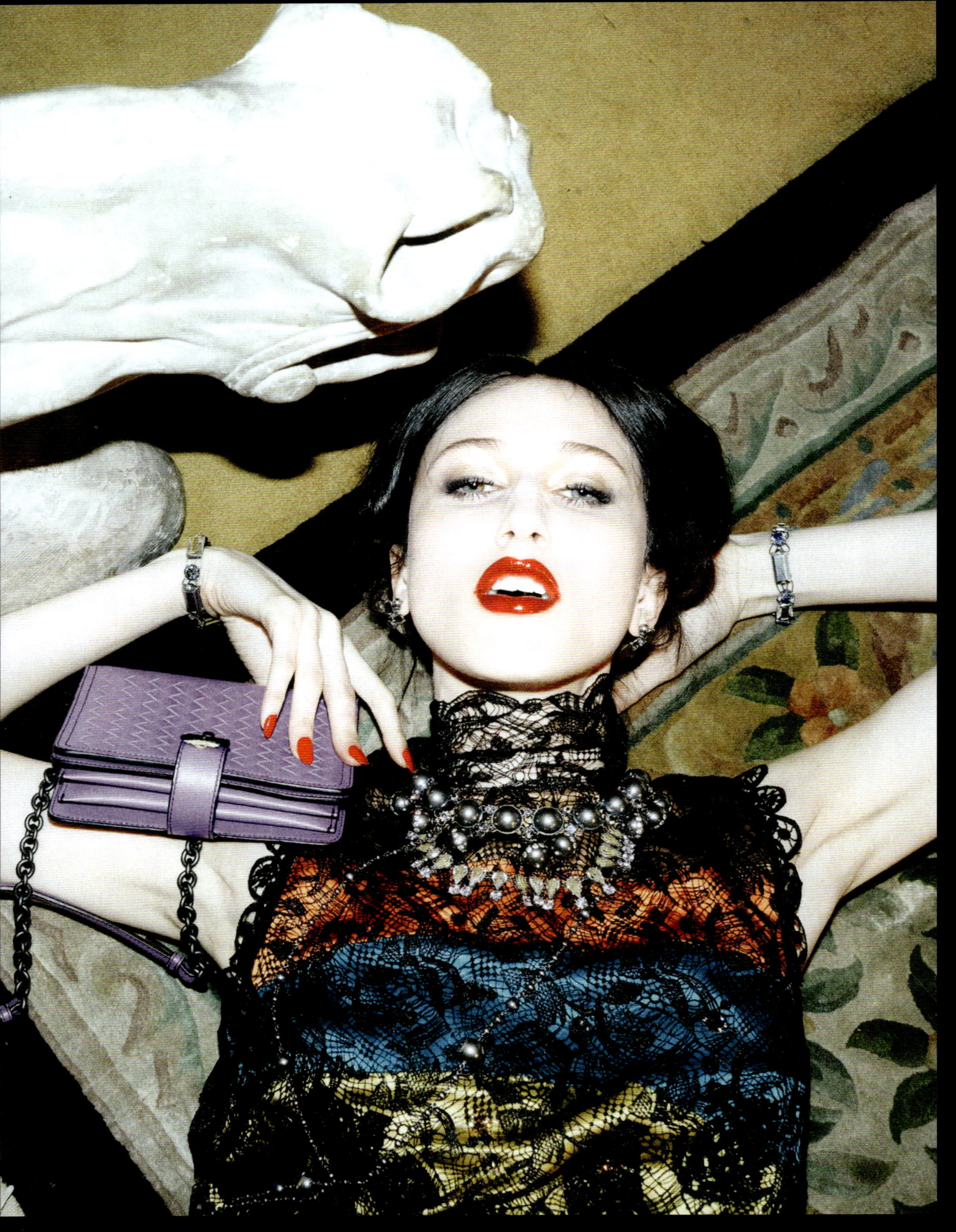

Bottega Veneta

INTRECCIATO, 1966

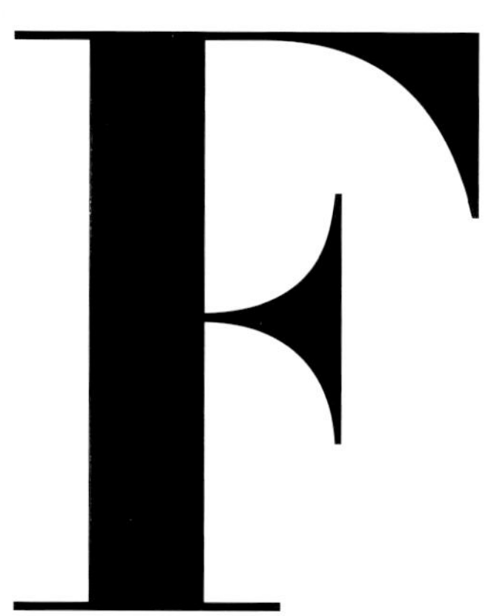

ounded by Michele Taddei and Renzo Zengiaro in 1966, Bottega Veneta is rooted in an understated artisanal style (*bottega* is Italian for "atelier"). When they set up shop in the Veneto, the region was renowned for its textile manufacturing—not leather goods. The local sewing machines weren't equipped to handle the thick saddle leather then used for handbags. This constraint forced the designers to change their approach to bag making: they began using thin, lightweight leathers cut into strips and woven into larger panels, not unlike weaving a tapestry on a loom. Afterward, another panel of cotton was glued to the back as a lining. This leather-weaving technique was called *intrecciato*, after the Italian word for "woven." The resulting design was a distinct, durable weave—one unique to Bottega Veneta.

Success came soon, as Bottega Veneta offered what the 1970s trends of flash and logomania did not: quiet refinement, an approach the company emphasized with the tagline "When Your Own Initials Are Enough." Bianca Jagger, Jacqueline Kennedy Onassis, and Andy Warhol became fans. Warhol, who lived near the New York store and often did his Christmas shopping there, even filmed a short promotional piece for the brand in 1980. That year, Lauren Hutton clutched a brick-red Bottega Veneta bag in the film classic *American Gigolo*.

Designer Tomas Maier assumed the role of creative director in 2001. His bags steer clear of any identifiable markers except the signature *intrecciato* technique. "Using the cloth-weight skins was a great—if accidental—departure that made a bag that was collapsible," he said in *Bottega Veneta* (2012). For his famously unlined bags such as the slouchy Cabat tote and the curved Veneta hobo, the process involves double-sided *intrecciato*, in which two strips of leather are glued together, eliminating the need for a lining. The artisans nimbly weave the leather at a rate of about an inch a minute and do so while standing, since that allows for the correct leverage and strength necessary to create the taut crosshatched effect. The extreme craftsmanship is what makes it a status symbol.

"I always like an object that is as beautiful on the inside as it is on the outside," said Maier in *Harper's Bazaar* (2008). "That's what luxury is all about. It's very personal. Nobody needs to know."

OPPOSITE:
Model Anna Cleveland with a Byzantine intrecciato nappa shoulder bag, Bottega Veneta, Fall 2015.

PAGES 40–41:
Top-handle python bag, Bottega Veneta, Spring 2014.

PAGE 42:
Intrecciato crocodile shoulder bag, backstage at Bottega Veneta, Spring 2015 ready-to-wear.

PAGE 43:
Intrecciato nappa double-micro shoulder bag, backstage at Bottega Veneta, Fall 2016 ready-to-wear.

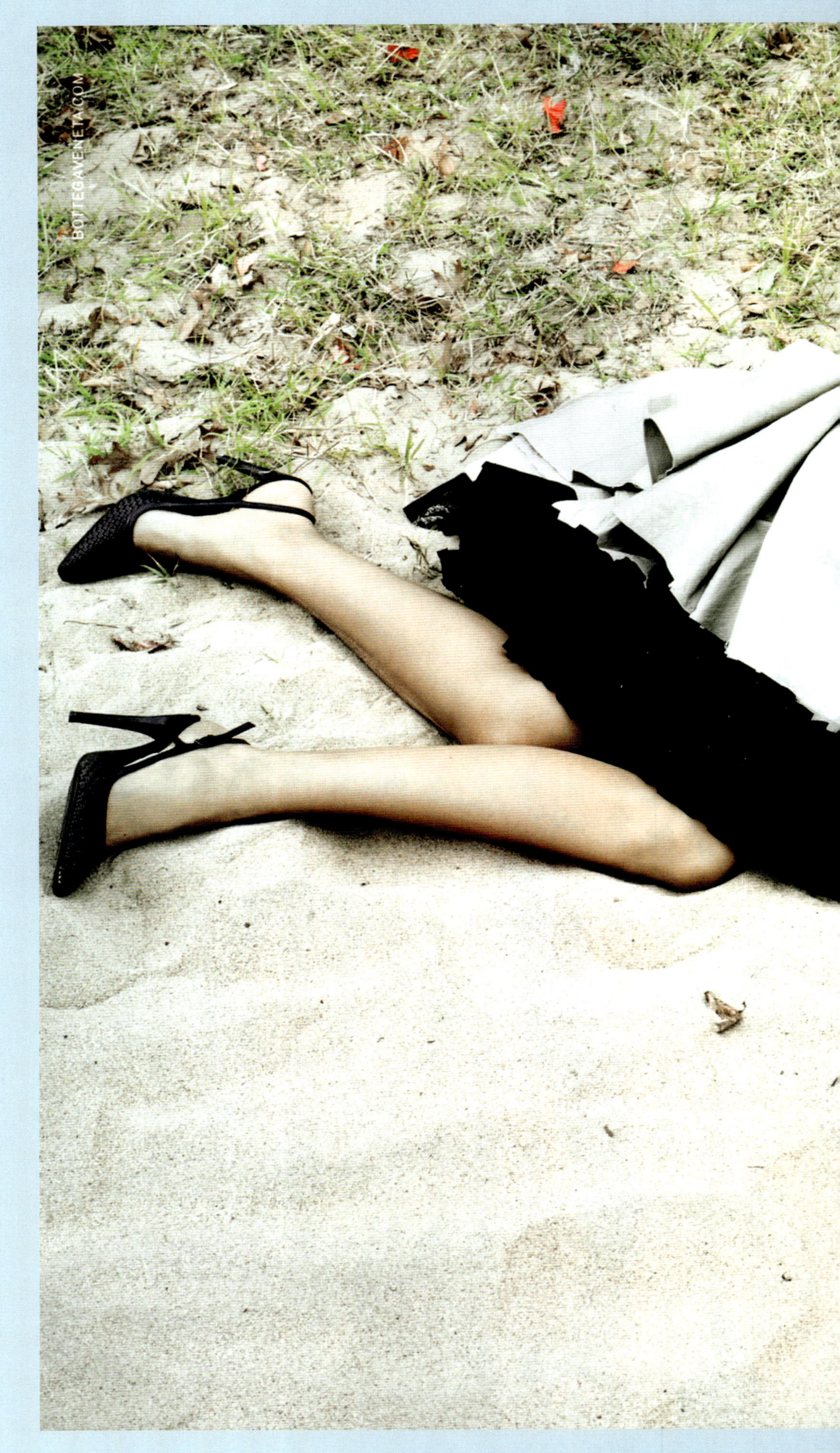
BOTTEGAVENETA.COM

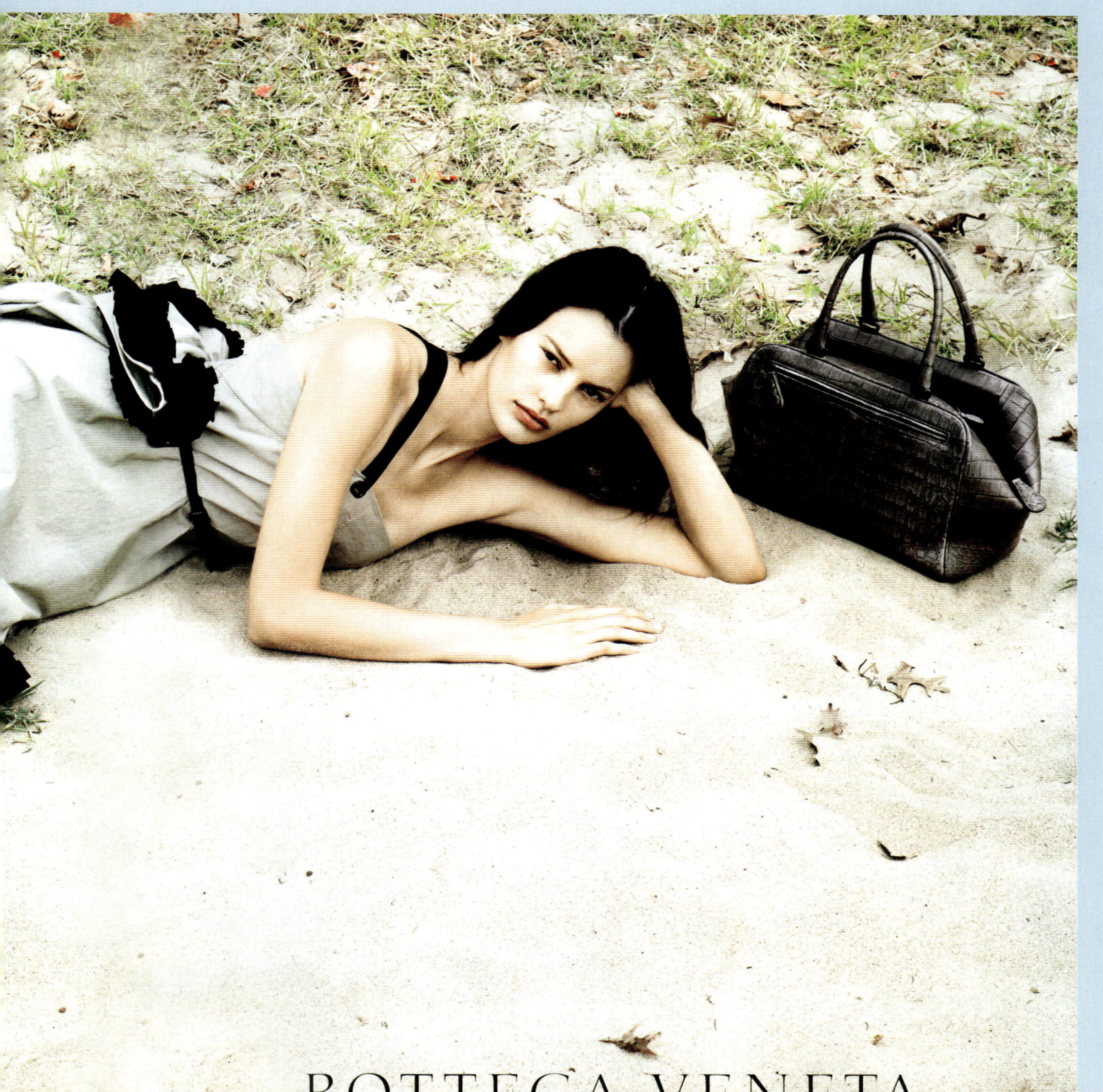
BOTTEGA VENETA

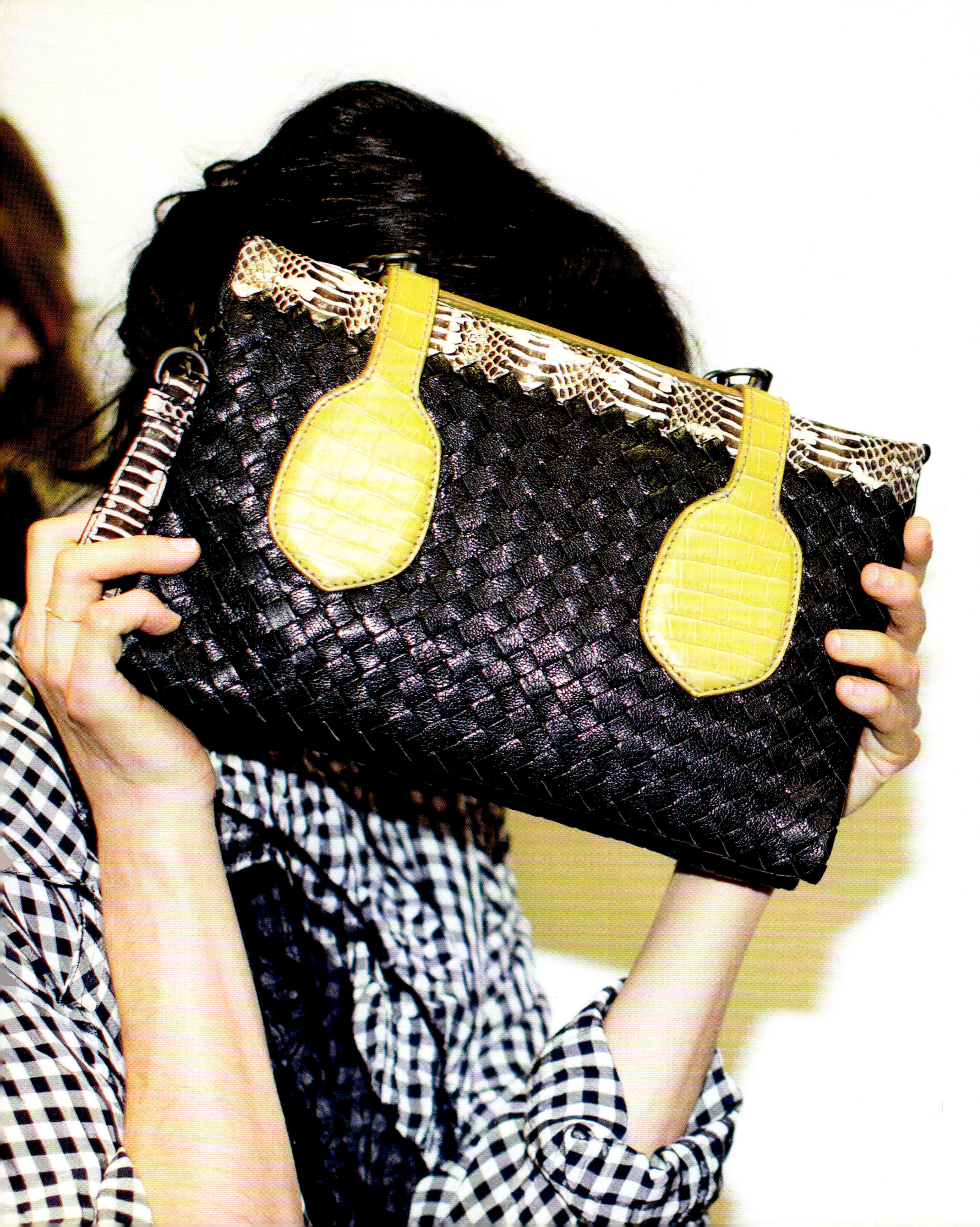

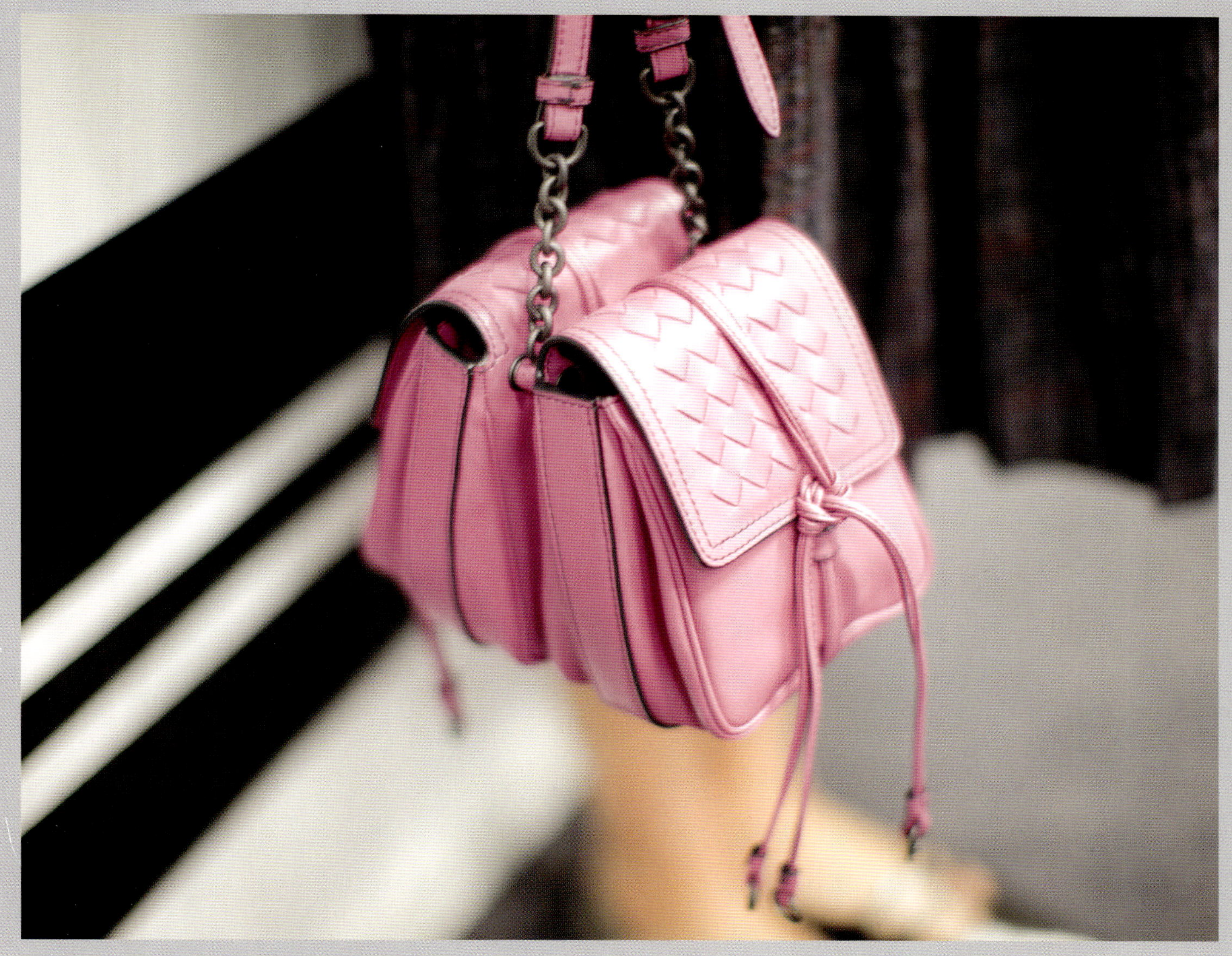

"Only people in the know will recognize what you have, and it's really just not relevant to other people."

—VALERIE STEELE on Bottega Veneta, *The New Yorker*, January 3, 2011

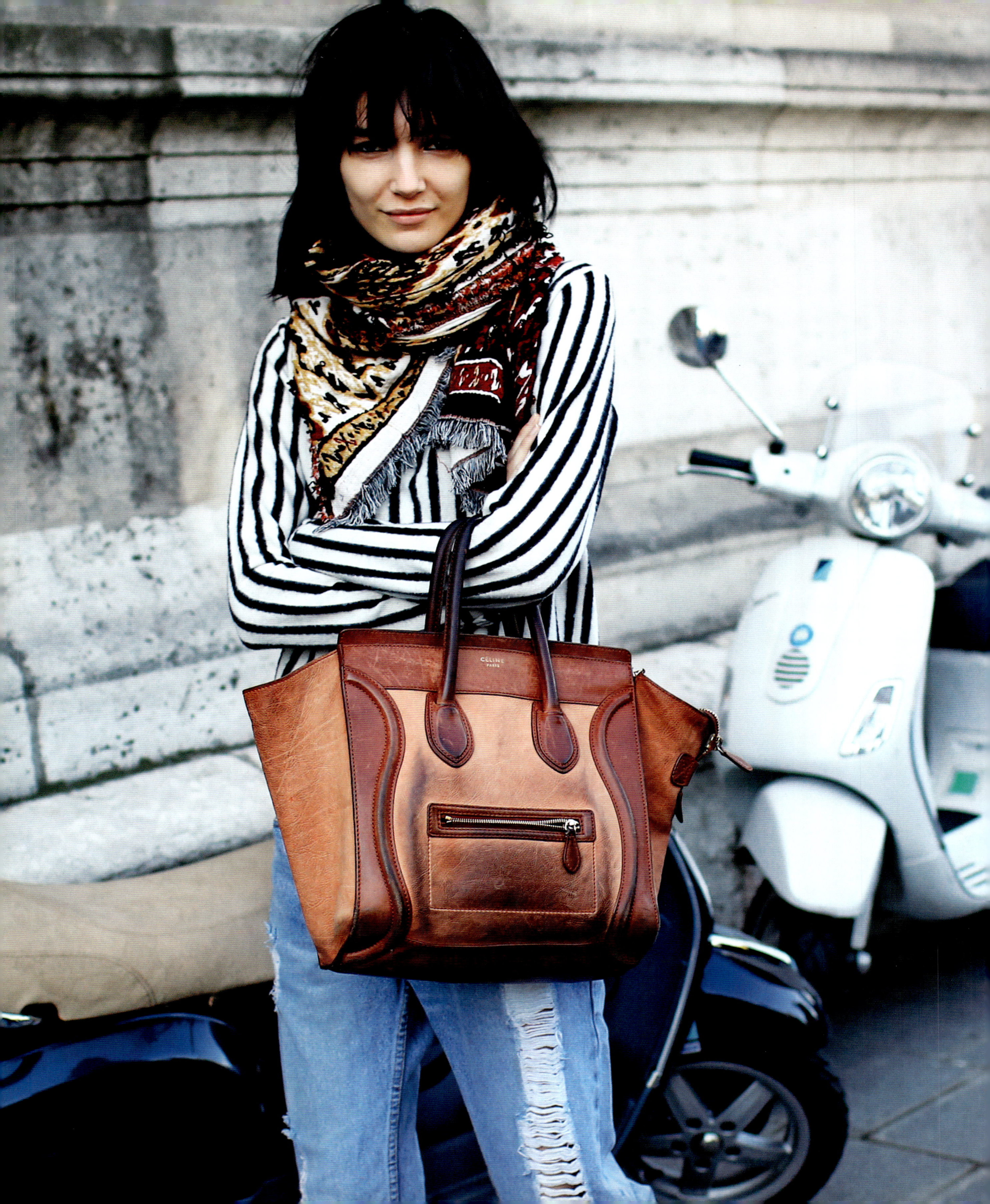
CELINE
PARIS

Phoebe Philo for Céline

BOX, 2010

LUGGAGE, 2010

CABAS, 2010

TRAPEZE, 2013

In 2006 Phoebe Philo was a design star when she decided to leave Chloé to focus on her family life. A favorite of editors, retailers, and handbag lovers, she had created the popular Paddington bag. After a three-year break, she decided to return to work in 2009, when she became the creative director of Céline. She soon put to rest any doubts about whether she still had the magic touch.

Her debut collection for Resort 2009, presented in an empty New York loft, was a quiet affair—simple, spare separates that exuded chic restraint. By the time Philo held her first full fashion show in October 2009, the consensus was in: "Triumphant return," declared the *New York Times*. A beautiful collection, with precision lines and a laser focus on modern minimalism, it created a tectonic shift in the fashionscape that introduced a new mode of modern dressing. Less was now undeniably more.

The Philo mindset extended to the handbags, which telegraphed her vision of pure design and also created a revolution in accessories by eliminating excessive hardware and froufrou in favor of clean, Spartan lines. The bags quickly became mainstays. The Box is a small flap style with soft-grained leather and a geometric double-square gold clasp. The Luggage satchel features distinctive curves and a zip on the front, while the Cabas tote is a purely reductive design. The Trapeze is sleek, with extra-wide "wings" that allow for intriguing color-block combinations. Designer after designer took their cue from Philo's approach for the next seven years, until longtime Gucci designer Alessandro Michele became the creative director in January 2015 and effectively swung the pendulum back a year later.

Céline's bags continue to sell out, and Philo isn't in the least bit concerned about the look-alikes. "I love it," she told *Vogue* in 2013. "I'm nothing but flattered. I've got friends with copied pieces. My mum's even got a knockoff bag!"

OPPOSITE:
Luggage medium tote, Céline, Paris, September 2014.

RIGHT:
Cabas Phantom tote, Céline, Fall 2016.

PAGES 46–47:
Luggage micro tote *(far left)*, Céline, Paris, October 2015.

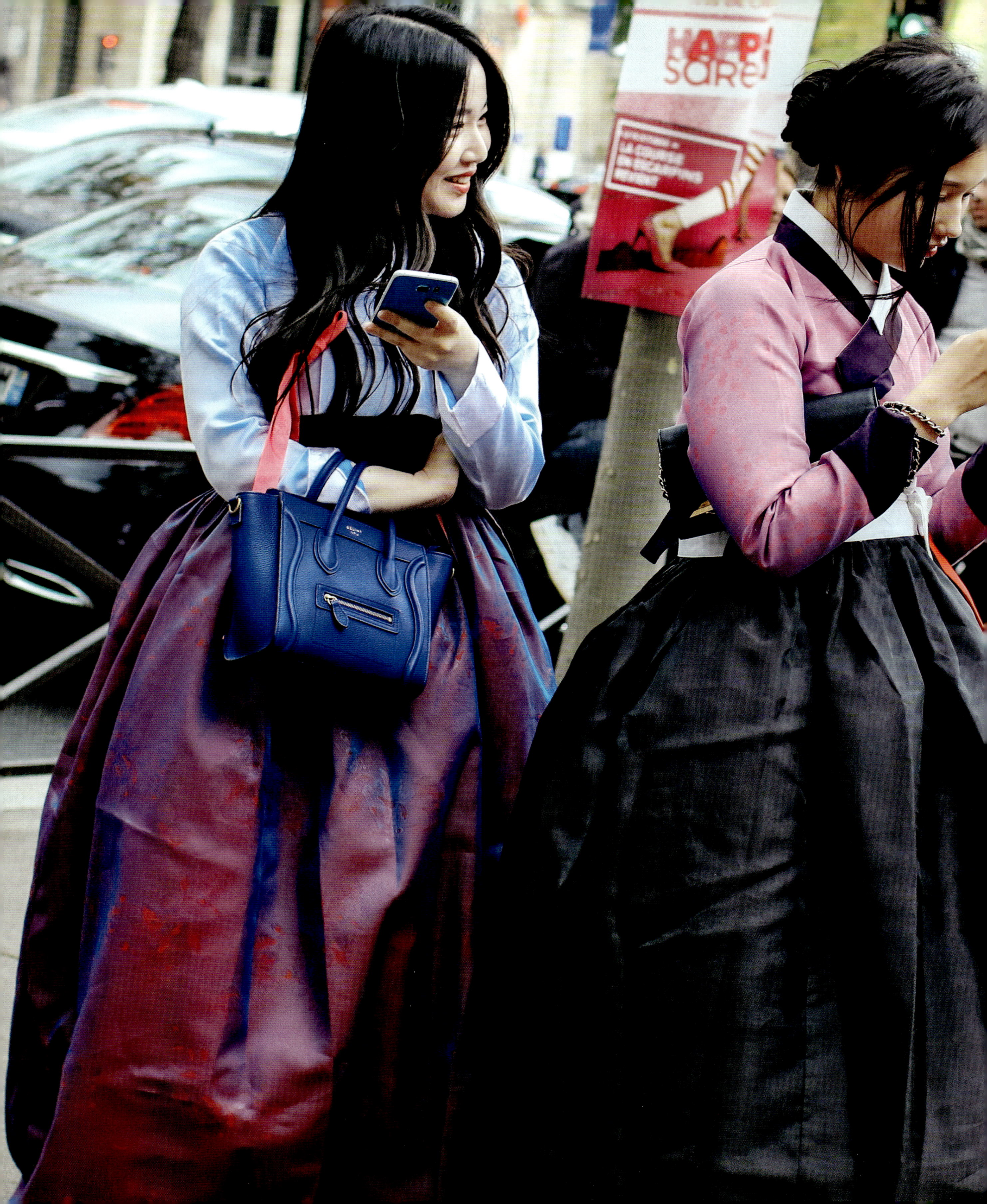

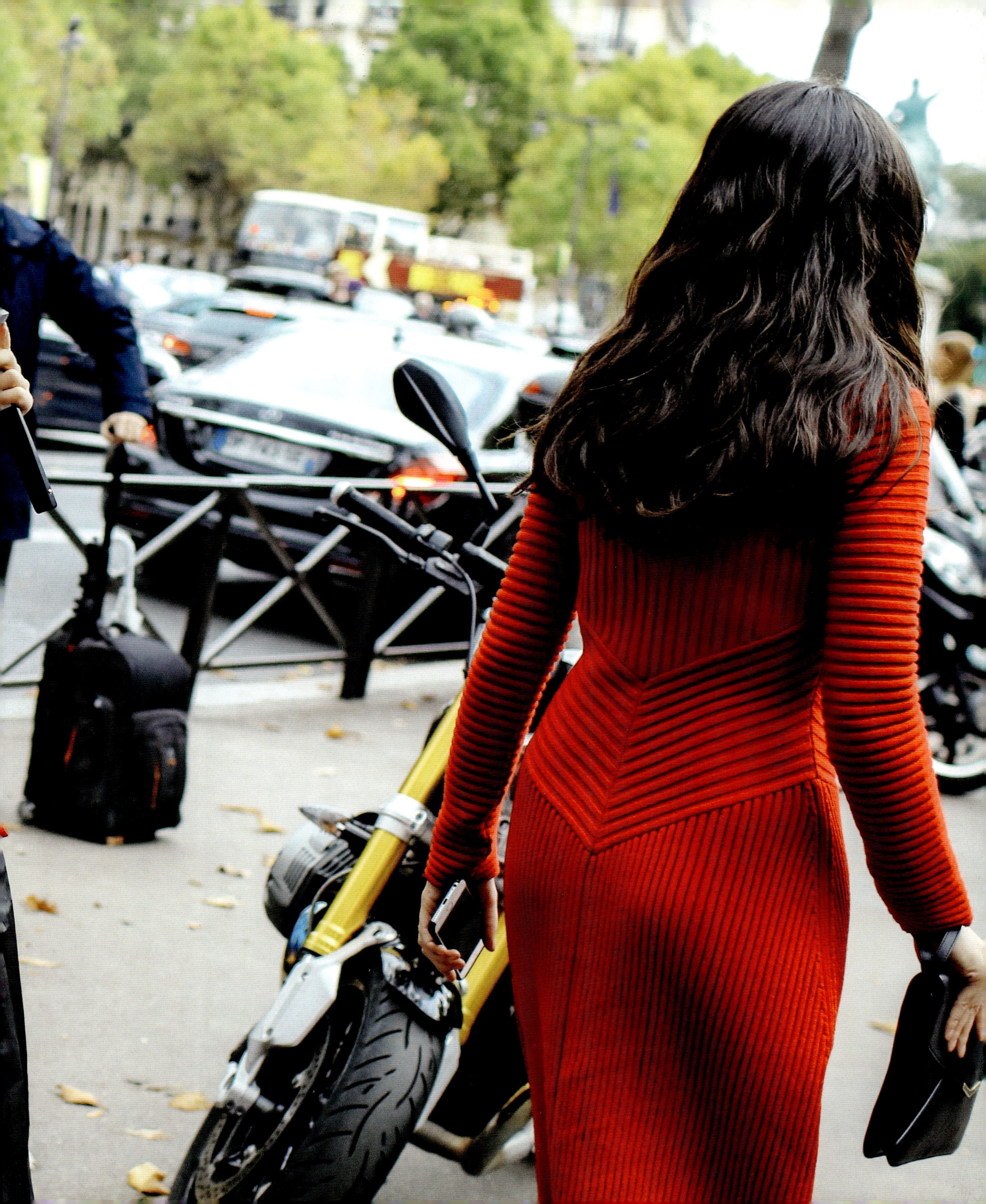

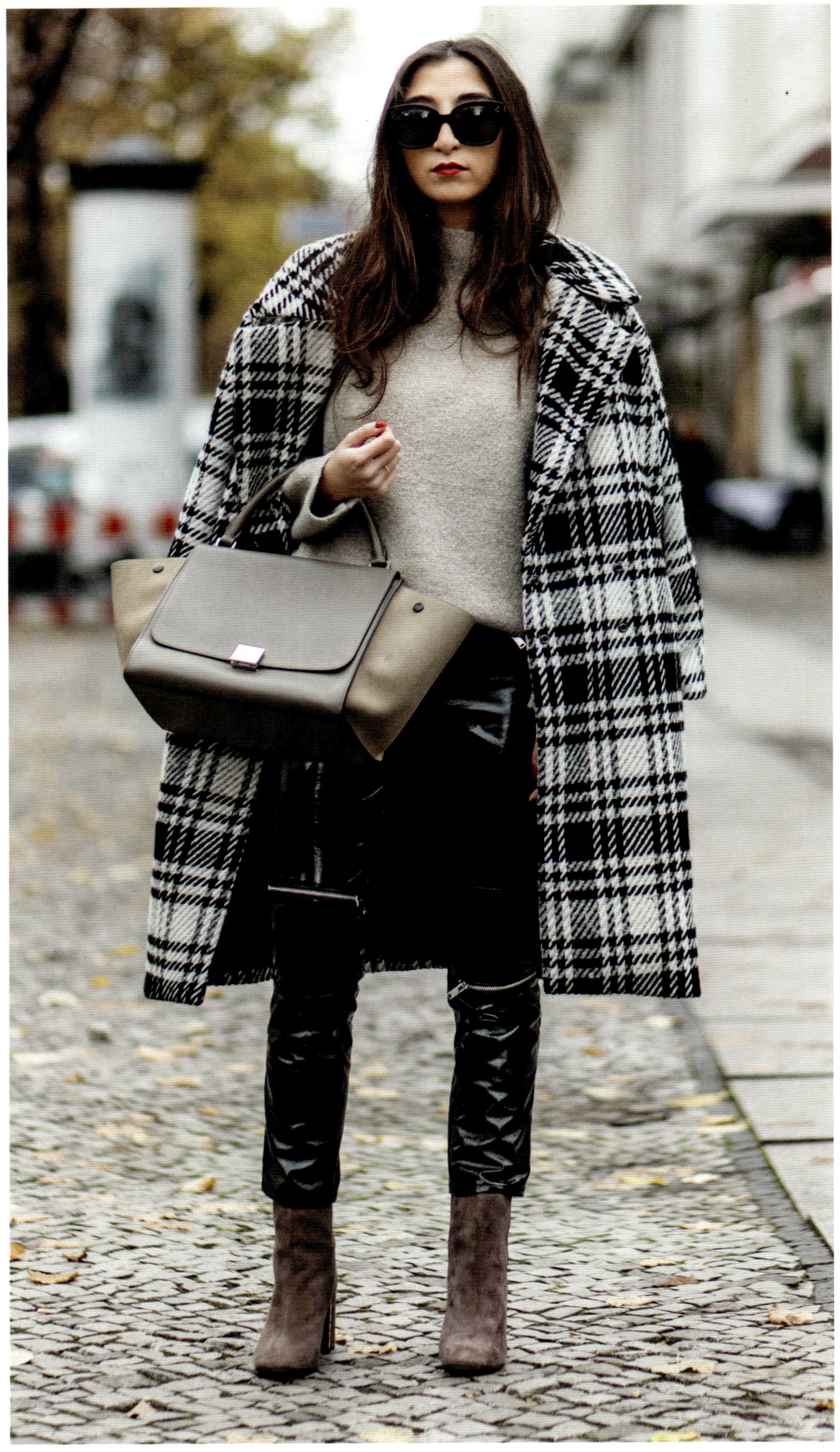

"The ultimate is when you see it on the street on someone who's wearing it, owning it, enjoying it, feeling good in it. I love that."

—PHOEBE PHILO
Vogue, March 2013

LEFT:
Trapeze bag, Céline, Berlin, November 2016.

OPPOSITE:
Luggage large tote *(foreground)*, Céline, Milan, June 2015.

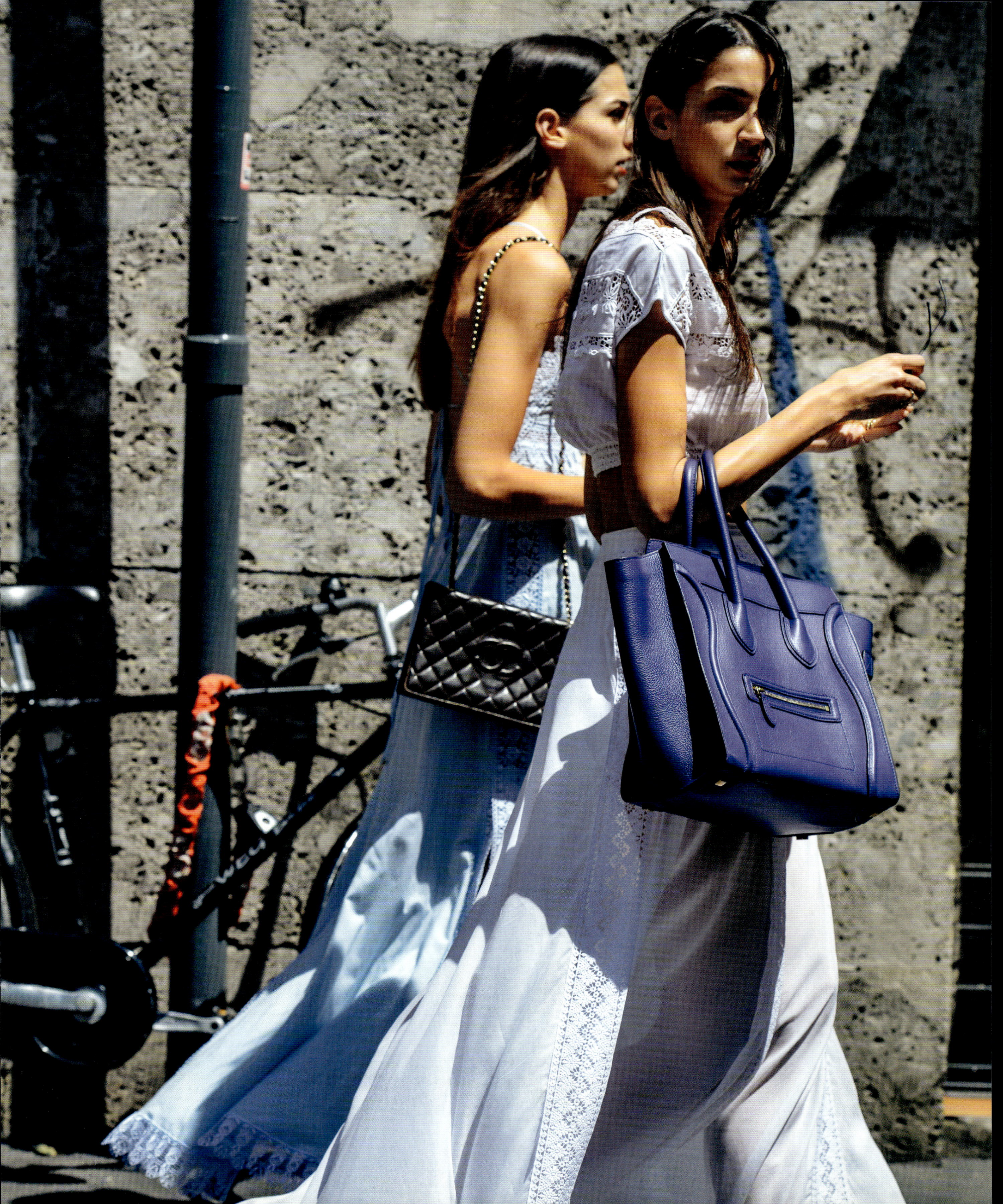

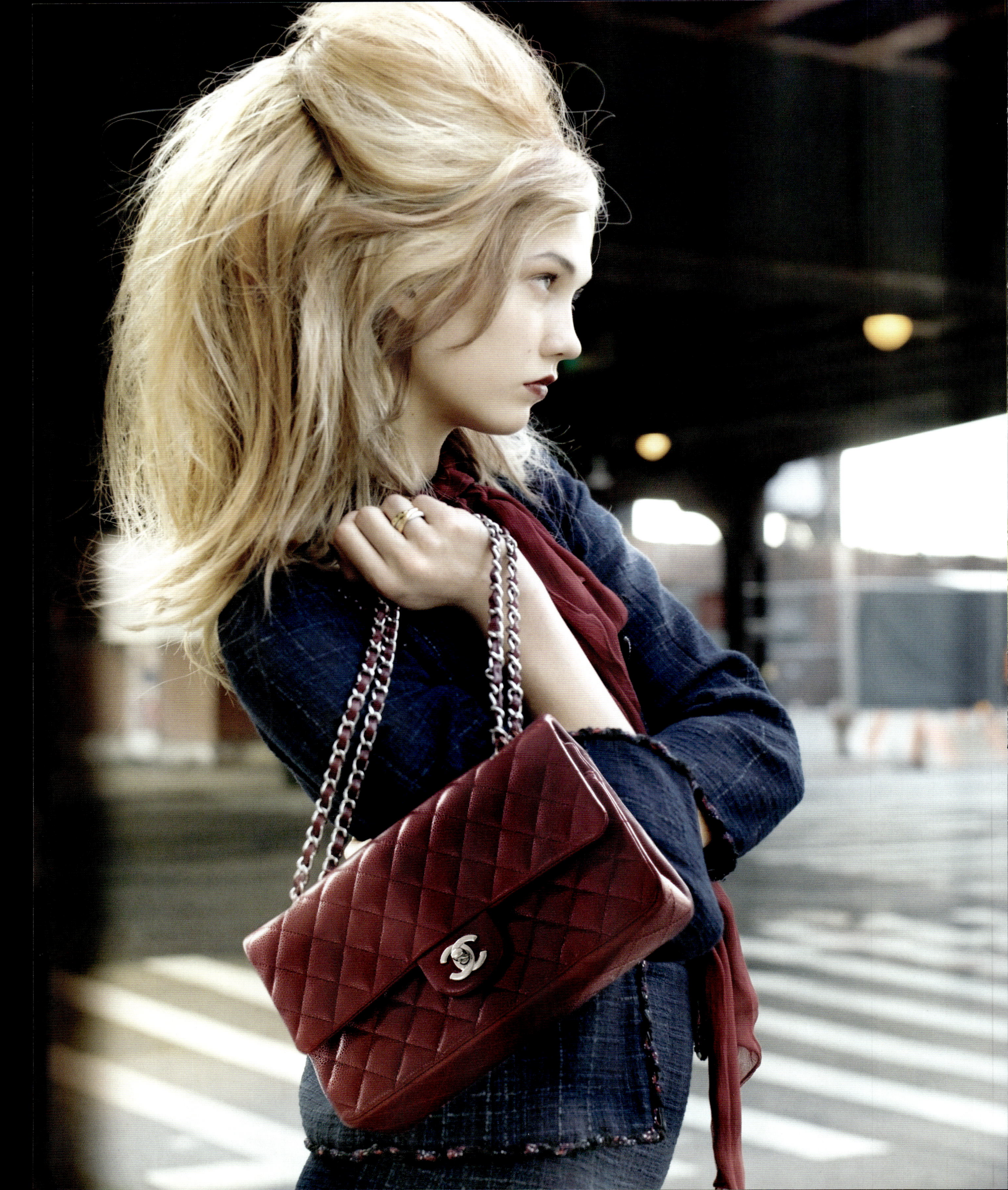

Chanel

2.55, 1955
BOY, 2011

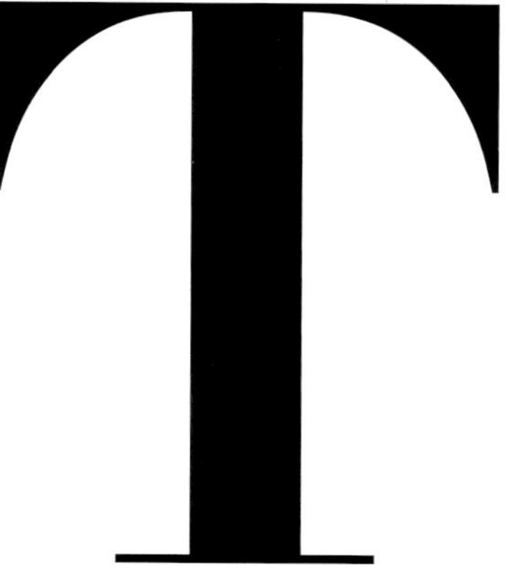he cultural impact of Chanel—as a house, a brand, a story, and a history—is unparalleled in the accessories world. People know there's a Coco behind Chanel and they recognize her codes: the LBDs, the pearls, the camellias, the two-tone ballet flats, and the tweed bouclé jackets. They resonate solidly throughout the world as a visual vocabulary that is *Chanel*. And prime among those Chanel pillars is the quilted 2.55 and its update, Boy.

The original design, created in 1929, liberated women in the same way Chanel's jersey dresses and tweed jackets offered an escape from hobble skirts and corsetry. By adding thin straps, inspired by those of soldiers' bags that you could sling over your shoulder, Chanel freed up the hand. The iteration we're familiar with today dates to February 1955, when she resurrected and updated the style as part of her postwar comeback; the bag's name stems from its date of rebirth.

There's a story behind every detail of the 2.55—from the burgundy lining, which represents the uniforms at the Aubazine convent where she grew up, to the gold chains inspired by those the nuns wore to hold their keys, to the front flap pocket where she allegedly placed her love letters. The iconic diamond quilting comes from her love of equestrian culture and jockey jackets, though some sources point to the cushions in her apartment, others to the stained-glass windows at Aubazine. The slim interior lipstick pocket was equally personal, as Chanel never went anywhere without her red lipstick.

Since taking over the design direction of Chanel in 1983, twelve years after Mademoiselle's death, Karl Lagerfeld has updated the classic 2.55. He replaced the original rectangular turnlock—known as the Mademoiselle Lock, an amusing reference to the fact that Chanel never married—with one flaunting the double-C logo. And he kept the 2.55 going strong, generating new takes season after season—hot pink, denim, embroidered, terry cloth, covered in 1970s-style crochet. There are also plenty of versions cut from that house staple tweed, which Chanel liked extra nubby, even though the irregularities were considered flaws in her day. In 2005 Lagerfeld reintroduced the original in celebration of its fiftieth anniversary.

The Boy redefines the 2.55 for a younger audience. It features the double-C logo atop a rectangular metal clasp and a front flap that goes all the way to the bottom, unlike the 2.55, which stops roughly two-thirds of the way down. The rest of the codes are there: the chain link; the East-West rectangular shape; and the quilting, with three additional quilted "stripes" bordering the edges. There's storytelling magic here, too. The elegant polo player "Boy" Capel was Chanel's great love and muse until he died in a car accident at age thirty-eight in 1919.

OPPOSITE:
Karlie Kloss with a burgundy Chanel 2.55, *Vogue*, August 2010.

PAGE 52:
Dress designs by Chanel. Illustrations from *Vogue*, April 1927.

PAGE 53:
Chanel advertisement, 1980s.

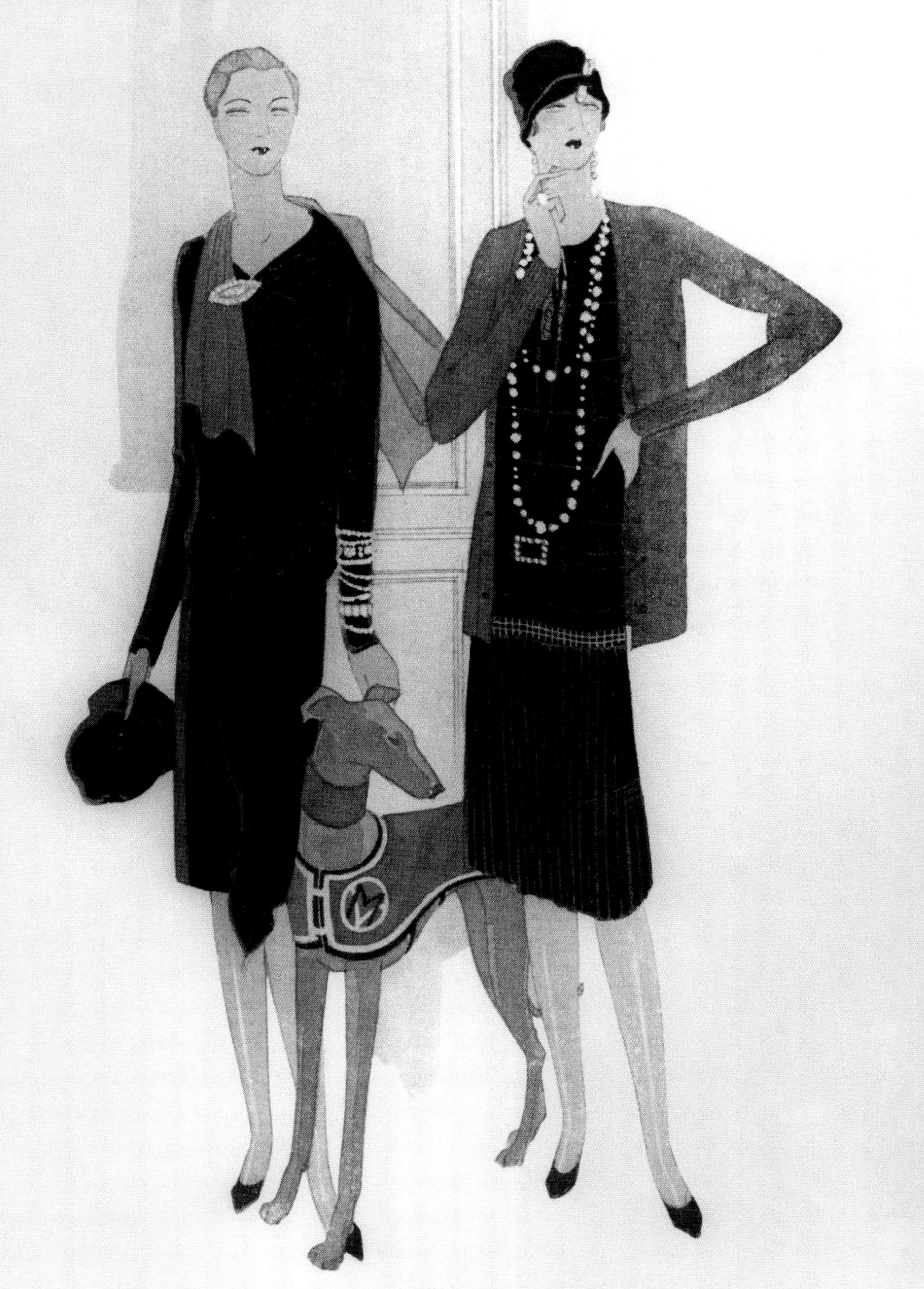

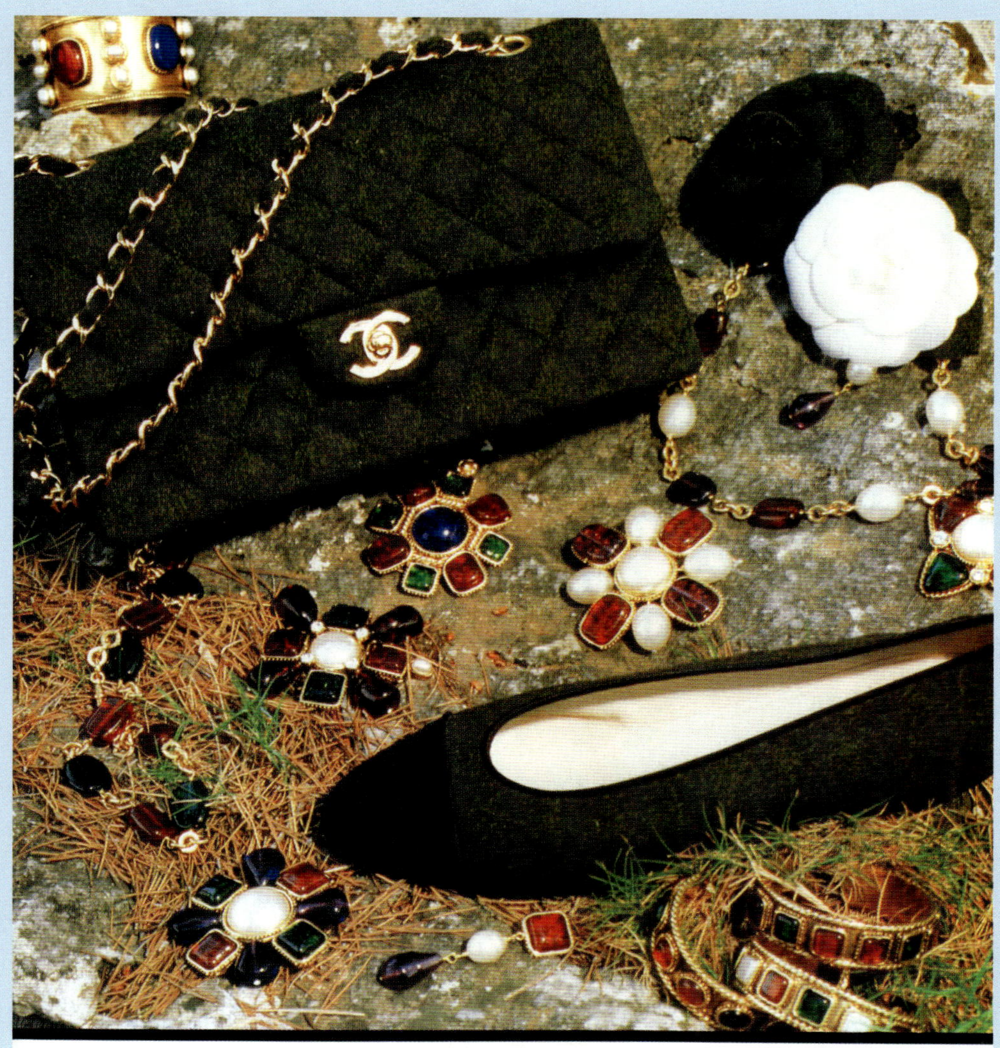

CHANEL
BOUTIQUE

26 OLD BOND STREET · LONDON W1
31 SLOANE STREET · LONDON SW1

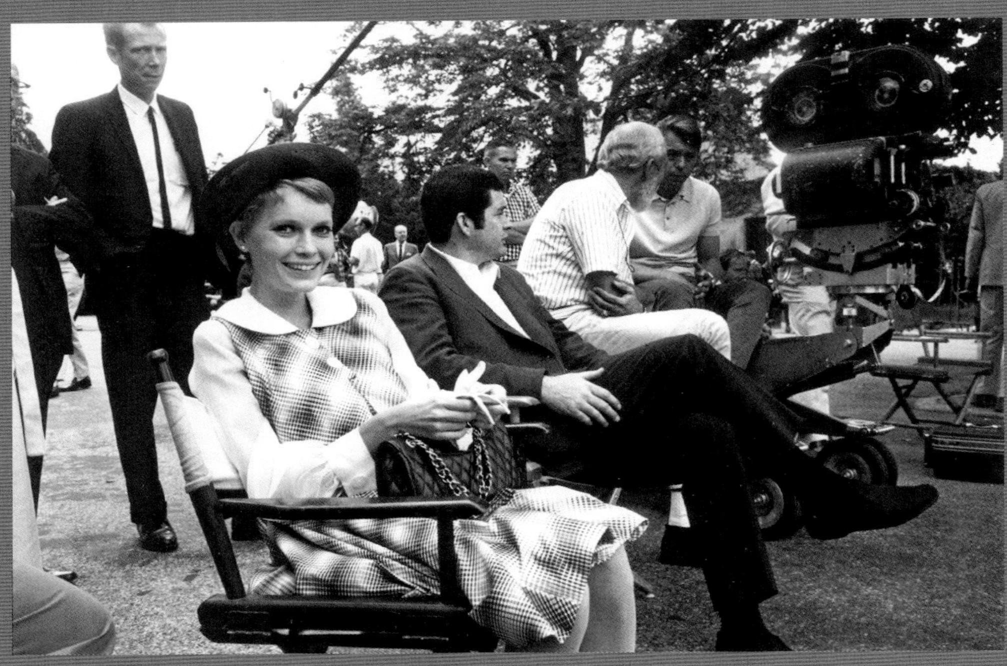

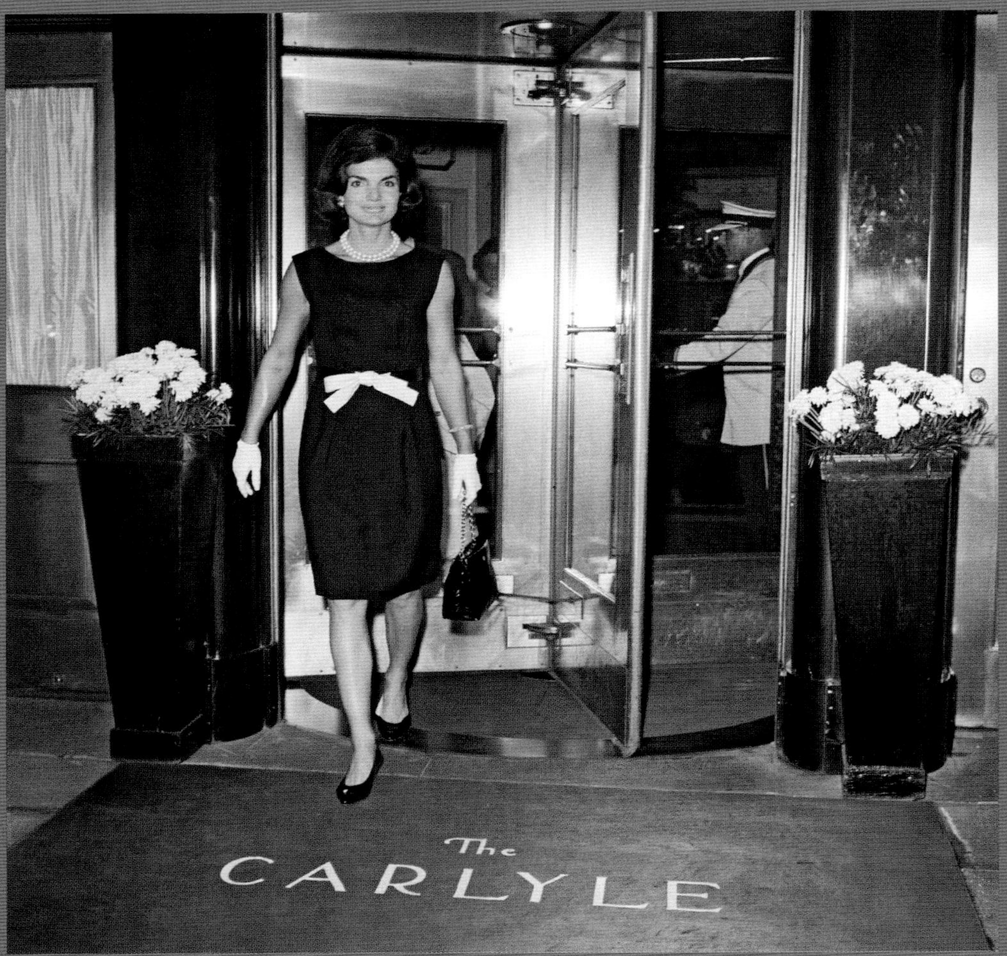

TOP: Mia Farrow on the set of *Rosemary's Baby*, 1967.

BOTTOM: Jacqueline Kennedy leaving the Carlyle Hotel, New York City, March 1962.

OPPOSITE: Boy bag, Chanel, *Numéro Tokyo*, July 2015.

PAGE 57: Coco Chanel in the Tuileries Garden, Paris, September 1957.

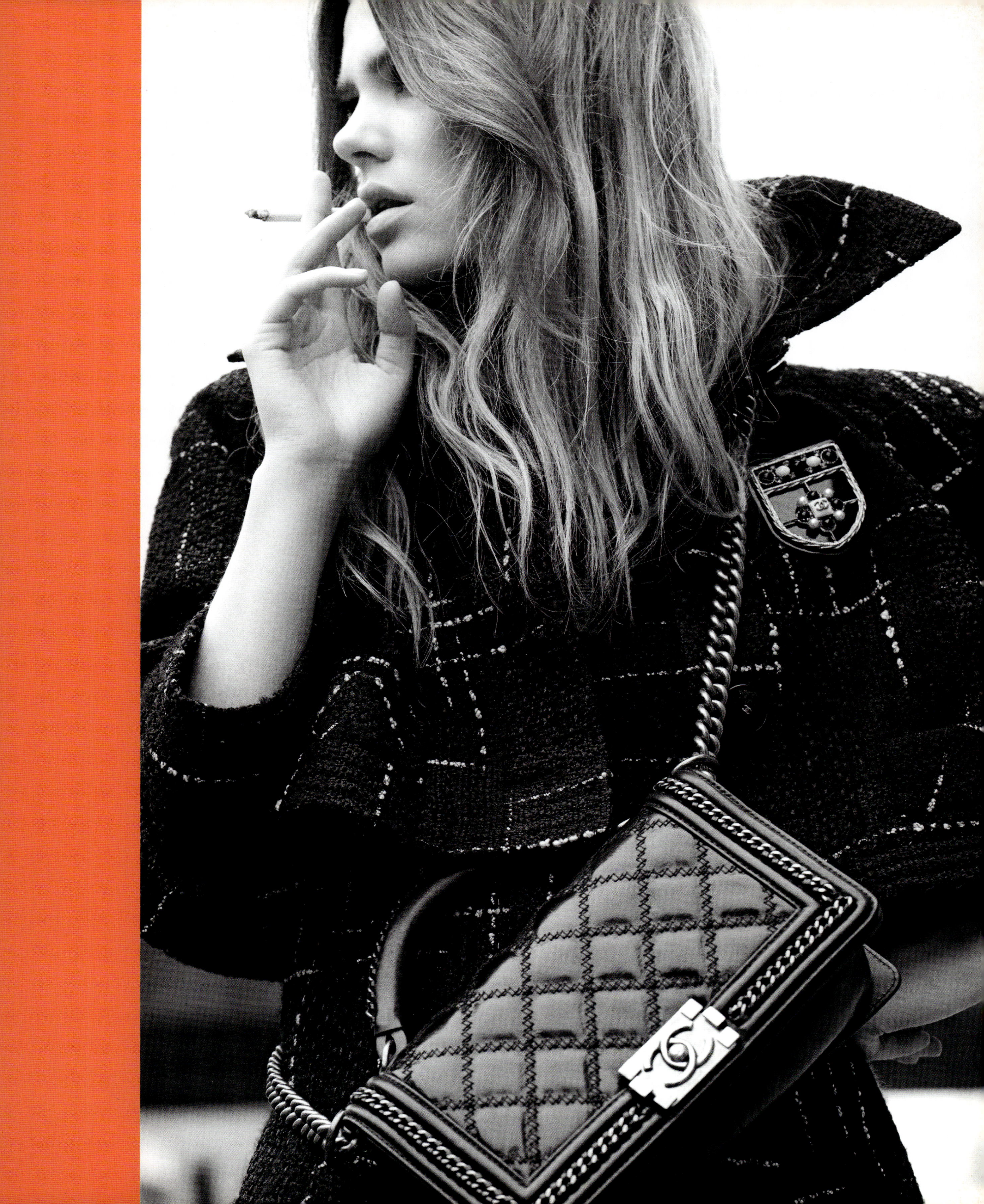

"Luxury is a necessity that begins where necessity ends."

—COCO CHANEL, from *The World of Coco Chanel: Friends, Fashion, Fame* by Edmonde Charles-Roux, 2005

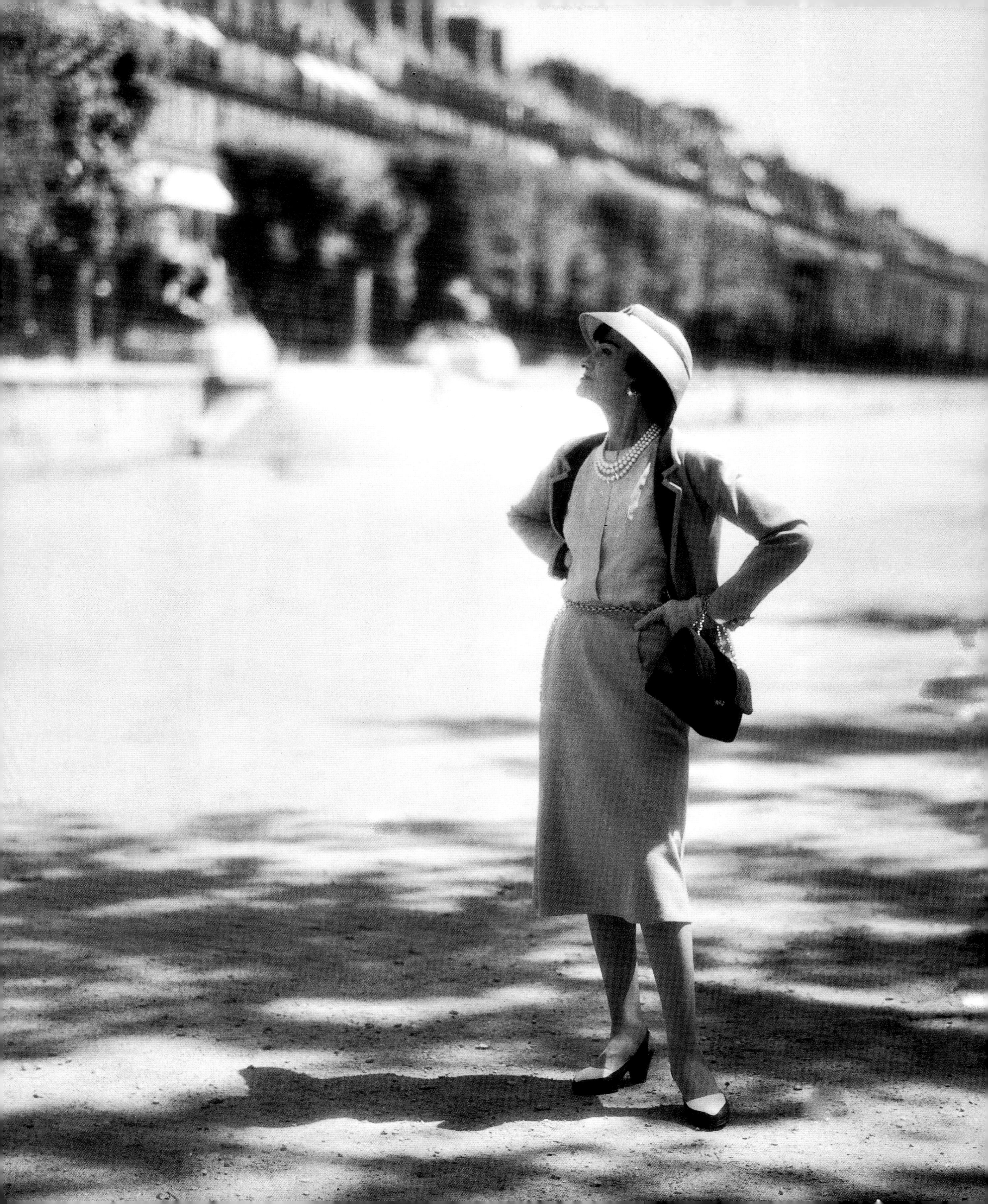

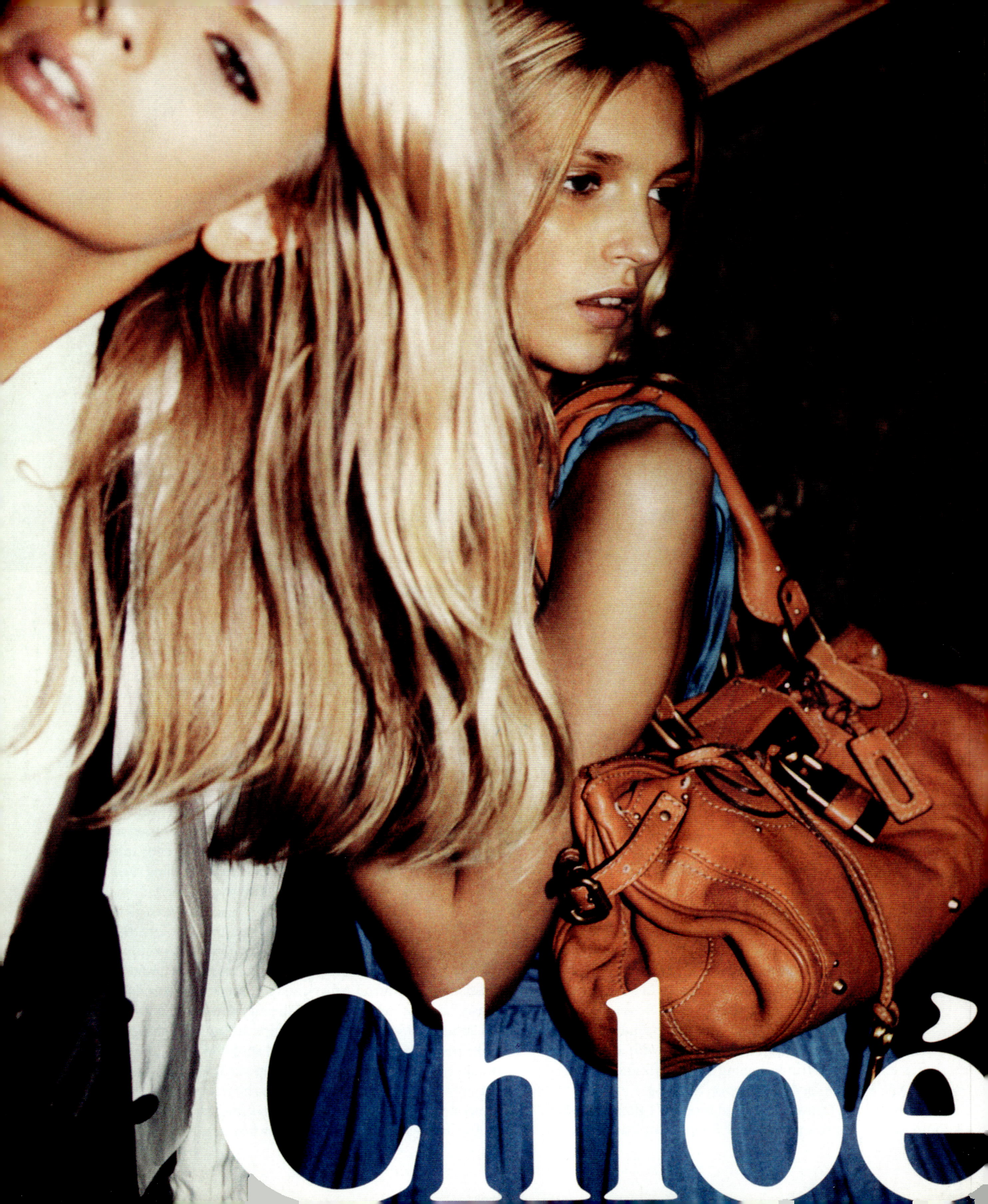
Chloé

Chloé

PADDINGTON, 2005
DREW, 2015

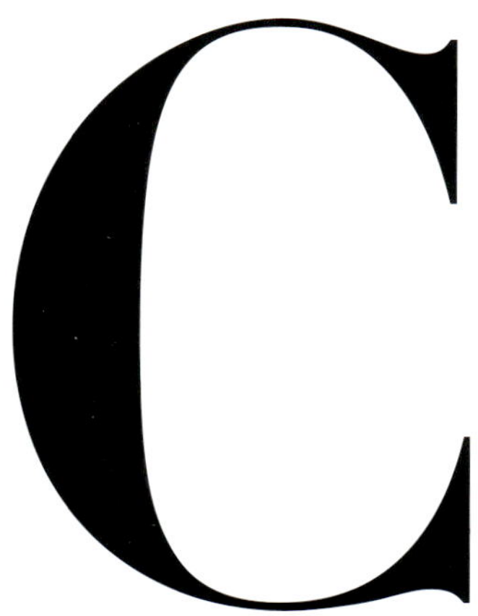

Chloé was founded in 1952 by Gaby Aghion, an Egyptian expatriate living in Paris who longed for something other than the skiff-skirted formality of Dior and Balenciaga. Given her station in life, Aghion wasn't expected to go into business. "I couldn't use my name in relation to my family, who, out of snobbery, were already talking about 'how Gaby was working,'" she recalls in journalist Sarah Mower's *Chloé: Attitudes* (2013). So she borrowed the name of a friend, "which I liked for the roundness of its letters," and made her mark by embracing a gentler side of femininity with cotton poplin dresses and crepe de chine blouses.

Aghion was also renowned for her support of bright, young talent. Karl Lagerfeld was her most famous hire—his softly cut, romantic bohemia for Chloé during the 1970s made fashion history. Even after Aghion sold the company in 1985, it continued to promote cutting-edge new talent, including best friends Stella McCartney and Phoebe Philo, who had studied together at Central Saint Martins College of Art and Design, London.

Philo, who took the creative reins from McCartney in 2001, ushered in an era of fresh-faced girlishness—flighty dresses, frilly blouses, and sweet eyelet jackets—that reconnected with the house's early years. For accessories, she smartly launched a behemoth of a bag to temper all the airiness. The Paddington was big and bulbous, with thick pebbly leather and a bulky brass padlock up top. "Phoebe had a knack for pushing her design to a level of exaggeration that dared girls to go further with every season," wrote Mower.

The handbag also dovetailed nicely with the nouveau boho trend on the rise, as seen in the countless tabloid shots of Sienna Miller and Kate Moss in breezy threads and layers, with their coffee in one hand and their Paddington in the other. Everyone lusted after the bag, even though it weighed three pounds when empty. "Loyal fans of outsize handbags tend to tick off their purse-induced woes like proud veterans of the football field," noted the *New York Times* in a 2006 article titled "Ouch! My Bag Is Killing Me."

OPPOSITE:
Paddington bag, Chloé, Spring 2005.

RIGHT:
Paddington bag, Chloé, Spring 2008.

PAGES 60–61:
Drew bag, Chloé, New York City, February 2015.

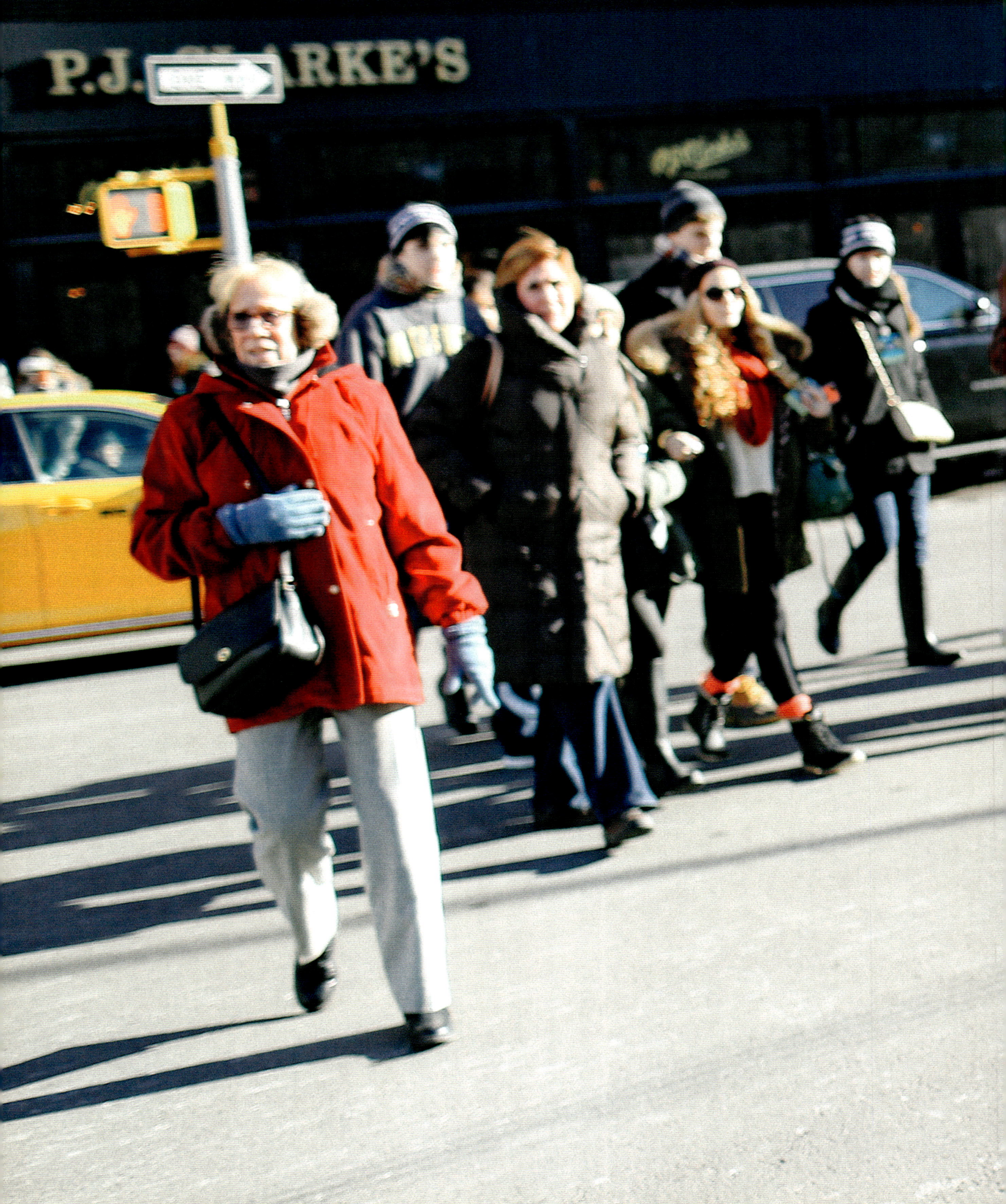
P.J.
ARKE'S

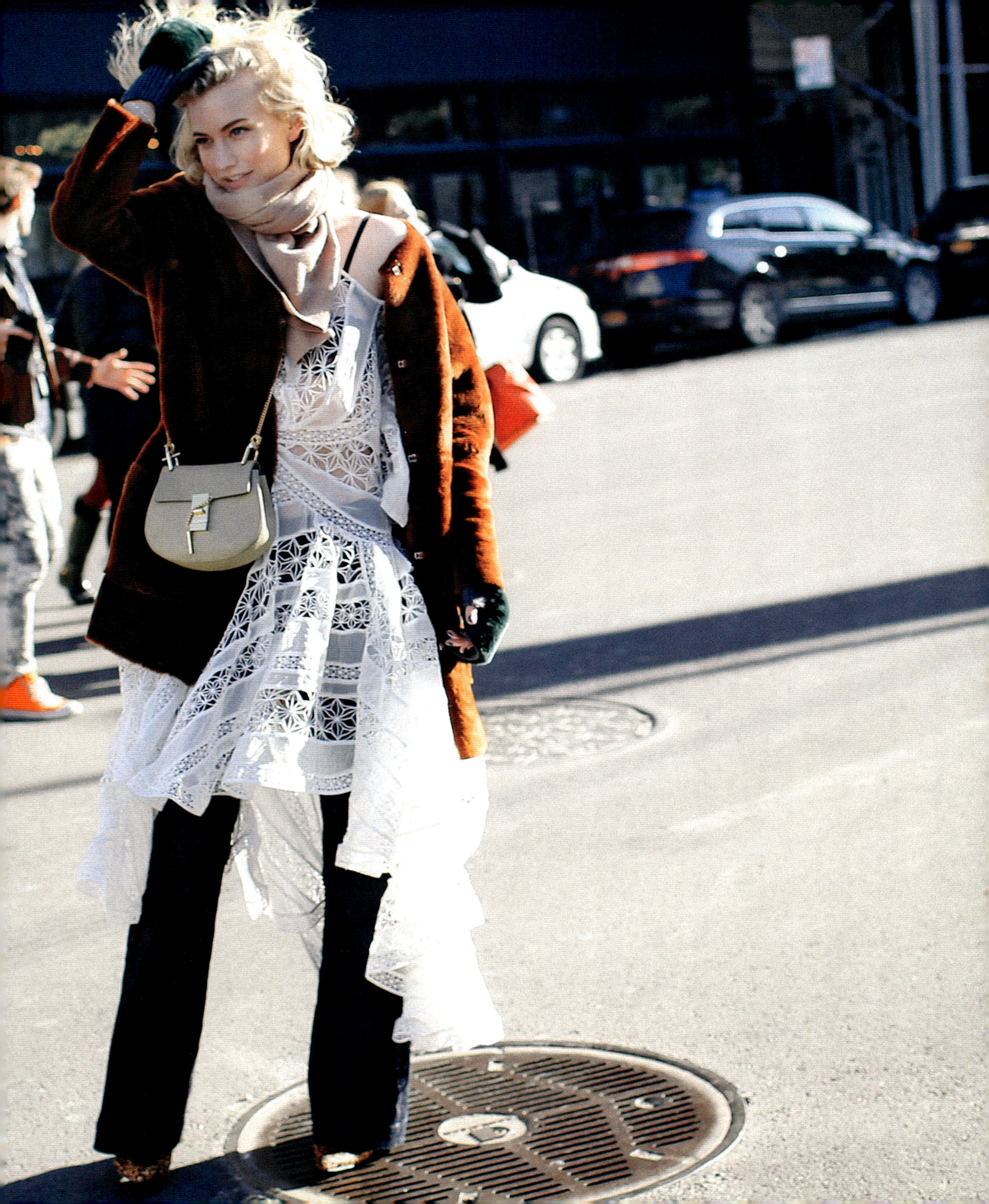

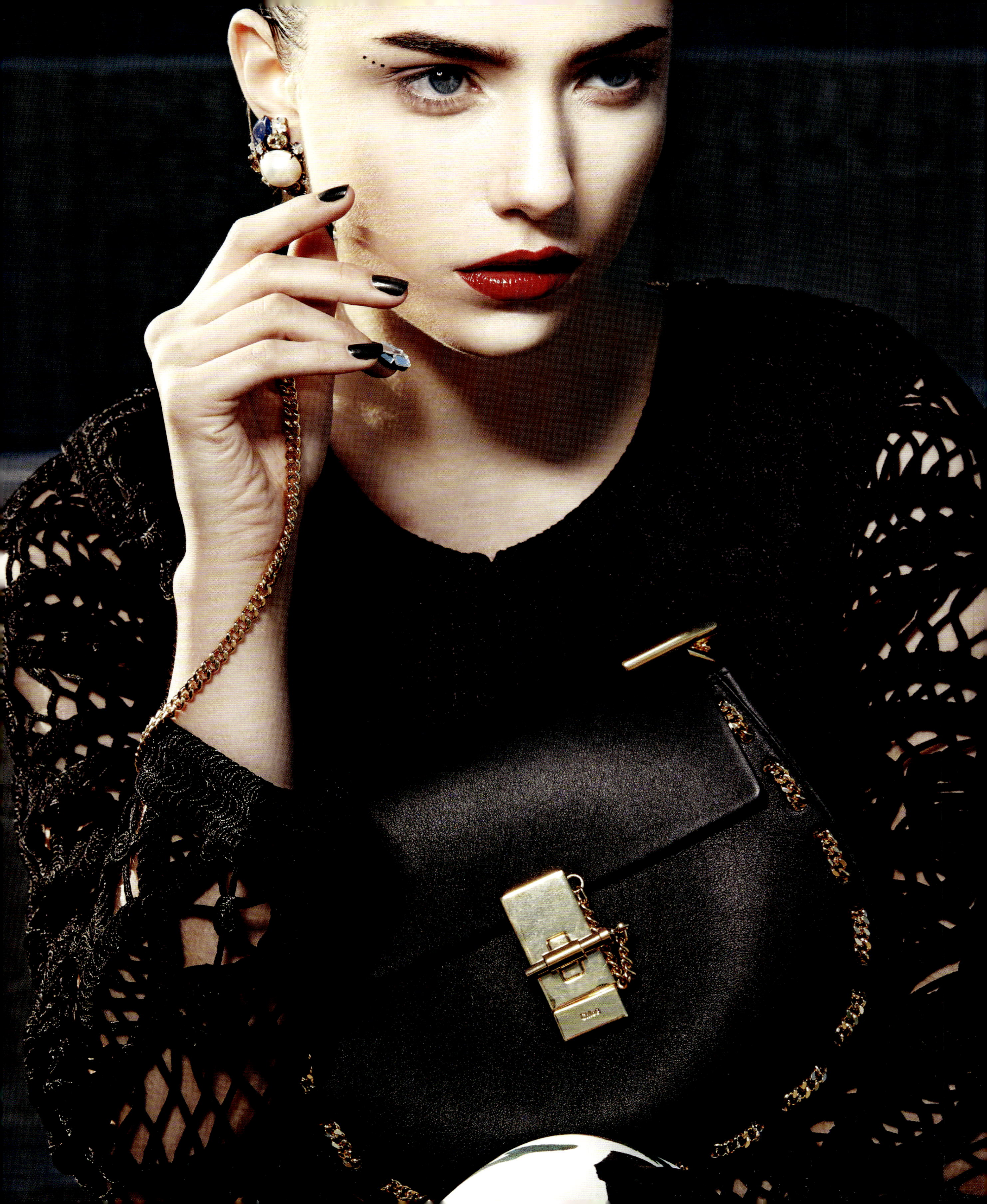

"I have often wondered if the enthusiasm with which some women embrace a backbreaker like the Paddington is a way of flaunting their vigor and strength, an advertisement of their youthful vitality."

—LYNN YAEGER, *The Atlantic Monthly*, April 2007

But the fashion pendulum swings, and by the end of the decade the heavyweight, hardware-loving bag was out. "Turning up . . . with a Chloé Paddington felt like walking into a romantic restaurant with a screaming infant in your arms," bemoaned the *Daily Telegraph* in 2011. After Philo left in 2006, the company circled through a number of designers before making Clare Waight Keller creative director in 2011. Keller introduced an It style of her own in the pre-Fall 2014 collection: the Drew bag. A pretty twist on the classic saddlebag that was popular in the 1970s and available in a few sizes, the Drew is feminine and modern, its half-moon shape a nod to the bohemian chic aesthetic associated with Chloé. The dainty pin closure adds an element of charm, while the long, slim gold chain allows for personalization; you can casually knot the chain, on one side or both, so the bag hangs higher. Whether crafted from smooth leather, suede, or a combination of the two, the Drew continues to seduce fashion editors and haute hippies alike with tactility and elegance, as Chloé introduces new interpretations often enough to tempt Drew devotees.

In 2017, Waight Keller left the company for Givenchy, ushering in a new era for the company. Natacha Ramsay-Levi, Nicolas Ghesquière's right hand at both Balenciaga and Louis Vutton, has taken the creative reins.

OPPOSITE:
Model Tess Finley with the Drew bag, *Elegant*, October 2015.

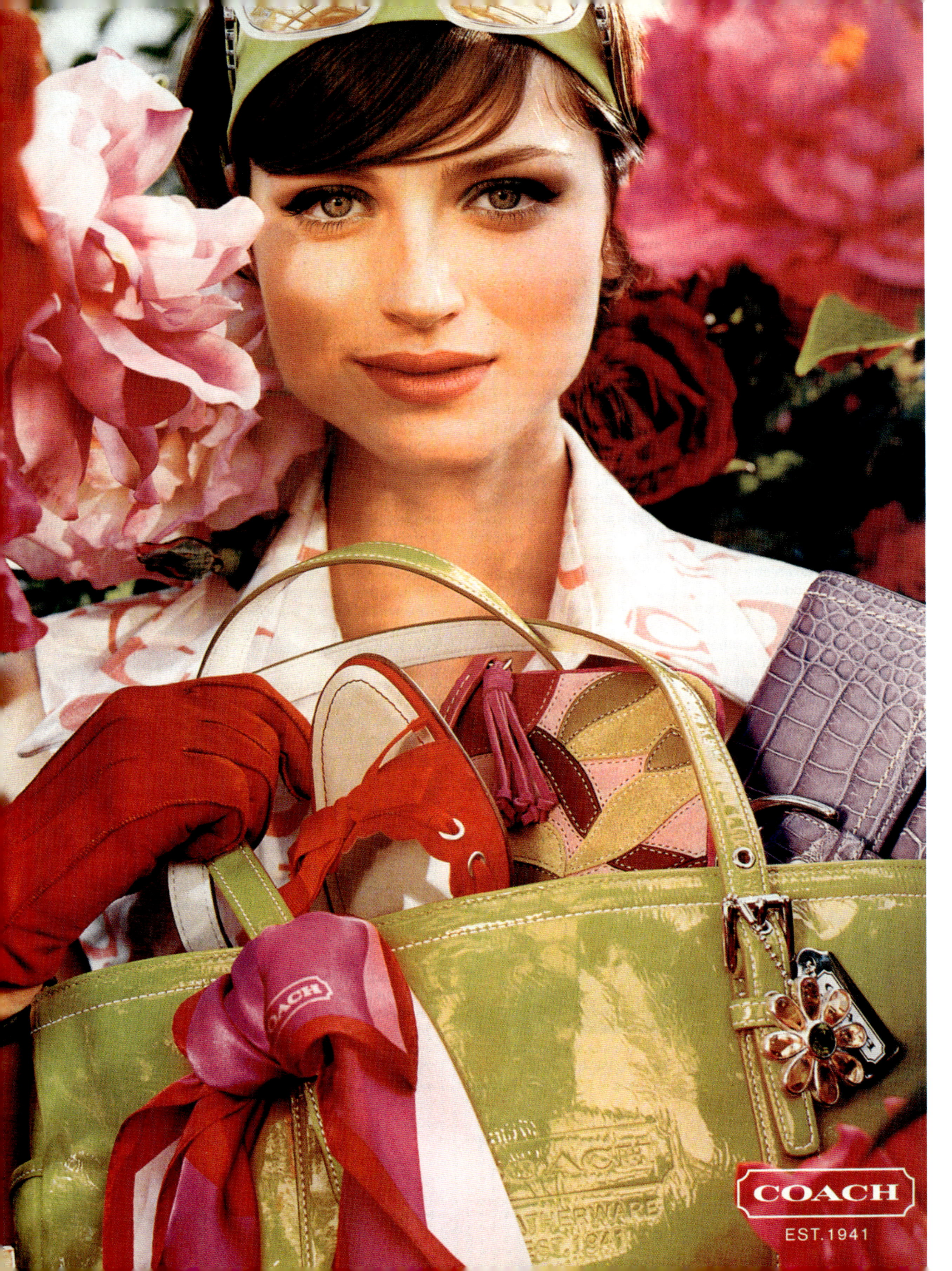
COACH
EST.1941

Coach

CASHIN CARRY SLING, 1962

CASHIN CARRY SHOPPING BAG TOTE, 1962

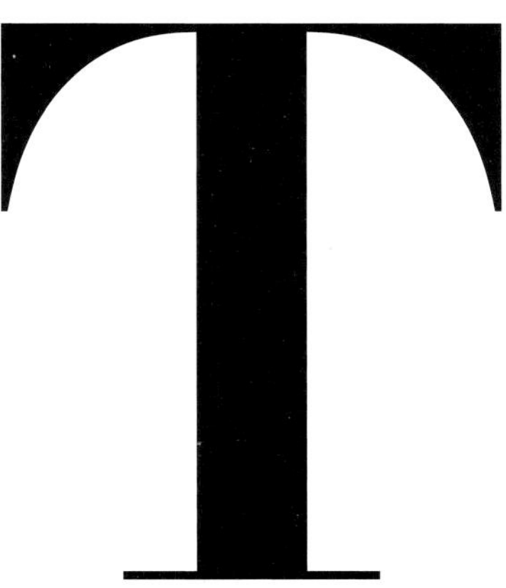

he Coach empire began in 1941 as Gail Leather Products, Inc., a small leather-goods factory on West Thirty-Fourth Street in New York, selling wallets, belts, and billfolds. Miles and Lillian Cahn joined the business in 1946 and, twelve years later, added men's handbags crafted from the same beautifully worn leather as a baseball glove. They were an instant hit. Like a catcher's mitt, they became softer, more supple with age and use. In 1961 the Cahns bought out the original owners and changed the company name to Coach. That December the Cahns hired designer Bonnie Cashin to create a women's line.

Cashin was already a celebrated name in the fashion industry. She had been a costume designer for both stage and film at 20th Century Fox; created uniforms for the armed forces; was the subject of her own Coca-Cola ad with the tagline "That Extra Something!"; and, since 1952, had owned her own fashion company.

The match was a brilliant one. The handbags that resulted from their thirteen-year collaboration forever changed the accessories landscape and catapulted Coach into the spotlight. Cashin's designs were streamlined, unfussy, and emphasized function and practicality. "I tried to get down to the unadorned basics of 'things to carry things in.' Could functional simplicity be retained with fashion?" mused Cashin—who found inspiration in paper bags and baskets—in the Fall 1964 Coach catalog. Among her most popular designs was a leather version of a shopping bag—which, Coach boasted, was the most copied bag in America—and slouchy sling-like styles with a coin purse attached to the exterior so women wouldn't have to rummage through their bags to find change. These practical outside "purse pockets" were a signature of Cashin's ready-to-wear, dating back to her years as a costume designer, when her mother sewed a purse to her daughter's jacket to hold her various supplies.

Cashin's designs for Coach gave handbags a jolt of levity and fun and offered an alternative to the more formal styles making waves in Paris. She used punchy colors like teal, mustard, pistachio, and cotton-candy pink and experimented with playful patterned linings. Her hardware treatments were novel: the firm's signature brass turnlock closure, for instance, was inspired by the hood fastenings on her 1940s convertible.

When Reed Krakoff arrived at the house in 1997, he made revolutionary changes. One of the first to corner the accessible luxury market and inject an element of desire, Krakoff didn't just reinvigorate the brand—he reinvented it.

OPPOSITE:
Coach, 2004 advertisement.

PAGES 66–67:
A Bonnie Cashin–inspired bag from Coach's limited-edition 70th anniversary collection, Milan, February 2012.

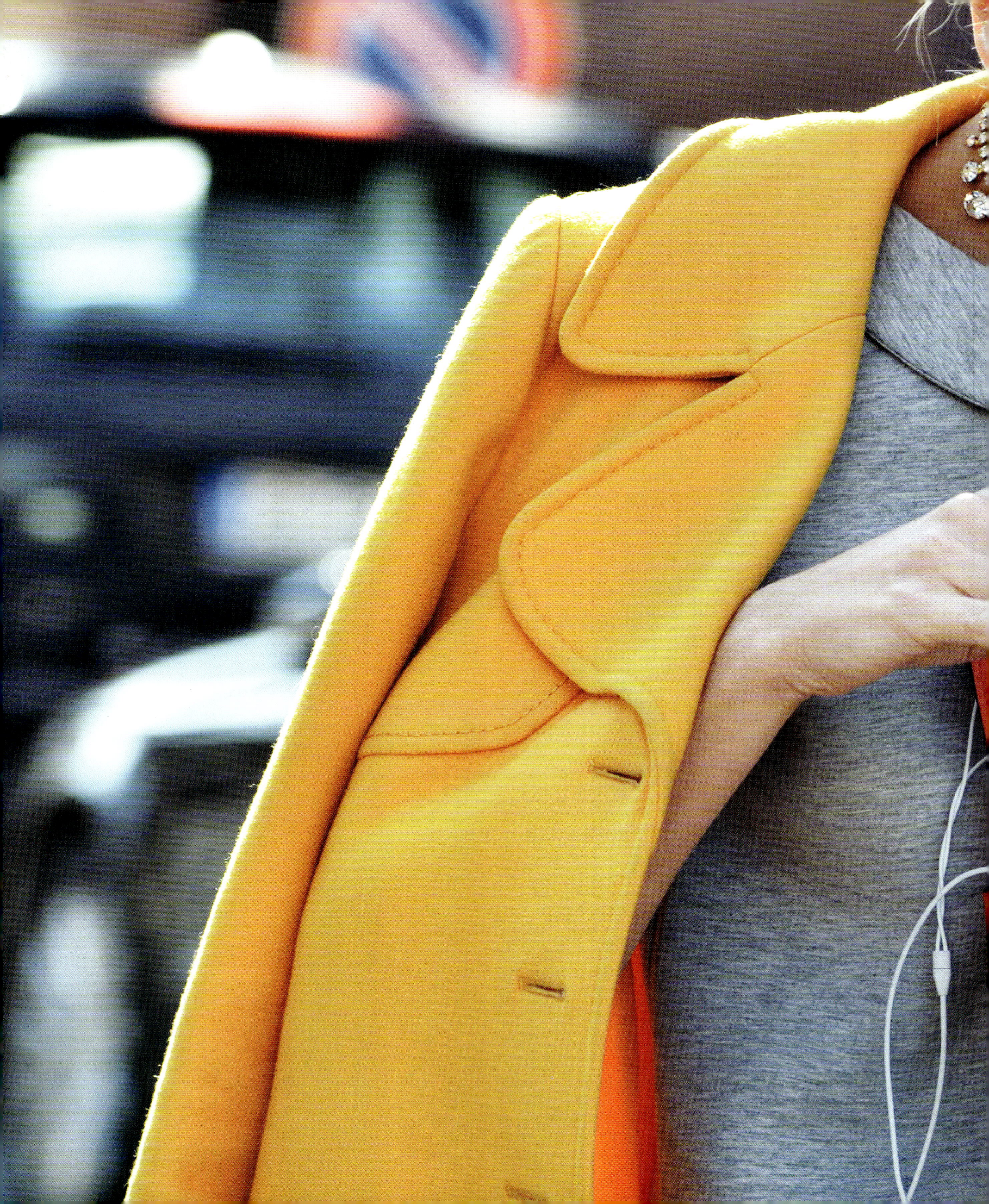

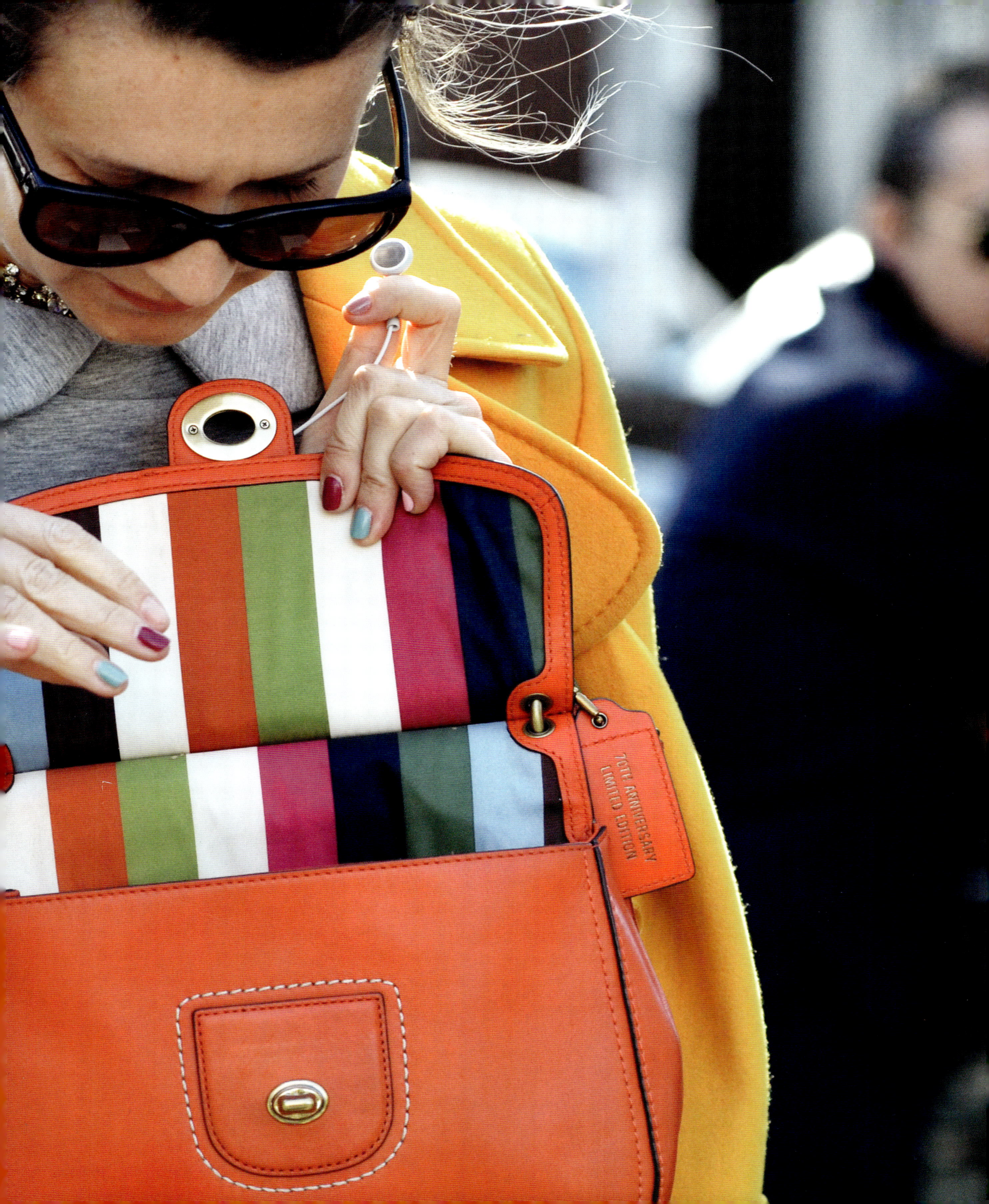
70TH ANNIVERSARY
LIMITED EDITION

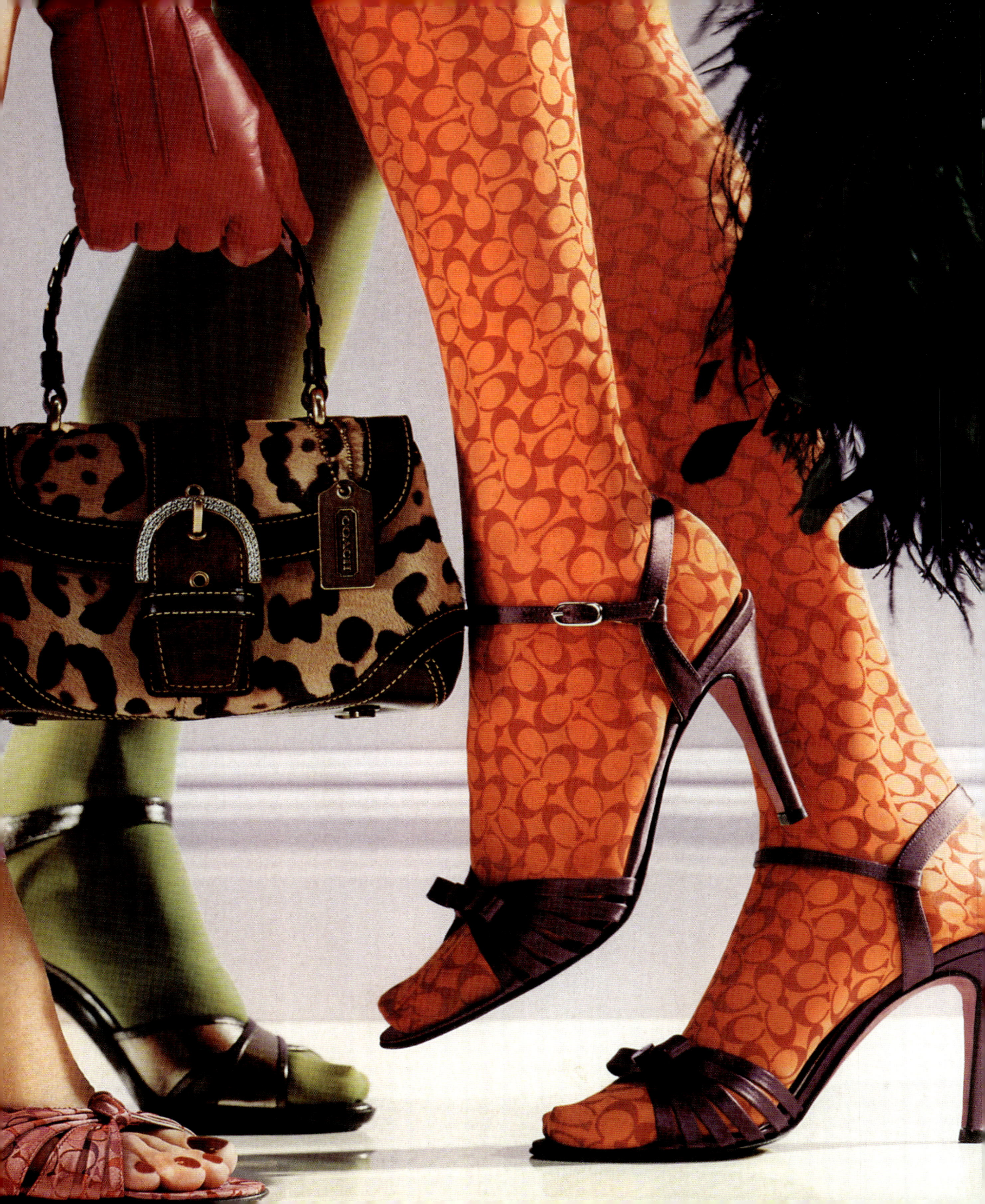
COACH

“When I imagine the kind of woman who carries a Coach bag, I think of chic women caught in all-American moments—barefoot on the docks in Nantucket or window-shopping down Fifth Avenue on a crisp autumn day. A Coach woman is Ali MacGraw in *Love Story*: breezy, laid-back, and drop-dead chic.”

—GLENDA BAILEY, from *Coach* by Orla Healy, 2002

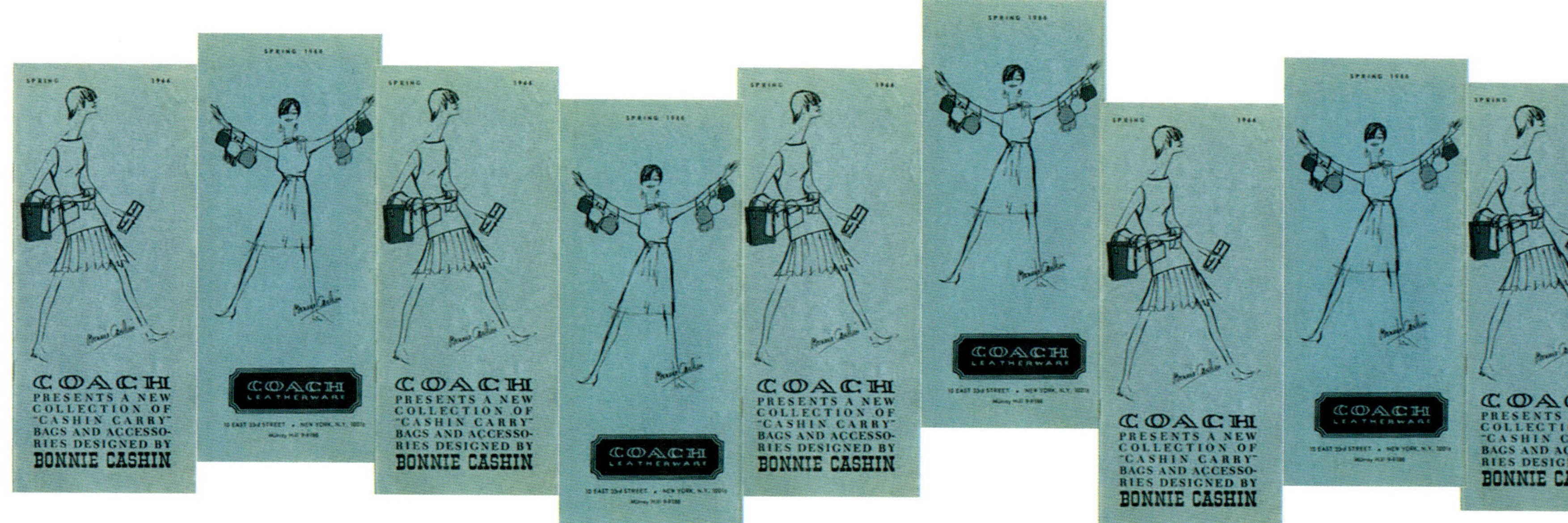

Back then Coach’s offerings were narrow, the styles were relatively conservative, and there wasn’t a constant turnover of new merchandise on the sales floor. So Krakoff—whose role extended beyond design to include all creative, from advertising to retail, also radical for that time—pumped up the fashion factor; introduced other categories such as eyewear, shoes, and umbrellas; and implemented seasonal collections “to create multiple visits by consumers,” as he recalled years later in *Women’s Wear Daily* (2011). His goal: get people to buy because of *want*, not need.

By boosting the collection and increasing the frequency of deliveries, Krakoff was also able to react to trends. When logos were hot, for example, he delivered monogram canvas bags with a C pattern, inspired by interior designer David Hicks’s alphabet prints. “We used to be a place where people went when they needed a bag,” he said in *Footwear News* in 2006. “Now, we’re where someone goes who just wants to see what’s happening in the world of fashion.”

That same year, Krakoff brought the brand full circle with the launch of Legacy, a collection based on Cashin’s original designs, complete with weathered brass hardware and hand-burnished leather for a vintage feel. His successor, Brit Stuart Vevers, took over in 2014 and infused the brand with a new youthfulness. Vevers’s first big bag was the Swagger, with thick pebbled leather and double turnlock hardware. Its name references “girl gangs, which Vevers feels are quite cool,” observed the *Independent* in 2016.

OPPOSITE:
Buckle flap bag, Coach, 2004.

ABOVE:
Illustrations by Bonnie Cashin for a Coach promotional piece, Spring 1966.

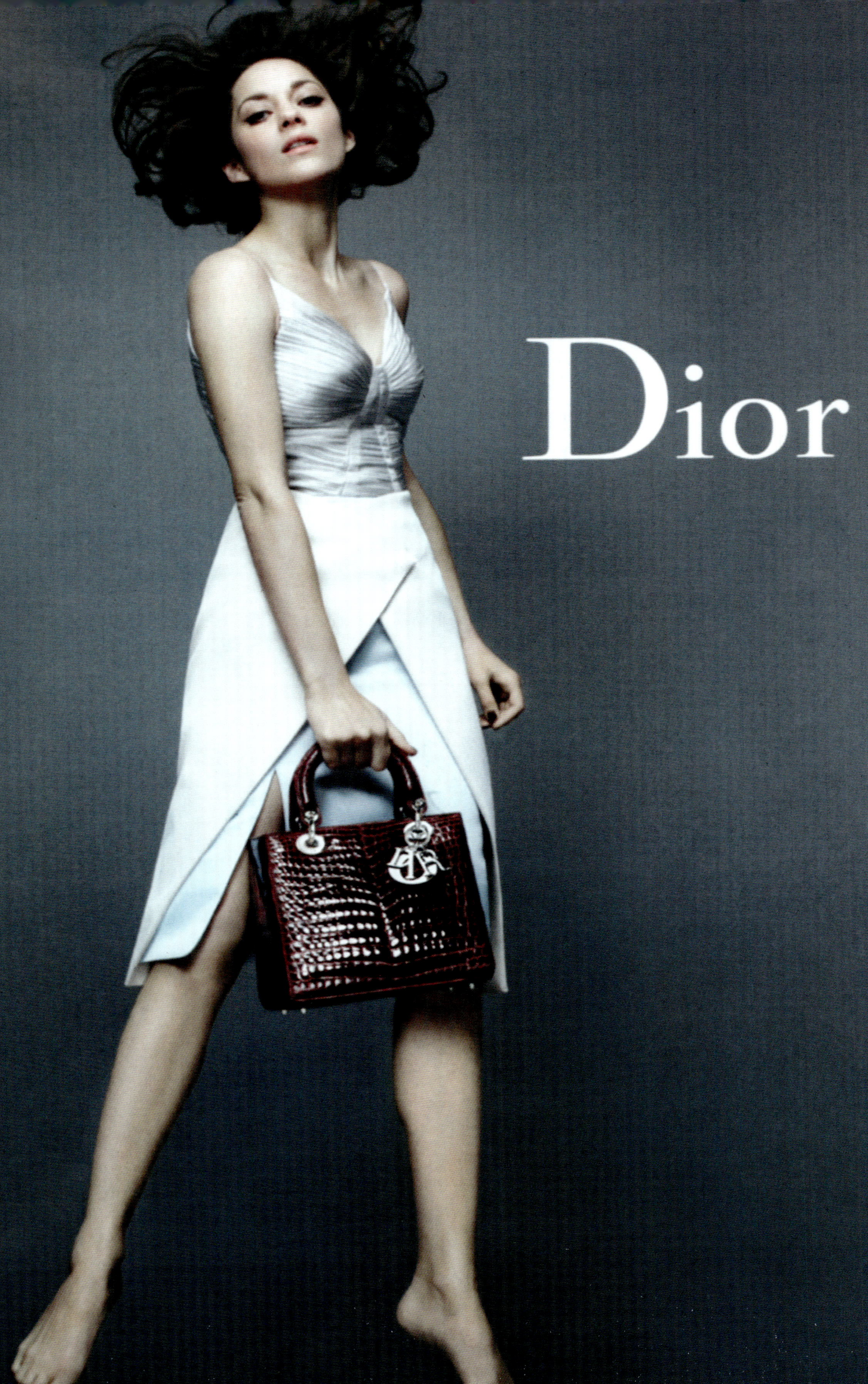
Dior

Christian Dior

LADY DIOR, 1995

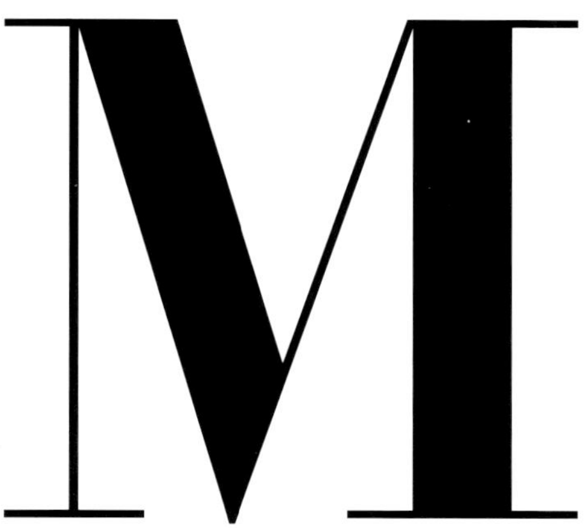

Much has been written about the revolutionary impact of Christian Dior's New Look collection, which debuted on February 12, 1947. The silhouette emphasized a heightened femininity, with nipped wasp waists and full, generously cut skirts, meant to soothe wartime memories. The New Look impacted accessories as well, with petite ladylike pochettes—roomier shoulder bags, with their straps reminiscent of soldiers' bags, were out. "Don't forget, a bag is not a wastepaper basket!" advised Monsieur Dior in his now-classic tome, *The Little Dictionary of Fashion* (1954). "You can't fill it with a lot of unnecessary things and expect it to look nice and last a long time."

Dior, one of history's leading fashion houses, did not have an iconic handbag until 1984, when Bernard Arnault, chairman and CEO of LVMH, acquired the firm. He did away with licensing obligations and focused on in-house production—the first step to the birth of the bestselling Lady Dior.

Princess Diana received Dior's black boxy quilted bag, originally named the Chouchou (French for "pet"), as a gift from French First Lady Bernadette Chirac at the opening of a Cézanne exhibition at the Grand Palais, Paris, on September 25, 1995. As luxury lore goes, Diana loved the handbag so much that she ordered one in every color and was soon photographed with it everywhere, from a business trip in Argentina to the Met Gala in New York, where she wore a blue bias-cut lace-trim gown by John Galliano for Dior. When photos were published of Diana carrying the bag during a visit to Birmingham in 1995, Harrods reportedly sold out of the style within hours. The following year, 140,000 bags were sold at $1,200 each. By this time, the company had smartly renamed the style—it was now the Lady Dior.

Over the years, the handbag has gone through countless permutations without losing any of the inherent elegance and simplicity that have made it such a favorite. There was the diamond-studded version, the collaboration with German artist Anselm Reyle (Dior's first with an artist), the mink version, and the ones in woven leather or embellished with petals or patch pockets. They all featured the house's trademark *cannage* pattern, metal rings connecting the handles to the body, and D-I-O-R logo letter pendants. *Cannage*, from the French word for "caning," was inspired by the caned seating of the chairs at the 1947 show.

"If it's an icon bag with a real story, people say, 'We are ready to invest in that,'" observed Sidney Toledano, president and CEO of Christian Dior, in *Women's Wear Daily* in 2010. "People are rediscovering that luxury has meaning only if it goes through a long process across time, which means you have to have heritage."

OPPOSITE:
Dior campaign, 2014, featuring Marion Cotillard.

PAGE 72:
Princess Diana carrying a black Lady Dior bag, London, March 1997.

PAGE 73:
Illustration by Christian Dior, *Vogue*, June 1947.

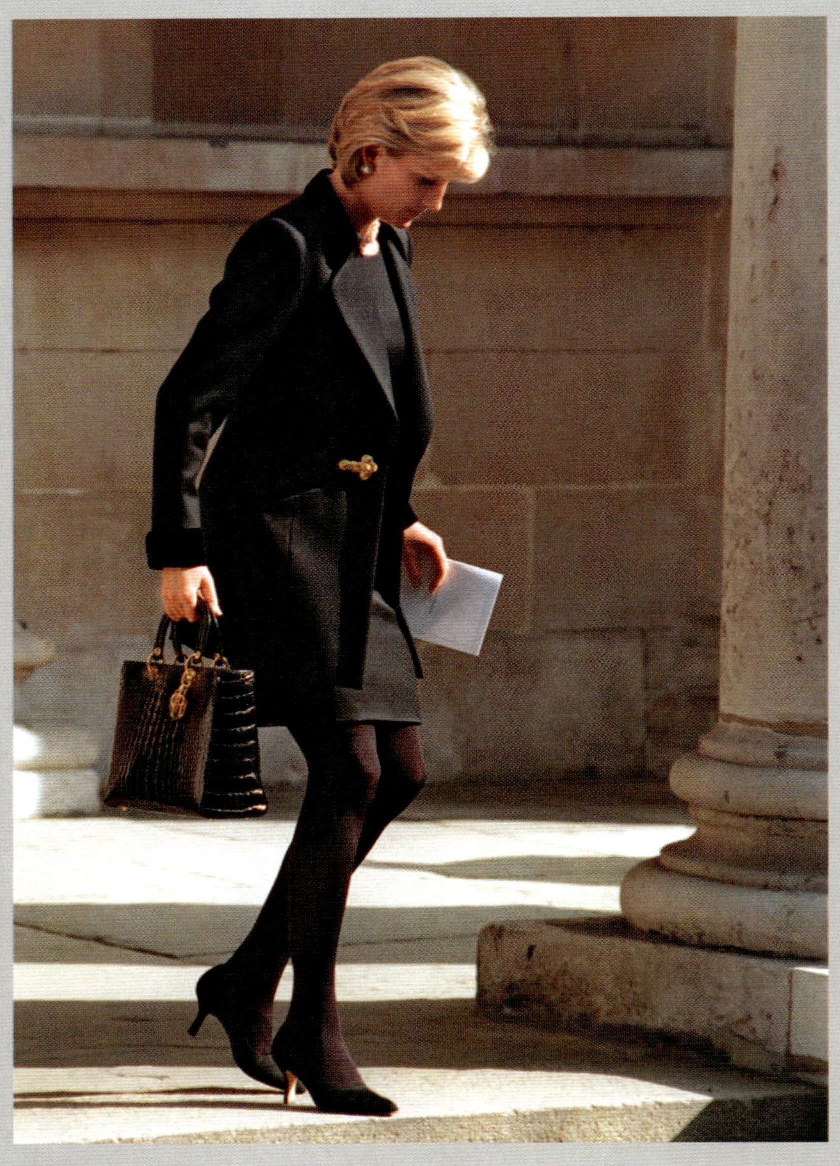

"There is nothing I would like better than to make every woman look and feel like a Duchess."

—CHRISTIAN DIOR, from *Vogue on Christian Dior* by Charlotte Sinclair, 2015

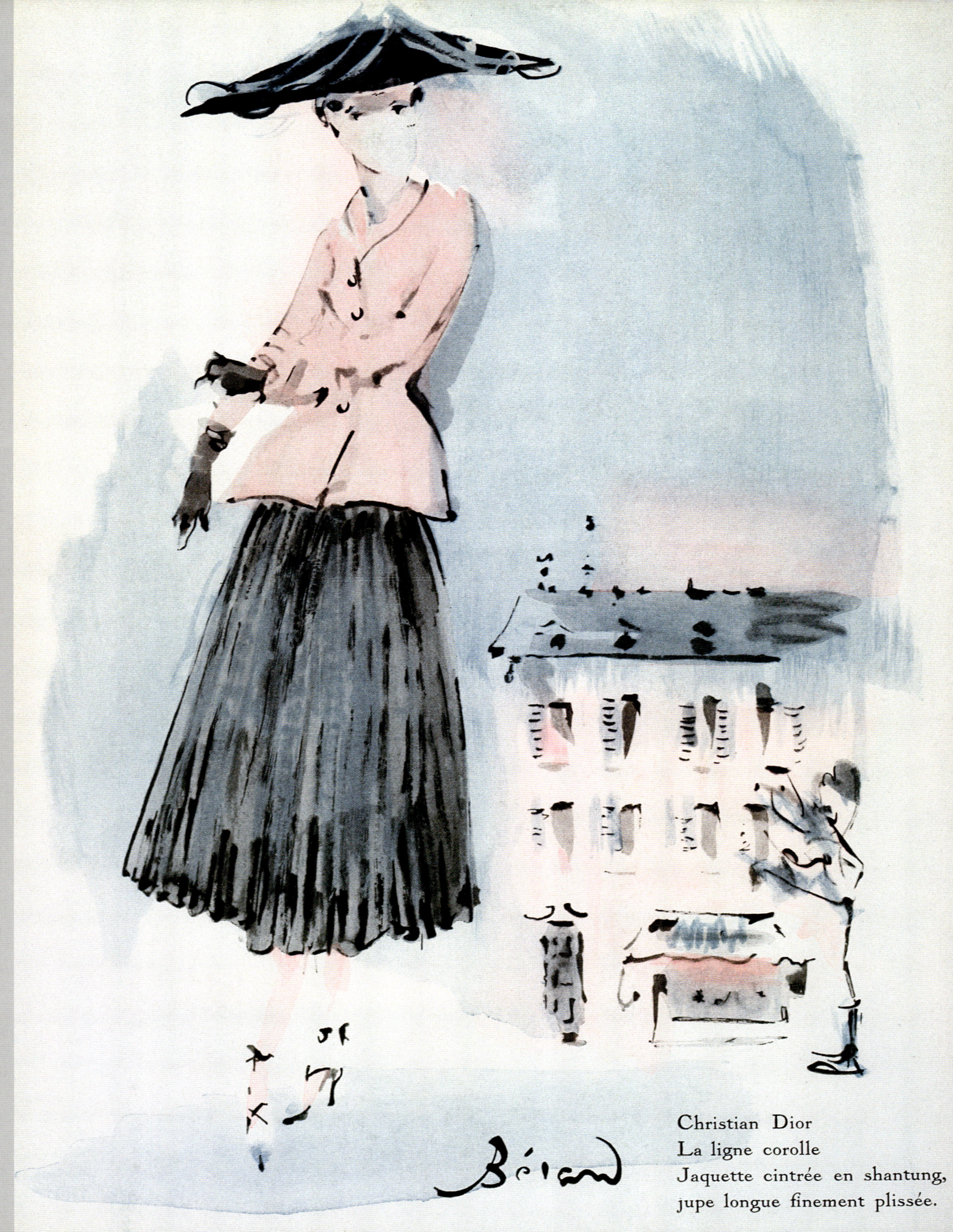

Christian Dior
La ligne corolle
Jaquette cintrée en shantung,
jupe longue finement plissée.

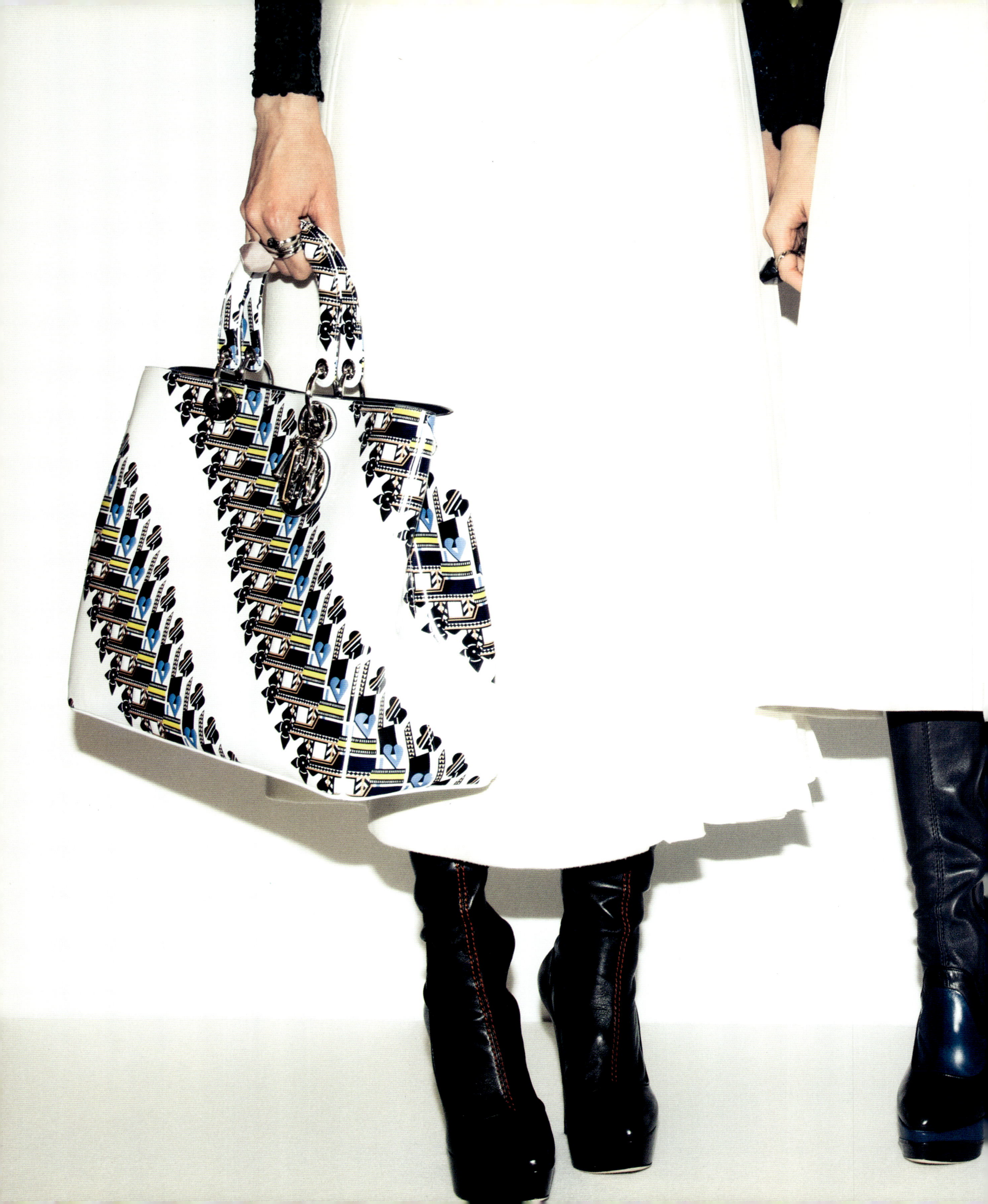

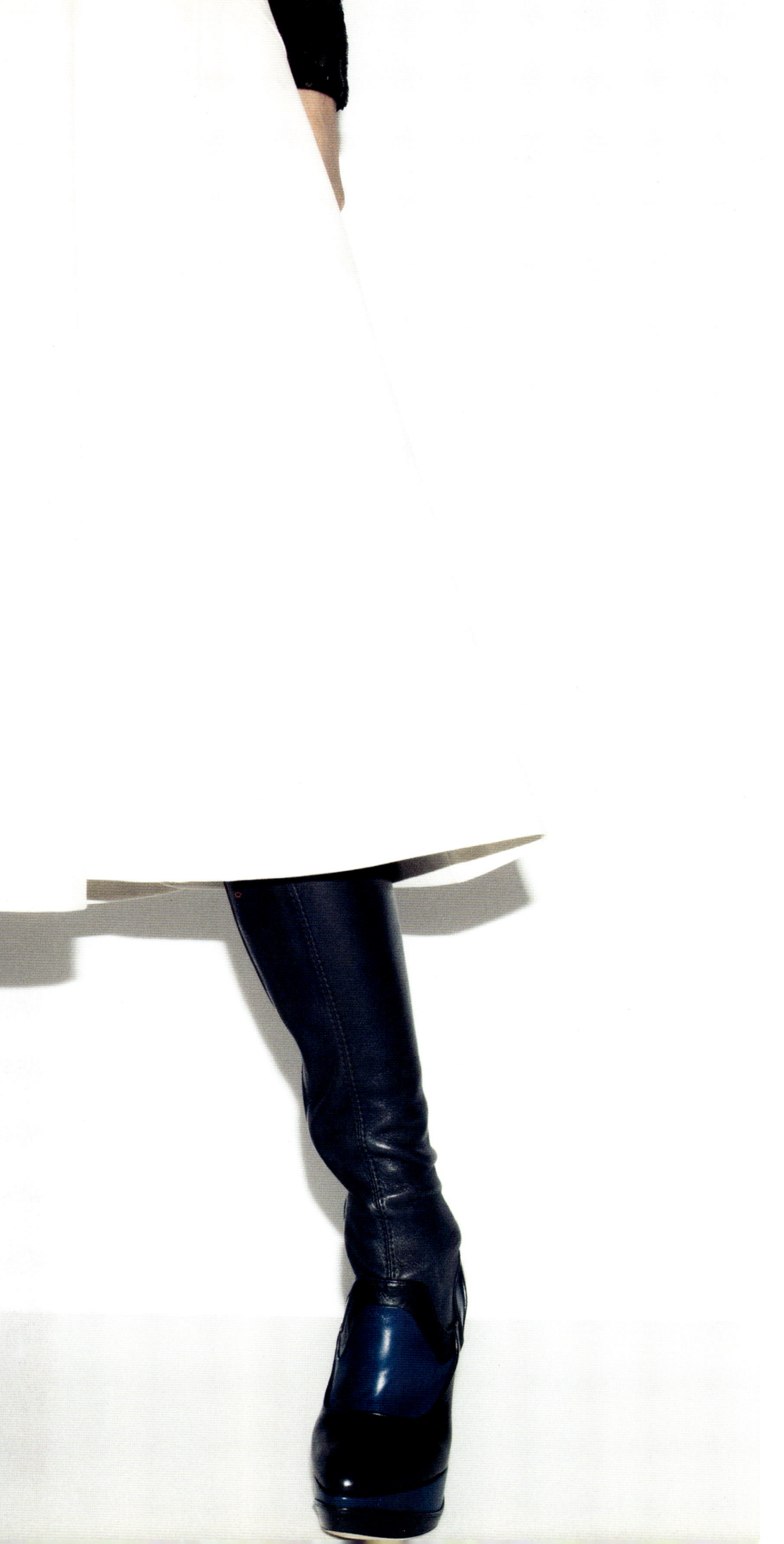

THIS PAGE:
Lady Dior, backstage at Christian Dior, Pre-Fall 2015 ready-to-wear.

PAGE 76:
Christian Dior advertisement, 1948.

PAGE 77:
Christian Dior, 1955.

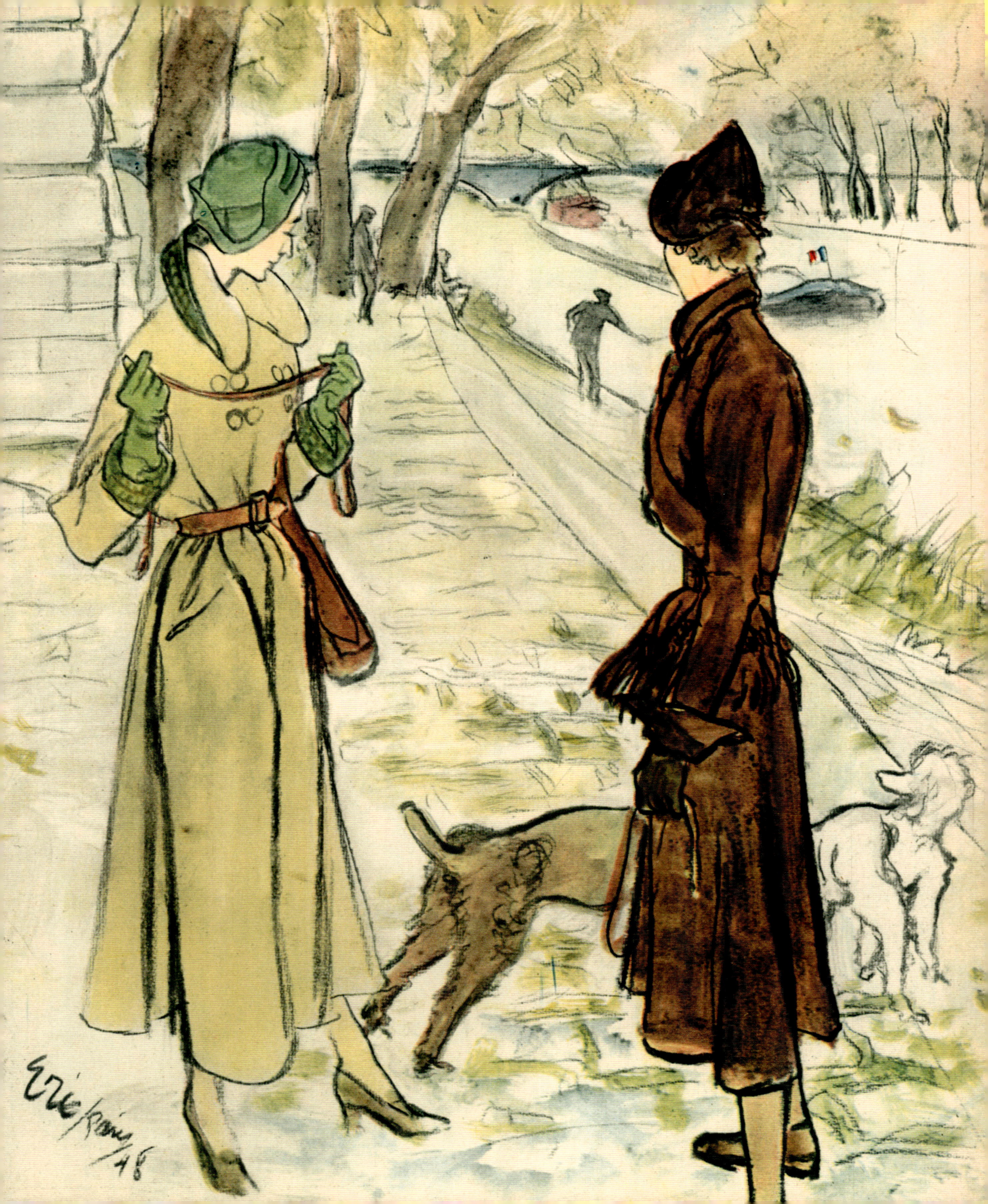

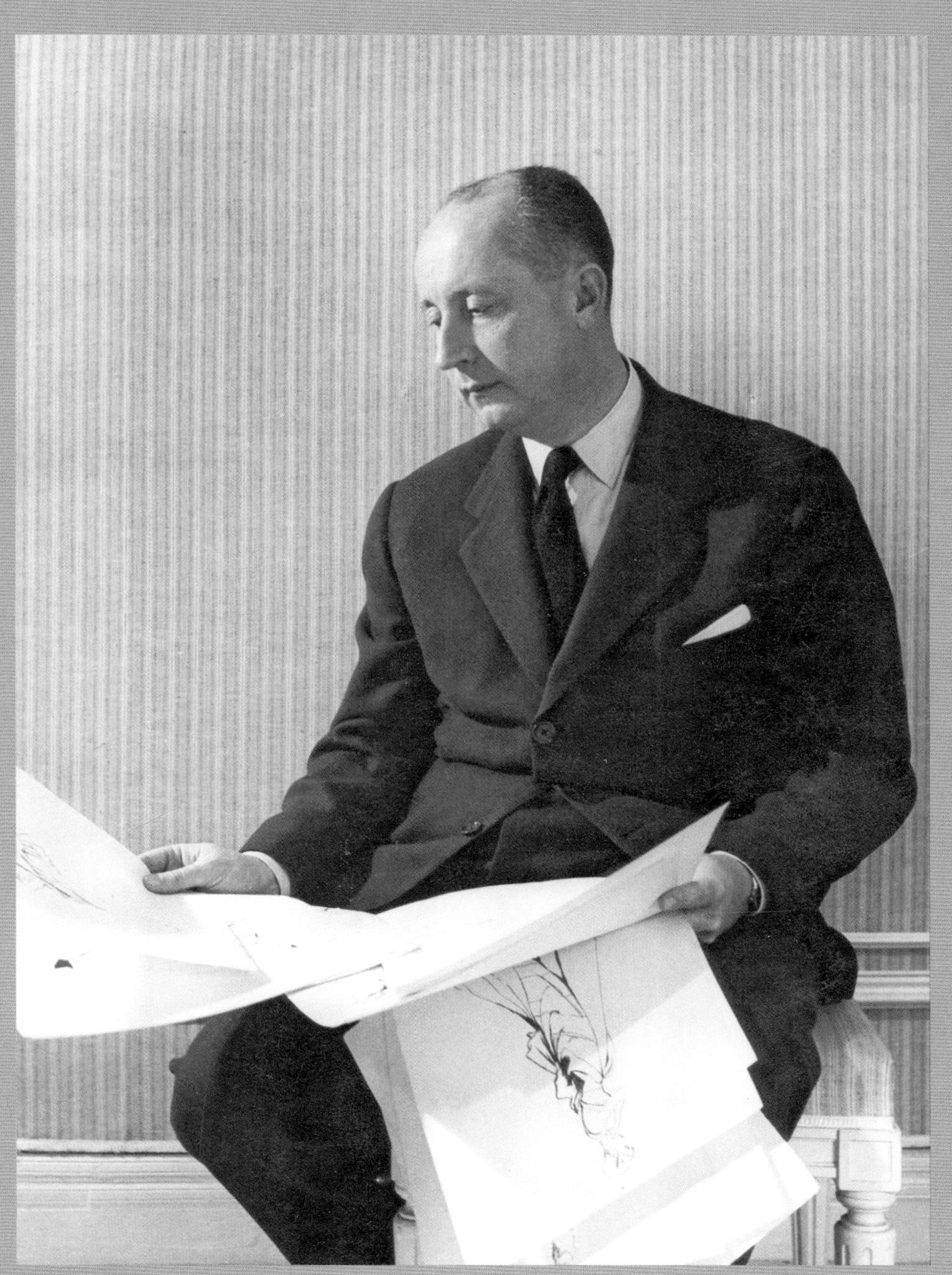

HANDBAGS IN FILM

In film, as in life, handbags announce a person's identity and style. A glimpse of Sarah Jessica Parker with her Fendi and Chanel in *Sex and the City* tells you all you need to know about her character, Carrie Bradshaw—she's fashion obsessed. In *Legally Blonde*, Reese Witherspoon's character, sorority-sister-turned-law-student Elle Woods, carries a bright red Bottega Veneta bag, perfectly telegraphing her character's optimism, drive, and love of a good luxury object. Handbags have been used cleverly throughout the history of cinema—here are some of my favorite moments.

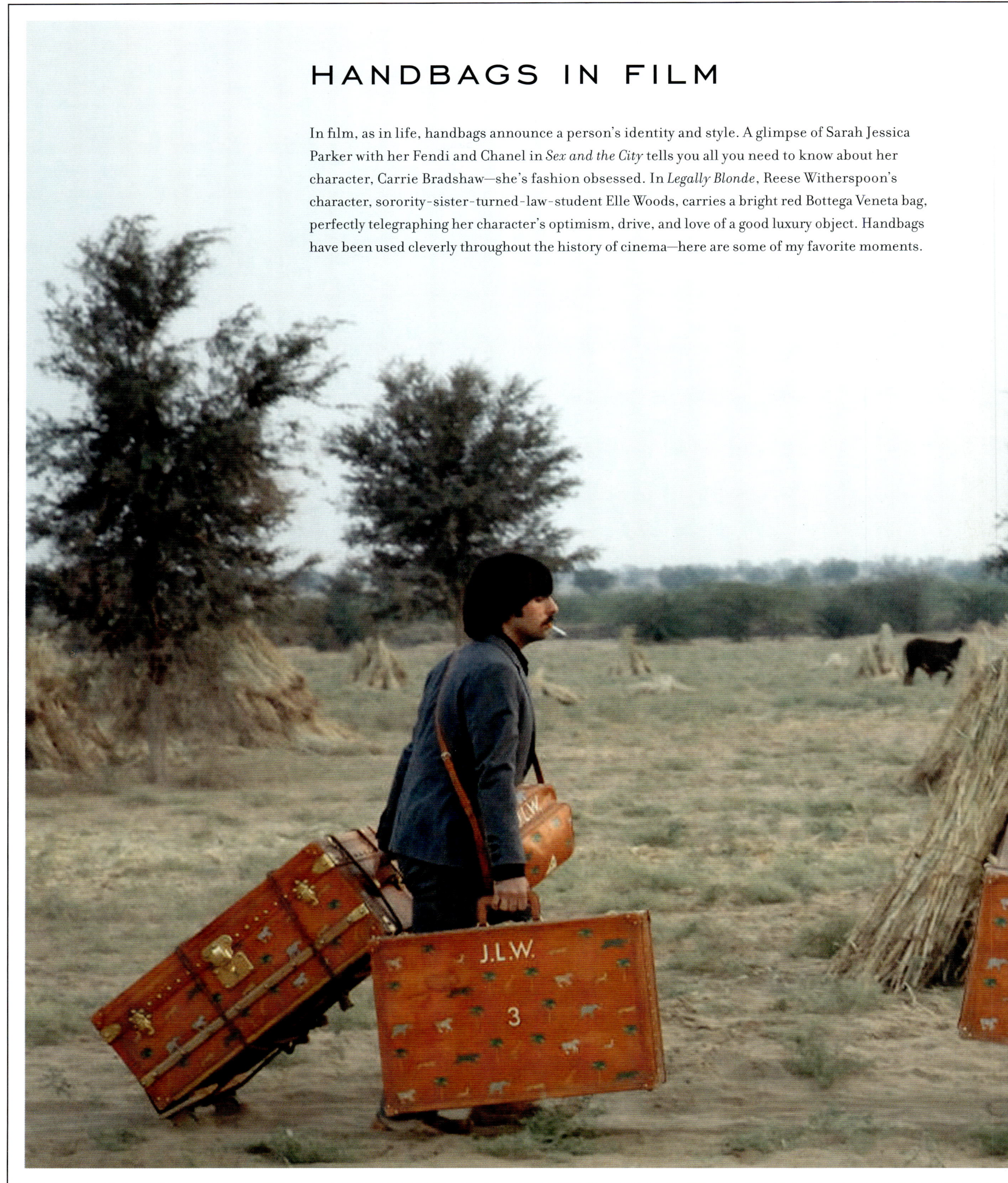

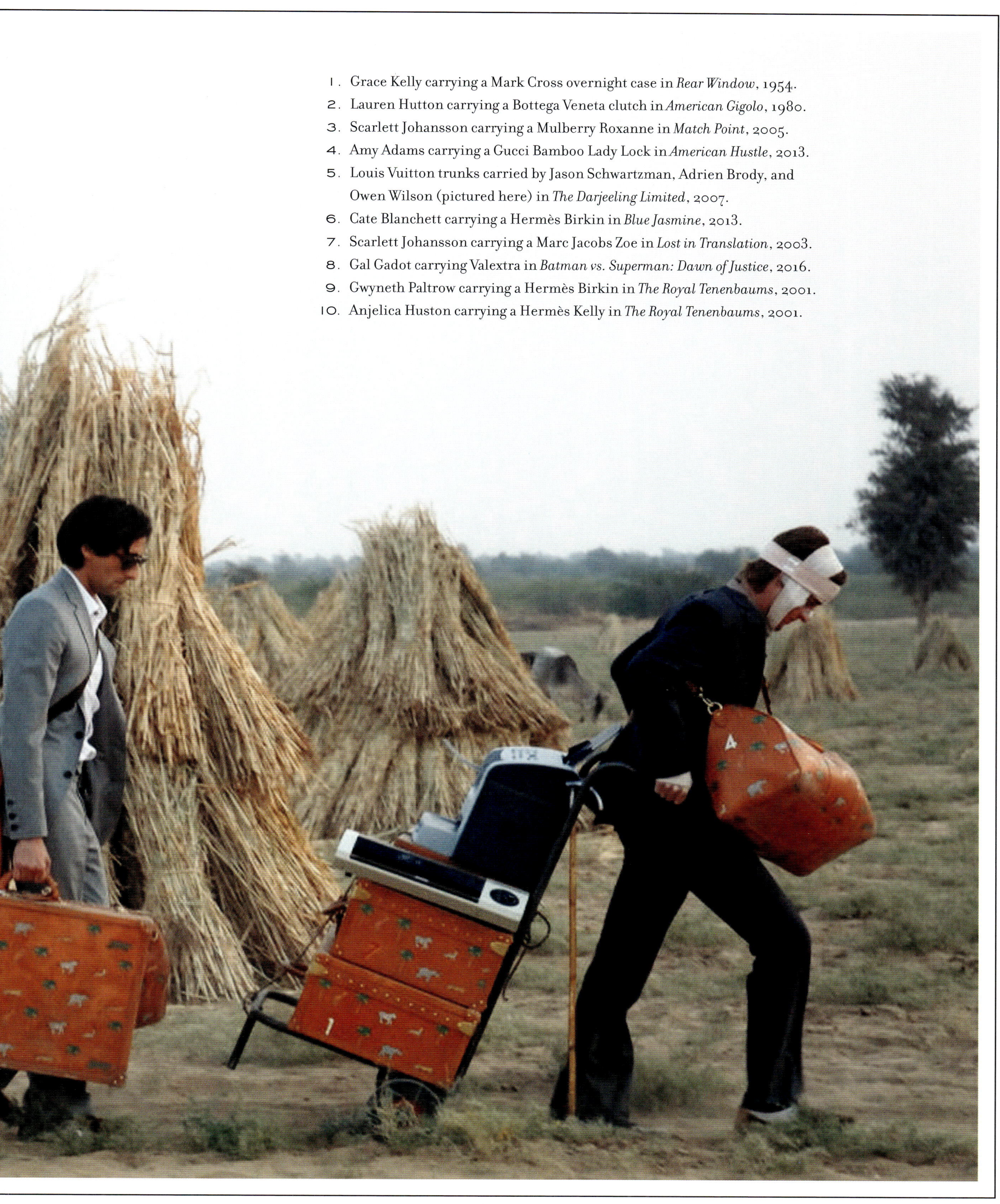

1. Grace Kelly carrying a Mark Cross overnight case in *Rear Window*, 1954.
2. Lauren Hutton carrying a Bottega Veneta clutch in *American Gigolo*, 1980.
3. Scarlett Johansson carrying a Mulberry Roxanne in *Match Point*, 2005.
4. Amy Adams carrying a Gucci Bamboo Lady Lock in *American Hustle*, 2013.
5. Louis Vuitton trunks carried by Jason Schwartzman, Adrien Brody, and Owen Wilson (pictured here) in *The Darjeeling Limited*, 2007.
6. Cate Blanchett carrying a Hermès Birkin in *Blue Jasmine*, 2013.
7. Scarlett Johansson carrying a Marc Jacobs Zoe in *Lost in Translation*, 2003.
8. Gal Gadot carrying Valextra in *Batman vs. Superman: Dawn of Justice*, 2016.
9. Gwyneth Paltrow carrying a Hermès Birkin in *The Royal Tenenbaums*, 2001.
10. Anjelica Huston carrying a Hermès Kelly in *The Royal Tenenbaums*, 2001.

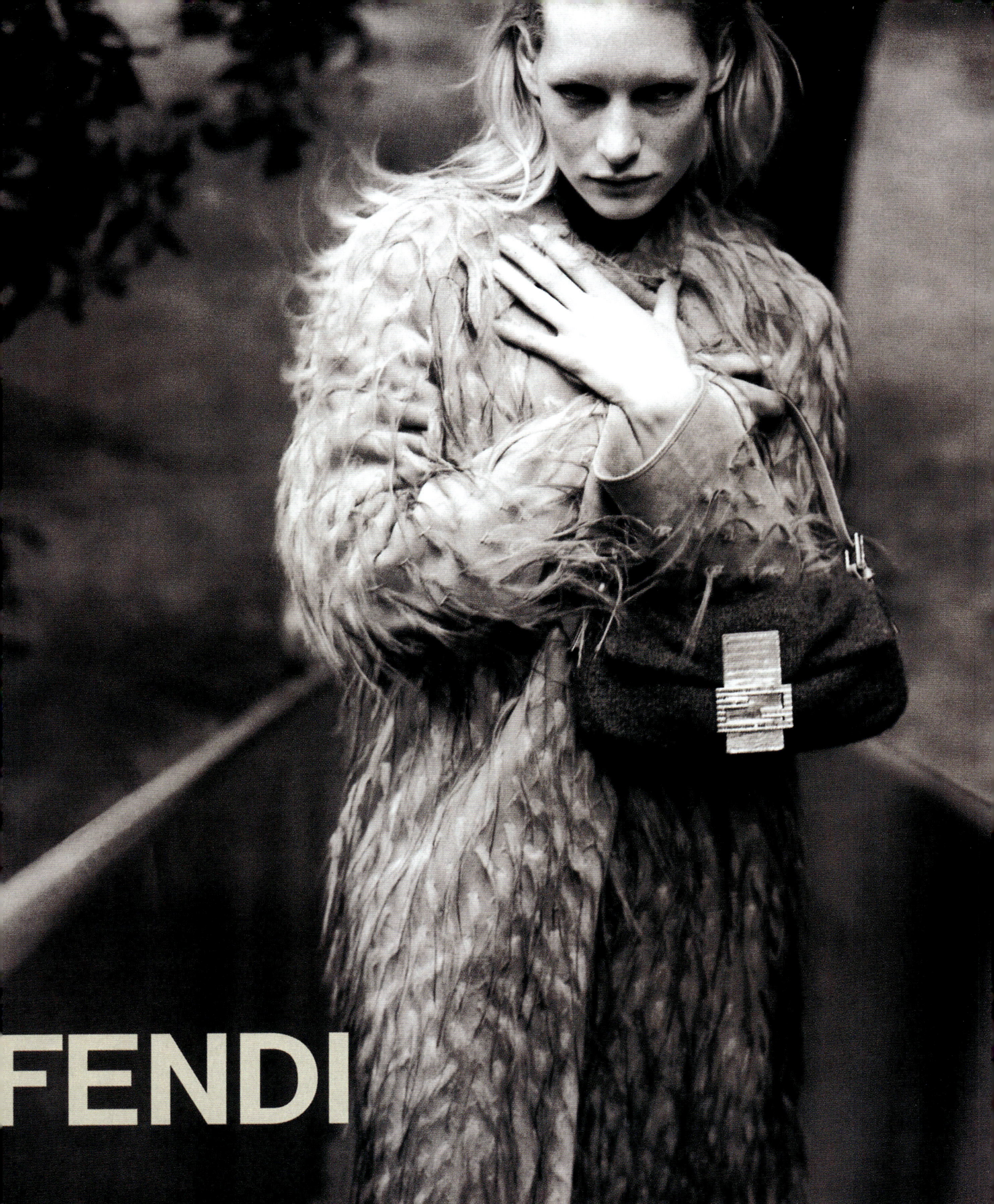
FENDI

Fendi

BAGUETTE, 1997

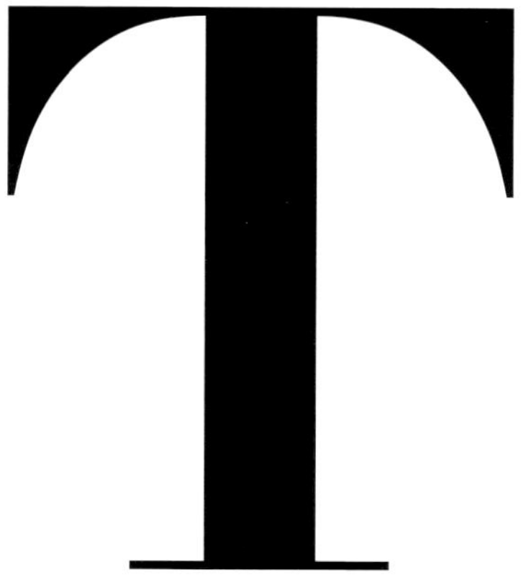

The Fendi Baguette is in a class of its own. Slim, with a short strap, and small enough to tuck under the arm like a loaf of French bread—hence the name—the Baguette triggered the It Bag craze. The Hermès Birkin predates the Baguette, as does Prada's nylon backpack, but it was the Baguette, launched in 1997, that sparked the must-have fever and the inevitable symptom—the waiting list.

The genius lies in the design's endless variations, some dripping with sequins and dangling beaded fringe, others a textural wonderland with three-dimensional embellishments and appliqués. There are bags that resemble grimacing cartoon faces with furry brows, re-create Cubist Picasso-like profiles, or are exquisitely painted or petaled. Fendi even sold a do-it-yourself Baguette kit—a white canvas bag with ten Pantone markers—that let customers doodle their own never-before-seen styles. With this kaleidoscope of colors, patterns, and materials, each bag became a special edition of sorts, though all were smartly branded and immediately recognizable with a huge double-F logo, an invention of creative director Karl Lagerfeld. The Baguette struck at just the right time, when the stylish set was tiring of 1990s minimalism and hungry for a bit of ostentation. The handbag was so successful that it's credited with reviving the Fendi firm.

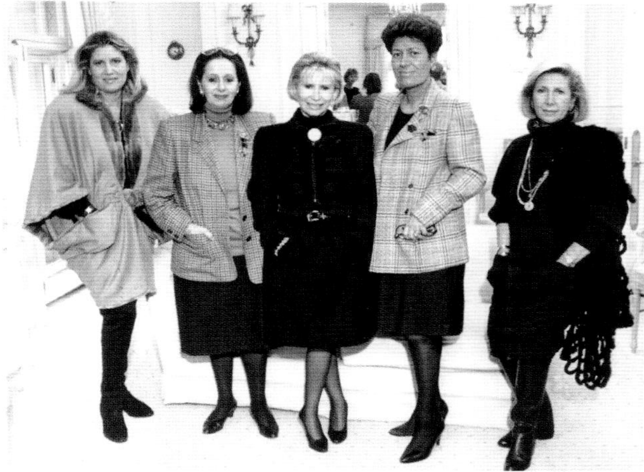

It is fitting, then, that the creator of the bag was none other than Silvia Venturini Fendi, the last remaining Fendi at the legendary Roman house. Founded by her grandparents Adele Casagrande and Edoardo Fendi in 1925, the leather and fur shop descended to their five daughters, each of whom oversaw a different part of the family business with the shared mantra "For women, by women." They're the ones who brought in Lagerfeld in the 1960s to head up ready-to-wear and be the company's public face. And they're the ones who gave Fendi its renown.

Venturini Fendi, whose mother, Anna, was the accessories designer, has gone on to create other cult items such as the Spy Bag (2005), with its woven handles and hidden compartments, and the Peekaboo (2009), which, with its discreet exterior that folds down just a bit to reveal a bold, luxurious interior, she has dubbed "the anti-Baguette."

There's a scene in the HBO series *Sex and the City* that aptly sums up the reverence evoked by the Baguette. Carrie Bradshaw, played by fashion icon Sarah Jessica Parker, gets mugged somewhere south of Houston Street. "Give me your bag," the assailant demands, aiming a pistol at her. Her first response is to correct him: "It's a *Baguette*."

OPPOSITE:
Baguette, Fendi 1990s.

RIGHT:
The Fendi sisters in Rome: *(from left to right)* Alda, Paola, Anna, Carla, and Franca.

PAGE 82:
Karlie Kloss carrying a Fendi leather-and-canvas logo bag, *Vogue*, August 2010.

PAGE 83:
Sequined Baguettes, *Vogue*, October 2012.

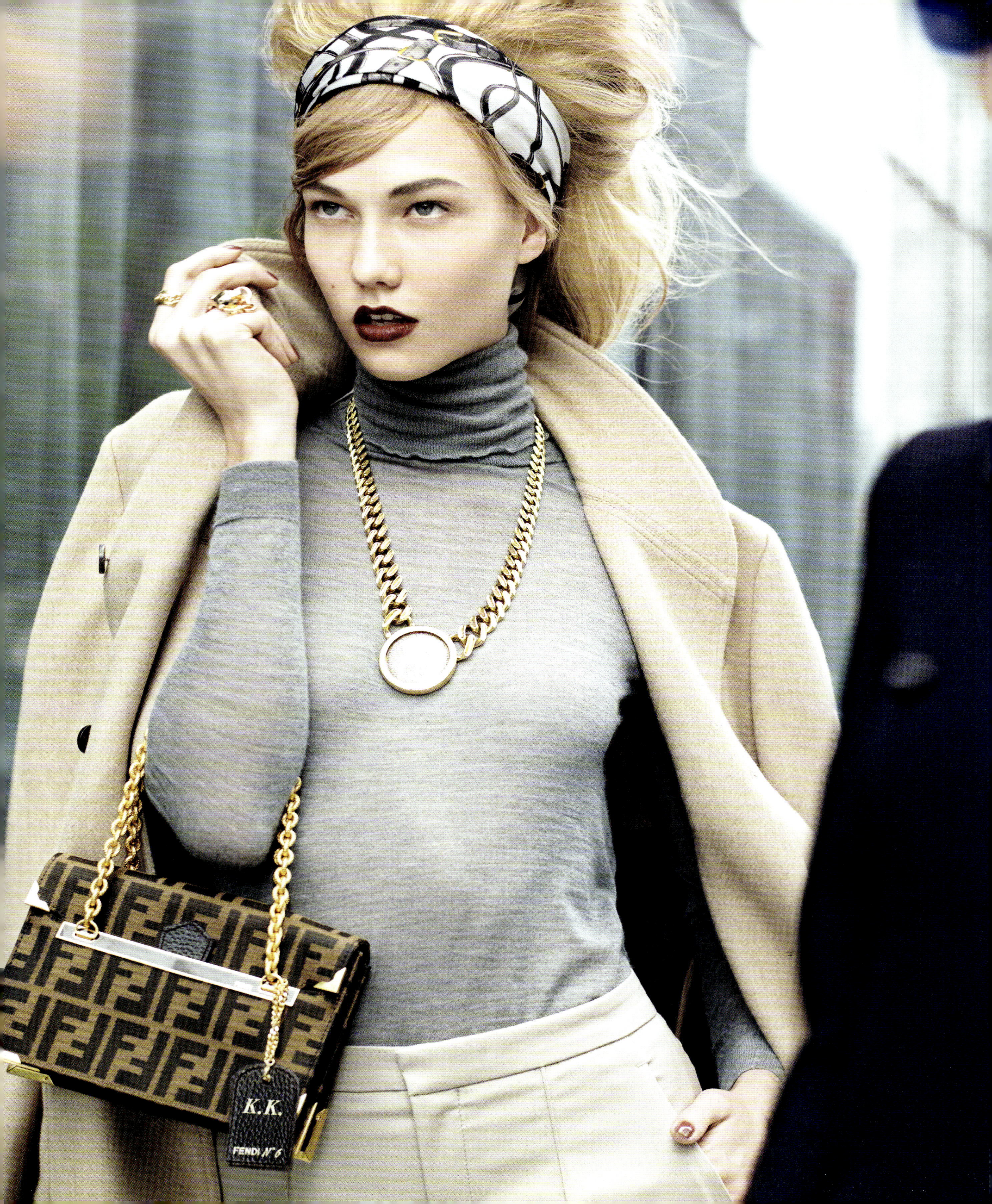
K.K.
FENDI N°6

“Every once in a while,
a girl has to indulge herself.”

—SARAH JESSICA PARKER, as Carrie Bradshaw on *Sex and the City*, 1998–2004

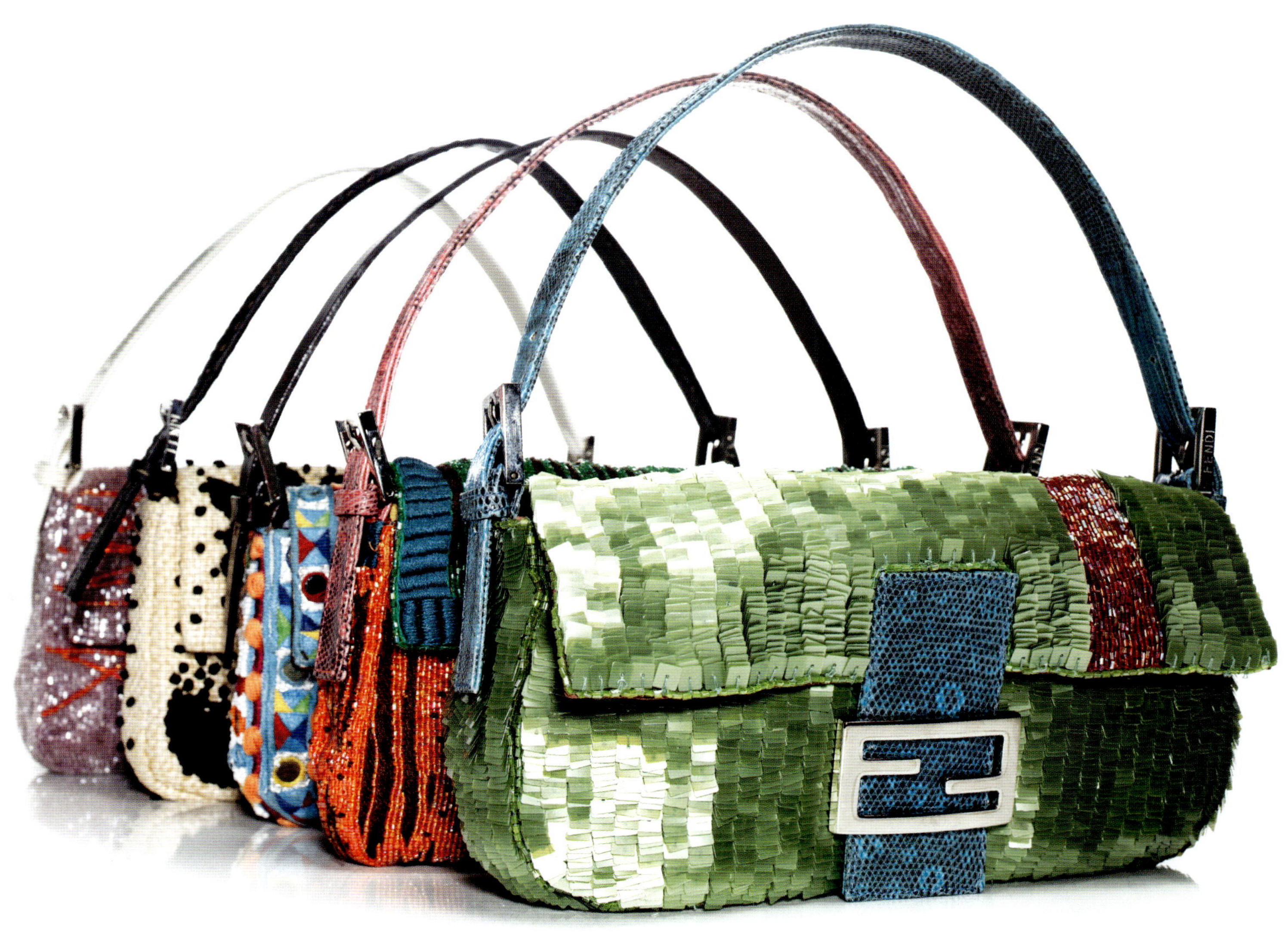

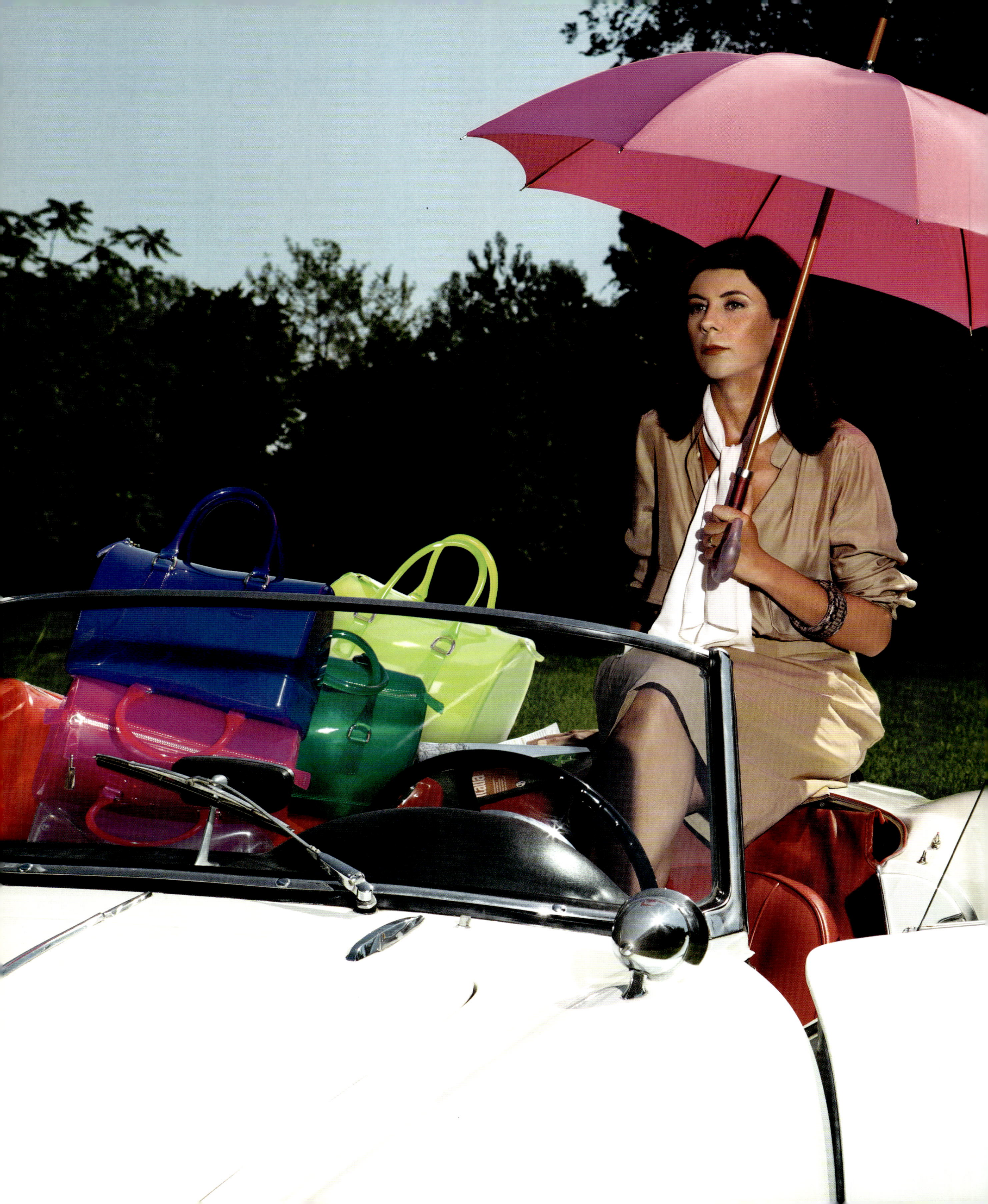
Italia

Furla

CANDY, 2011

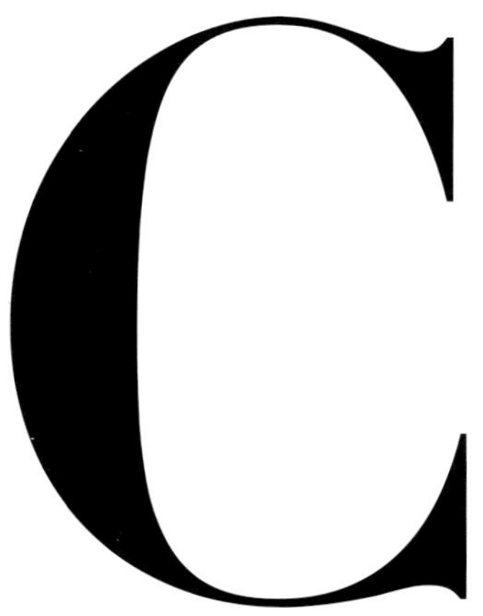

onsidering Furla is one of Italy's family-run heritage firms, it's somewhat surprising that their blockbuster Candy satchel is made from the synthetic called PVC (polyvinyl chloride). Founded in Bologna in 1927 by Aldo Furlanetto, what began as a small store that sold knickknacks, costume jewelry, linens, and small leather goods morphed, once his children became involved in the 1970s, into a full handbag collection. But even back then, the Furlanettos were forward thinking—some of their early styles featured industrial rubber and nylon. Through the years, they've created transparent bags for easy airport security (the Boarding Bag), seamless one-mold rubber shoppers (the Gummy), and handbags tricked out with an interior light that comes on briefly every time the bag opens (the Greta).

The popular Candy style was the 2011 brainchild of Giovanna Furlanetto, Aldo's only daughter, and was aimed at the younger customer. And what twentysomething—or older, for that matter—could resist? Bright and shiny, in cheerful candy colors, the PVC bags were the accessory equivalent of happy pills. Since successfully introducing the Candy, Furla has continued to launch various incarnations of it. Some are more playful, manufactured in glitter-infused or translucent ombré PVC, so if your smartphone happens to be in the bag when it rings, the resulting flash of light illuminates the interior. Others incorporate fun details like a snakeskin-printed base or metal studs trimming the bottom. There's even an amusing version covered in beast-like shaggy blue-and-white fur. A nostalgia factor enhances the bag's appeal, too, as the brightly colored squishy texture reminds many women of their youth, whether it's through an association with jelly sandals or jellied candy, be it jujubes or gummy bears.

The company promoted the launch with the Candy Brissima tour, a series of worldwide events hosted by local celebrities. At each stop, Furla enlisted artists to customize a bag that was then displayed in a Furla store. In Tokyo, for instance, illustrator and nail artist Nagisa Tsukishima added handprints decorated with intricately painted acrylic nails. Furla encouraged fans to join the conversation on Twitter and Instagram with the hashtag "candycool."

OPPOSITE AND PAGES 86–87:
Candy bags, Furla, Spring 2011.

"'Candy power!' said Mr. Wonka. 'One million candy power!'"

—WILLY WONKA, from *Charlie and the Chocolate Factory* by Roald Dahl, 1964

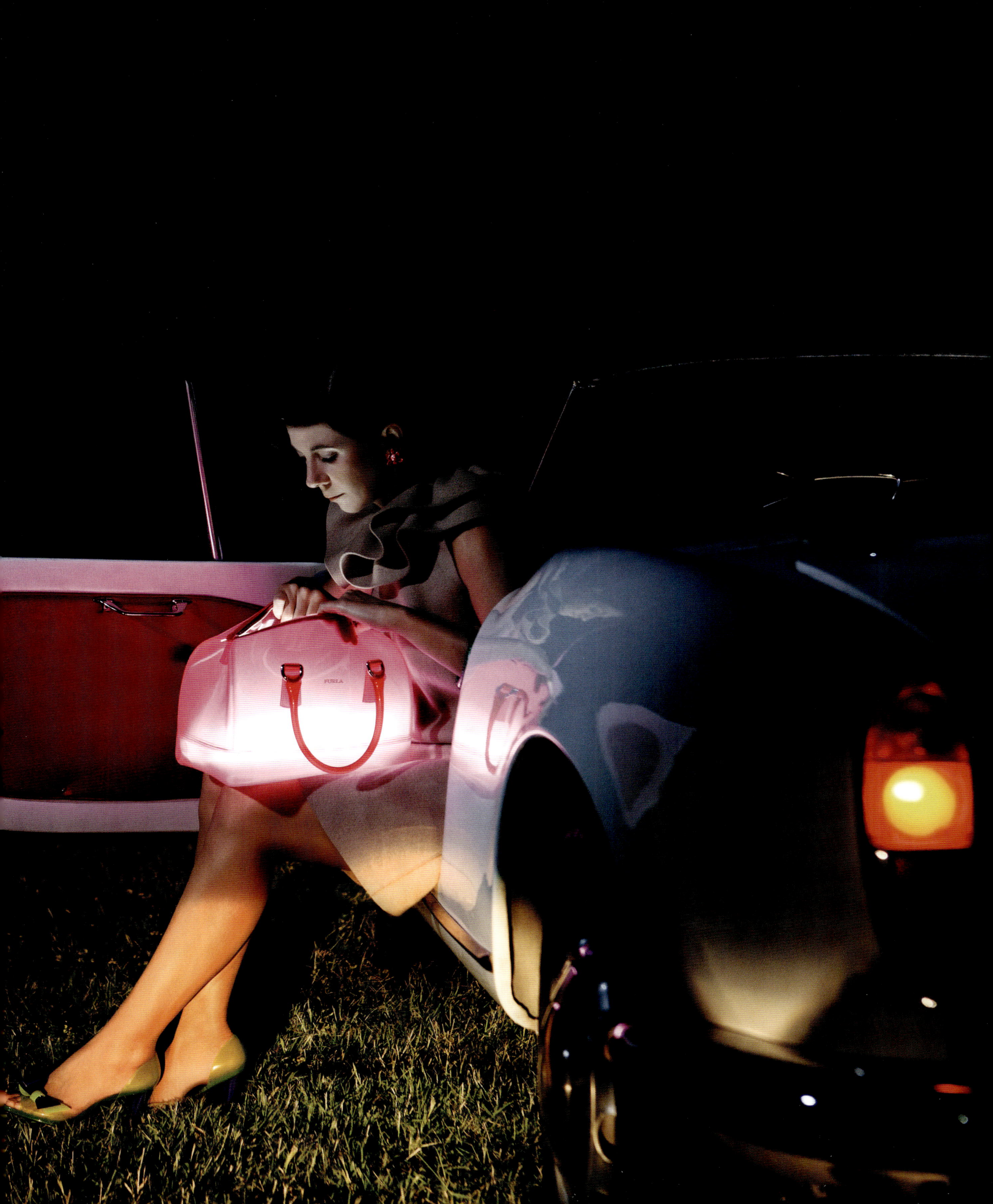
FURLA

Riccardo Tisci for Givenchy

NIGHTINGALE, 2006

ANTIGONA, 2010

PANDORA, 2010

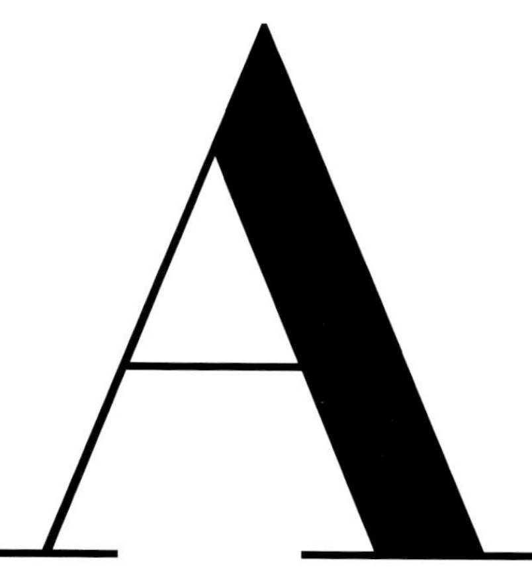

fter the legendary Hubert de Givenchy stepped down as director of the eponymous couture house he founded in 1952, he was followed by John Galliano, Alexander McQueen, and Julien Macdonald, none of whom could match his success. When Riccardo Tisci arrived at Givenchy in 2005, the fashion industry was skeptical that the thirty-year-old Italian, who had only two collections under his belt, would succeed either.

The reviews of his first outings were brutal. "There's only one way to sum up what went on at Givenchy: It was painful," jabbed *Vogue* in 2005. "Riccardo Tisci of Givenchy has the pretension to be a couturier but not the discipline or the honest imagination," sniped the *New York Times* in 2006. Yet, after a few seasons, all those critics who questioned what his vision had to do with the Givenchy heritage found themselves coming over to his side. "Sometimes you need to see a movie three times before you understand it," Tisci said. "I think it's the exact same style it always was, but now everyone is used to it." And, indeed, Tisci's hybrid of goth, romance, and power aggression came to be celebrated editorially and commercially as a revival triumph.

Tisci's golden touch carried to the accessories, which capitalize on street appeal and luxe sophistication. The Nightingale, named after Florence Nightingale, made a splash when it debuted on the runway: Naomi Campbell carried one in each hand, as did other models. The shots went around the world, and the rounded supple satchel that originally had a logo embossed on the handles became the house's first great hit. The style was updated in 2015—the perpendicular cross-seams and logos were eliminated to achieve a more streamlined look, the clean curved contours recalling Givenchy's pioneering couture line.

Part satchel, part messenger bag, the Pandora made headlines for its unusual angled double-zip top, which playfully riffs off the Greek myth of Pandora's box. The Antigona, a more structured, angular, and architectural style, comes in a variety of extreme versions with goat hair and Rottweiler prints for more outré clients, including Marina Abramović, Mariacarla Boscono, Madonna, Rihanna, and Florence Welch. As he told *Women's Wear Daily* in 2016, "I was born a daring designer and I'm going to die a daring designer. That is me." The following year, he left and was replaced by Clare Waight Keller of Chloé, who is the first woman to step into the creative director role.

OPPOSITE:
Nightingale bag, Givenchy, Fall 2007 advertisement.

PAGE 90:
Dress design by Hubert de Givenchy, *L'Officiel*, March 1953.

PAGE 91:
Nightingale bag, Givenchy, Spring 2009 advertisement.

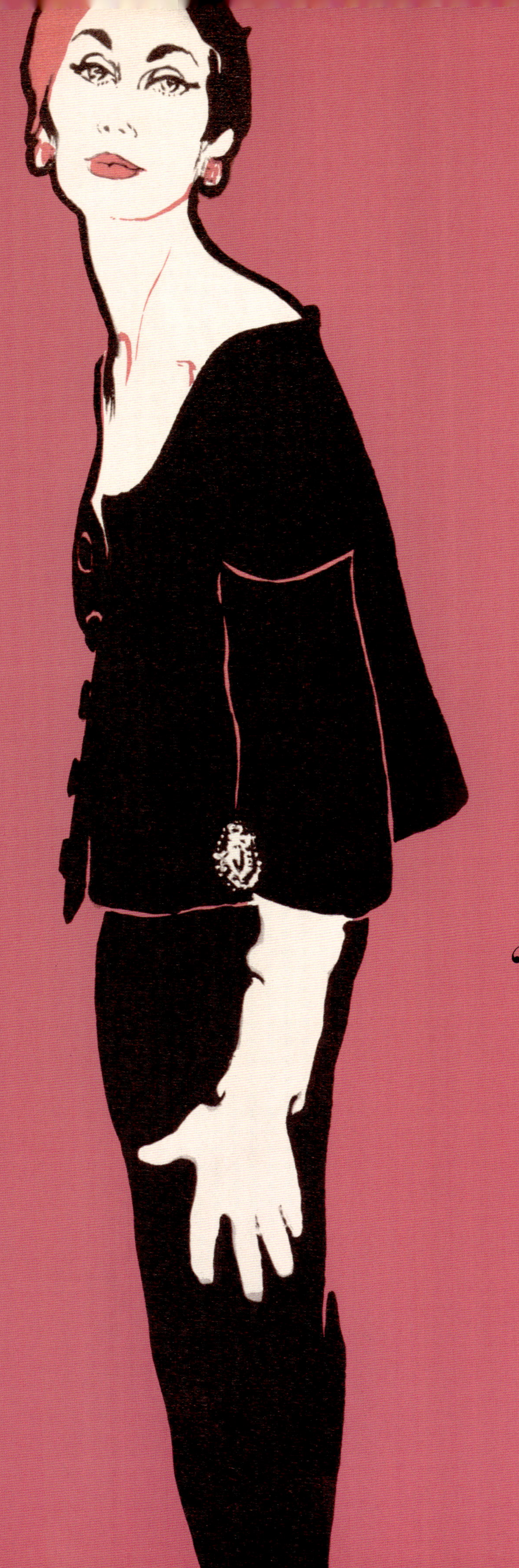

"He needed to create his own world, and now people have fallen in love with it."

—MARIACARLA BOSCONO,
on Riccardo Tisci, *Harper's Bazaar*, October 2008

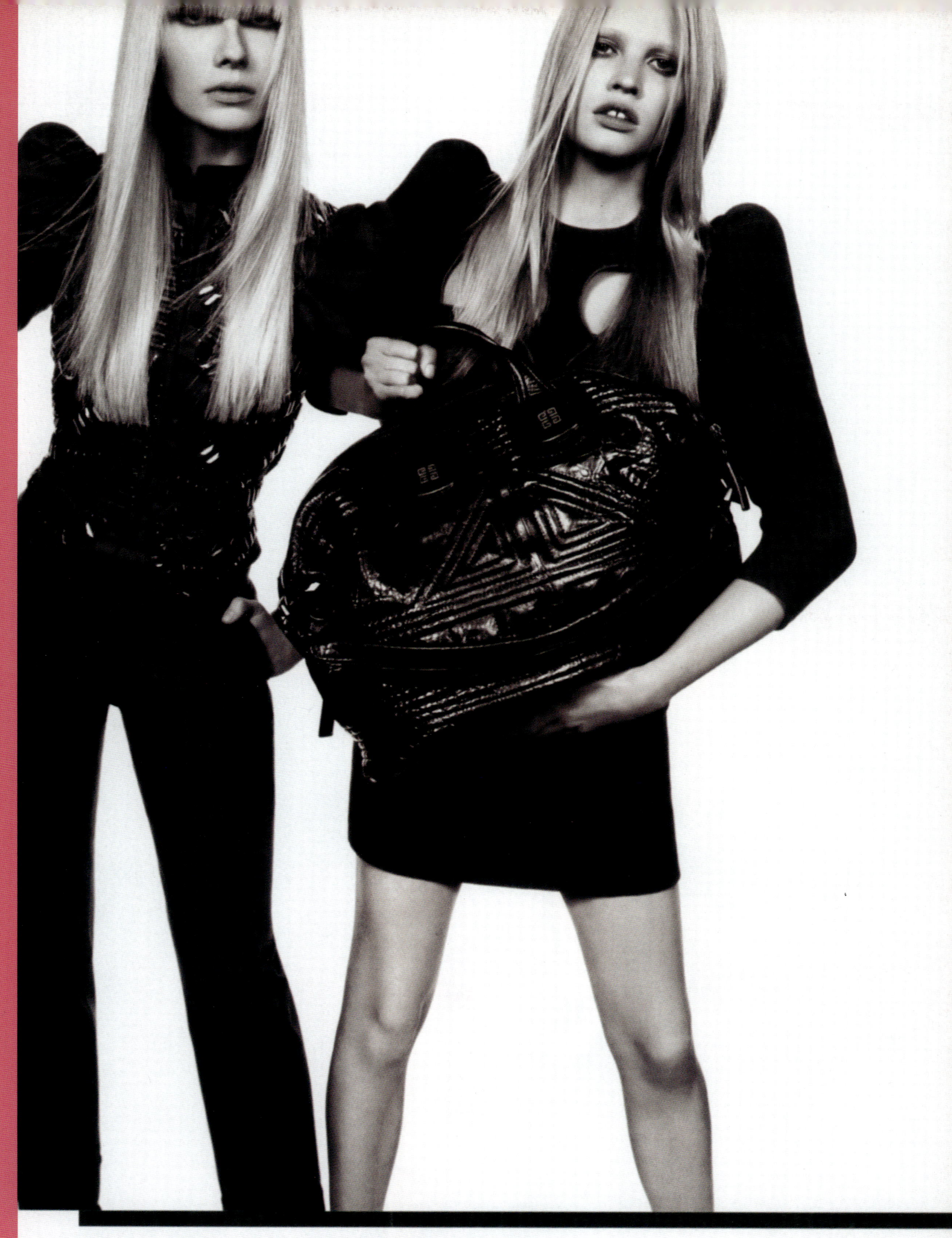
GIVENCHY

“She had no more money, and a terrible

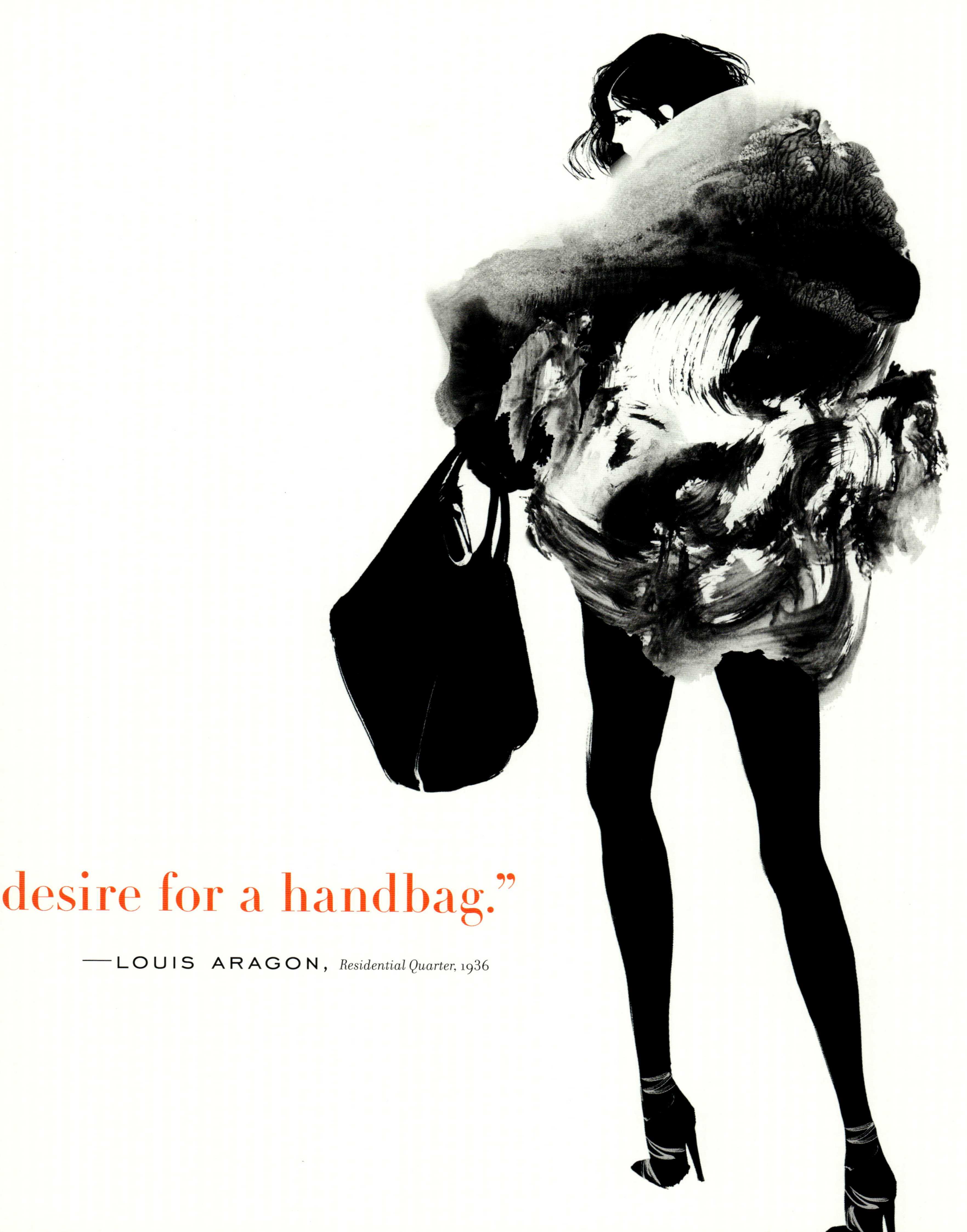

desire for a handbag."

—LOUIS ARAGON, *Residential Quarter*, 1936

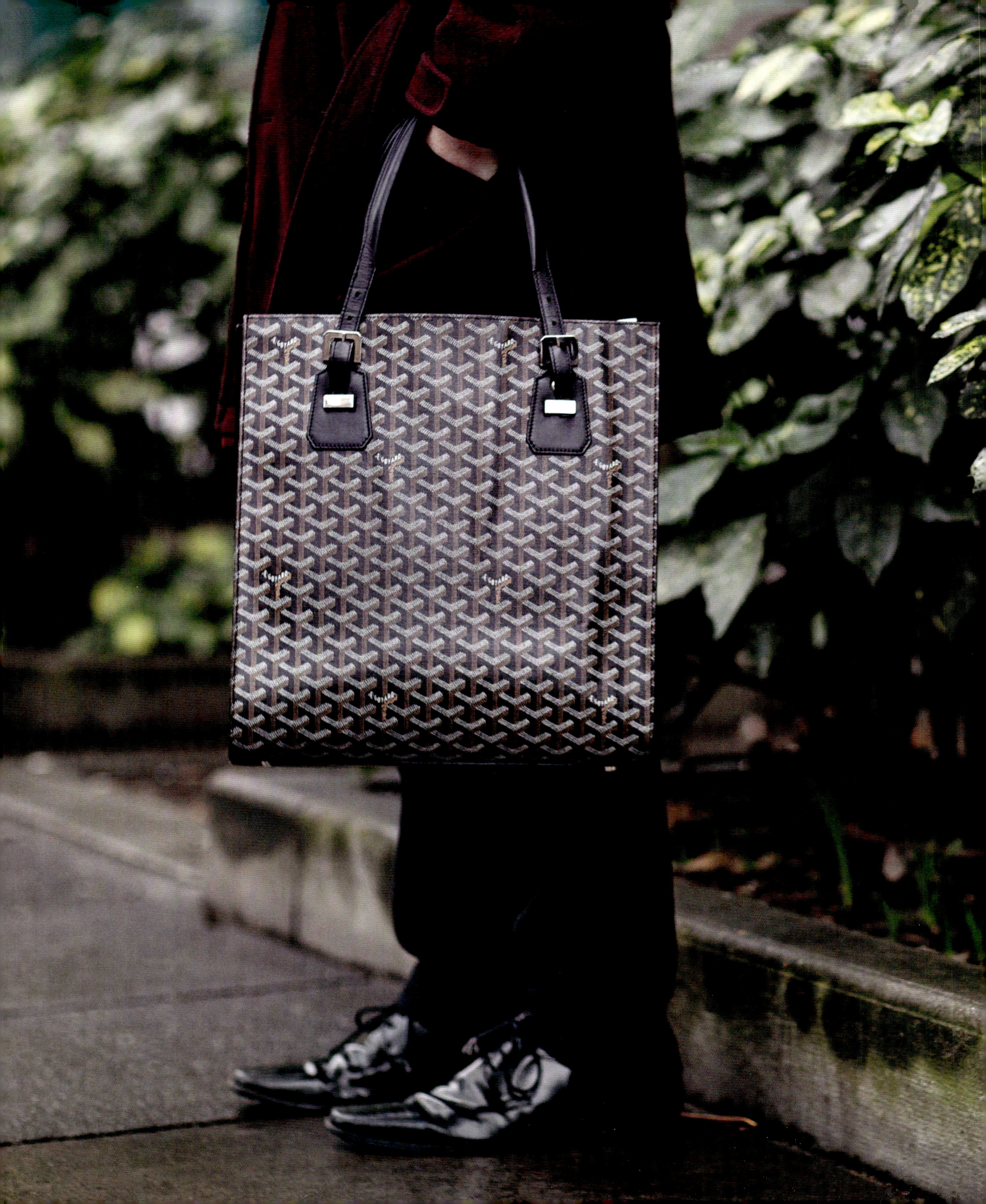

Goyard

ST. LOUIS, 1998

In 1792 trunkmaker Pierre-François Martin founded the House of Martin, and his fine handcrafted designs soon made him a favorite of the aristocracy, becoming a royal supplier to Marie-Caroline de Bourbon-Siciles, Duchess of Berry. Martin handed down the company to trusted employee Louis-Henri Morel, who successfully ran the business, renaming it Maison Morel, until his death in 1852, when he bequeathed it to his twenty-four-year-old apprentice François Goyard. In 1853 the Goyard era officially began.

In 1885 Goyard's eldest son, Edmond, took the reins, opening stores in Biarritz, Bordeaux, and Monte Carlo; he's the one who introduced Goyardine, the firm's signature Y-pattern canvas cloth. The Y shape is composed of tiny dots meant to subtly reference his ancestors, log drivers in Burgundy. Through the years, the company descended from one Goyard generation to the next, garnering a luminous clientele: Catherine Deneuve, Barbara Hutton, Pablo Picasso, Cole Porter, the Rockefellers, and the Duke and Duchess of Windsor, among many others. Goyard was especially known for its custom creations, from a portable writing desk for Arthur Conan Doyle to a cheetah carrier for Josephine Baker.

By the 1990s, however, the firm had slumped and had only one shop, on the rue Saint-Honoré, and a single salesman. And it would have stayed that way if not for businessman Jean-Michel Signoles. He had been an avid Goyard collector since 1974, after falling in love with a trunk at a flea market in Port-de-Lanne. He became fanatical about the brand—"I bought all of its records, traced back its registered models, and got to know the dealers who sold Goyard items," he told the *International Herald Tribune* in 2009—and began contacting its owners in the mid-1990s to sell. For Signoles, restoring a legendary French firm wasn't such a stretch—he had modernized and revived the 1909 Hôtel de la Cité in his native Carcassonne. By 1998 he convinced the owners—fifth-generation Goyards—to sell and opened a new workshop in Carcassonne.

Signoles sparked a revival, introducing new shapes and colors, but never gave in to the brashness and bling that dominated the competition. It was luxury done with a wink and a whisper—to this day, there are no advertisements, no e-commerce—with the sole identifying factor being the discreet Y-shaped chevron pattern.

Soon, with women feeling logo-mania fatigue, the St. Louis was everywhere. From Paris to New York, you couldn't turn a corner without seeing the tote, cut from a coated linen-cotton-hemp hybrid. "And the winner of the handbag classic is: Goyard by a mile!" exclaimed a 2006 *New York Times* feature by photographer Bill Cunningham, who dedicated an entire spread in his "On the Street" column to Goyard sightings.

Adding to the brand's air of desirability was the ability to order a customized bag—a trunk for your saddle and polo equipment or a bag personalized with hand-painted initials, stripes, or your family coat of arms. It was, in fact, this anti–It Bag that gave birth to the monogramming trend followed by countless houses, including Dior, Prada, and Louis Vuitton.

OPPOSITE:
Comores bag, Goyard, London, January 2016.

PAGE 96:
Pharrell Williams carrying a Goyard Goyardine Ambassade bag, New York City, October 2013.

PAGE 97:
Senat pochette, Goyard, Rome, January 2014.

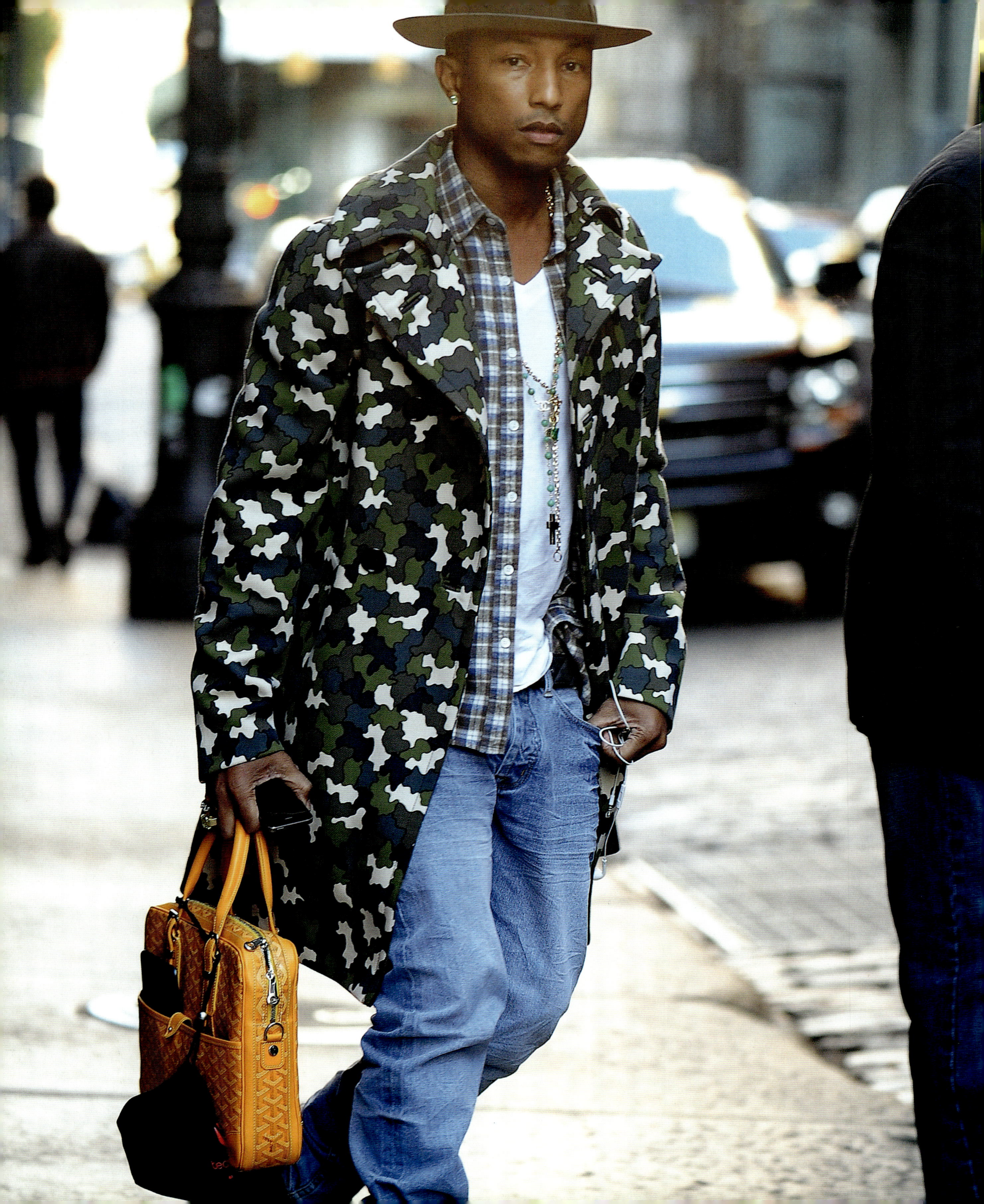

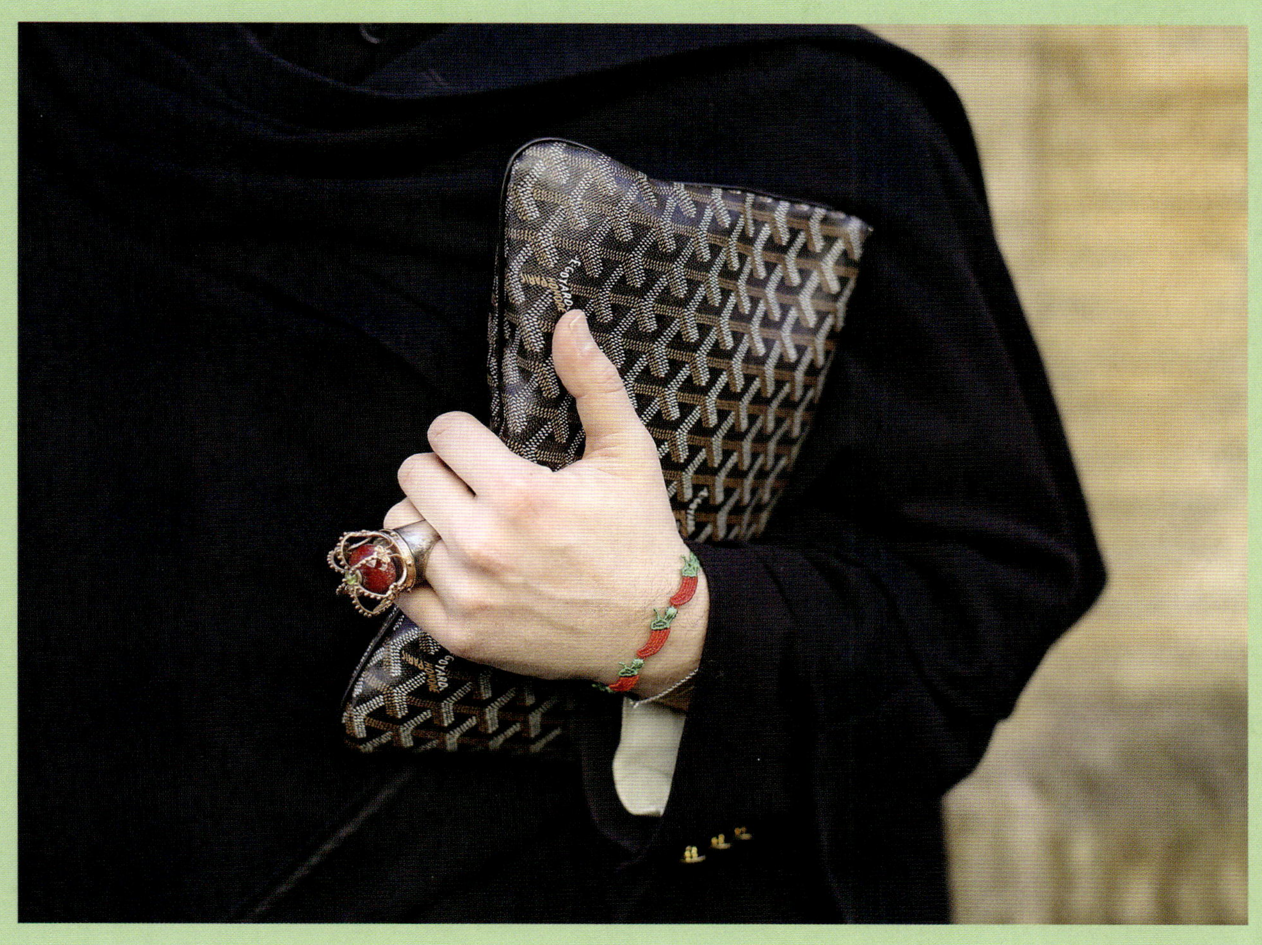

“She took a handbag—that is all. She will send for her trunk.”

—HORATIO ALGER, *Adrift in New York*, 1903

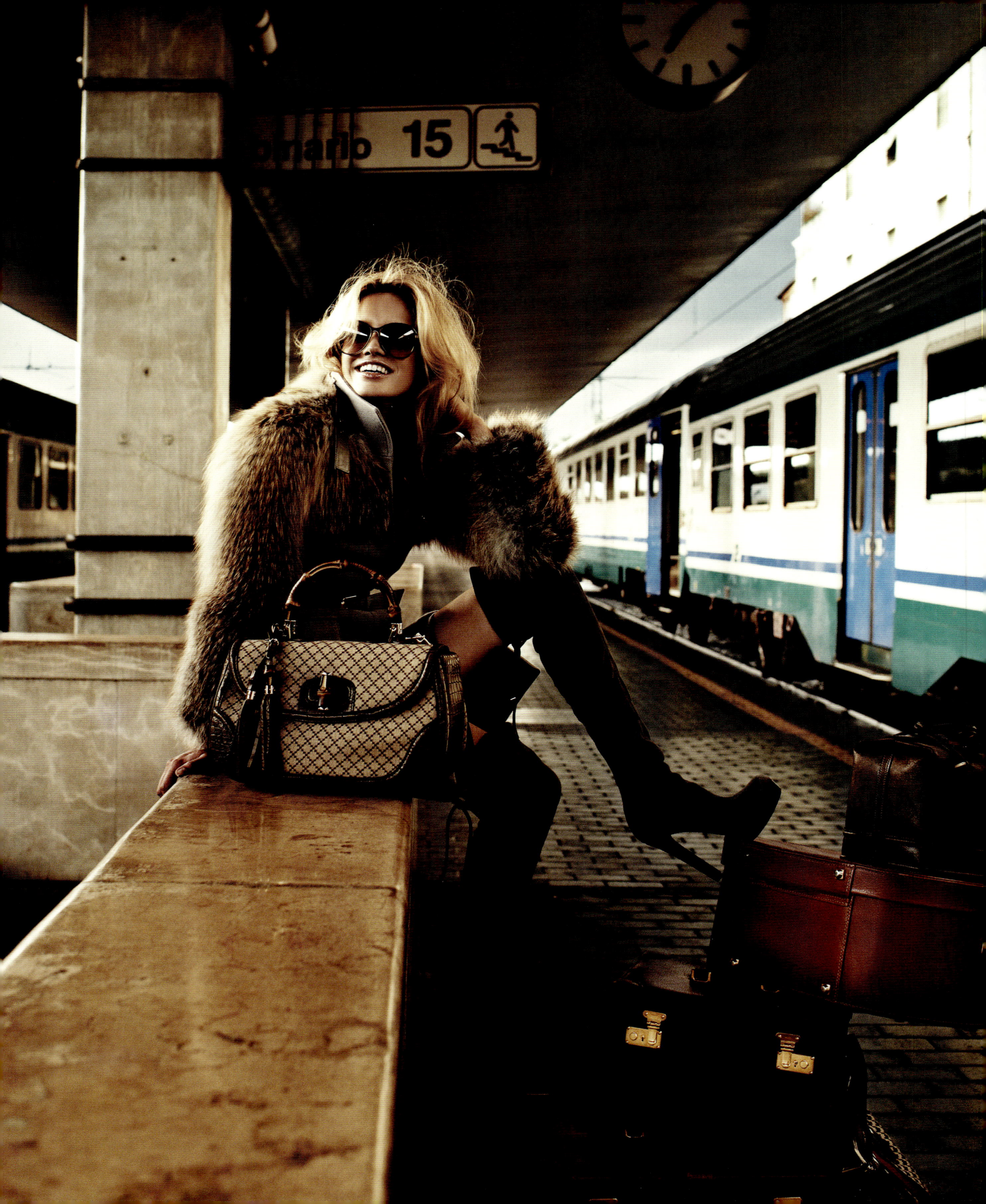
15

Gucci

BAMBOO, 1947
JACKIE, 1960s
DIONYSUS, 2015

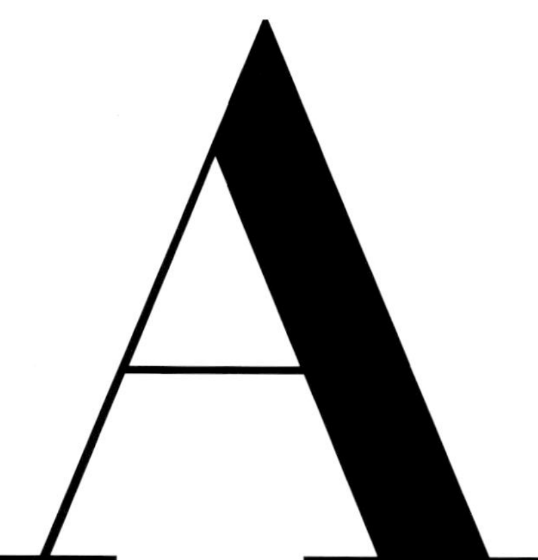

s one of Italy's great fashion houses, founded by Guccio Gucci in 1921, Gucci has had myriad brand-defining chapters—not to mention turbulent years of takeover bids and soap-opera-come-to-life family fights, back stabbings, and contract killers. But the different creative reigns have had one thing in common: they've all circled back to the firm's rich jet-set past and iconography.

Gucci has had the celebrity blessings of Lauren Bacall, Grace Kelly, Sophia Loren, Romy Schneider, Elizabeth Taylor, and, most famously, Jacqueline Kennedy Onassis, who was snapped so often carrying one of the firm's shoulder bags, with its rounded edges and push-lock closure, that it named the style after her.

Designer Tom Ford resurrected the Jackie bag in 1999 in an assortment of colors and treatments, and he brought back the traditional monogram canvas that the firm had allowed to languish during the minimalist 1990s. It was the right move. Those double-Gs caught on like wildfire. Together with Fendi's double-Fs and Louis Vuitton's interlocking LVs, they pioneered the logo letter craze of the late 1990s—a prime status moment for the masses.

Eventually, logo ubiquity arrived, banishing those double-Gs to the back of women's closets, but Gucci's other iconic bags continued to do well, with each designer adding his or her own touch. The New Jackie was introduced in 2009, which eased the silhouette and gave it a stylish slouch; the New Bamboo, updated in 2010 from the 1947 original, is now composed of 140 pieces hand-assembled by craftsmen in the Florence workshop. The house is flush with heritage motifs such as the horse bit, which first appeared on loafers in the 1950s; the bamboo handle; and the green-red-green stripes inspired by canvas saddle girths. Both the bamboo and the striped canvas were developed in the postwar years, when luxury materials were scarce.

For all the romancing of an equestrian heritage—such as the horse-bits and stripes and the classic Stirrup Bag, launched in 1975 and reintroduced in 2012, Gucci's origin story never actually involved horses. Founder Guccio Gucci had once worked at London's Savoy Hotel and was inspired by the culture of English horse riding and nobility. "I wanted the truth to come out," said his daughter Grimalda Gucci in Sara G. Forden's *The House of Gucci* (2001). "We were never saddlemakers."

OPPOSITE:
Bamboo top-handle bag, Gucci, *Elle Italia*, December 2011.

But when Alessando Michele—a longtime Gucci employee dating back to the Tom Ford era who worked in the firm's leather goods studio—took over as creative director in 2015, his appointment brought about a sea change at the house. The once-passé logo became au courant again, and maximalism sent minimalism packing.

For Michele's blockbuster Dionysus handbag, a structured trapezoidal frame with a sliding chain strap, the designer piled on wild embellishment: florals, and patches, along with a heavy use of embroidery, and an ample use of the logo. "I couldn't wait to get my hands on the logo," he said in a video interview at the 2016 New York Times International Luxury Conference. "It's like drawing on the Mona Lisa. The double-G is like a hieroglyph that everyone knows, and I use it as the cherry on top of my designs."

The Dionysus resonated with women because it allowed them to flaunt their individuality, a welcome change after years of chic anonymity made fashionable by Phoebe Philo at Céline. By early 2017, there were ninety versions available of the Dionysus, and that's not including those created through Gucci's do-it-yourself service program, which lets you customize your own Dionysus bag with embroidery, patches, trims, hardware, and monograms. There is one constant, though: the double tiger-head clasp, which is a reference to the bag's namesake, the Greek god Dionysus, as the tiger is one of his sacred animals.

BOTTOM, LEFT:
Jacqueline Bisset carrying a Gucci tote, London, April 1976.

BOTTOM, RIGHT:
Elizabeth Taylor, her Gucci bag, and Paul Newman on the set of *Cat on a Hot Tin Roof*, 1958.

OPPOSITE:
Model Veruschka with a Gucci shoulder bag and travel bag, Borghese Gardens, Rome, *Vogue*, April 1971.

PAGES 102—103:
Jacqueline Kennedy Onassis carrying the Jackie bag, Capri, August 1970.

PAGES 104—105:
Dionysus bag, Gucci, Düsseldorf, August 2016.

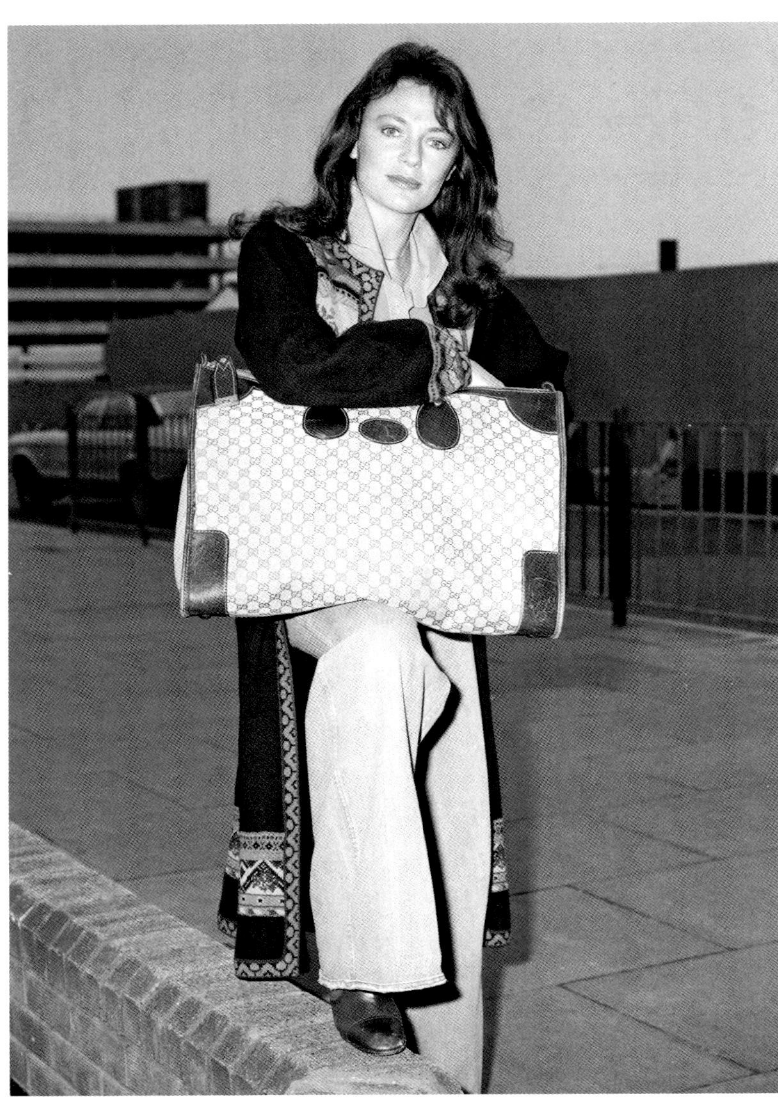

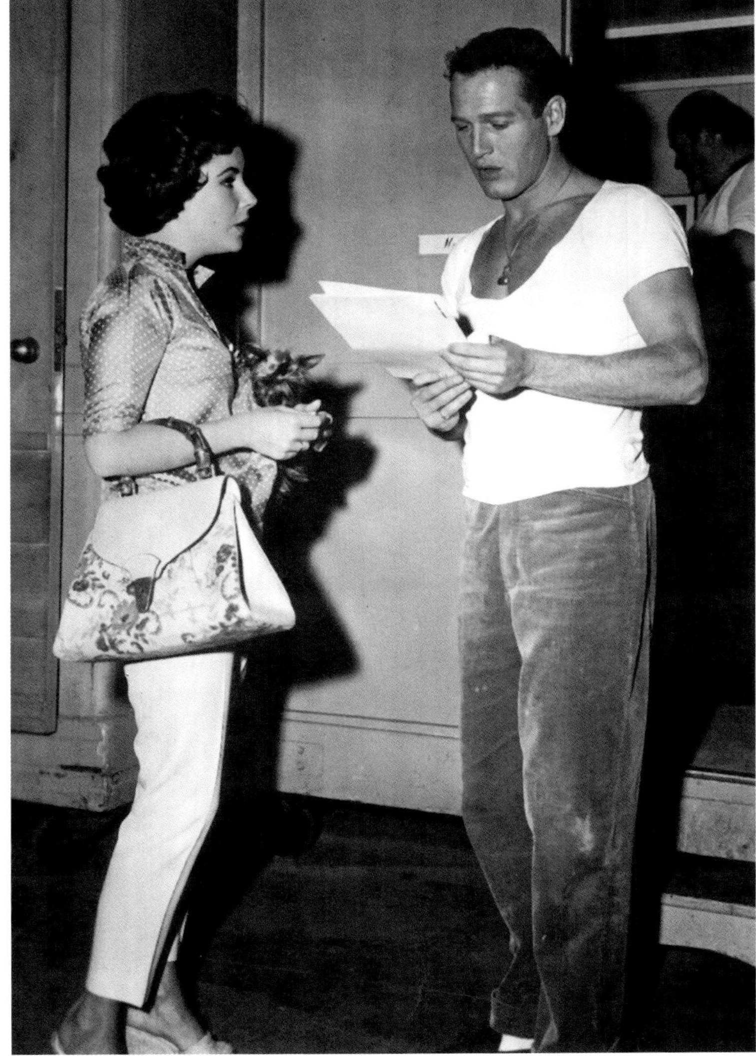

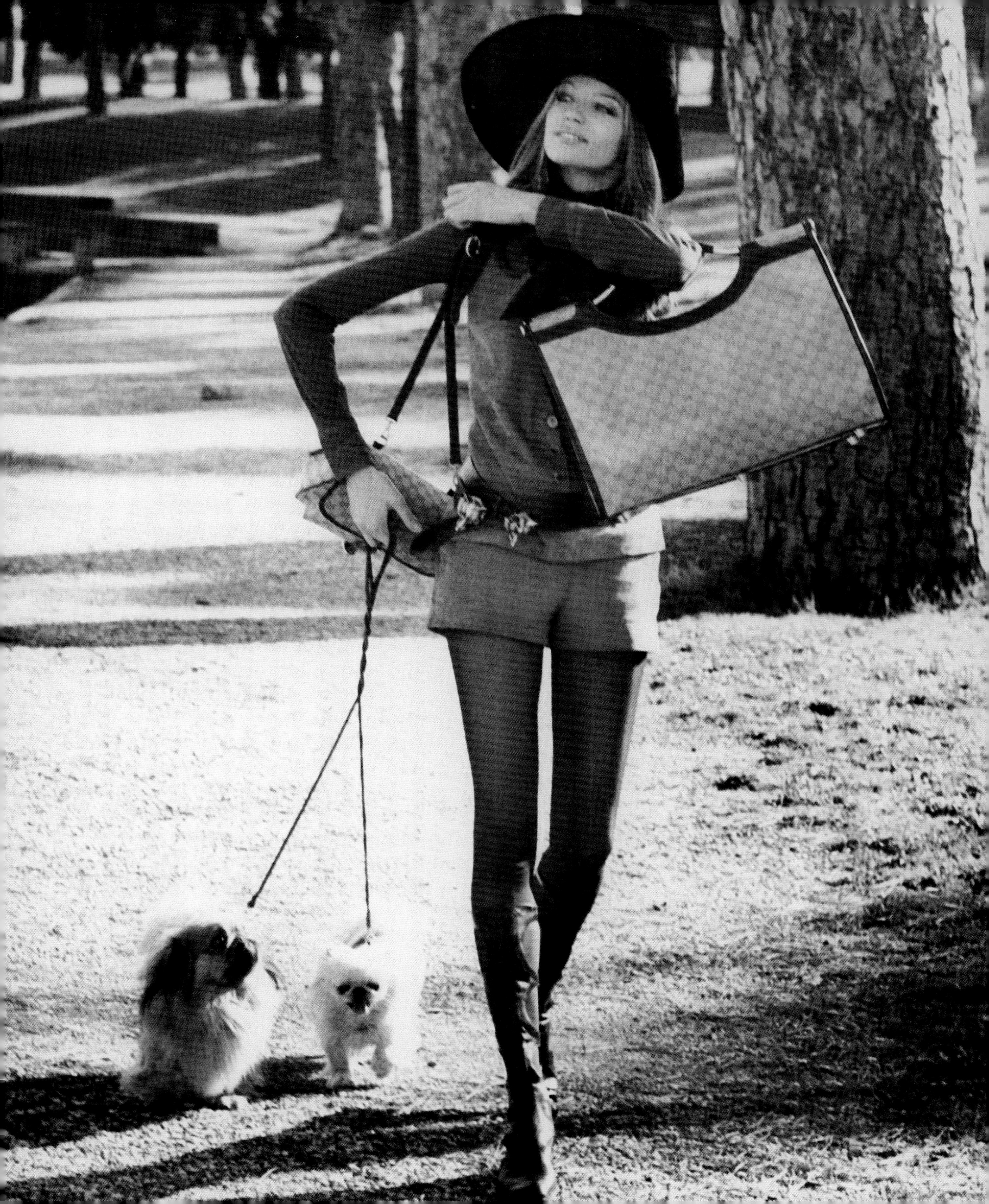

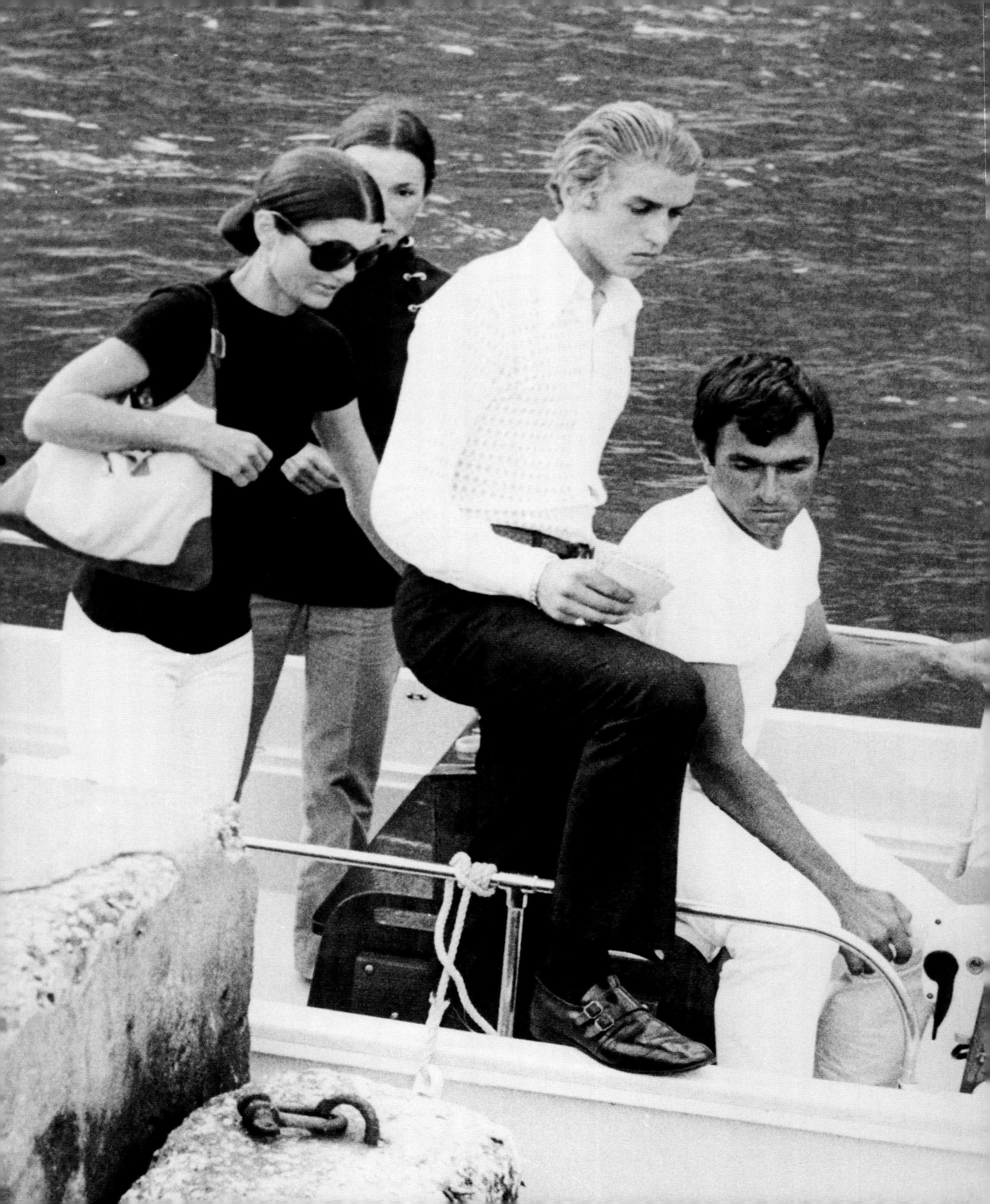

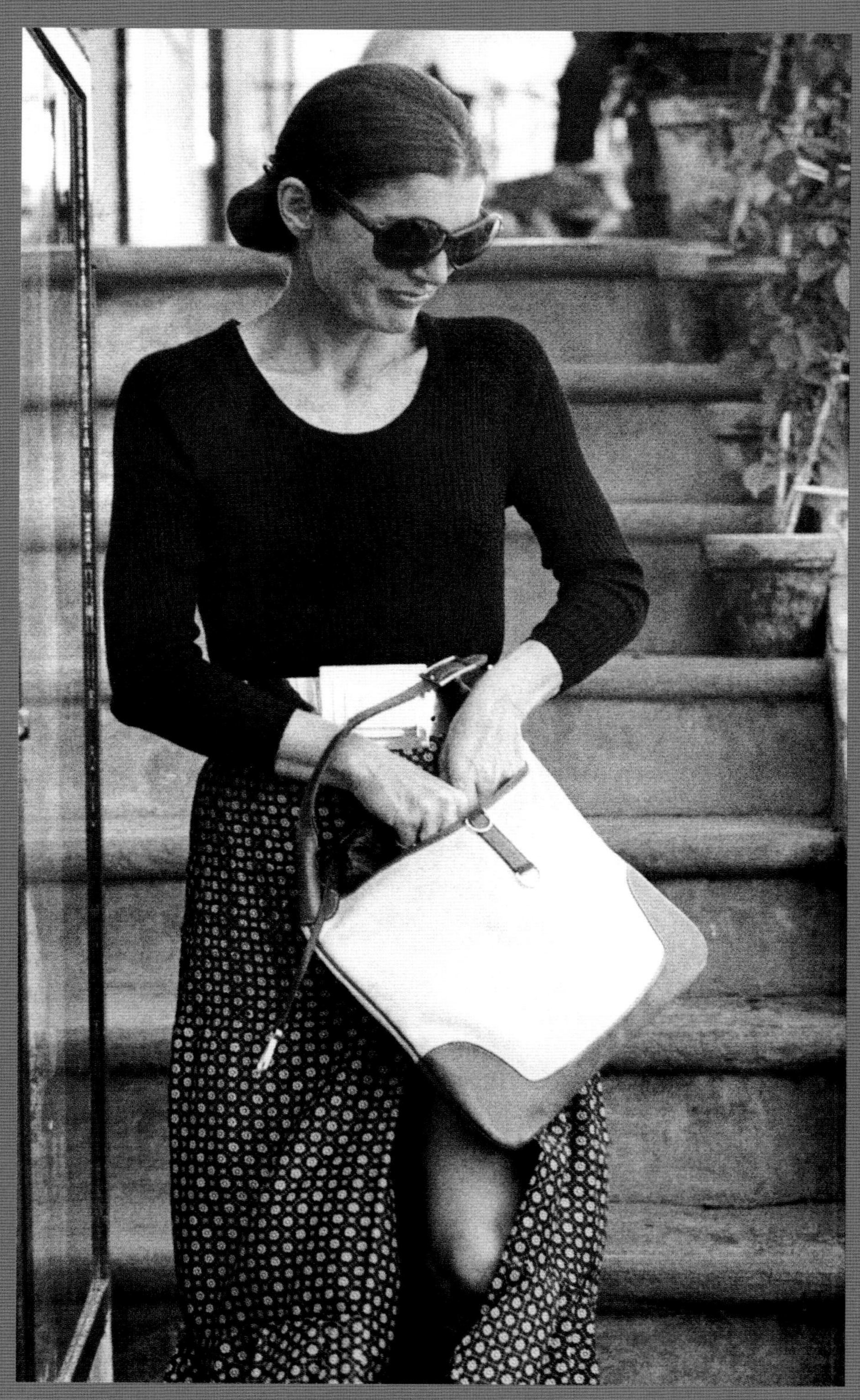

“Gucci represented a glamorous brand from glamorous Italy, where movie stars vacationed and movies were made.”

—VALERIE STEELE, *Women's Wear Daily*, June 5, 2006

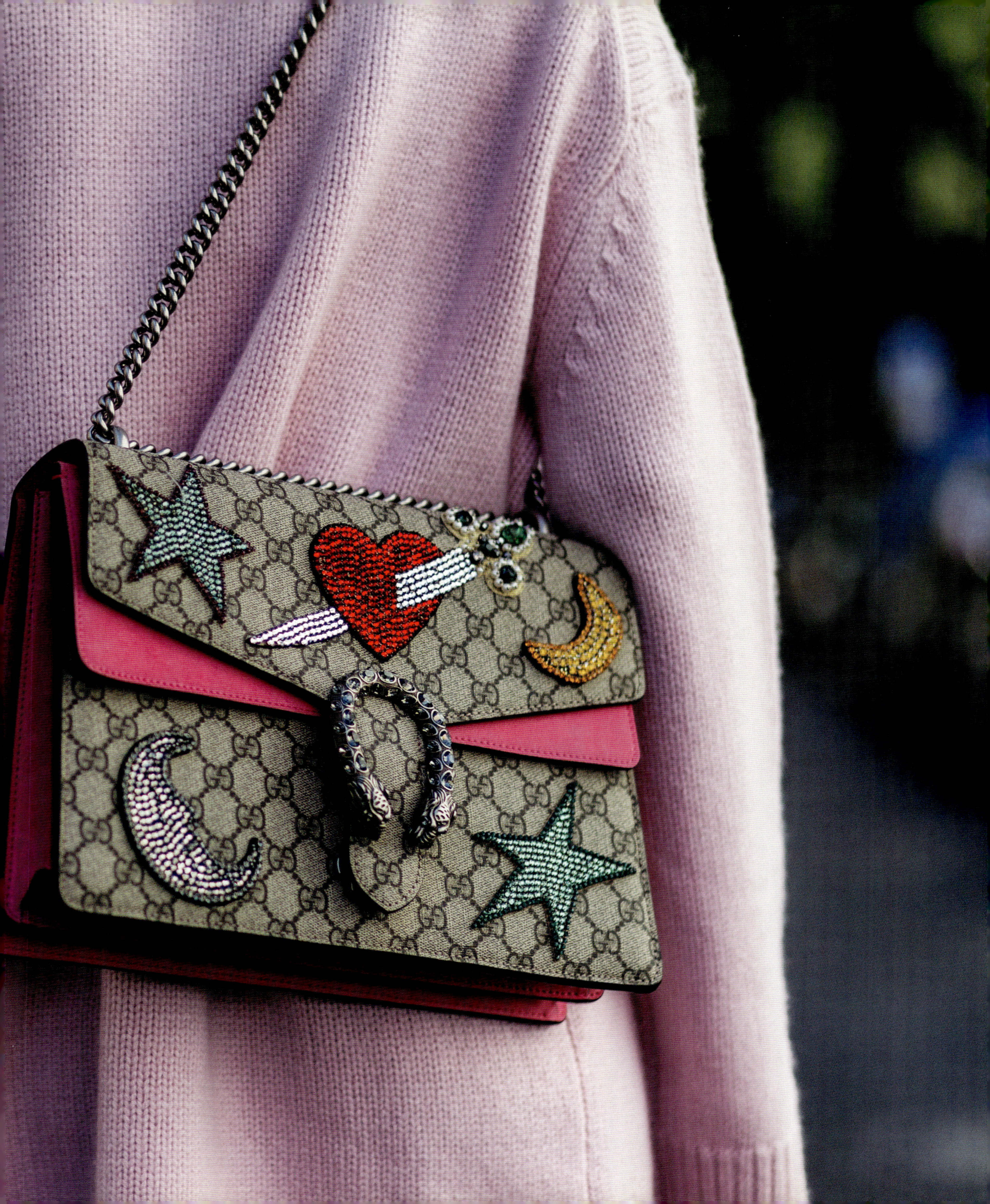

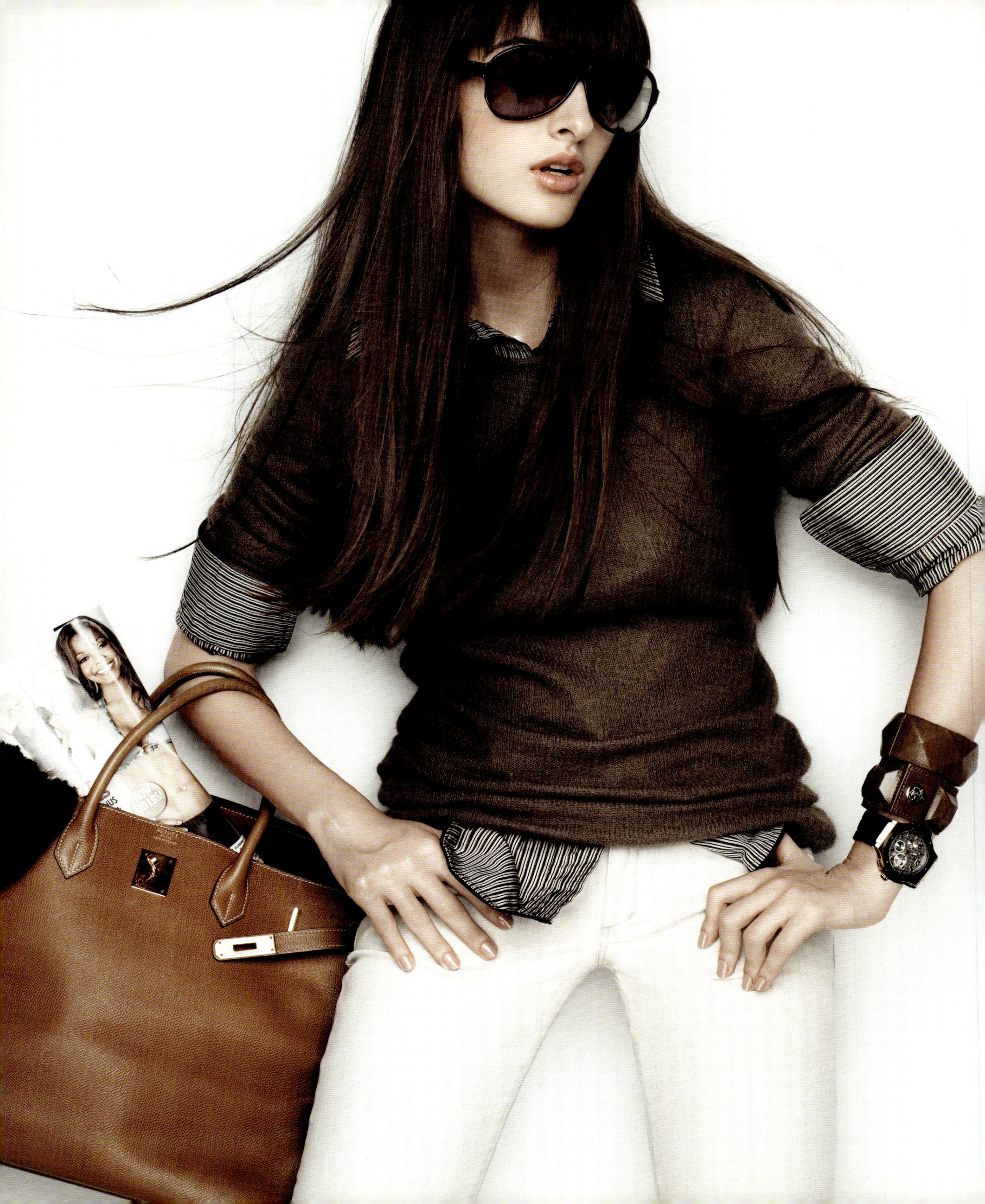

Hermès

KELLY, LATE 1800S
BIRKIN, 1981

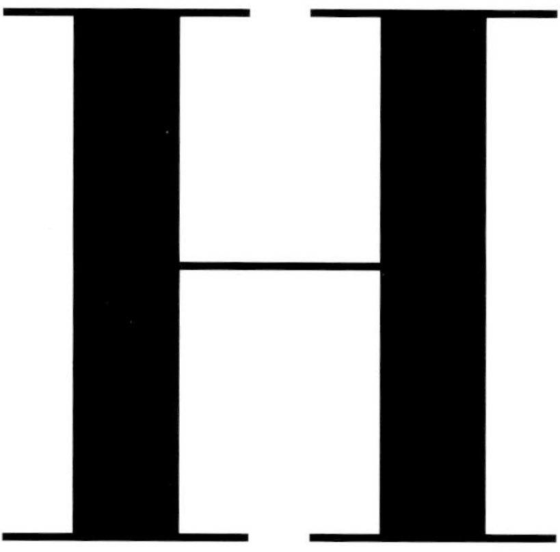

ermès is the luxury firm that all other luxury firms aspire to be. Its reputation is unchallenged.

At Hermès, product rules. "We don't have a policy of image, we have a policy of product," former chairman Jean-Louis Dumas told *Vanity Fair* in 2007. Its bags are still made the same way they have been for decades, from the best exotics and completely by hand, stitch by stitch. If a product is imperfect, it's destroyed. You can wait years for a bag, and that's after you've handed over six figures for it.

The Hermès story began in Krefeld, Germany, northwest of Düsseldorf. When the French citizen Thierry Hermès was born there, the land was still under Napoleon Bonaparte's control. By the 1820s this son of an innkeeper had made his way to Paris, where he got a job in leatherwork. In 1837 he opened his own shop specializing in carriage harnesses for the aristocracy.

The family-run company has been led by a number of top industry names, including Martin Margiela, Jean Paul Gaultier, Christophe Lemaire, and, today, Nadège Vanhee-Cybulski. While it has expanded to include everything from scarves to ready-to-wear, its reputation is still very much in leather and in two bags in particular, the Kelly and the Birkin, both of which have their own captivating stories.

The slightly trapezoidal Kelly, with two slim straps at the top and a single handle, is the successor to the Haut à Courroies, originally a revised saddle holder from the late 1800s. The defining moment came in 1956, the year actress Grace Kelly became the Princess consort of Monaco after marrying Prince Rainier III, and pregnant with Princess Caroline, used hers to hide her belly bump from the paparazzi; the shot made it onto the cover of *Life* magazine, immortalizing the design and forever linking the two. In 1977 the Haut à Courroies—which required 680 hand stitches and took one craftsman two weeks to complete—was officially renamed in her honor.

OPPOSITE:
Birkin bag, Hermès, *A* magazine, April 2007.

PAGE 108:
Hermès advertisement featuring the Kelly, 1957.

PAGE 109:
Newlyweds Prince Rainier III of Monaco and Grace Kelly (with her eponymous bag), 1956.

"I imagined the Queen of the Queen bees trying to brush by me and getting stuck in her gut with my boxy Birkin. Really, you couldn't put a price on that."

—WEDNESDAY MARTIN, *Primates of Park Avenue: A Memoir*, 2015

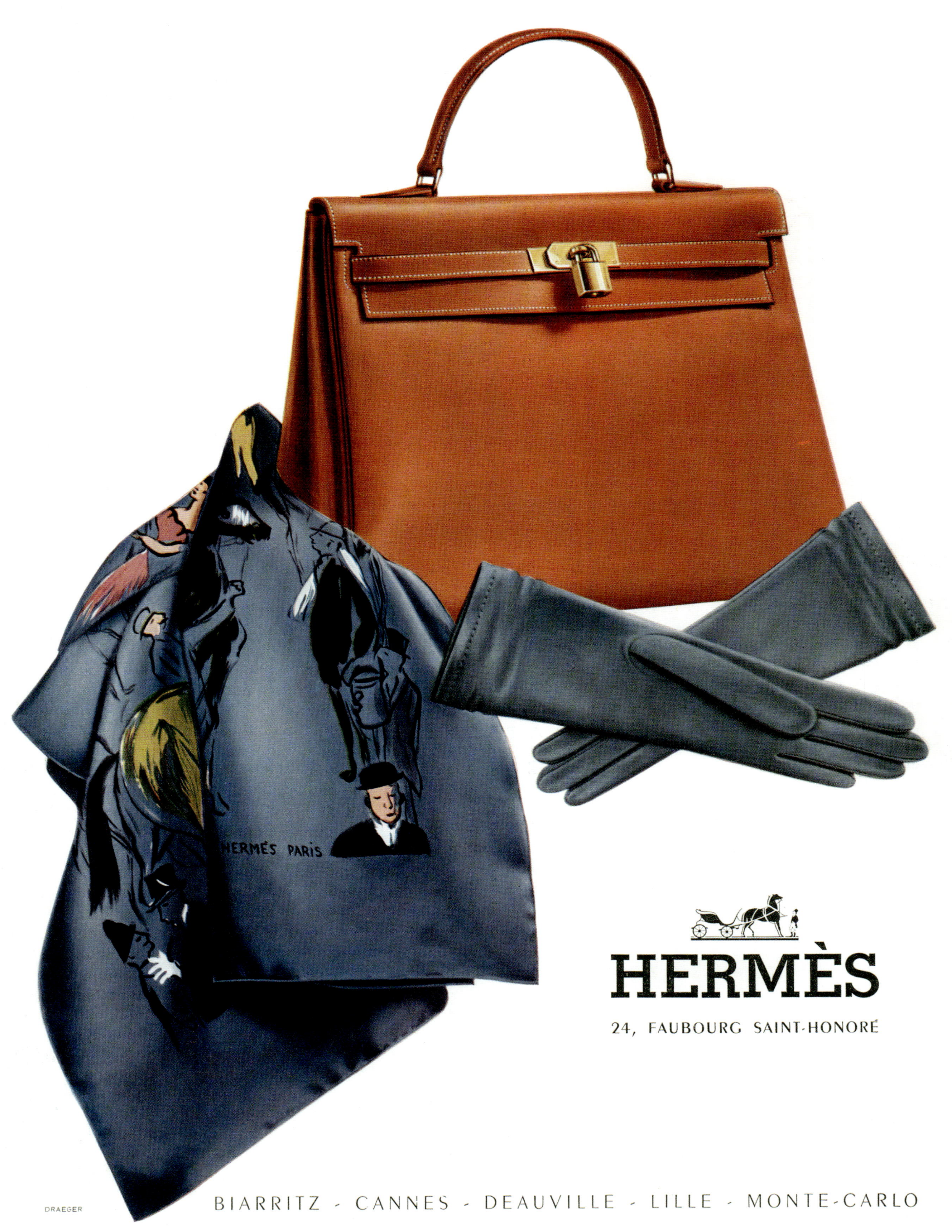
HERMÈS PARIS
HERMÈS
24, FAUBOURG SAINT-HONORÉ
BIARRITZ - CANNES - DEAUVILLE - LILLE - MONTE-CARLO
DRAEGER

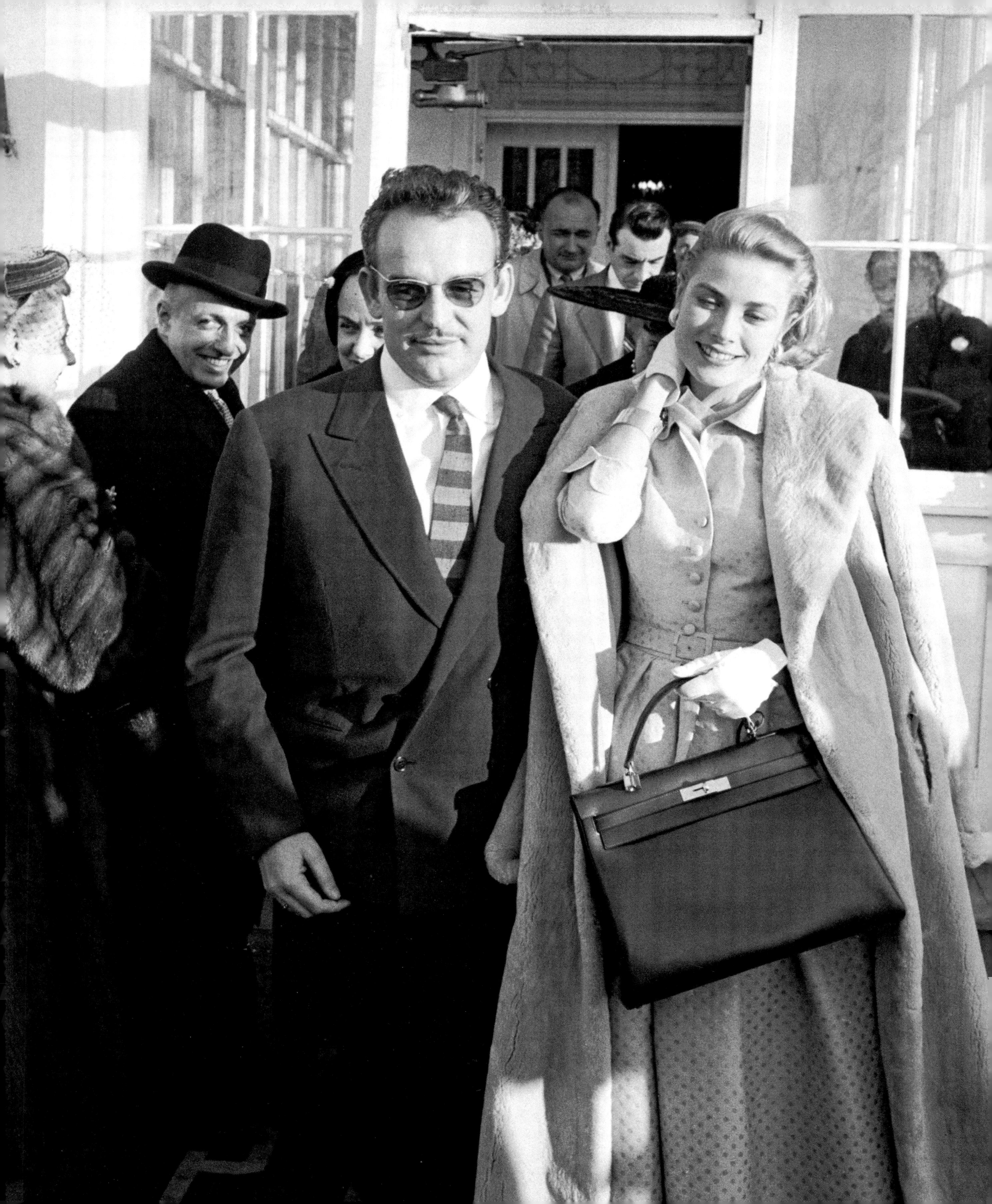

The tale behind its slightly larger cousin, the Birkin, with two top handles, involves the iconic fashion muse Jane Birkin, who found herself sitting next to Jean-Louis Dumas on a flight from Paris to London in 1981. As the story goes, Dumas noticed her overstuffed straw bag and told her, "You should have one with pockets." "The day Hermès makes one with pockets, I will have that," she answered. His reply: "But I am Hermès." Dumas invited her to the workshop to design one; she agreed. Reportedly, the initial sketch for the Birkin began on that fateful flight, drawn on the motion-sickness bag.

In 2015, after PETA (People for the Ethical Treatment of Animals) uncovered abuses at a crocodile farm, Birkin asked the firm to take her name off the bag. "I have asked Hermès to debaptize the Birkin Croco until better practices in line with international norms can be put in place," she said in a statement quoted by the *New York Times* in 2015. The ruckus died down pretty quickly, however, after Hermès investigated the farm and released a statement saying that "the crocodile skins supplied are not used for the fabrication of Birkin bags." So the handbag muse and the handbag house made peace.

The year 2016 brought yet another historical milestone: a red crocodile Birkin, with 18-karat white gold and diamond hardware, sold for a record-breaking $298,000.

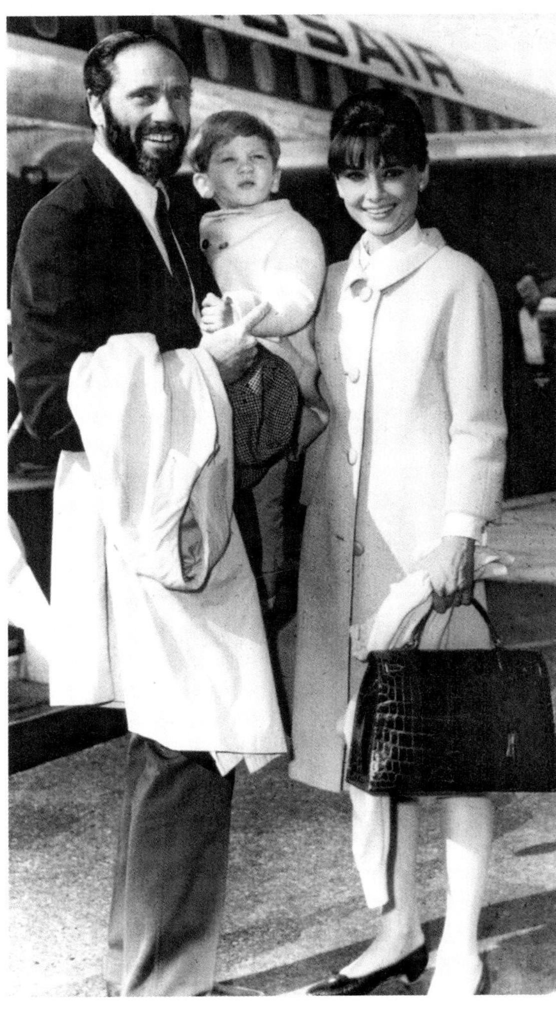

BELOW, LEFT:
Audrey Hepburn, carrying a crocodile Kelly, with husband Mel Ferrer and their son, Sean Hepburn Ferrer, at New York's International Airport, May 1963.

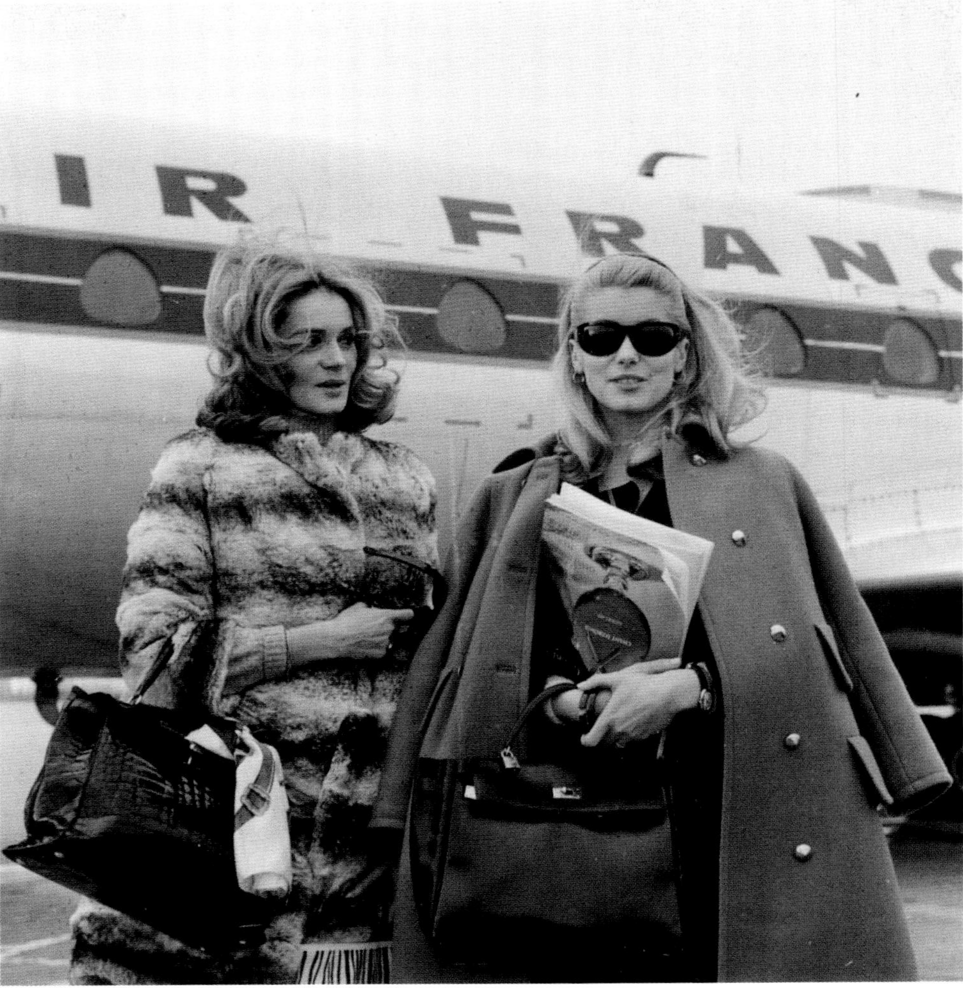

BELOW, RIGHT:
Catherine Deneuve *(right)* and her sister Françoise Dorléac, both with Kelly bags.

OPPOSITE:
Jane Birkin, toting her famous basket bag, and Serge Gainsbourg arrive in London, April 1977.

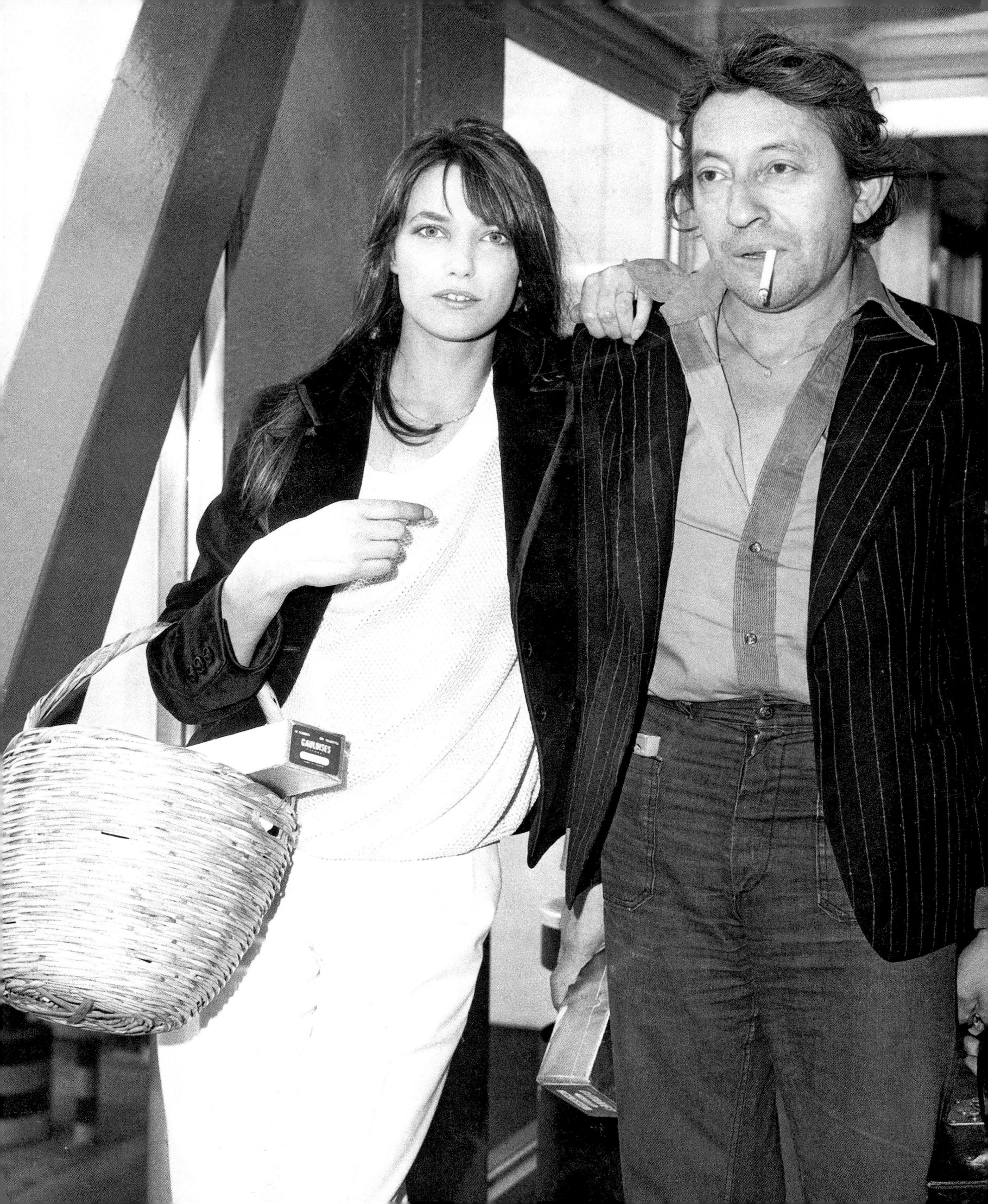
GAULOISES

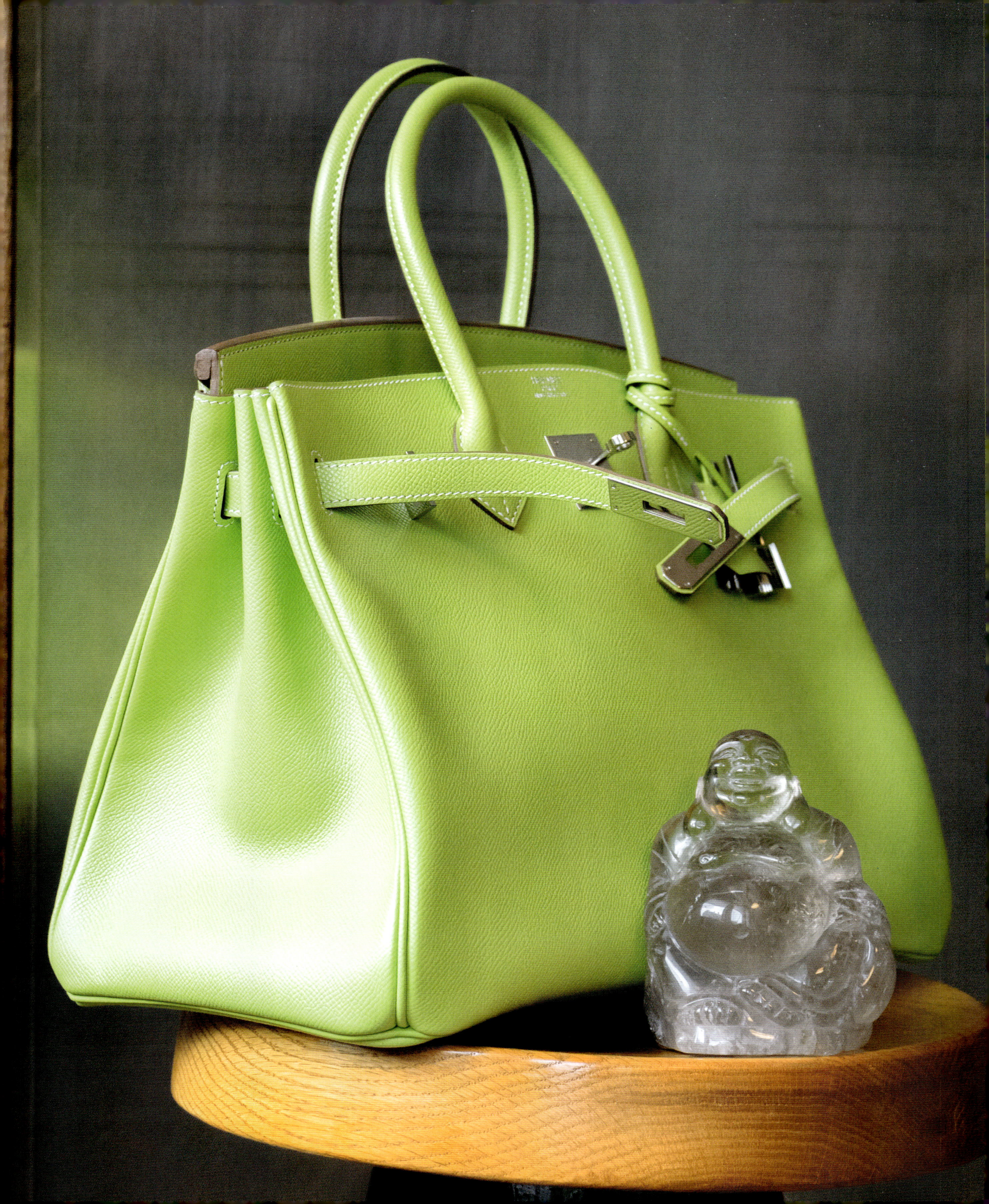

MAD ABOUT THE BIRKIN

LORI GOLDSTEIN

One of the fashion industry's premier editors and stylists, Lori Goldstein is an image maker extraordinaire. She's served as fashion editor-at-large at *W* and *Elle* and has styled editorials for every top magazine in the industry worldwide, from *i-D* and *Harper's Bazaar* to virtually every international edition of *Vogue*. Throughout her career, she has collaborated with a constellation of celebrated photographers, including Richard Avedon, Patrick Demarchelier, Steven Klein, Annie Leibovitz, Steven Meisel, Herb Ritts, Paolo Roversi, Mario Testino, Inez and Vinoodh, and Bruce Weber. She is also the author of *Lori Goldstein: Style Is Instinct* (2013) and the designer of LOGO by Lori Goldstein for QVC.

She's a passionate collector of the Hermès Birkin. Here are her thoughts on the bag and a sampling of some of her favorites.

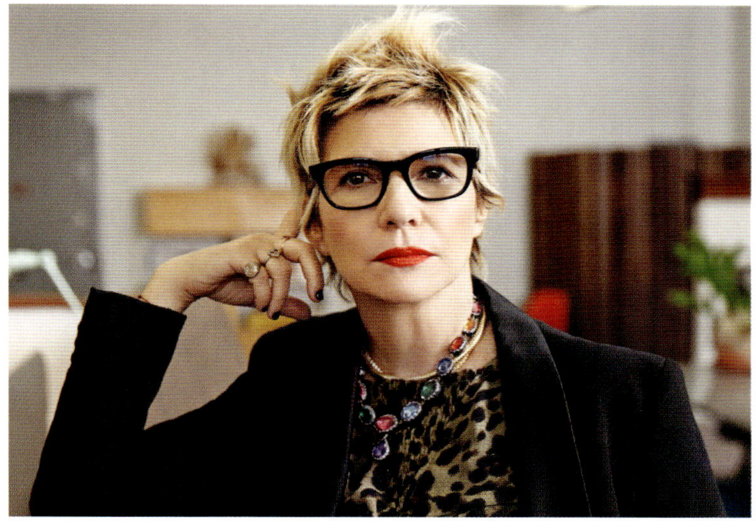

What was the first bag you fell in love with?

The Hermès Birkin. Everything, from the craftsmanship to the exotic skins and colors to their scarcity, really intrigued me.

What bag means the most to you?

The Hermès Birkin is still the most memorable bag for me. I'm a schlepper and a New Yorker. I love function and beauty, and this is the perfect bag. The Birkin is the chicest of them all. Over time, a single Birkin has turned into a true collection—a selection that is very specific to me—that I love.

Do you have any handbag style tips?

More is more! And bags are like clothes: you need a wardrobe of them, even if it's small, because what works for weekdays and workdays is not what you want to carry at night and on weekends, thank goodness!

As someone who has a lot of bags, do you have a storage system?

The Birkins are on shelves. I should treat them with more respect, but I want to see them, so they are not in dust bags. I also have an area for all my Chanel backpacks. I collect those, too. I have a hook area for bags with long straps. It's an organized mess!

What is one thing about handbags that only a true handbag lover would understand?

Collecting. I feel some people couldn't possibly understand why one would purchase the same handbag in different skins and colors and sizes, but when you love something, you end up gravitating toward it, wanting it in that new color, size, or skin—it's a problem! A true handbag lover understands this.

If there were a handbag named after you . . .

It would probably be a backpack in an amazing exotic skin, but it would be totally functional with outside pockets and so comfortable you would never take it off.

THIS PAGE: Lori Goldstein, 2014.

PAGES 112–117: Selections from Lori Goldstein's Hermès Birkin bag collection.

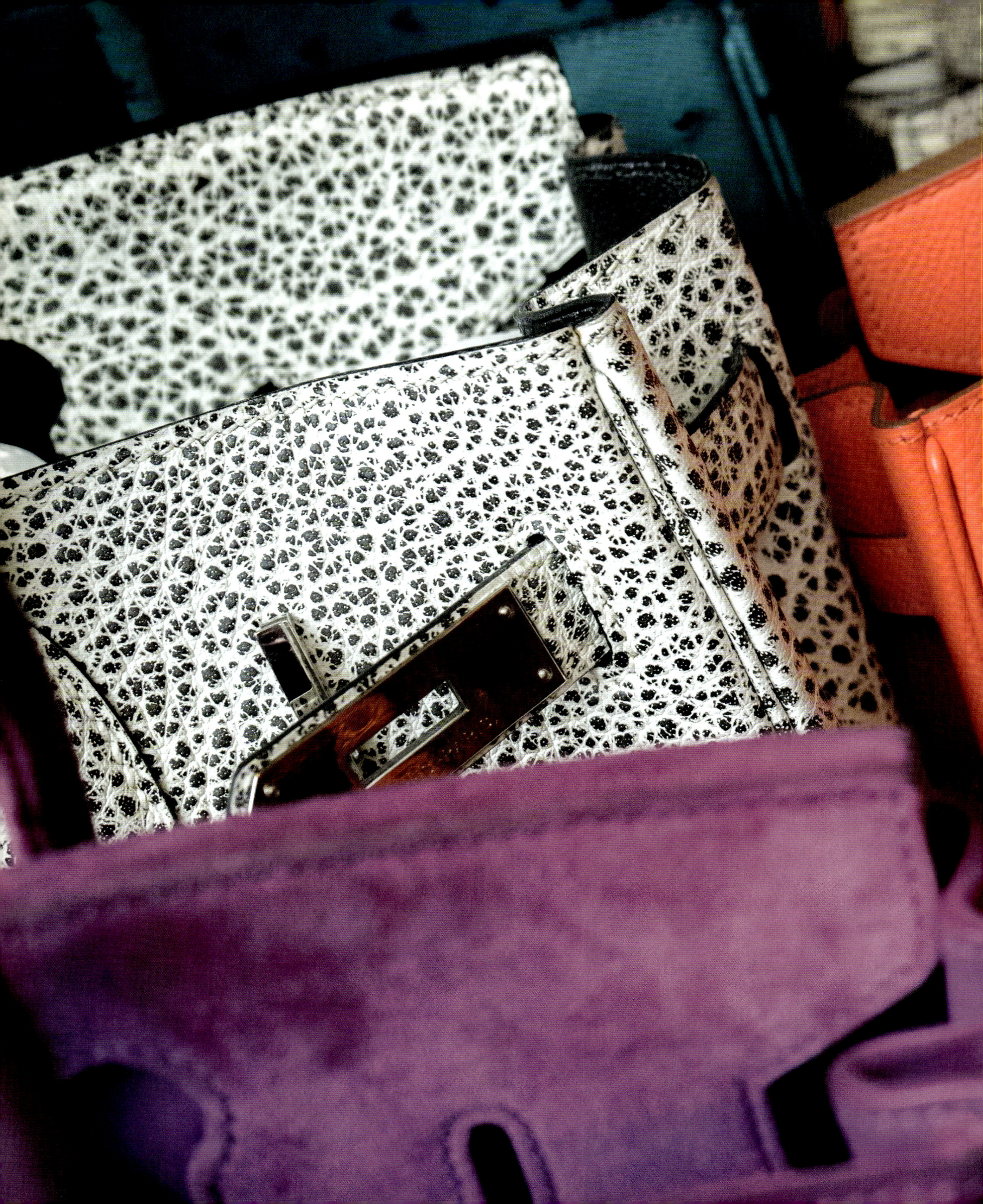

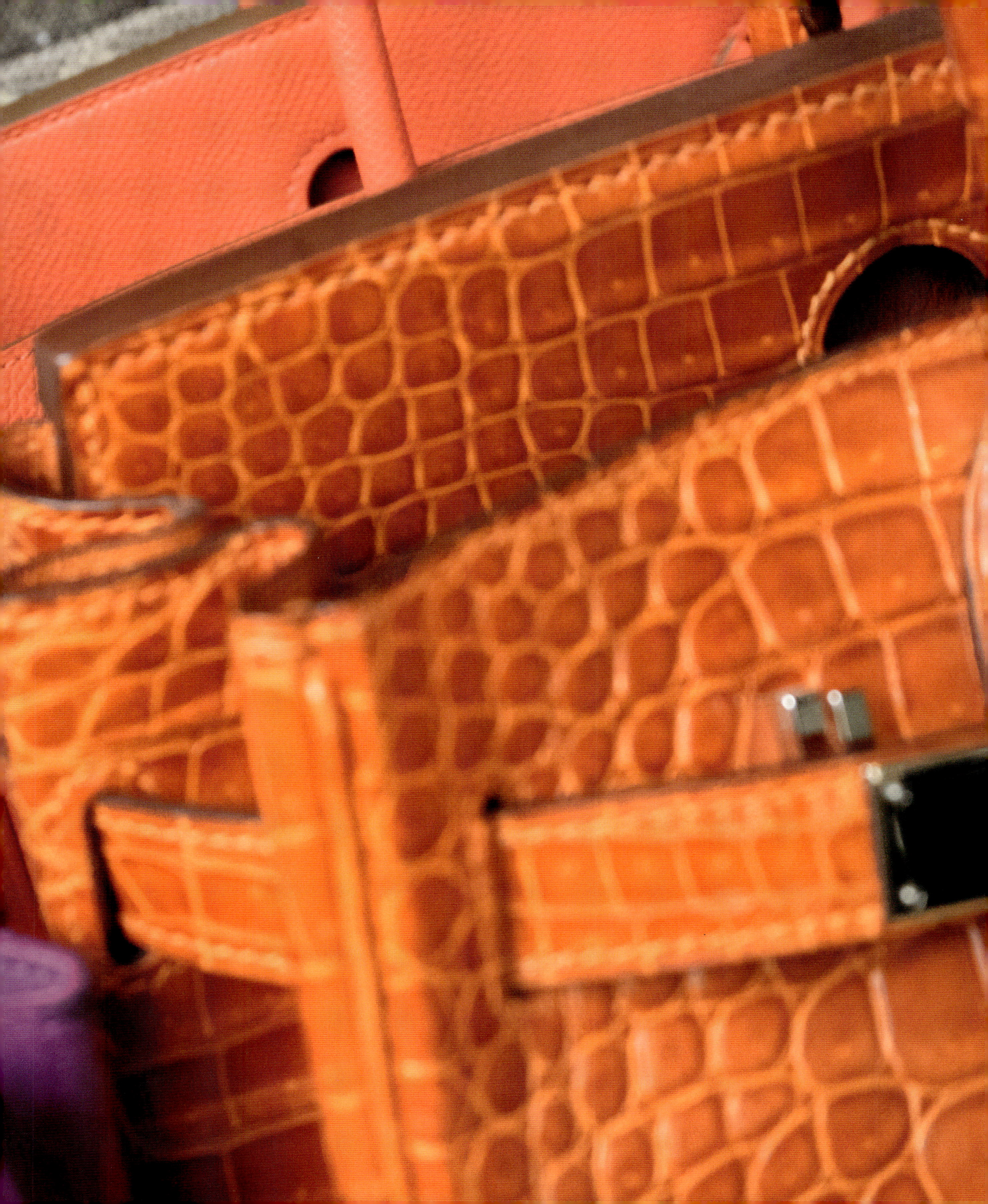

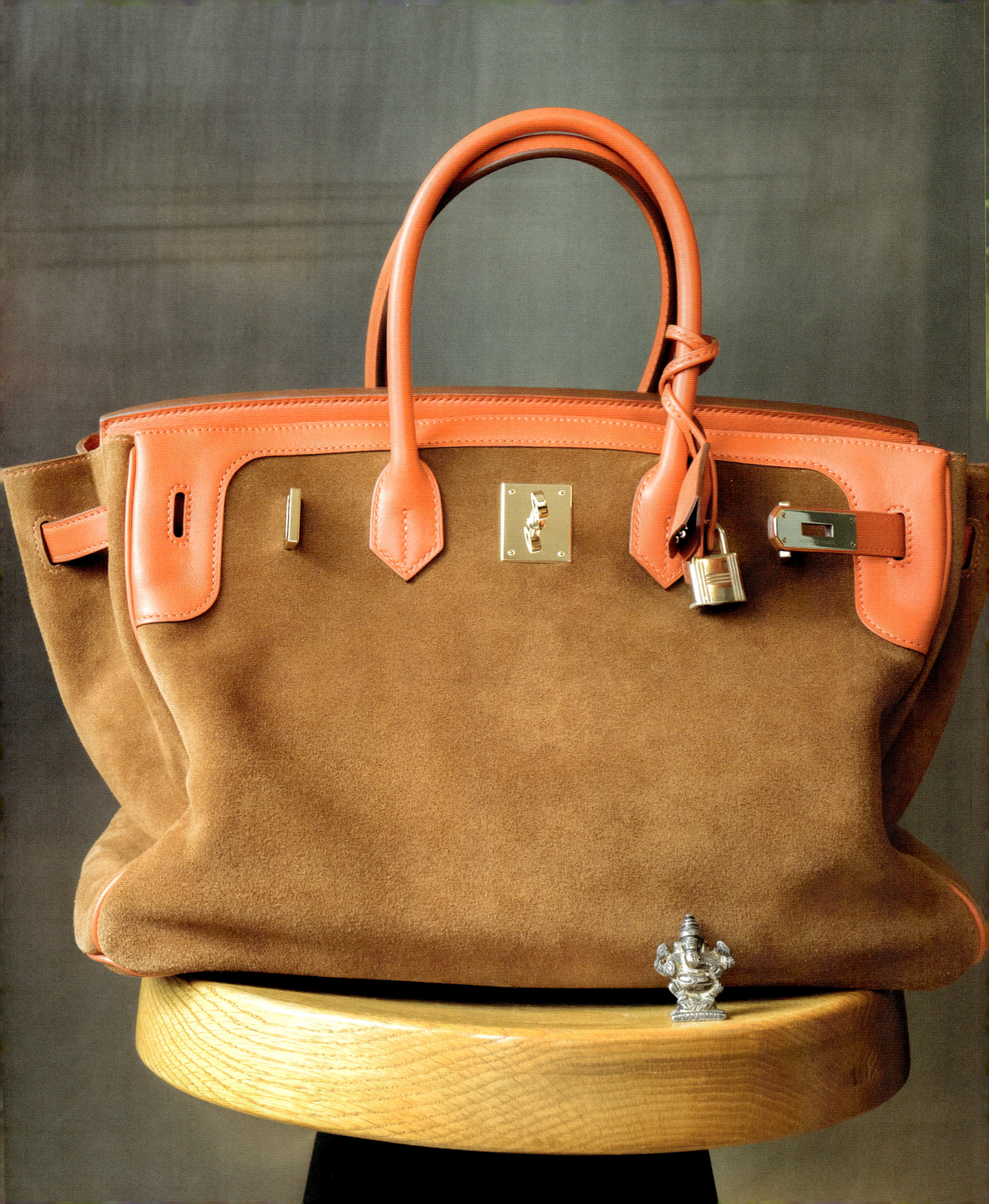

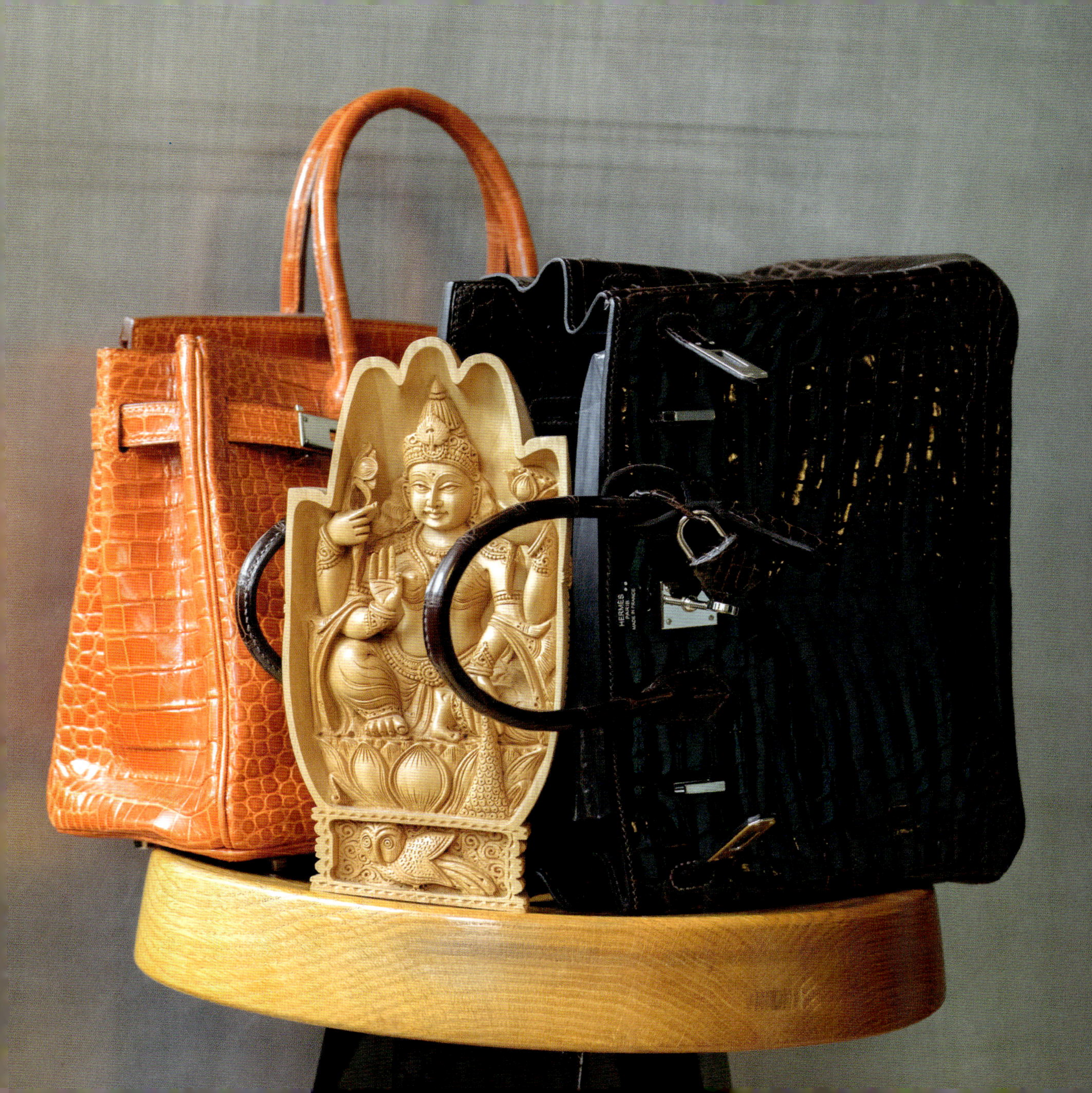
HERMES
PARIS
MADE IN FRANCE

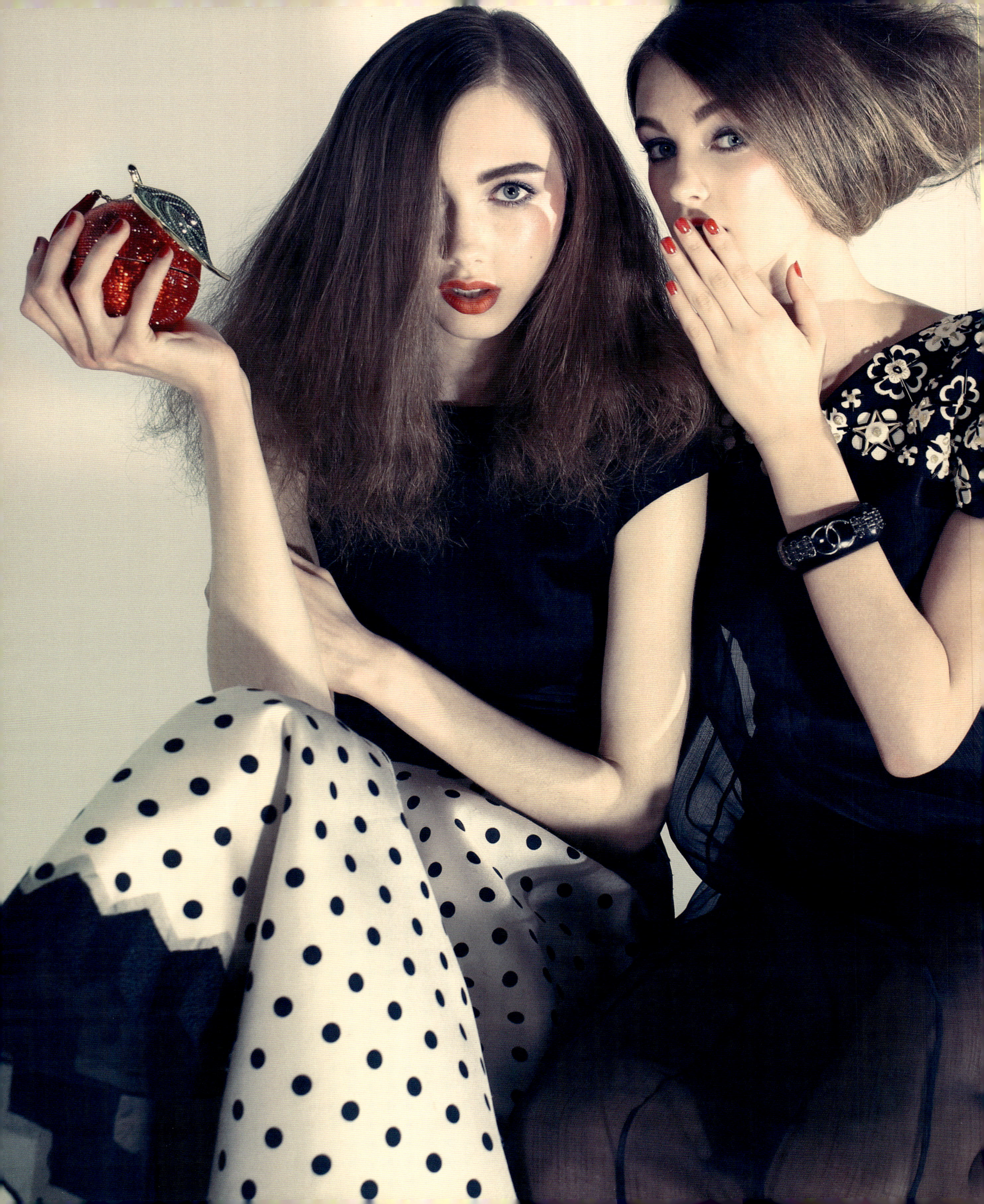

Judith Leiber

CRYSTAL MINAUDIÈRE, 1966

Born into an upper-middle-class Jewish family in Budapest in 1921, Judith Peto was studying chemistry in London with her sights set on a career in cosmetics—"I could have been Estée Lauder," she told *Moment* in 2012—when World War II broke out. Home for the summer, she decided to stay. With the number of opportunities for Jews now limited, she got a job at Pessl, a local handbag company, working her way up from sweeping floors and cooking glue to becoming the first female apprentice. Along the way she learned every step in the bag-making process.

When the Nazis entered Hungary, Judith's family escaped with the help of an uncle employed by the Swiss consulate and moved into Swiss-protected housing. When the Russian army closed in, they were forced into hiding. Terrible memories haunted her—hiding in basements, smelling burning flesh outside. Once, on a rare outing, she was hit in the left arm by a bullet. "I tried to fall asleep by dreaming of making handbags," she recounted in the biography *No Mere Bagatelles* (2009).

After the war, she returned to what she knew: handbags. But Pessl was no more; the owners had been sent to a concentration camp. So Leiber opened her own business, working with whatever materials were available. In 1945 Allied soldiers arrived, including Signal Corps sergeant Gerson Leiber. On his second day in Budapest, he met Judith. "I saw the girl of my dreams, it was love at first sight," he recalled in *Judith Leiber: The Artful Handbag* (1995) by Enid Nemy. The young couple wed the following year and set sail for the United States, settling in the Bronx.

Leiber's first job was at a union handbag factory. "The owner said to me, 'You remember how you made bags in Hungary, all the hand work? Well, that's not how we do it here. Here we bake them like strudel in sheets,'" Leiber said in *The Artful Handbag*. "I was used to handling each bag like a baby and I couldn't stand it." She eventually found herself a position with American fashion designer Nettie Rosenstein in Manhattan and in 1953 got her big break when Rosenstein was tapped to create Mamie Eisenhower's inauguration dress; Leiber made the matching bag. In 1963 Leiber struck out on her own, and in 1966 she created what would become her signature and her claim to fame: the crystal-covered minaudière.

OPPOSITE: Red Apple bag, Judith Leiber, *Lula* magazine, Fall/Winter 2011.

PAGES 120–121: A selection of Judith Leiber's more inventive crystal minaudières throught the years.

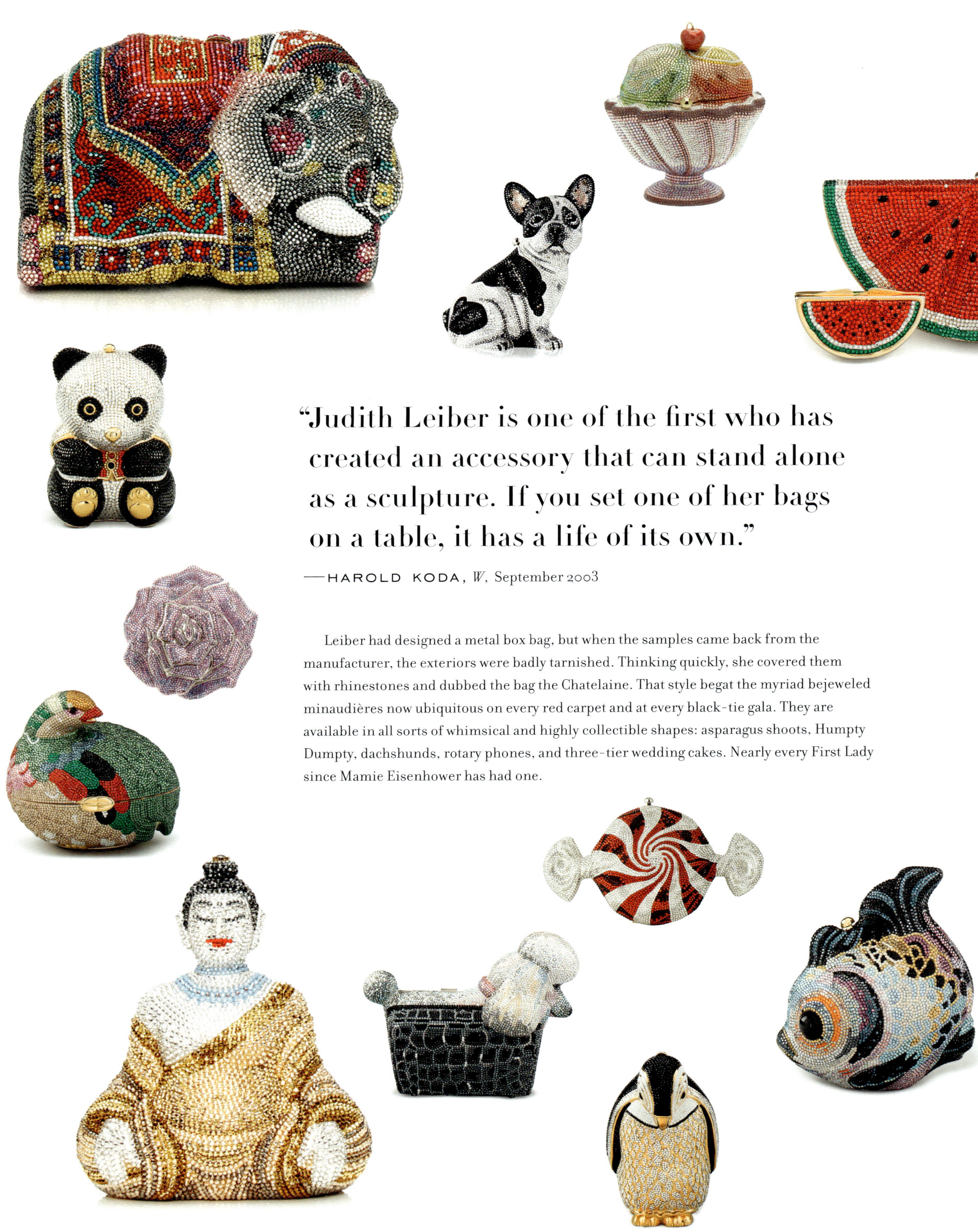

"Judith Leiber is one of the first who has created an accessory that can stand alone as a sculpture. If you set one of her bags on a table, it has a life of its own."

—HAROLD KODA, *W*, September 2003

Leiber had designed a metal box bag, but when the samples came back from the manufacturer, the exteriors were badly tarnished. Thinking quickly, she covered them with rhinestones and dubbed the bag the Chatelaine. That style begat the myriad bejeweled minaudières now ubiquitous on every red carpet and at every black-tie gala. They are available in all sorts of whimsical and highly collectible shapes: asparagus shoots, Humpty Dumpty, dachshunds, rotary phones, and three-tier wedding cakes. Nearly every First Lady since Mamie Eisenhower has had one.

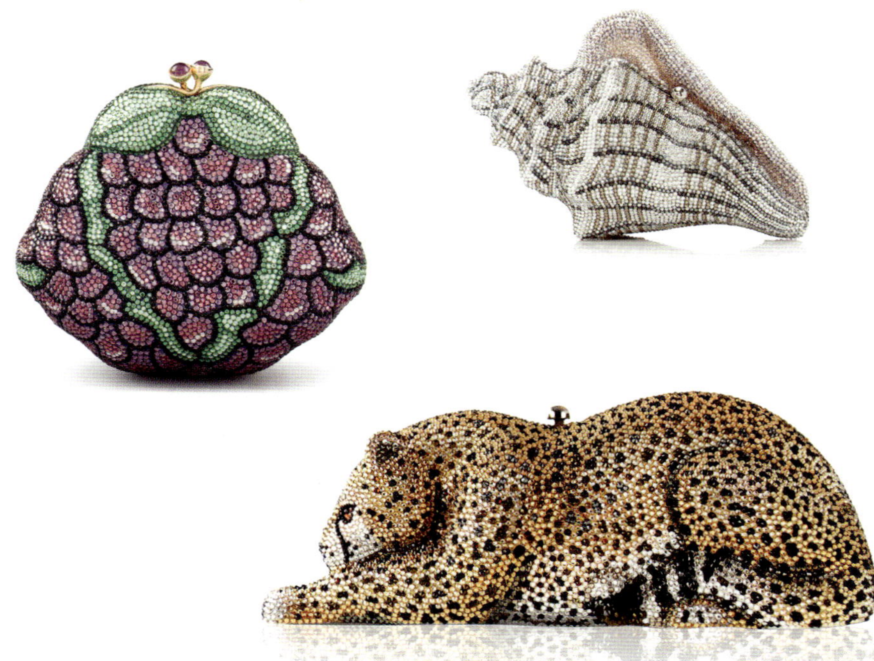
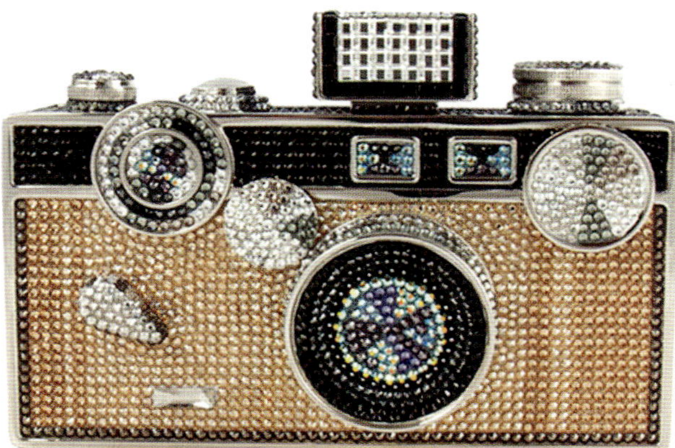
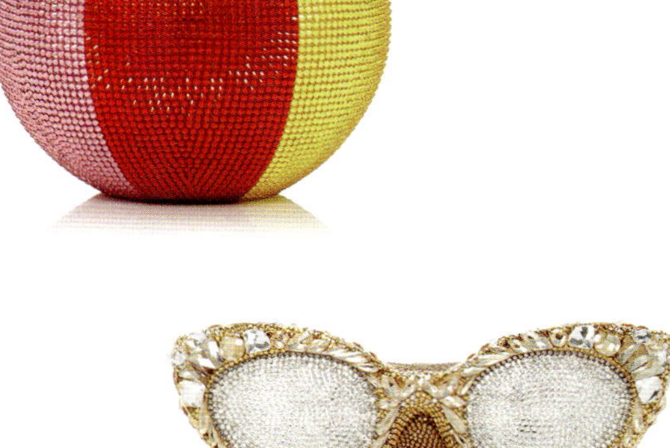

Leiber has designed some four thousand different styles, from animals and musical instruments to Fabergé-like eggs. Depending on the intricacy of the bag's form, models are made in either cardboard or wax. The forms are used to create molds, which ultimately are cast in brass, then gold-plated on the outside and lined with kid leather on the inside. They are painted before being festooned, most commonly with crystals, though gold and silver mosaics, precious stones, beads, and shells have adorned them, too.

Leiber fans are many, and her bags are red-carpet favorites, spotted on Zsa Zsa Gabor, Jennifer Lopez, Joan Rivers, and Elizabeth Taylor. In 1998 the *New York Times* noted that Bernice Norman, a patron of the arts in New Orleans, had nearly three hundred; the late opera singer Beverly Sills owned more than seventy.When Leiber retired in 1998, her company changed hands and shortened the name to simply Leiber, but her legacy endures on television, red carpets, and runways. For instance, designer Jeremy Scott sparked a renaissance when he attended a Chanel couture show in 2000 wearing a sparkly Leiber teddy bear as a pendant. In 2005, Judith and Gerson, an artist, built a Renaissance-style Palladian museum dedicated to a retrospective of their careers.

"When I'm wearing one of her egg designs, people ask me if it's a Fabergé egg," Sills is quoted in *The Artful Handbag*. "To me, it's just as valuable, it's a Leiber egg."

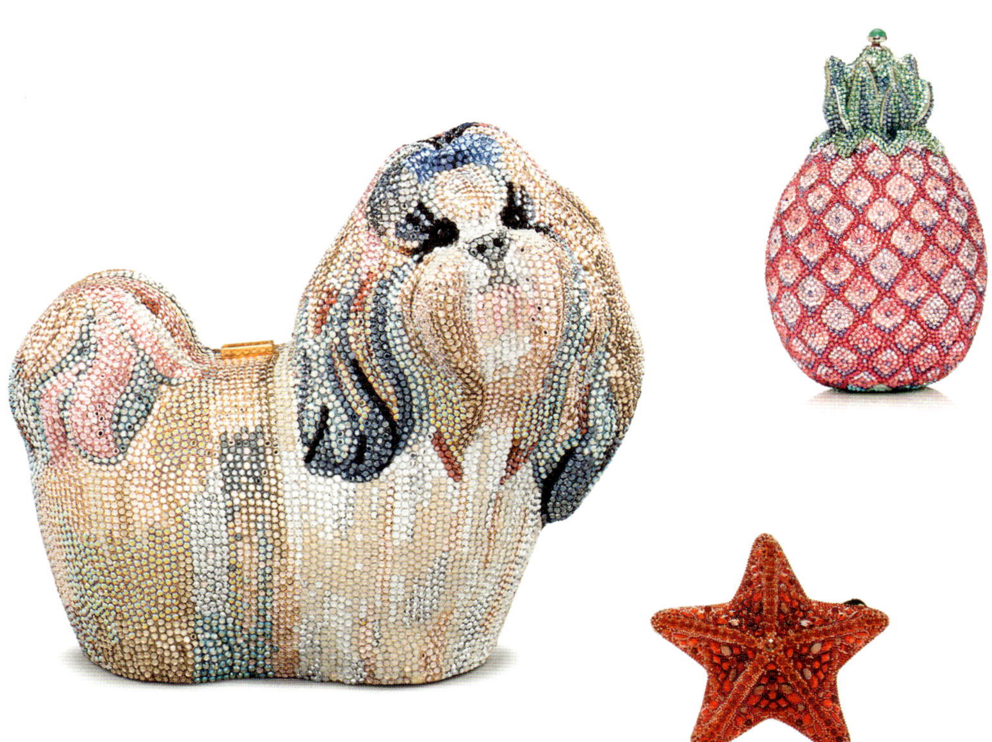
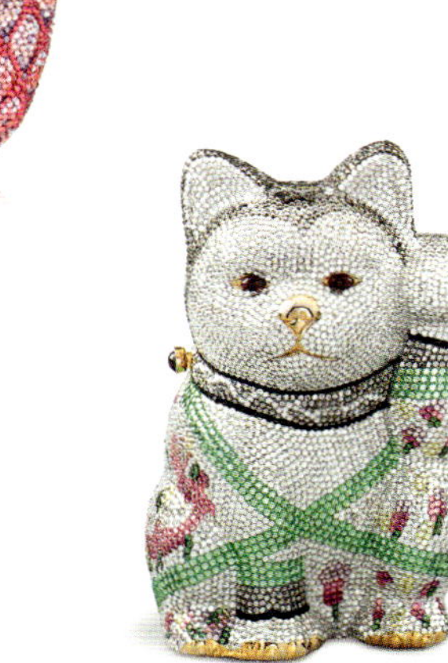
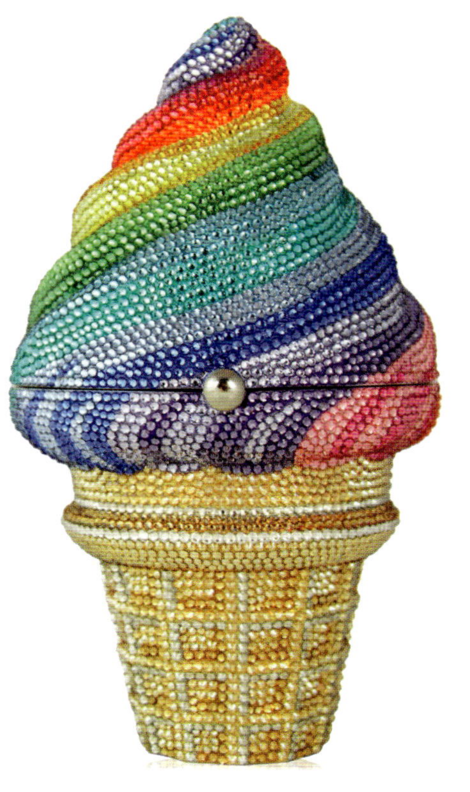

Loewe

AMAZONA, 1975

Loewe began in 1846 as a small workshop, shared by José Silva and Florencio Rivas, dedicated to small leather goods such as men's wallets and cigar holders. Based in the heart of Madrid, they worked quietly for the next twenty or so years until the German leather tanner and bag designer Enrique Loewe Roessberg joined the atelier, initially working as a producer of pistol holders. By 1872 Roessberg became their principal business partner, and by 1892 the firm was born. Loewe cultivated a reputation for high-quality leathers and exotics—iguana, snake, crocodile—and for fine craftsmanship. In 1905 the company was named an official supplier for the Spanish royal family. In five short years, they were renowned throughout Spain.

Loewe became synonymous with luxury and glamour. It's reportedly where Ernest Hemingway brought Ava Gardner for a little retail pick-me-up after her split with Frank Sinatra. Marlene Dietrich, Rita Hayworth, and Sophia Loren were all fans.

While Loewe, nicknamed the "Hermès of Spain," has had a roster of bestsellers—including the Cruz bag, designed in collaboration with the Spanish actresses Penelope and Monica Cruz—it's the Amazona that earns the top spot here. Big, soft, and rectangular, with leather patches at the bottom corners, the style, introduced in 1975, just as the country was emerging from the Franco era, has been a must-have for decades. The substantial size was deliberate. Stuart Vevers, the brand's former creative director, explained to *Harper's Bazaar* in 2013, "It was designed to celebrate the new freedom that women had—working and traveling by themselves for the first time. So it was big enough to hold all their belongings."

In recent years, the Amazona has had a resurgence outside Spain, thanks to new creative heads such as Vevers and Jonathan Anderson. They revamped the style with new color combinations, fabrics, and prints and toyed slightly with the silhouette while always keeping an eye on its roots in a sporty classicism. "When I arrived, there was an attitude of: 'Can you design us an It bag please, to put us on the map?'" recalled Vevers in the *Telegraph* in 2012. "But I felt it was very important to get away from all that. I consider the Amazona more of an emblem. I wanted a bag that could evolve year after year. It had to be more than something you just chucked a load of bling at."

The Amazona wasn't the only Loewe icon to get an update. In 2014 Anderson replaced the font used for the logotype with a new one, moving from Bembo to Pegasus, created by German typographer and calligrapher Berthold Wolpe in 1937. Designed by creative agency M/M (Paris), it's a subtle nod to Enrique Loewe Roessberg's German roots.

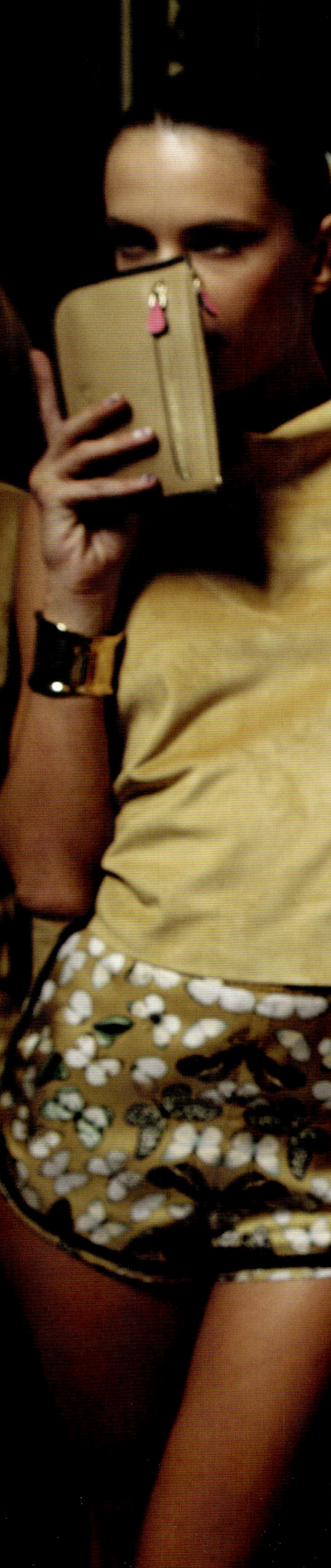

OPPOSITE: Amazona bag, backstage at Loewe, Spring 2011 ready-to-wear.

PAGES 124–125: Model Rosie Huntington-Whiteley carrying an Amazona bag, London, October 2011.

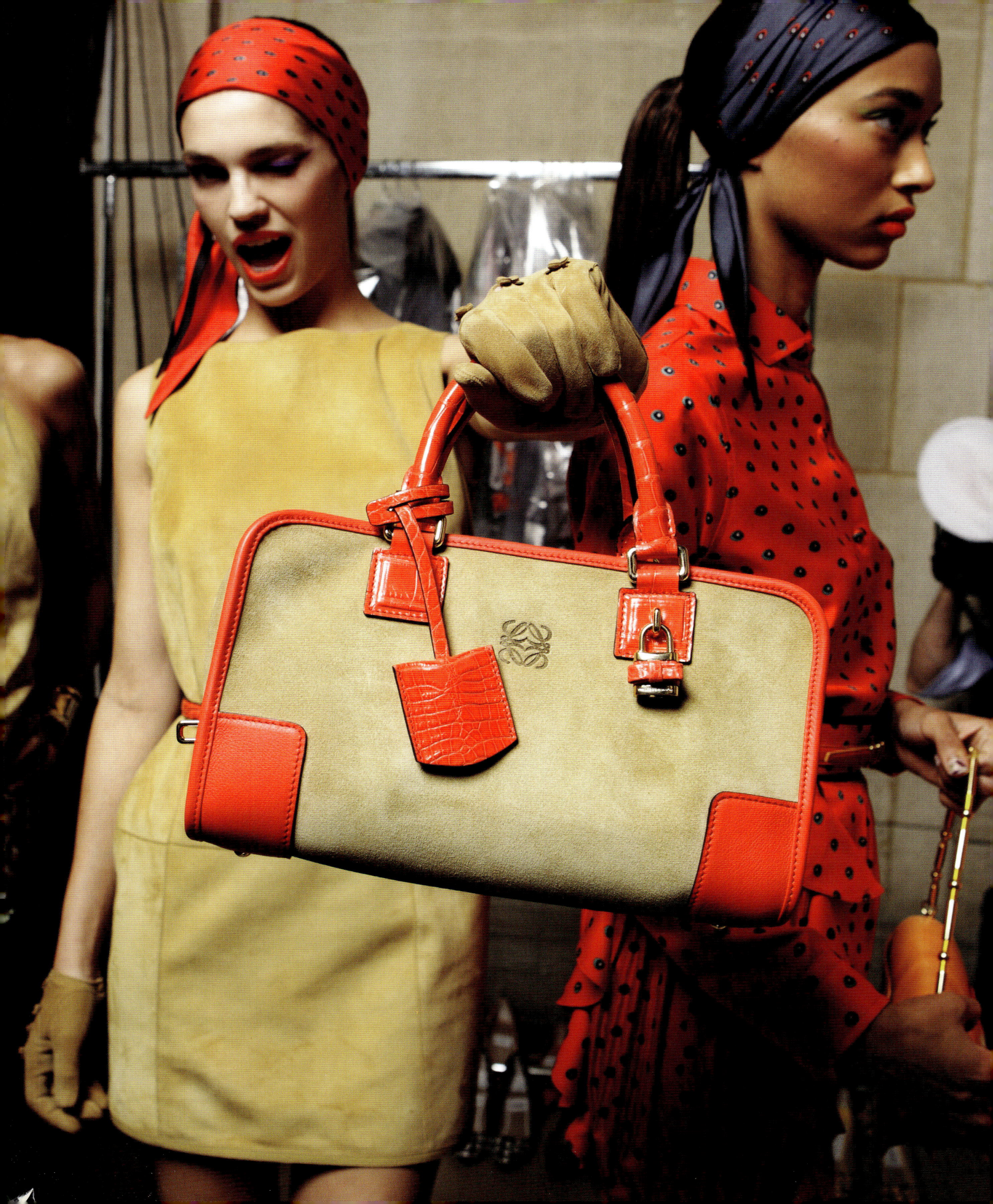

"For me, Loewe's Spanishness is what makes it so unique and intriguing. The management might be international but the 200 artisans are all Spanish. That shows in everything they do. It's not delicate or light. It's strong and bold. These bags couldn't come out of any other country."

—STUART VEVERS, *The Telegraph*, May 23, 2012

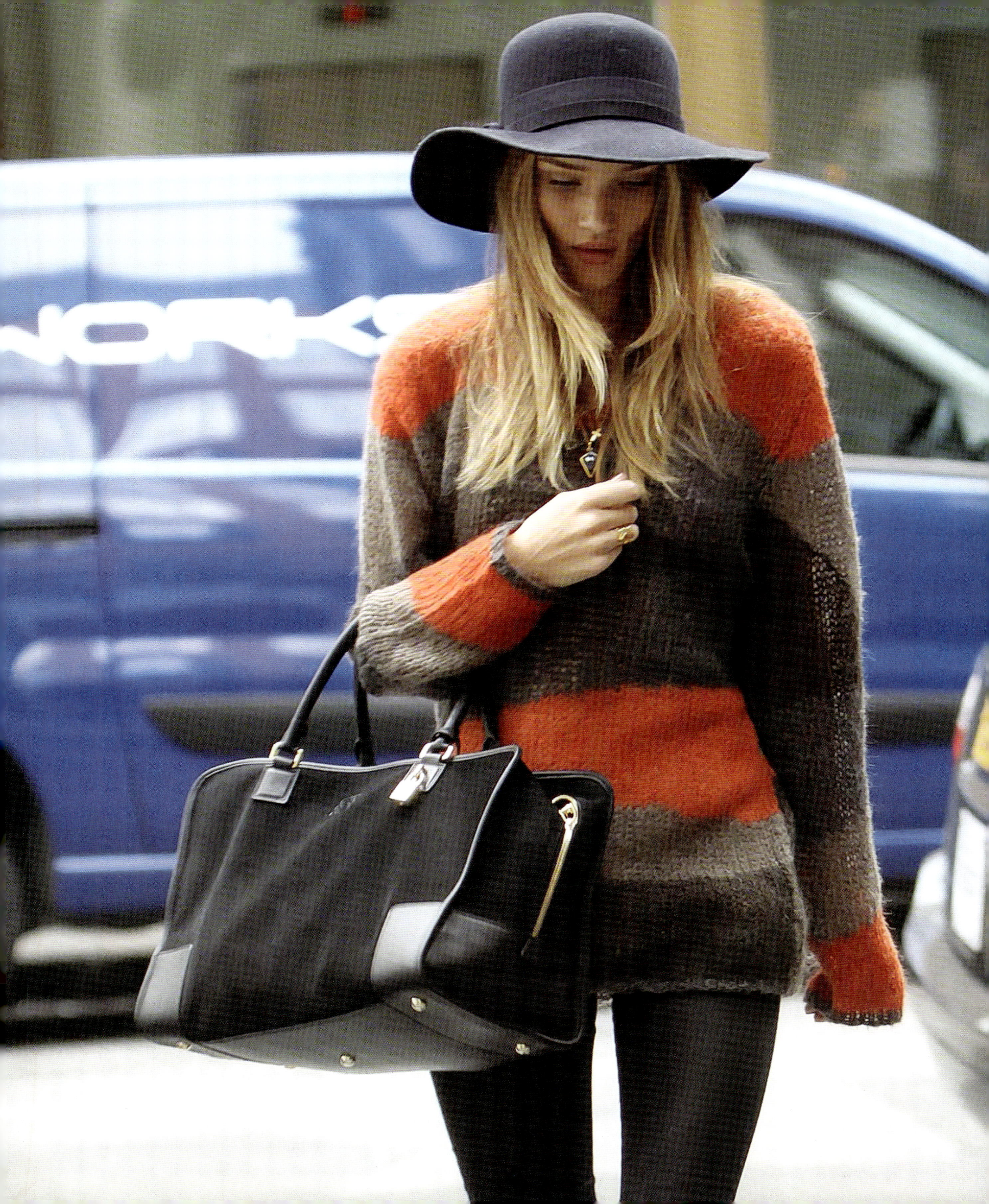

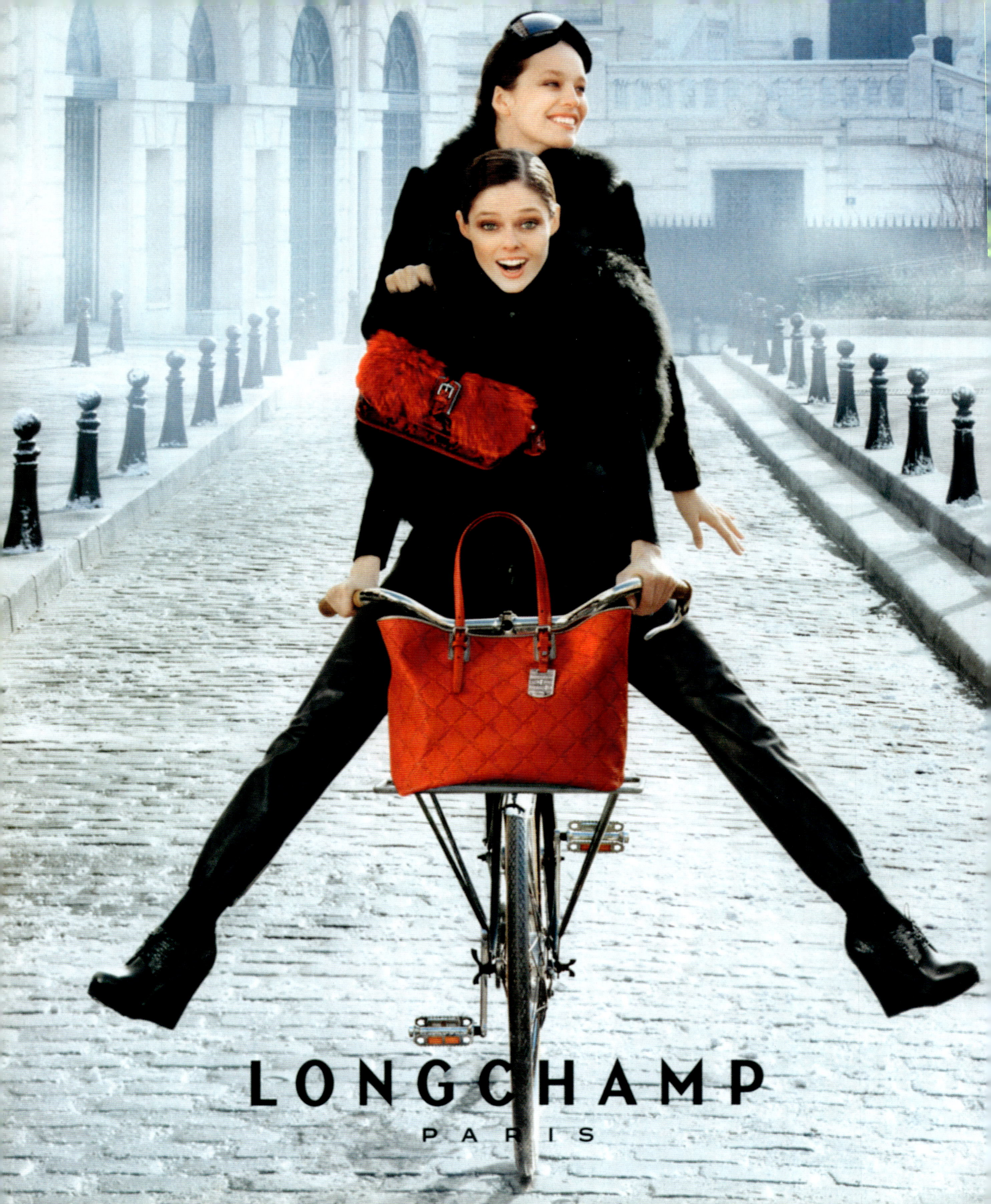
LONGCHAMP
PARIS

Longchamp

LE PLIAGE, 1993

Inspired by the Japanese art of origami, Longchamp's Le Pliage tote is a fairly simple, even plain, design: a slightly trapezoidal nylon body, with a leather clasp and handles, that you can easily fold into a small rectangle. No extra hardware, no doodads, no frills. Ultralight and available in an assortment of colors, the roomy bag is a godsend for travelers, new mothers, gym goers, and city dwellers. The bag is popular because it's chic, durable, and wonderfully utilitarian. It appeals to women of multiple generations and styles, especially the college set, who helped boost its visibility most recently.

There were limited-edition collections by Tracey Emin (2004), Jeremy Scott (2006), and Mary Katrantzou (2012), upping the cache just when it seemed the bag had reached its saturation point. You can now customize your own Pliage—size, color, handles, lining—on the Longchamp website. To date, more than 31 million Le Pliage totes in more than 150 colors have sold worldwide.

While its bestseller might be a versatile nylon tote, the firm's heritage is actually in leather. Founder Jean Cassegrain started working at his father's tobacco shop at 9 bis boulevard Poissonnière in Paris, a popular haunt for Allied soldiers during the postwar era. As the servicemen inevitably began to head home, the enterprising Cassegrain decided to start a new business: leather cozies for tobacco pipes, created using saddle-making techniques. In 1948 Longchamp was born.

Cassegrain initially named his business Jean Cassegrain et Compagnie, but a cousin already had a motorcycle business under that name. So he thought of mills—*cassegrain* literally meaning "to break grain" in French—particularly a mill located next to the Longchamp Racecourse on the outskirts of Paris. Cassegrain seized on the name Longchamp, which added an instant equestrian heritage—one the business-savvy Frenchman amplified with a logo of a galloping horse.

Longchamp continues to build on its heritage to this day, most recently with the 2012 Le Pliage Héritage, which has the familiar shape of Le Pliage but is crafted from exquisite top-stitched cowhide. The collection adds structure—and the legacy of Longchamp leathers—to the iconic packable nylon design.

OPPOSITE:
Longchamp Fall 2012 advertisement featuring models Coco Rocha *(front)* and Emily DiDonato.

PAGES 128–129:
Le Pliage *(left)*, Longchamp, Paris, March 2016.

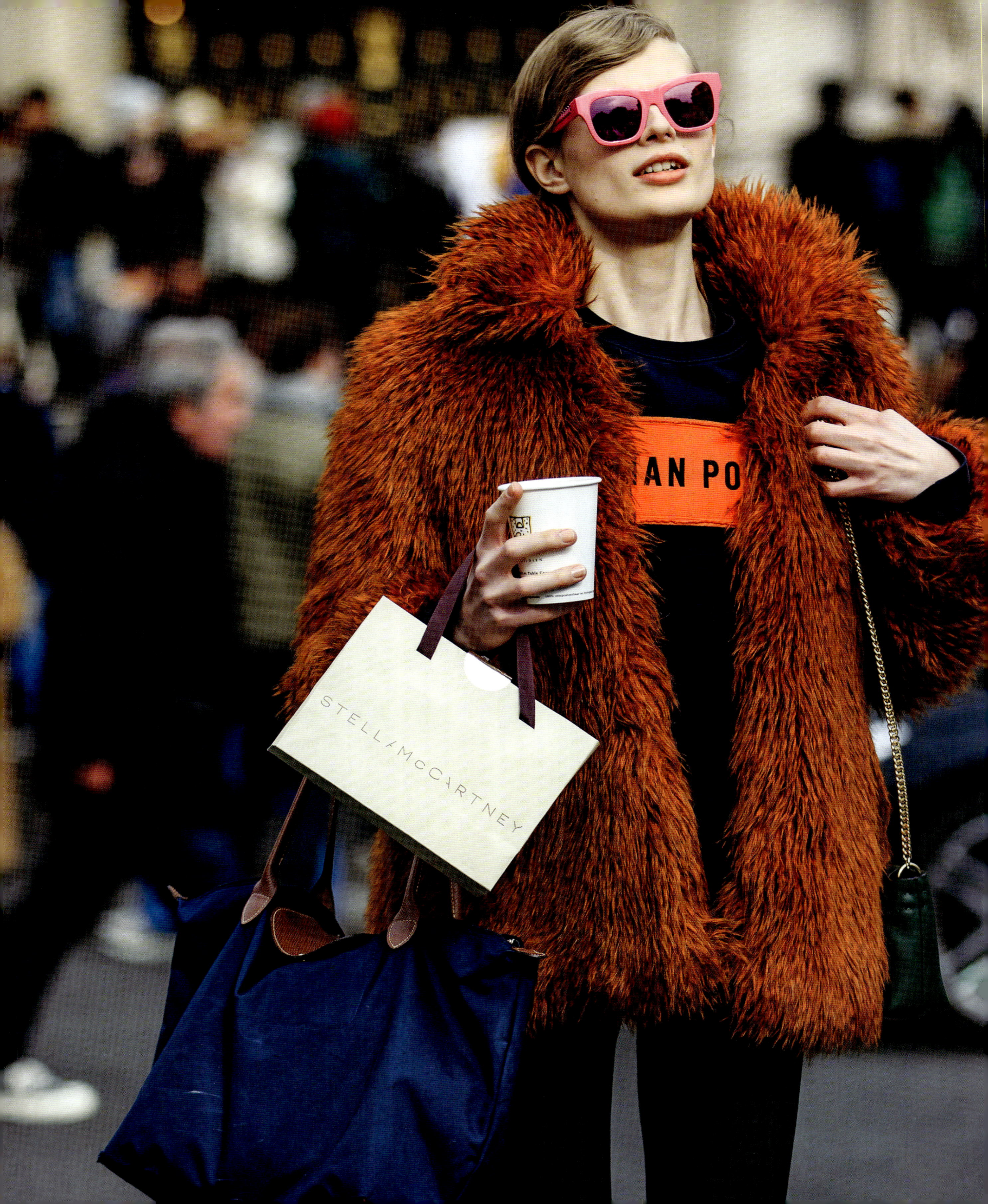
STELLA McCARTNEY

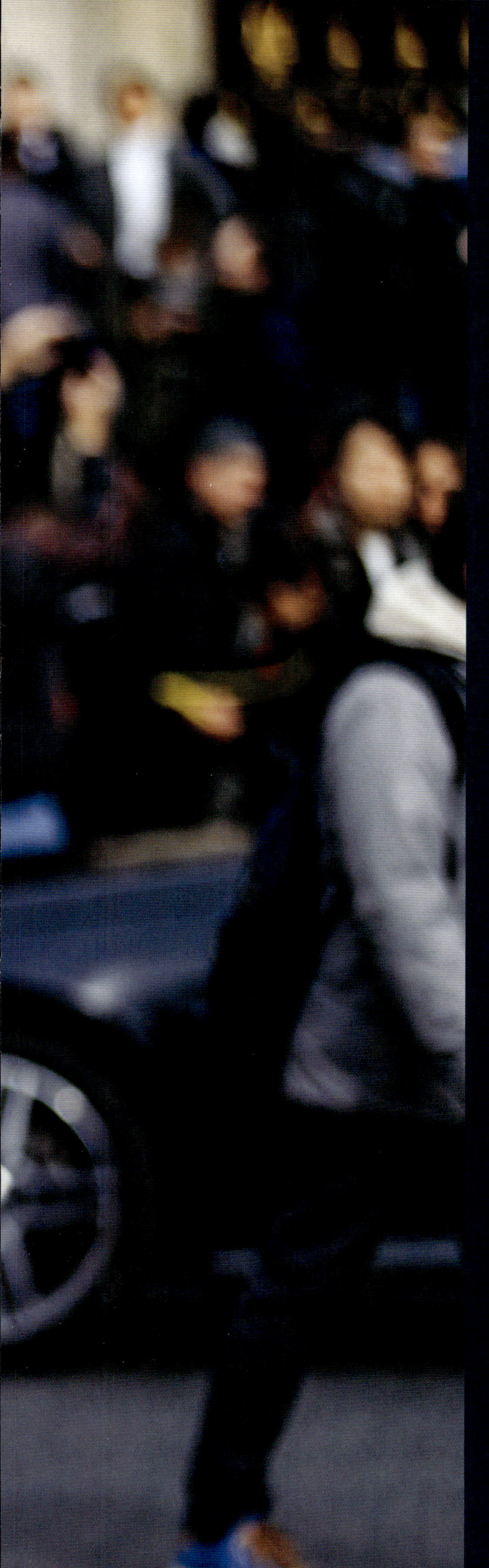

“No introduction required. Le Pliage is to Longchamp what the madeleine is to Proust.”

—MARIE AUCOUTURIER, *Longchamp*, 2008

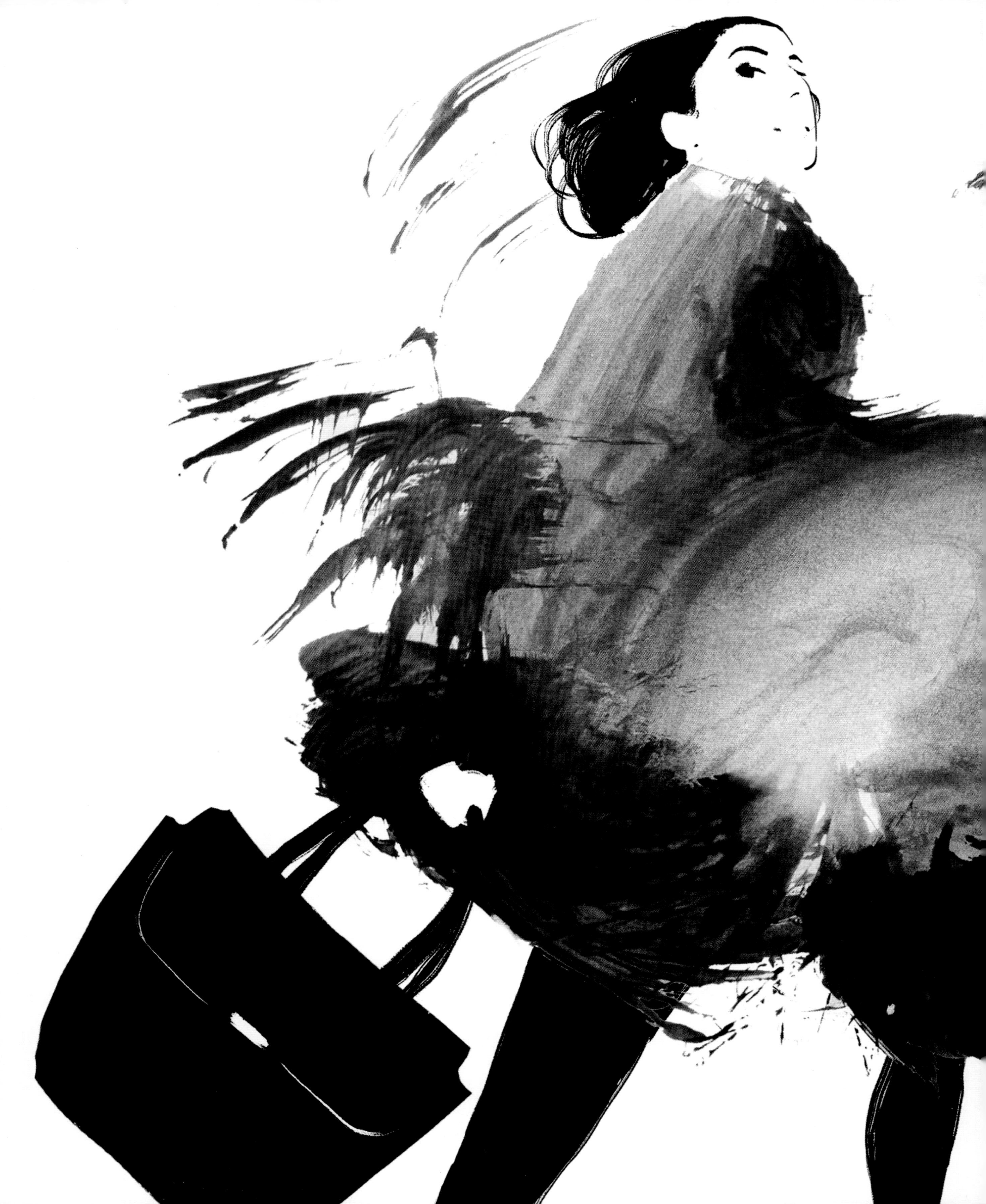

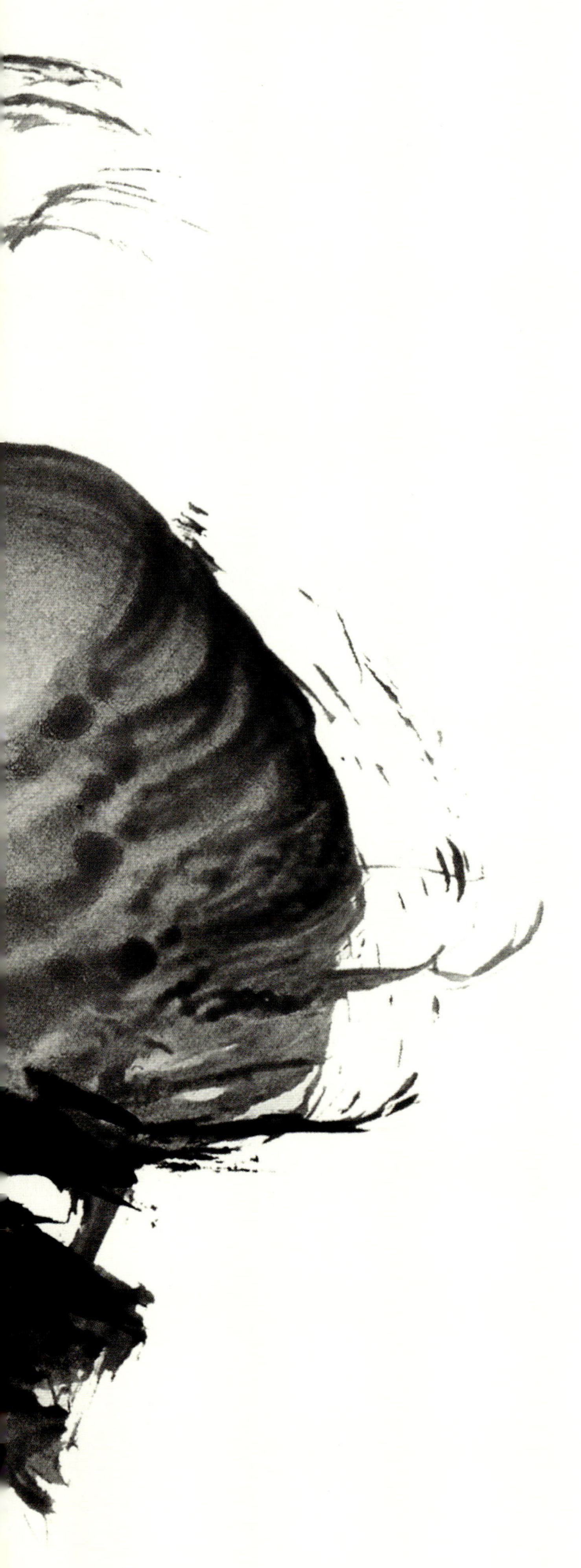

"While men have their hands in their pockets so grand, ladies have pockets to wear in their hand."

—IMPERIAL WEEKLY GAZETTE, 1804,
from *Handbags: The Power of the Purse* by Anna Johnson, 2002

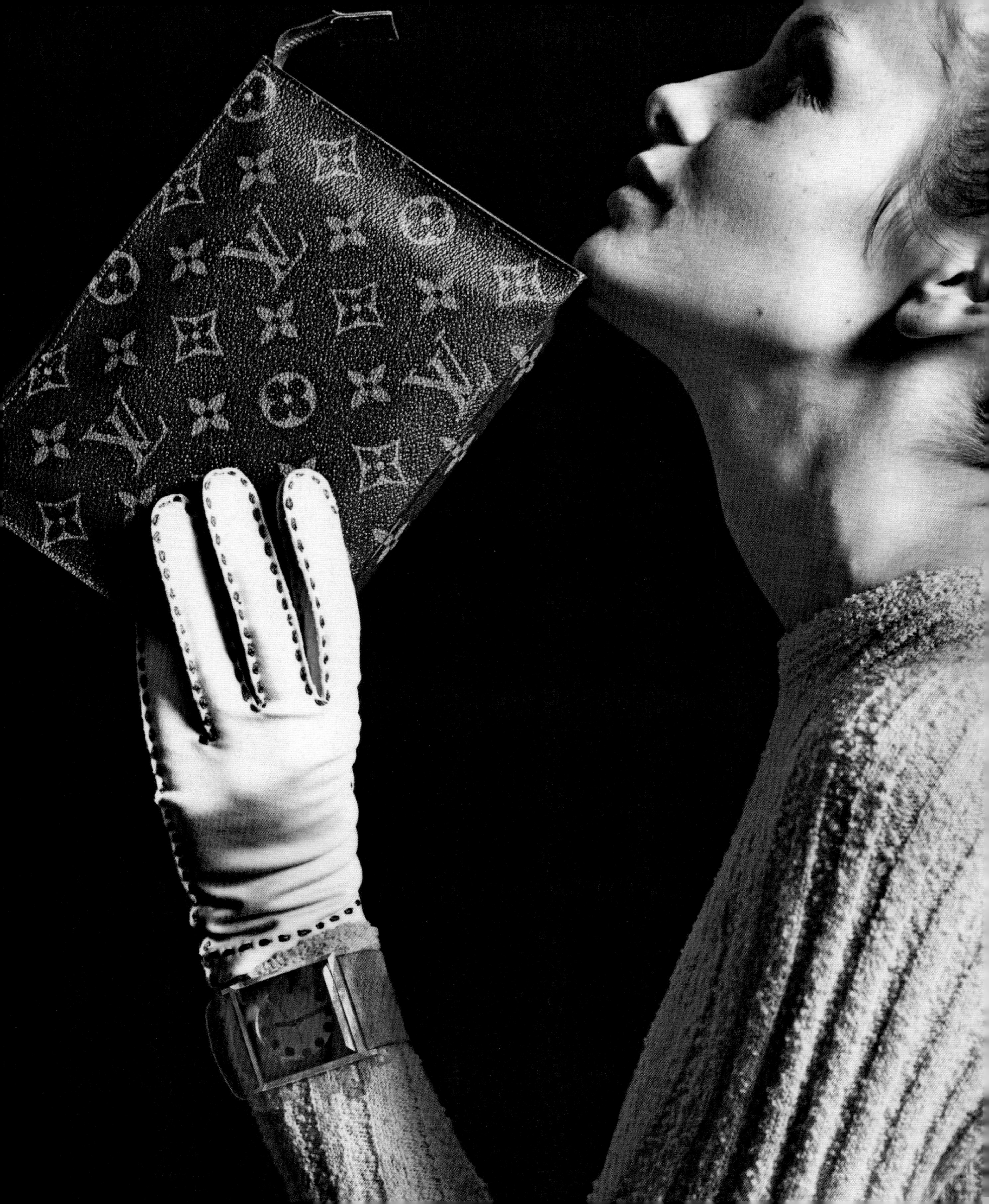

Louis Vuitton

SPEEDY, CA. 1930

NOÉ, 1932

PAPILLON, 1966

NEVERFULL, 2007

Founded by Louis Vuitton in 1854, this French company has long been one of the world's great luggage makers, with clients ranging from Czar Nicholas II to Charles Frederick Worth—the father of haute couture—to the Duke and Duchess of Windsor, who traveled to New York City's Waldorf Astoria every year with some ninety bags, more than sixty of which were Vuitton. The eponymous firm started out making trunks painted light gray. There were soon imitators, so in 1872 the trunks were decorated with stripes—first, red and beige, and, four years later, the now-trademark light-and-dark beige. Nevertheless, copies persisted, and in 1888 the company created the checkered pattern known as the Damier canvas. In 1896 came the Monogram canvas that featured the interlaced initials LV and three stylized floral motifs. Louis was the hand behind all these changes to prevent forgeries, save for the Monogram, which was the invention of his son, Georges.

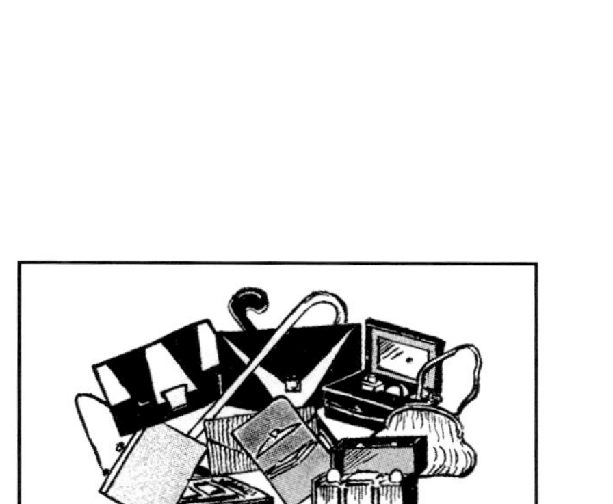

OPPOSITE: Twiggy with a Louis Vuitton Toilette pochette, *Vogue UK*, November 1967.

ABOVE: Louis Vuitton advertisement, 1925.

PAGES 134–135: Assorted Louis Vuitton bags and luggage, *Vogue Japan*, April 2012.

PAGES 136–137: Selections from "The Imaginary Voyages of Louis Vuitton" campaign, 1995.

PAGES 138–139: Catherine Deneuve *(left)* with an array of luggage and a Manhattan bag, and Scarlett Johansson with a Neverfull bag, Louis Vuitton, Fall 2007.

"[Georges] was overjoyed when . . . the Americans copied his products and in their ads called their Louis Vuitton counterfeits French trunks," wrote Paul-Gérard Pasols in *Louis Vuitton: The Birth of Modern Luxury* (2012). "This really made him feel he had won, not only for his own company but for all French trunk manufacturers."

The company is also known for its easily recognizable signature styles such as the Noé, a bucket shape inspired by a five-bottle champagne case made by the firm in the early days; the wide Neverfull tote; and the Papillon. The Speedy, a smaller version of its Keepall travel bag, was created in the 1960s for Audrey Hepburn, who requested a smaller style to match her petite frame; the name also nodded to the fast-paced life of modern times. Cut from the same trunk canvas, now coated in PVC for a moldable, supple effect, the styles all sported the checkered and monogram patterns. By the 1960s and 1970s these bags became a signifier of haute luxury, boosted by images of the era's glitterati living the good life with a Louis Vuitton by their side—Twiggy posing seductively in a 1967 issue of *Vogue*, Sophia Loren photographed stepping out of a hotel in Nice in 1977.

In 1996 Louis Vuitton celebrated the 100th anniversary of the Monogram canvas by inviting seven designers to reinterpret the icon. Azzedine Alaïa wrapped an Alma bag in panther skin; Helmut Lang created a DJ case equipped to hold seventy vinyl records; and Vivienne Westwood designed a rounded bustle-like fanny pack. The arrival of Marc Jacobs in 1997 transformed the company into a fashion force and resulted in a new set of creative collaborations (see "Marc Jacobs's Art Trek for Louis Vuitton" on page 140). Nicolas Ghesquière, formerly of Balenciaga, took over Jacobs's practice in 2014. His debut coincided with the brand's 160th anniversary and, in a repeat of the 1996 campaign, Ghesquière gave six designers carte blanche to rework the classic monogram, pushing it to new inventive heights. Fellow designer Karl Lagerfeld's submission was a boxer's leather punching bag covered in the initials LV.

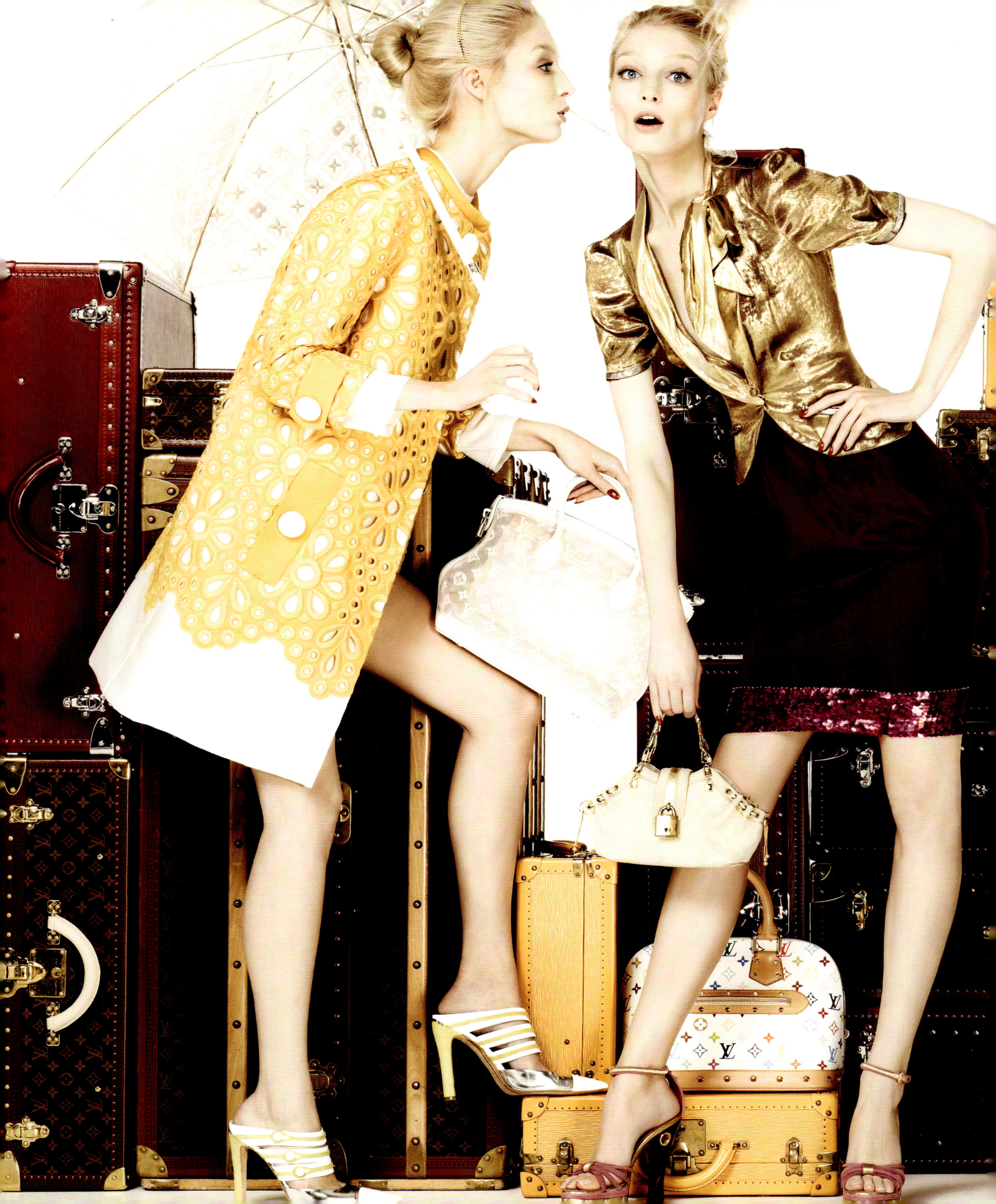

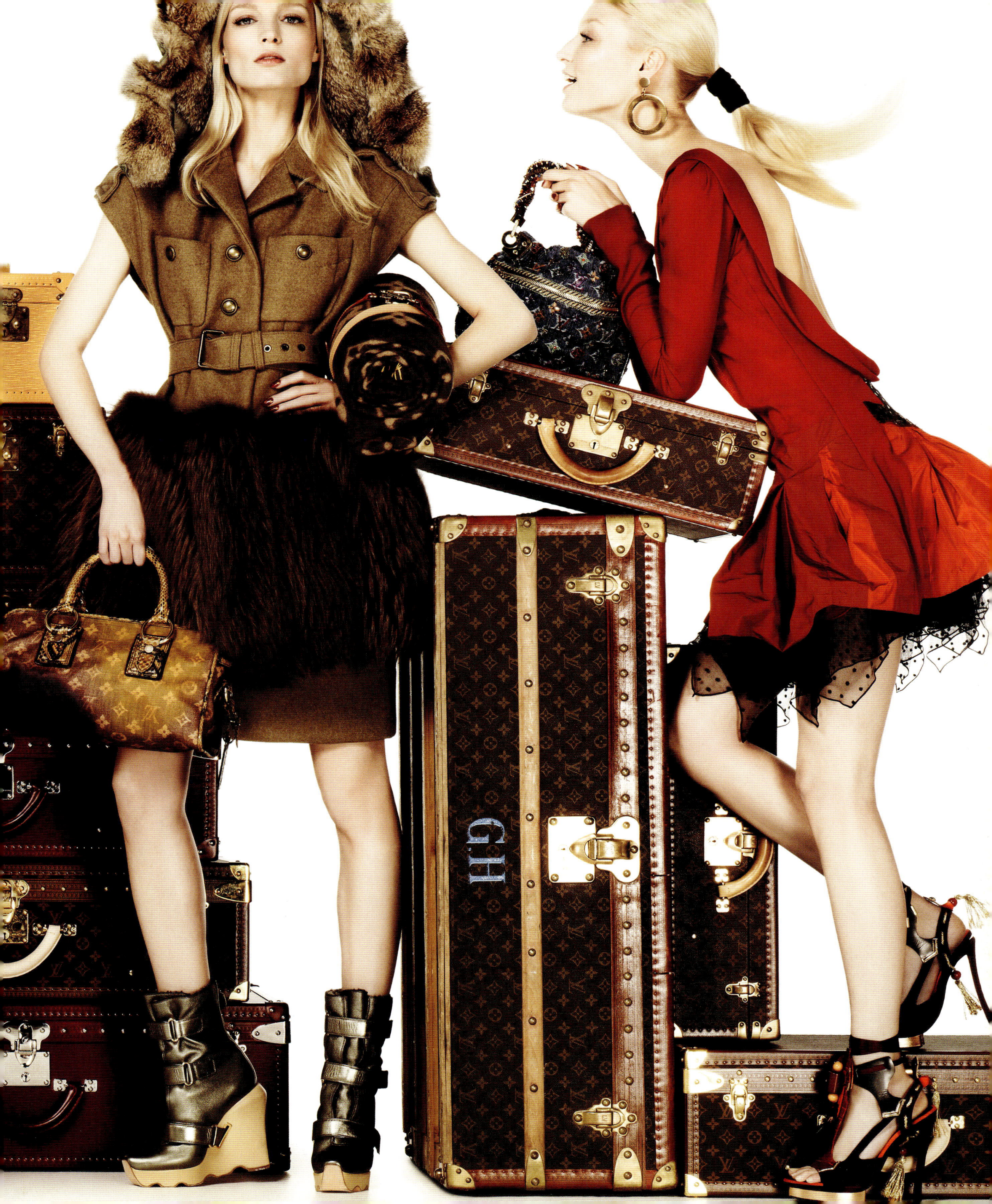
G.H

Louis Vuitton. Since 1854, always the unexpected.

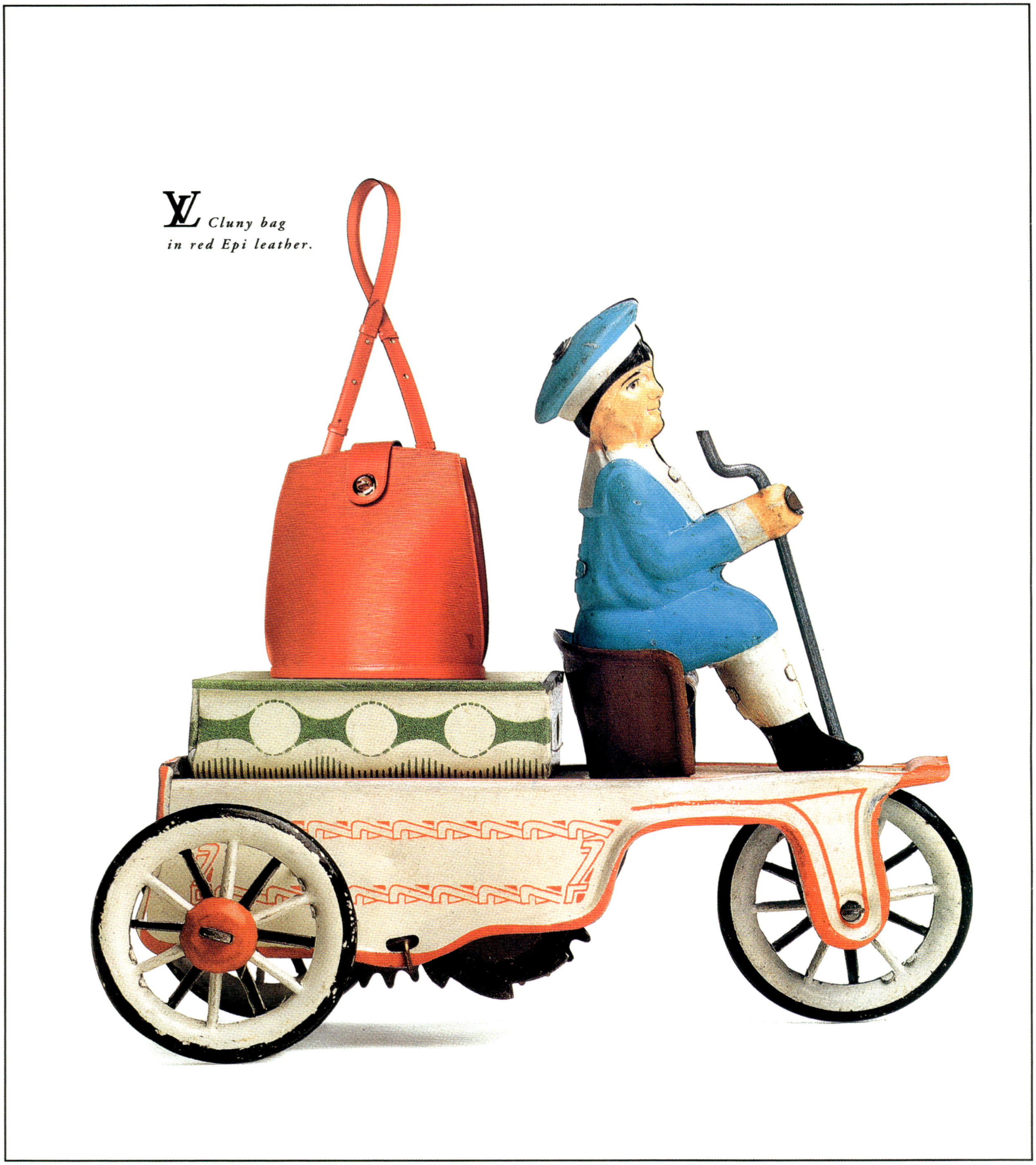

Cluny bag in red Epi leather.

Lenox Square Atlanta 404-266-3674

Available exclusively at Louis Vuitton shops and select department stores.
For more information or the store nearest you, please call: 1-800-458-4136.

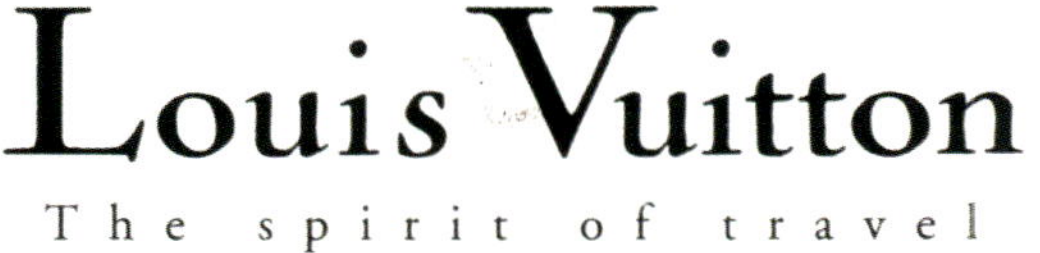

Louis Vuitton. Since 1854, always the unexpected.

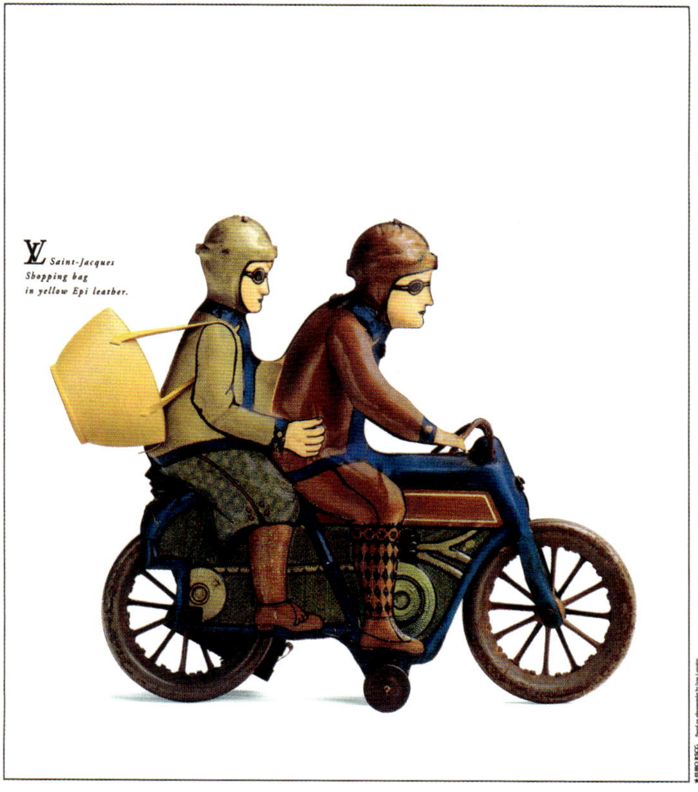

Available exclusively in Louis Vuitton shops and select department stores.
For more information or the store nearest you, please call: 1-800-458-4130.

Louis Vuitton
The spirit of travel

Louis Vuitton luggage: always the unexpected, since 1854.

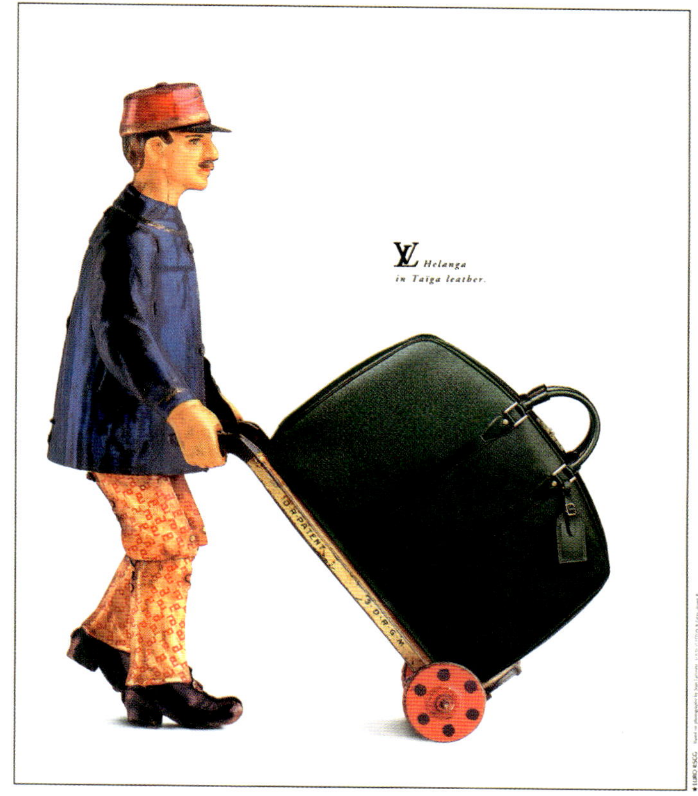

Available only in Louis Vuitton shops and select department stores
For more information, please call: 1-800-458-4131.

Louis Vuitton
The spirit of travel

Louis Vuitton luggage: always the unexpected, since 1854.

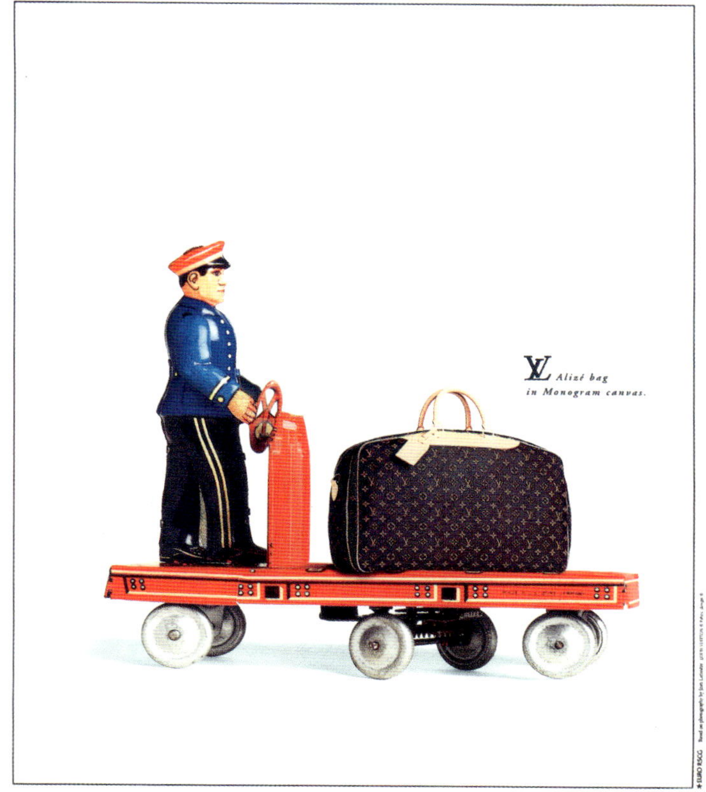

Available only in Louis Vuitton shops and select department stores.
307 North Rodeo Drive, 310-859-0457 • South Coast Plaza, 714-662-6907 •
I. Magnin Beverly Hills.

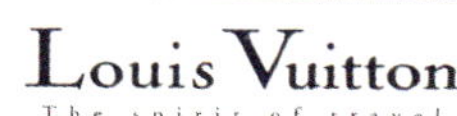

Louis Vuitton bags: always the unexpected, since 1854.

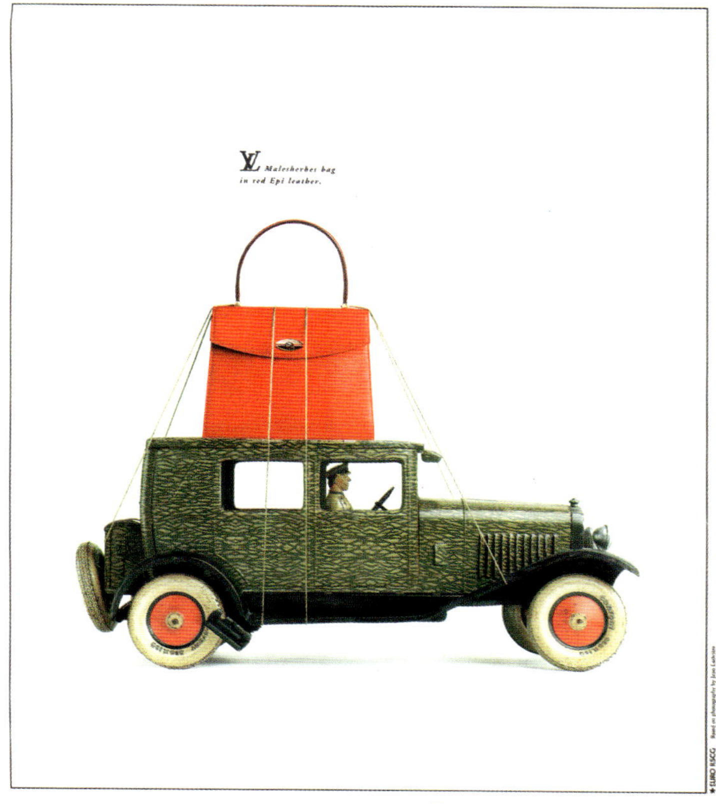

Available only in Louis Vuitton shops and select department stores.
For more information, please call: 1-800-458-7961.

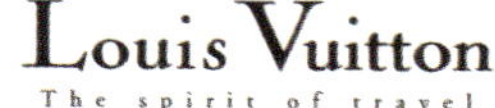

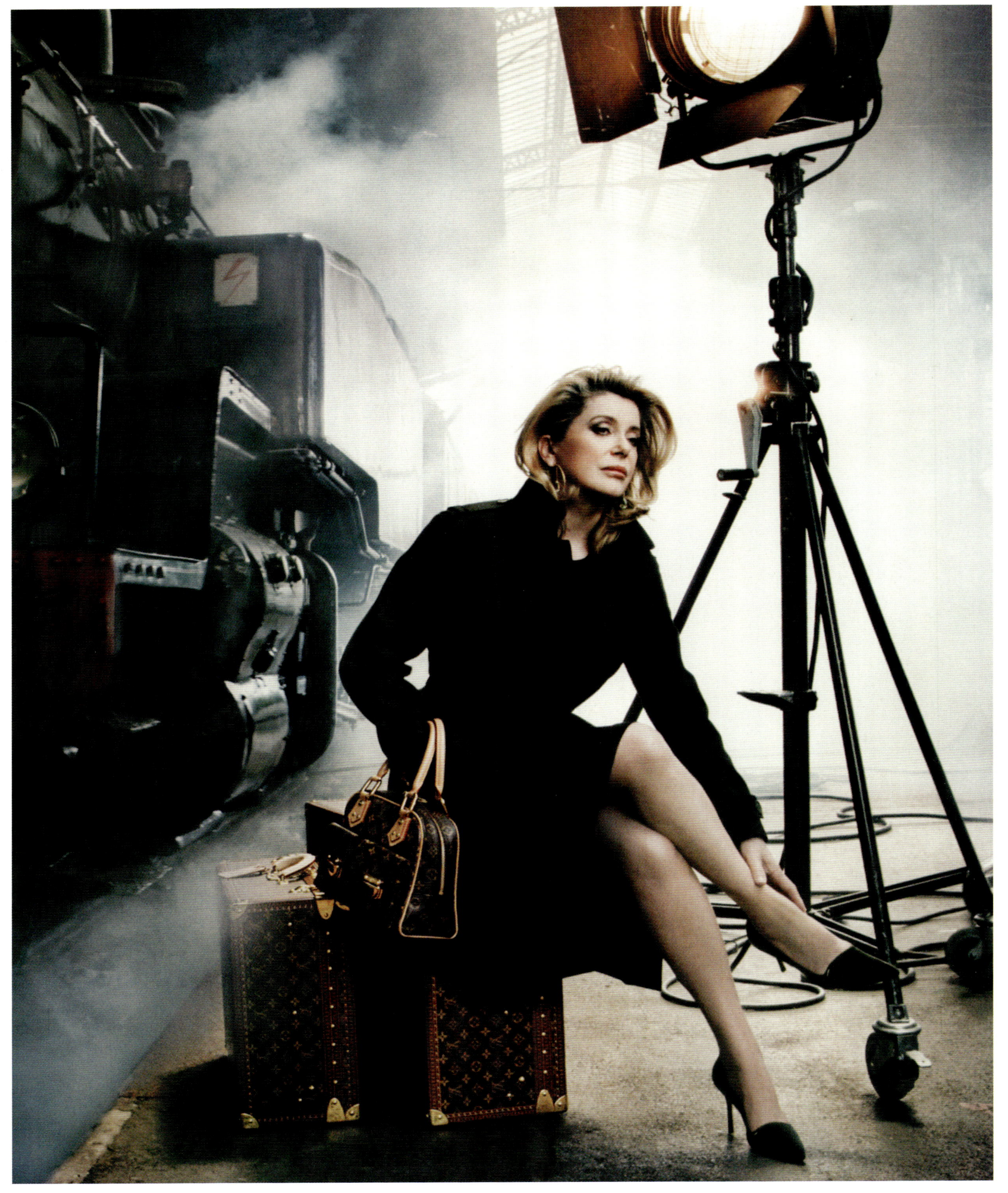

LOUIS VUITTON

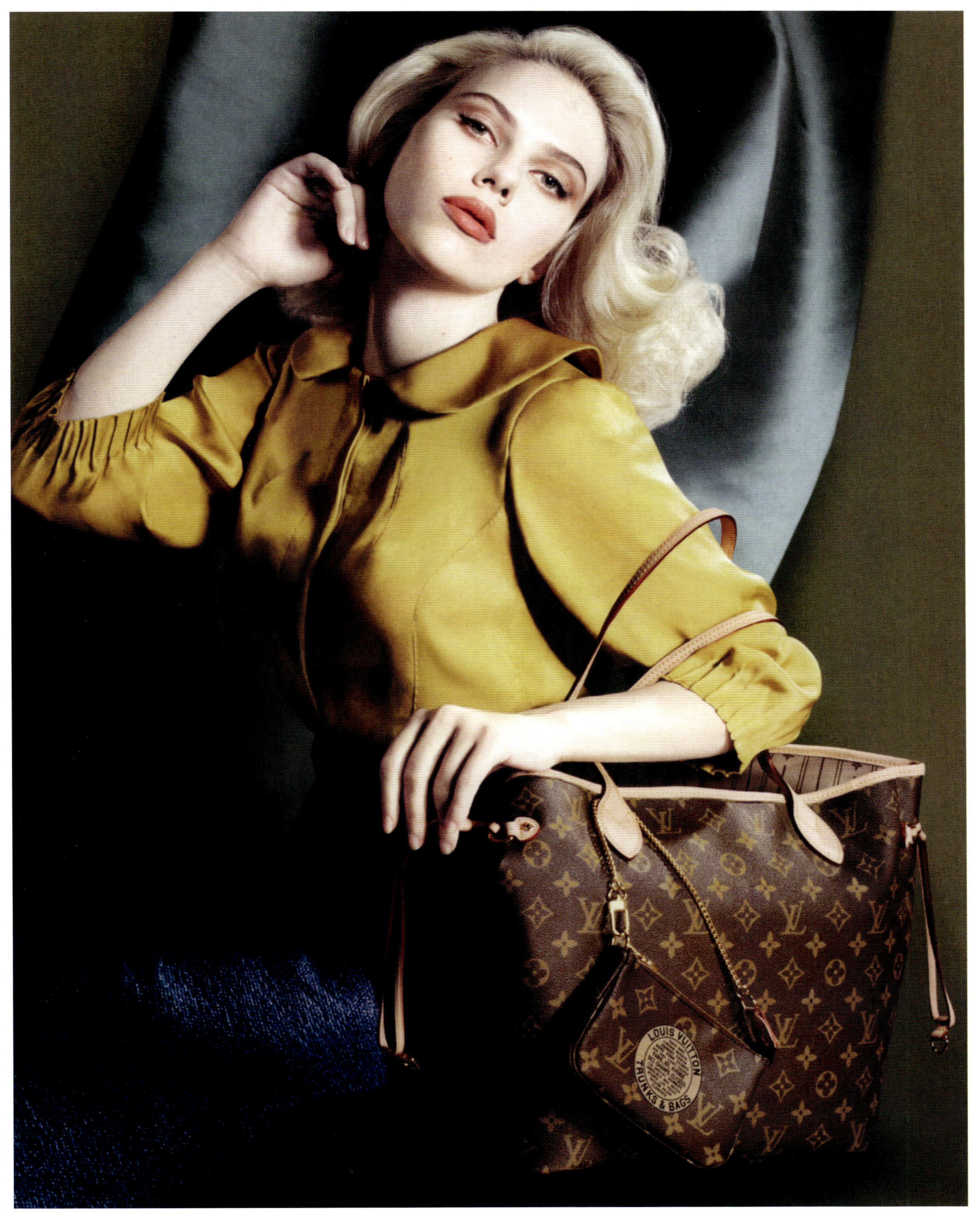

LOUIS VUITTON

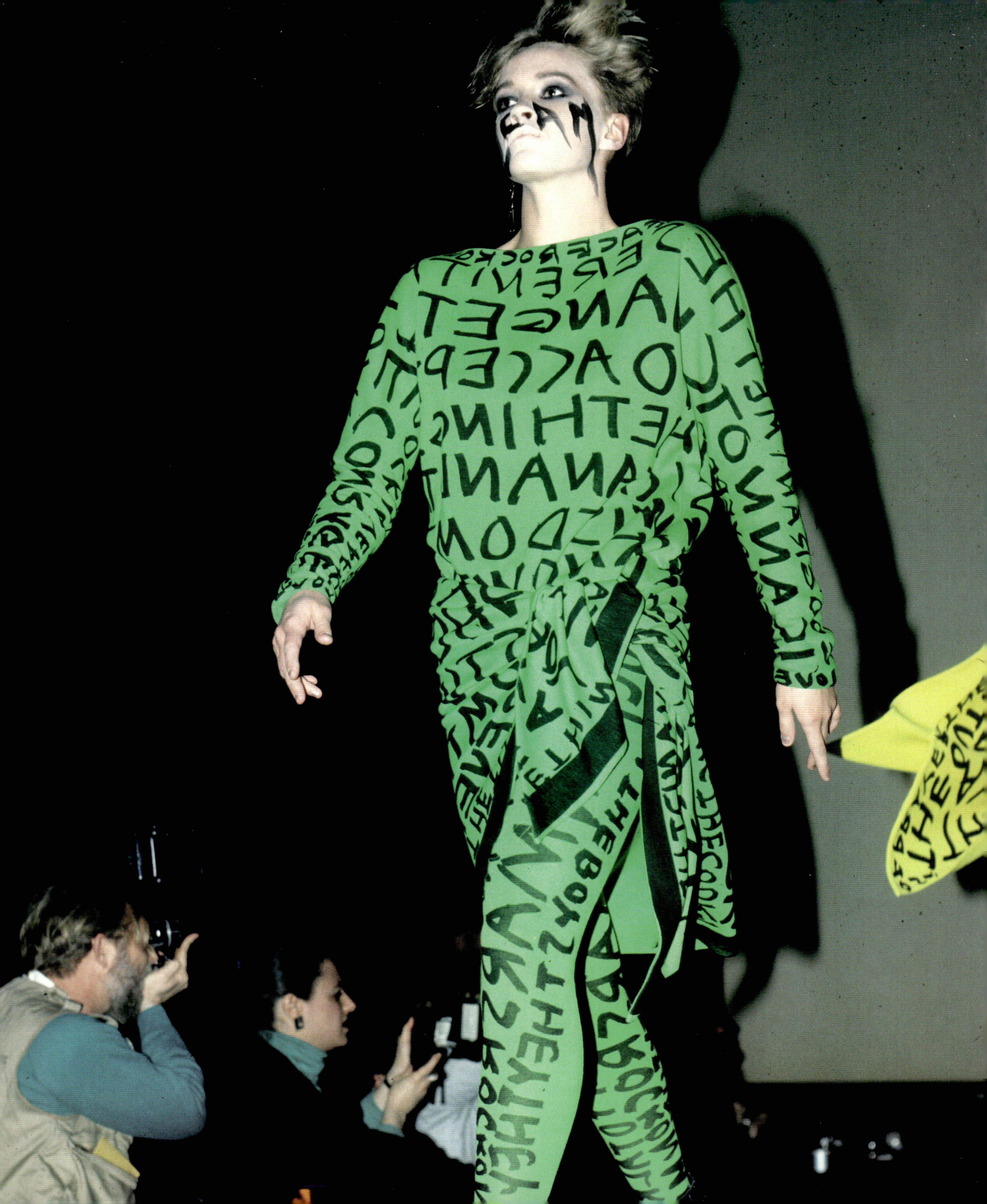

MARC JACOBS'S ART TREK FOR LOUIS VUITTON

When Marc Jacobs became artistic director in 1997, his challenge was to launch the luxury leather luggage firm's first ready-to-wear line. His first outing, in 1998, was a minimalist affair. He was, in effect, beginning with a blank slate, all clean shapes and pure lines. There was only one handbag on the runway—a white messenger bag with the monogram discreetly embossed on it. "I was told that I was not allowed to change the monogram, or do anything to it," Jacobs recounted to the *Daily Telegraph* in 2008. "But at one point I just said, 'I'm going to do what I want.'" And "what I want" translated into a series of revolutionary—and, saleswise, absolutely explosive—collaborations. Here's a look at Jacobs's top art-fashion partnerships.

> "I'm not really rebellious, but it was kind of a clever solution to doing what we were told by a certain old guard at Louis Vuitton we couldn't do: 'You don't deface the Monogram; you don't change the Monogram.'"
>
> —MARC JACOBS, from *Louis Vuitton/Marc Jacobs* by Pamela Golbin, 2012

STEPHEN SPROUSE

SPRING 2001

The inspiration behind Marc Jacobs's Spring 2001 collection was mere happenstance. Once, when Jacobs visited actress Charlotte Gainsbourg at her Paris apartment, he noticed a Louis Vuitton trunk that her father had painted black. He liked the way her father had taken something iconic and tampered with it. That act reminded him of one of his favorite works, a Readymade by Marcel Duchamp, *L.H.O.O.Q.* (1919), a postcard depicting Leonardo da Vinci's portrait of the *Mona Lisa* that Duchamp "defaced" by adding a mustache and a beard and scribbling in the title of the work. The black trunk also reminded him of fellow designer Stephen Sprouse—of his way of reframing and shaking up fashion standards, though rather than defacing the iconic, he took inspiration from the street and made it art.

Jacobs decided to vandalize the tony Vuitton monogram and enlisted Sprouse to do it. What was supposed to be a collection just for the runway and editorial shoots became a commercial blockbuster for Vuitton. It gave Jacobs the creative freedom to blur the lines between art and fashion, resulting in one hit bag after another. "To this day some of those bag souvenir places right by our offices in Paris have these little nylon bags that are so clearly taken from that Sprouse graffiti," Jacobs said in *Louis Vuitton/Marc Jacobs* (2012). "They say things like 'Paris France' written in a style that's obviously imitating Stephen's in the way we presented it."

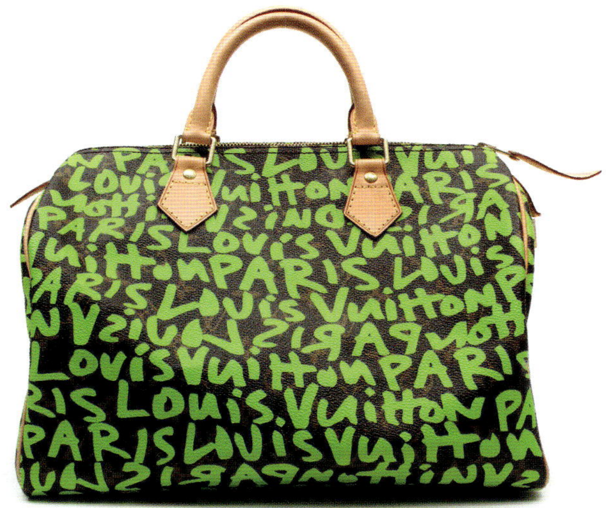

OPPOSITE: Stephen Sprouse, Fall 1984 ready-to-wear.

RIGHT: Speedy bag, Stephen Sprouse for Louis Vuitton, 2001.

TAKASHI MURAKAMI

SPRING 2003

In 2001 Jacobs went to an exhibition featuring the bright and buoyant art of Japan's Takashi Murakami at the Cartier Foundation in Paris. Taken by the artist's colorful pop sensibility, he approached him to do a collaboration. "When Marc asked if I would be interested in working with Vuitton, the offer was quite abstract but very creative," Murakami said in *Louis Vuitton/Marc Jacobs* (2012). "This Western icon brand was willing to take a risk and if I lived up to the expectations, I could escape Andy Warhol's phantom of supposedly not being able to bridge high art with the commercial." Murakami reinterpreted the classic monogram in bright candy colors, sprinkling long-lashed cartoon eyeballs into the pattern. There were floating pandas, grinning flowers, and cherries, too. The joyous collection resulted in one of the biggest It Bag sensations of the early 2000s.

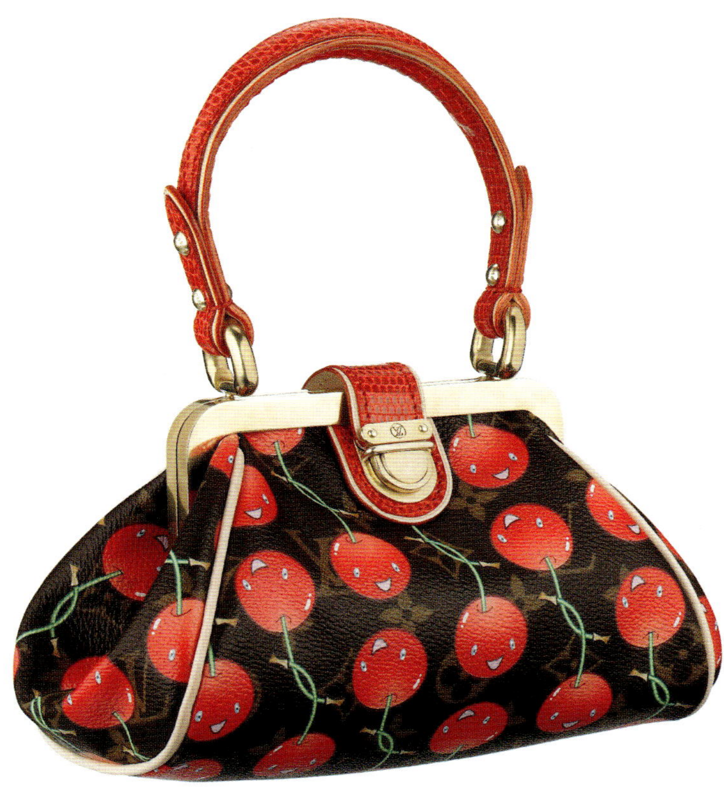

ABOVE: Sac Fermoir, Takashi Murakami for Louis Vuitton, Spring 2005.

OPPOSITE: Installation view of the © *MURAKAMI* exhibit at The Geffen Contemporary at Museum of Contemporary Art, Los Angeles, October 2007.

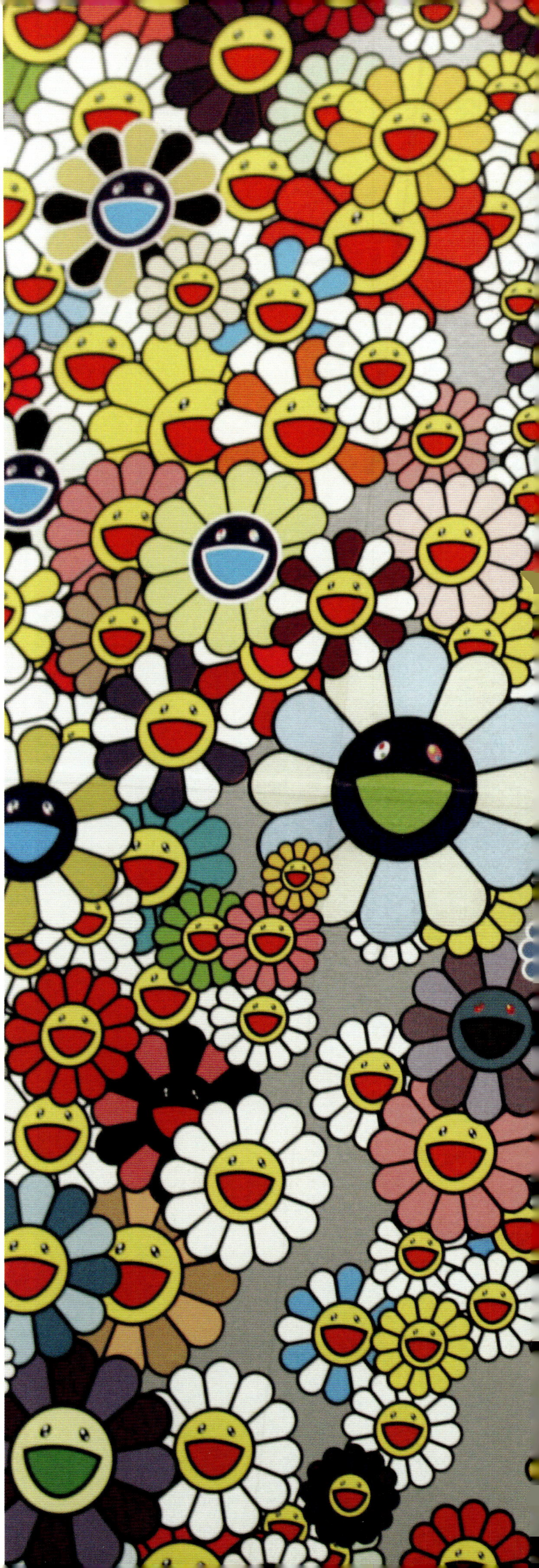

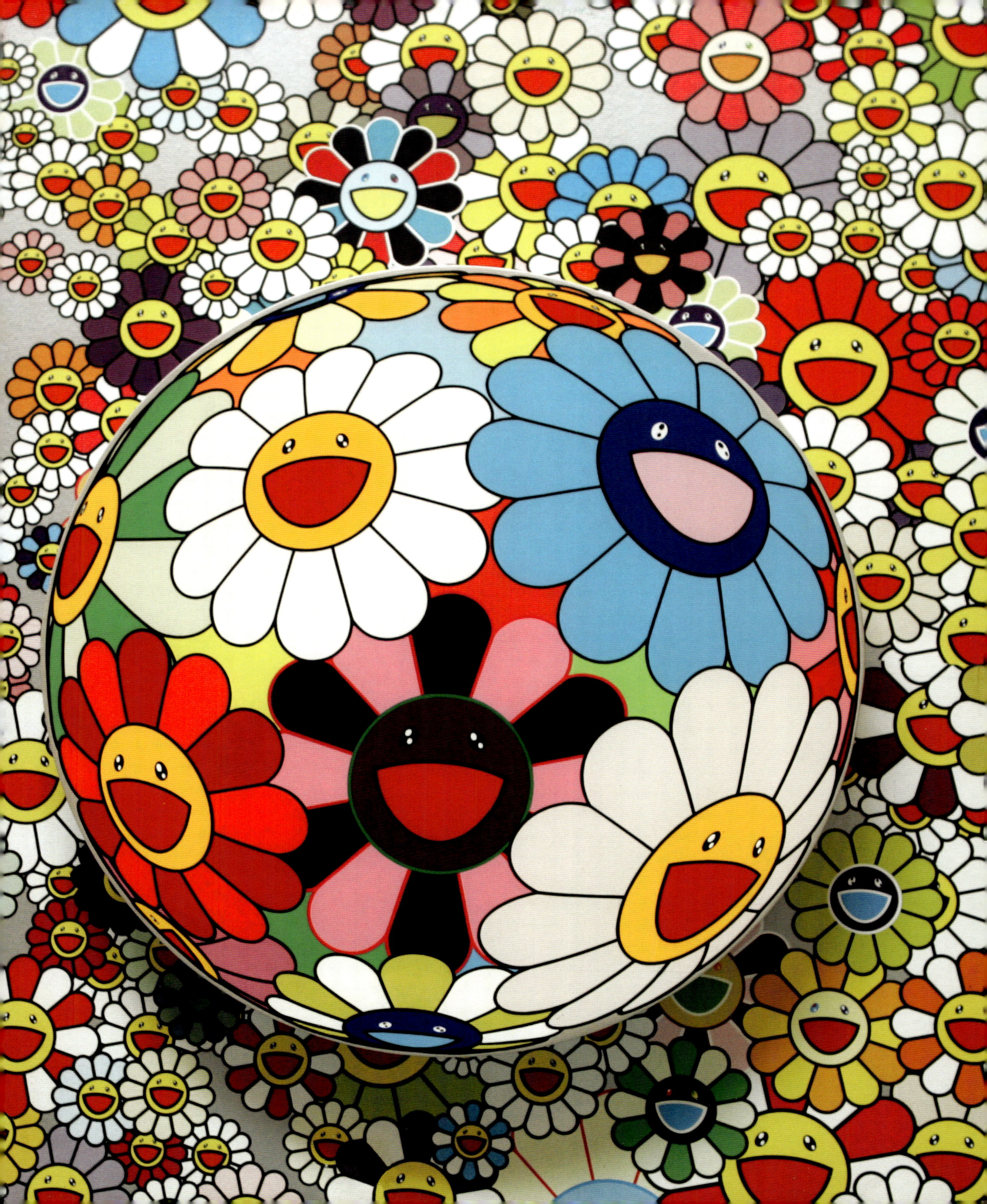

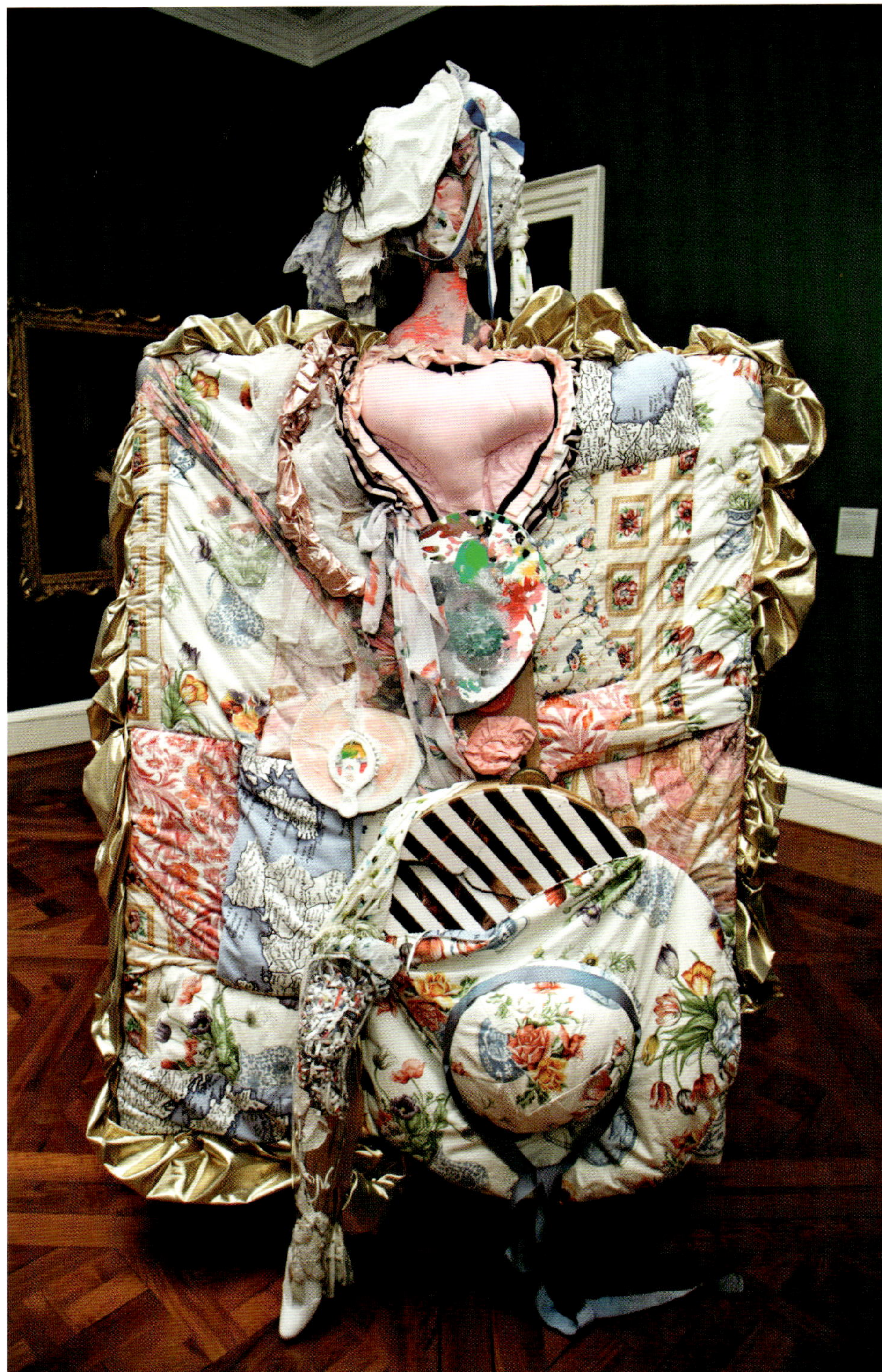

JULIE VERHOEVEN

SPRING 2002

Jacobs's collaborator after Stephen Sprouse was Julie Verhoeven, British illustrator and former assistant to John Galliano. Her collection for Louis Vuitton was on the whimsical side, using collaged appliqués to create fantasy scenes on the handbags, like a colorful turtle walking a path beneath a rainbow or a psychedelic mushroom dreamscape. "A friend of mine had this funny, sweet collage bag," Jacobs explained to the *Guardian* in 2002. "And then one of our designers saw this picture of Olivia Newton-John with a denim bag with an appliqué. And we thought that Julie would be great, because she has such a quirky charm. So we asked her to use the different monograms—the vernis, the mini, regular and graffiti monograms—to make a scene. It was a nice idea, and it worked."

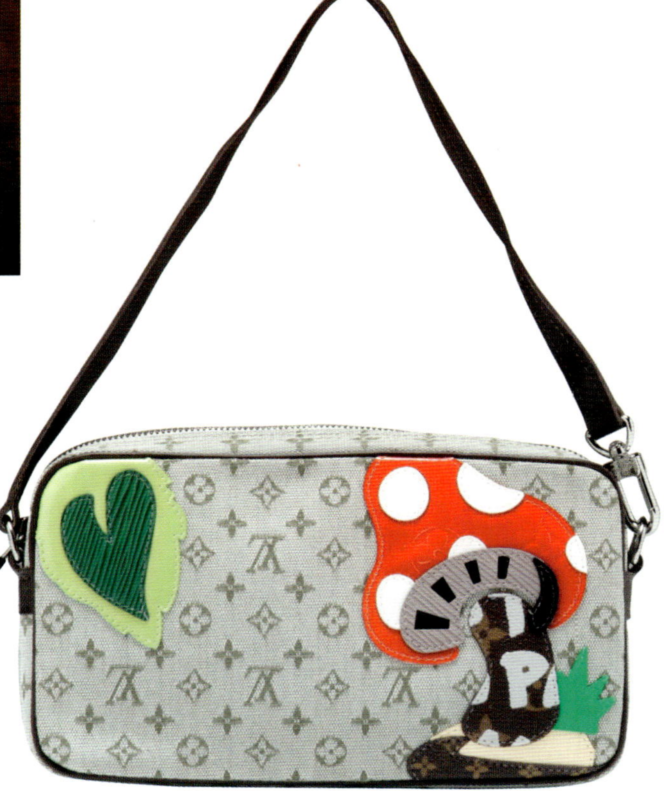

ABOVE: Julie Verhoeven, *Ladies, Let's Rip!*, The Holburne Museum, Bath, England, April 2013.

RIGHT: Pochette bag, Julie Verhoeven for Louis Vuitton, Spring 2002.

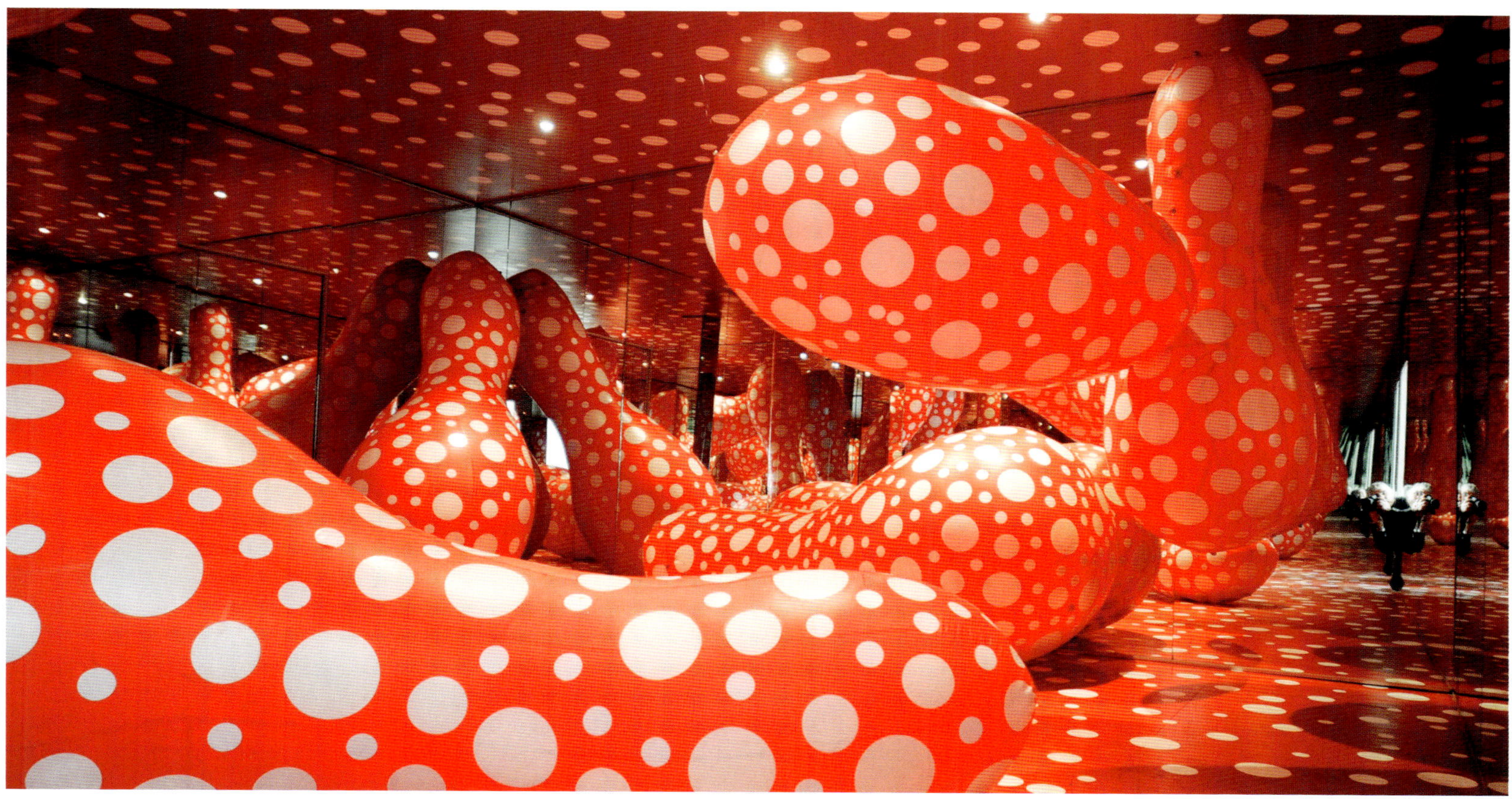

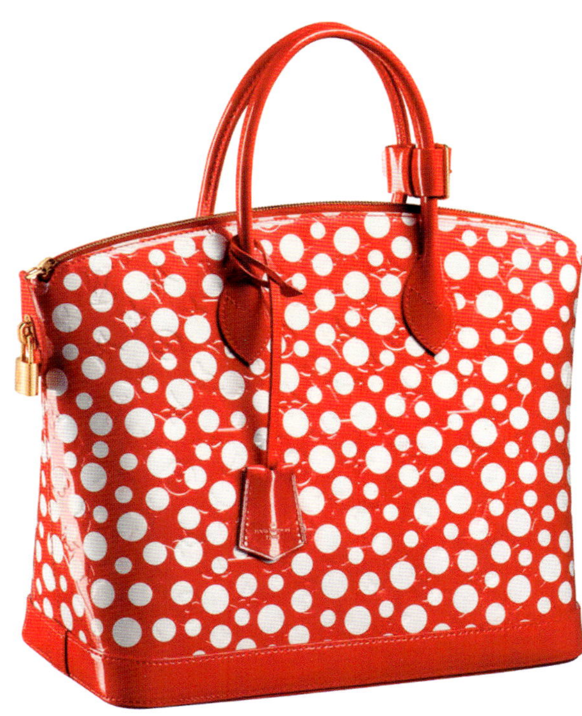

TOP: Yayoi Kusama, *Dots Obsession: Infinity Mirrored Room*, Contemporary Art Center Biennal, Le Havre, France 2008.

BOTTOM: Lockit bag, Yayoi Kusama for Louis Vuitton, 2012.

YAYOI KUSAMA

SPRING 2012

Marc Jacobs and Yayoi Kusama first met in 2006. The designer was in Tokyo during the filming of the documentary *Marc Jacobs & Louis Vuitton* (2007) by Loïc Prigent. Jacobs visited her studio and brought her flowers; the space was across the street from the Seiwa Hospital for the Mentally Ill, where, in 1973, Kusama had voluntarily checked herself in. She, in turn, excitedly showed him a Speedy she had hand-painted. In 2011 Louis Vuitton sponsored a traveling retrospective of her work, and Kusama created a limited-edition collection for the luxury firm. In 2012 Jacobs launched the collection to coincide with the opening of the exhibition at its final venue, the Whitney Museum of American Art in New York. Kusama had covered not only Vuitton handbags with her signature dots—which the artist uses as a means toward self-obliteration—but also an entire line of shoes, bags, dresses, pajamas, trench coats, and knits.

"When I look at her career and her different vehicles for expressing herself—from her early performances staged at MoMA, to her sculptures, paintings, canvases, Infinity nets, and her endless polka dots—I find a sort of simplicity, naivety and passion," Jacobs told the *New Zealand Herald* in 2012. "The fact that she never veers from her vision is really admirable."

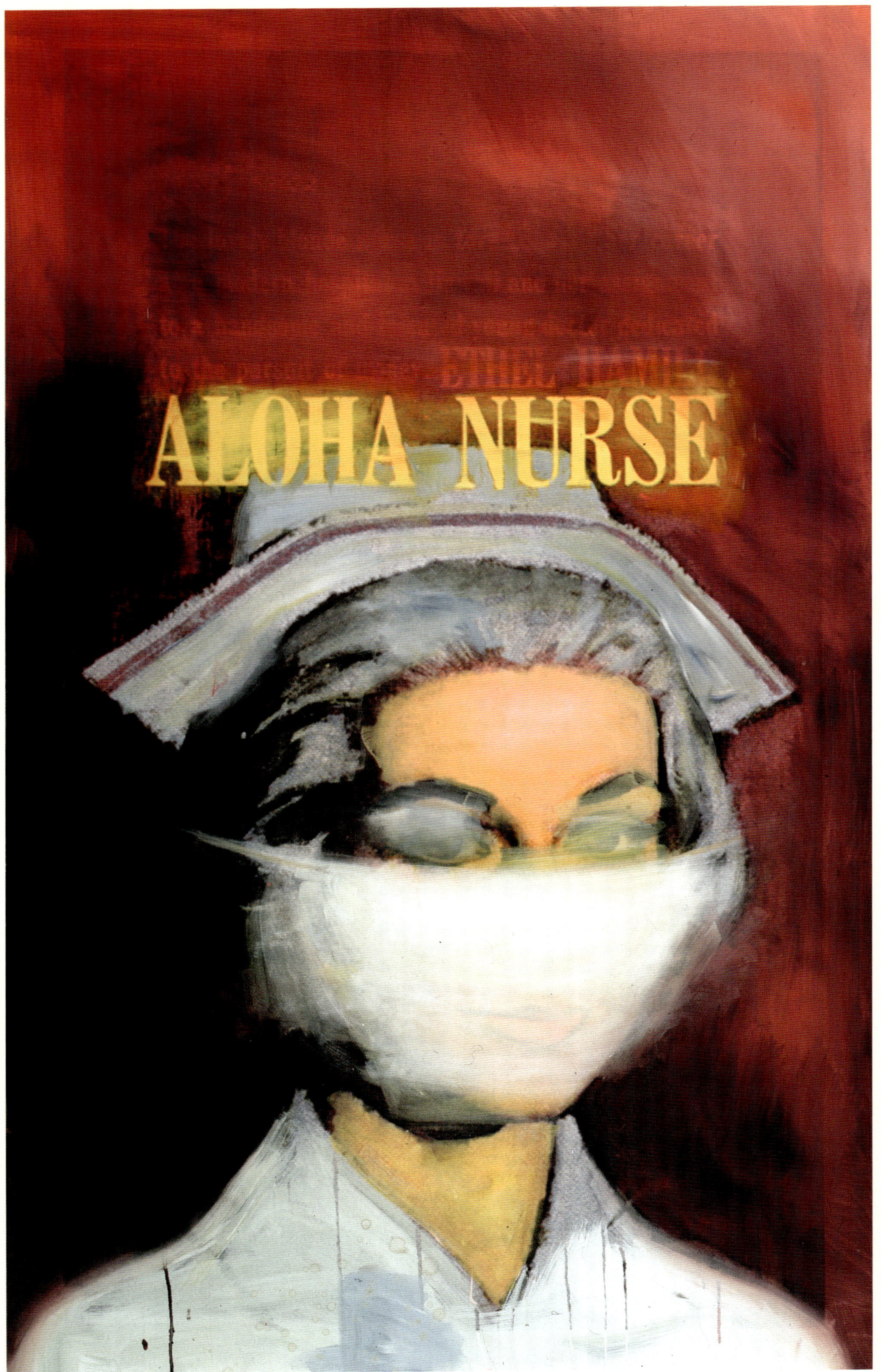
ALOHA NURSE

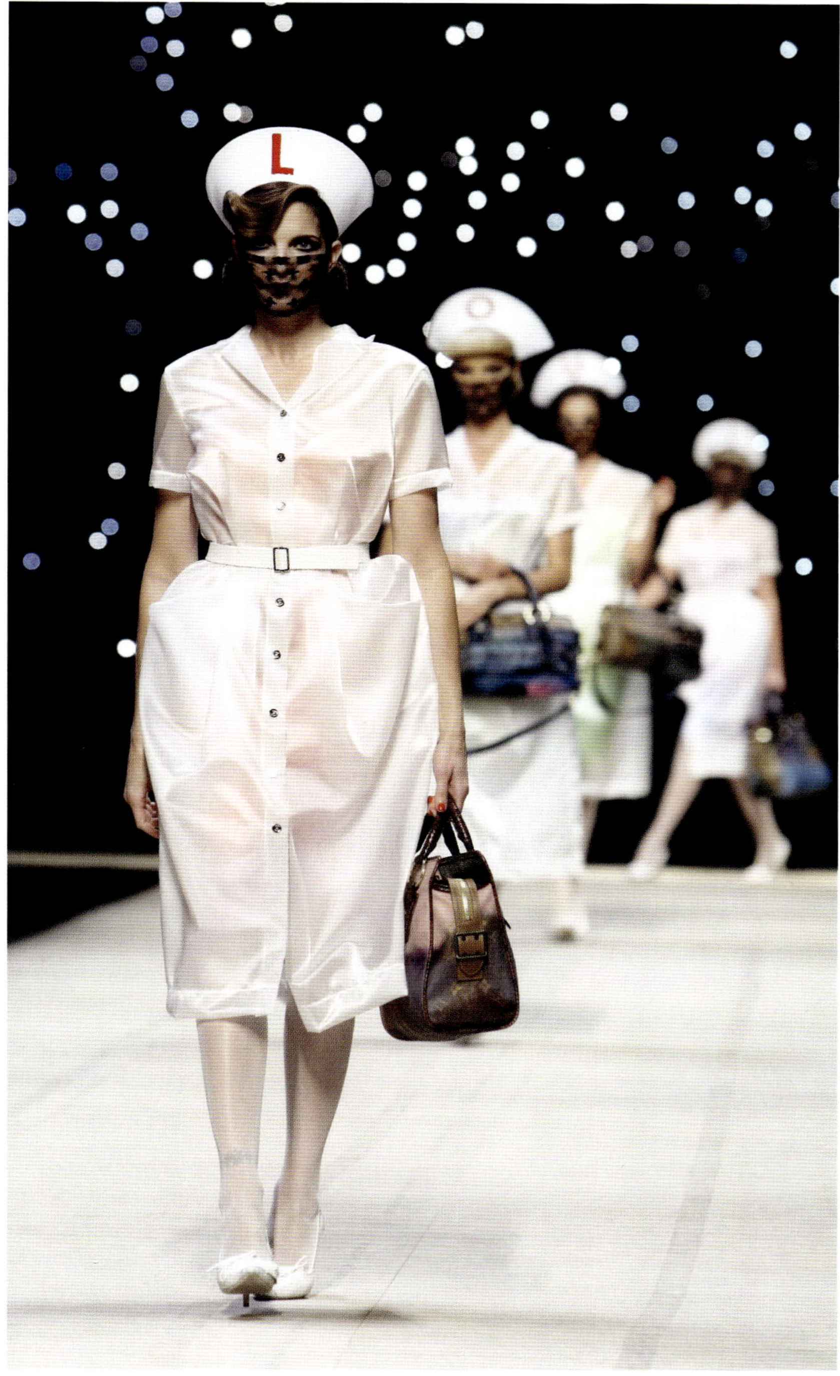

RICHARD PRINCE

SPRING 2008

When looking for an artist to collaborate with for Spring 2008, Marc Jacobs perused his own art collection for inspiration—he owns works by Georges Braque, John Currin, David Hockney, Ed Ruscha, Richard Prince, and Andy Warhol—and ultimately decided on Prince. The result was a collection inspired by Prince's nurse paintings and Monochromatic Jokes series. A canvas bag, for instance, is printed with Prince's partially legible jokes: "Every time I meet a girl who can cook like my mother, she looks like my father" and "My wife went to the beauty shop and got a mud pack. For two days she looked beautiful. Then the mud fell off." Prince appealed to Jacobs in part because he is an appropriation artist. "That's an approach I understand very well," Jacobs said in *Louis Vuitton/Marc Jacobs* (2012). "My big love is fashion and I look at iconic clothes from different designers from different periods, and I try to think of how I can kind of take it, change it, and redo it."

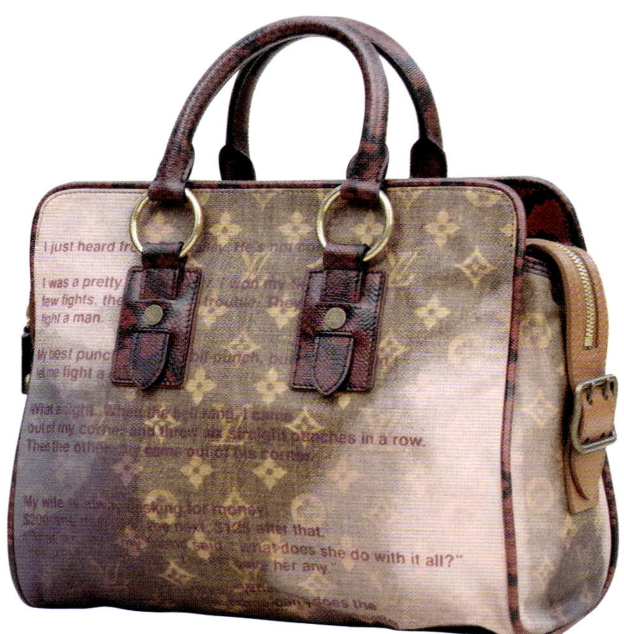

OPPOSITE: Richard Prince, *Aloha Nurse*, 2002.

ABOVE: Richard Prince's handbags on the Spring 2008 runway at Louis Vuitton.

RIGHT: Graduate Jokes bag, Richard Prince for Louis Vuitton, Spring 2008.

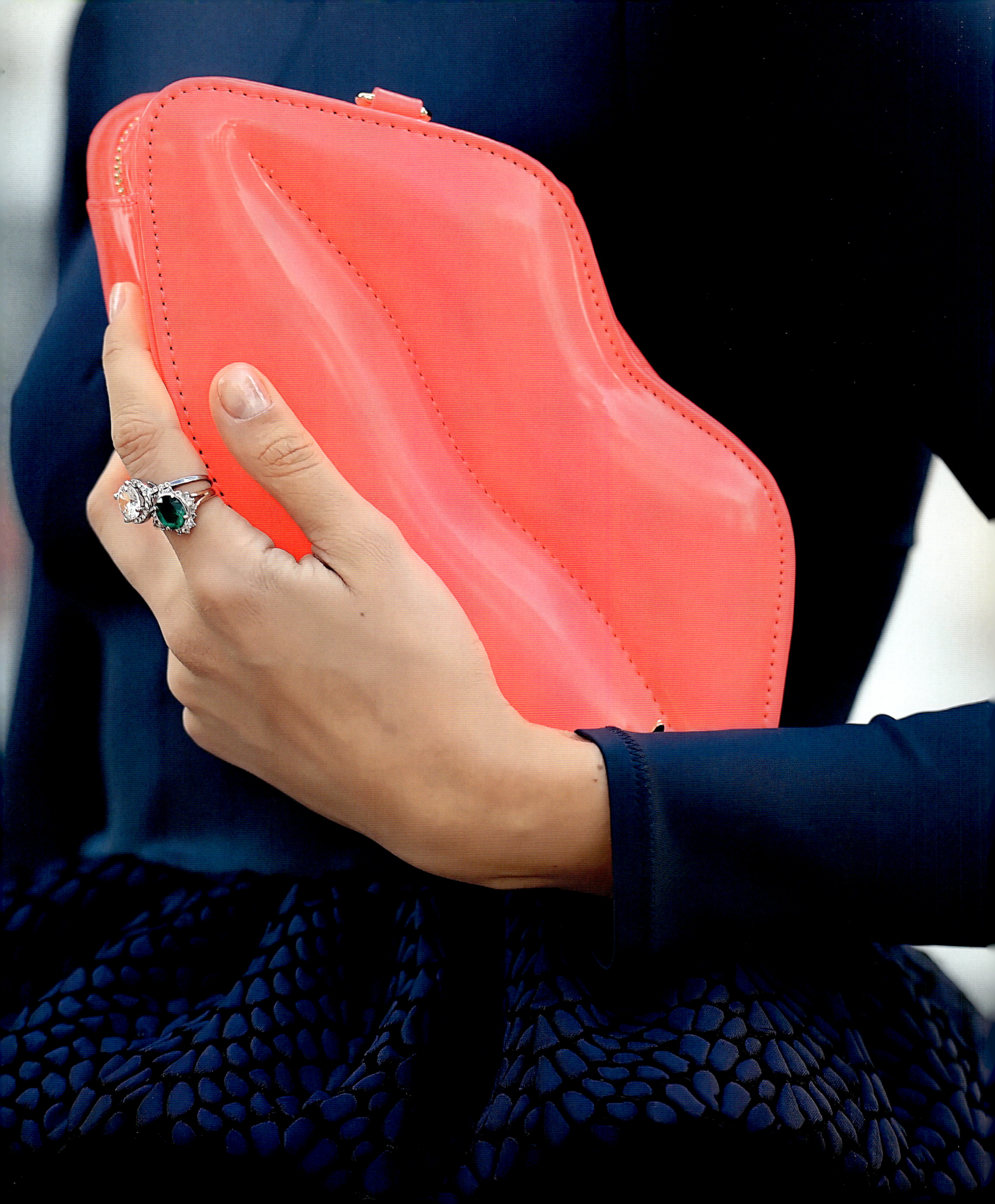

Lulu Guinness

LIPS, 2004

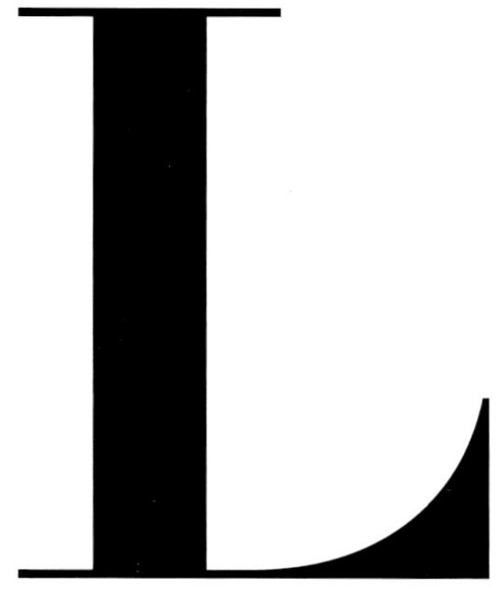

Lips have long been a beloved motif in art—just think of Man Ray's *Observatory Time: The Lovers* (1936), Salvador Dalí's *Mae West Lips Sofa* (1937), and René Magritte's *Shéhérazade* (1950). While countless designers have incorporated them into their work—Diane von Furstenberg, Yves Saint Laurent, and Elsa Schiaparelli—Lulu Guinness has made puckered lips all her own.

Guinness's iconic Lips clutch made its debut in 2004 in red-and-gold padded snakeskin before spinning off into more than thirty versions, such as Swarovski-studded or with flag appliqués, as well as jewelry and cosmetic cases in a vanity travel collection. The popular molded Perspex model of 2008 features an equally wide range of variations—from a rubberized "matte" Lip to the 25th Anniversary edition of 2014 with a silver mirrored finish—each created from a bespoke mold. The motif is such a signature that Guinness has recast the lip into zip pulls and Christmas ornaments. For Guinness, lips are fun, playful, glamorous, and flirtatious. Her Lip clutch is all those things—and it makes you smile.

And that is precisely the ethos behind her line, founded in 1989. She has designed bags in the shape of a house, featuring embroidered windows, climbing ivy, and a cat; a box of chocolates, complete with the individual chocolates up top; and a pail filled with red roses, now in the permanent collection of the Victoria & Albert Museum. "I don't like being too serious about design. Which is why minimalism really turns me off. It's too cold. I like humor," Guinness told the *Straits Times* in 2000. Guinness, like her designs, is unapologetically feminine, with a girlish 1950s vintage streak.

OPPOSITE:
Lips bag, Lulu Guinness, New York City, September 2013.

"I love the unexpected. . . . I like working out how a bag will open and close, that you lift up a skirt, or it stays shut by putting the roof on top of it. Trying to have an idea that's never been had before. That's the sort of thing I've loved, having moments of inspiration. And I still do."

—LULU GUINNESS, *Vanity Fair*, January 2006

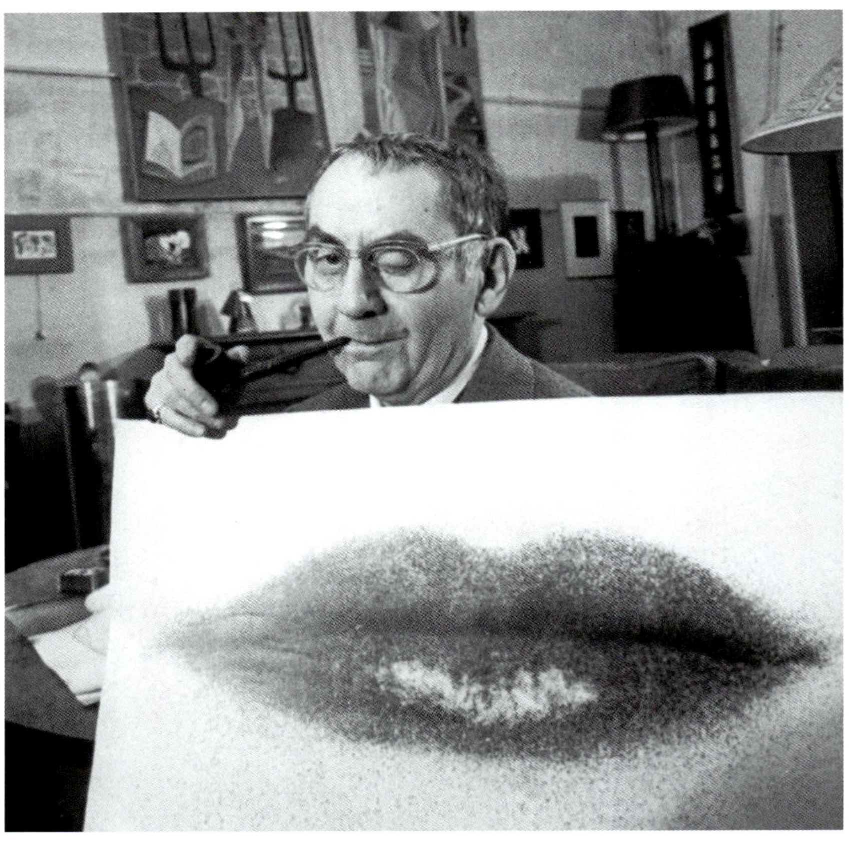

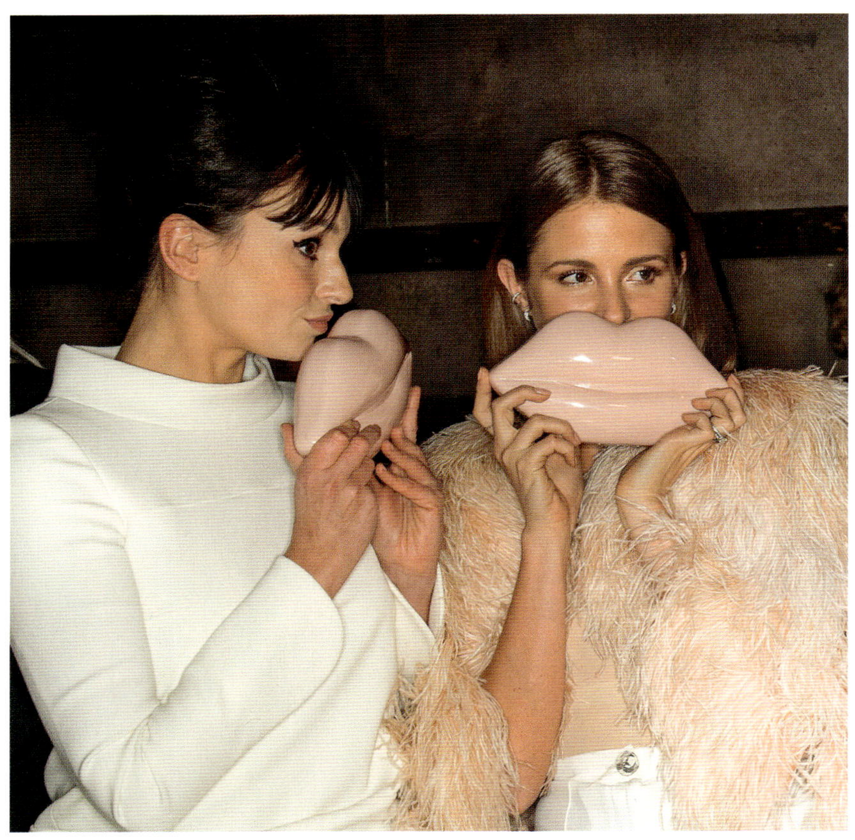

TOP:
Man Ray with his *Lips* print, 1961.

BOTTOM:
Lips bag, Lulu Guinness, London, February 2015.

OPPOSITE:
Salvador Dalí, *Mae West Lips Sofa*, 1938, at the *Surreal Things: Surrealism and Design* exhibition, Museum Boijmans, Rotterdam, Netherlands, September 2007.

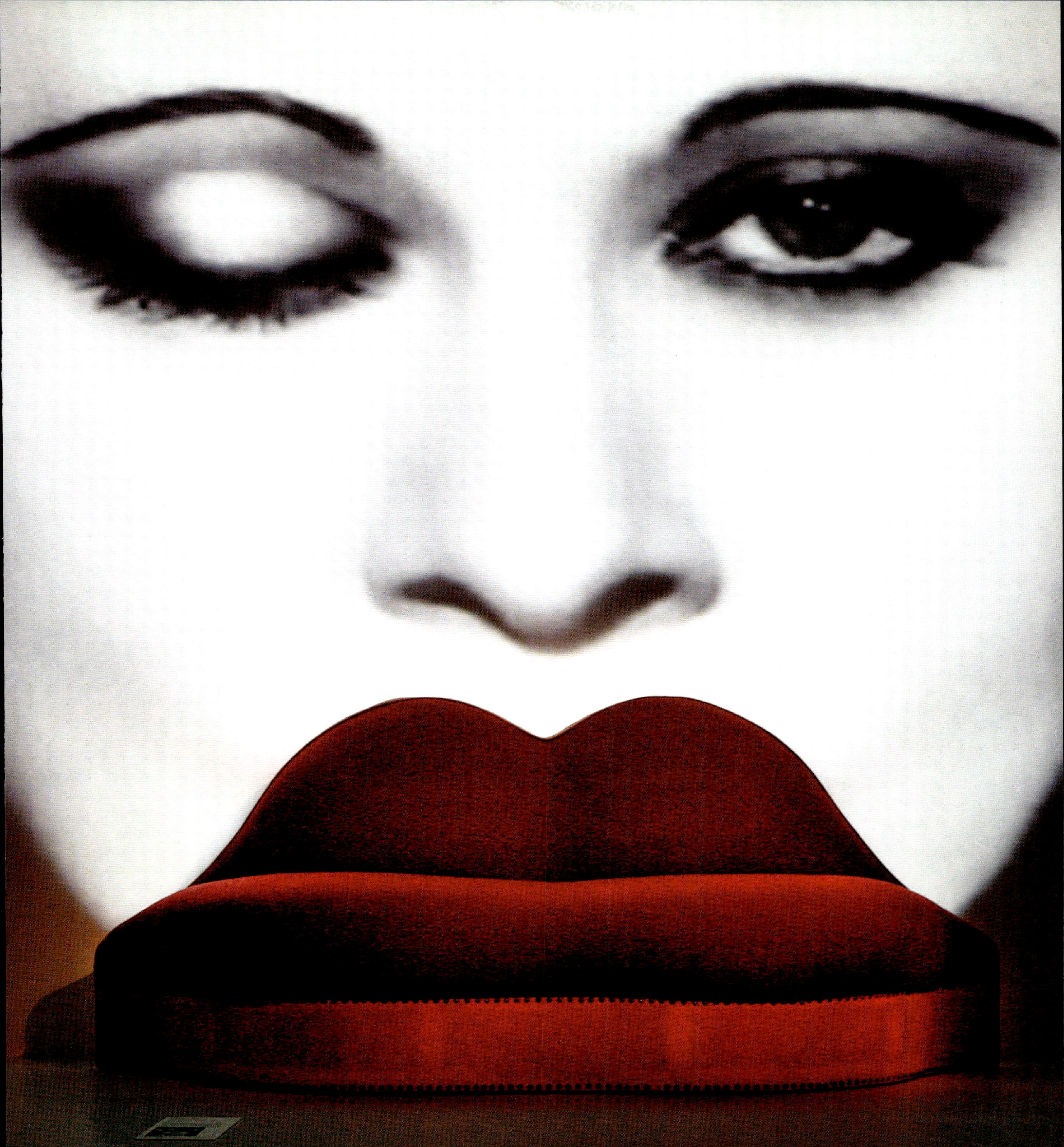

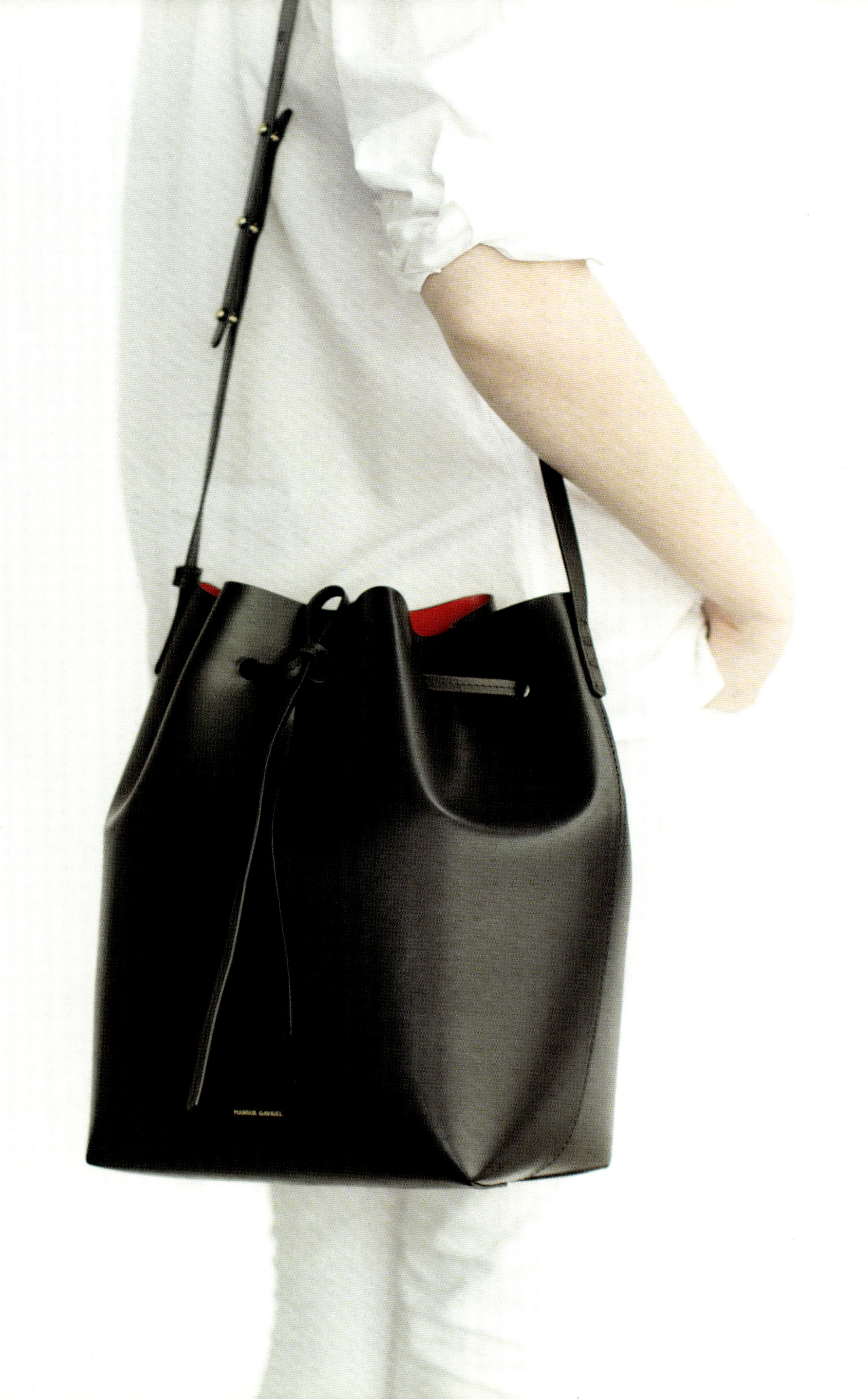

Mansur Gavriel

BUCKET, 2013

Rachel Mansur and Floriana Gavriel met in 2010 at a concert in Los Angeles and soon became friends. They had a shared aesthetic and both were in the world of fashion—Mansur had studied textile design at the Rhode Island School of Design and Gavriel had interned at Lanvin. The very day they met, they decided to launch a line. By 2012, after a couple of years of lively exchanges via email and a shared Tumblr account, both had relocated—Mansur from Los Angeles and Gavriel from Berlin—to New York to start what they had decided would be a handbag line. "We didn't know where to begin, but we knew what we identified with intuitively." And that was something "beautiful and clean but also had a warmth to it," as they recalled in "Happy Bags Happy Girls" on wmagazine.com in 2016.

In June 2013 they launched their business with the Bucket. With money they had saved, they had the first prototypes made at a factory in East Los Angeles. A month later, there were waiting lists, which is astounding, given that the brand and its designers were unknown.

The structured Bucket bag, which is clean and elegant, without hardware or logos, and with just a peek of vibrant color on the inside, turned into a cult item seemingly overnight, thanks in part to social media—most notably, a beautifully curated Instagram account that combined images of flowers, art, and deftly styled bags. In December, when Mansur Gavriel announced the arrival of a new shipment of multiple styles, 95 percent of the stock sold out within an hour. The audience helped sales, too, as those who were able to get their hands on a bag posted on Instagram to flaunt their wares, stirring up the frenzy even more.

The power of the Bucket is its ability to ignite an It Bag moment during an era that is decidedly post-It. The bag is impeccably crafted in Italy—beautiful architectural construction, minimal seams, smooth vegetable-tanned cowhide—and still affordable. Plus, the designers also recognize the power of intense color and incorporate extremely saturated hues not usually seen on accessories, like Indian spice and bright azure, both inside and out. Beloved by major retailers, the distinct style of colorful simplicity continues to entice, even as the firm expands into other styles—including clutches and backpacks—and categories. What everything has in common is the ability to resonate on an emotional level through pure color and design.

OPPOSITE:
Bucket Bag, Mansur Gavriel, 2013.

"It's better to own one good bag than half a dozen of inferior quality."

—ELSA SCHIAPARELLI, from *Couture Confessions* by Pamela Golbin, 2016

ROLE MODEL

COCO ROCHA

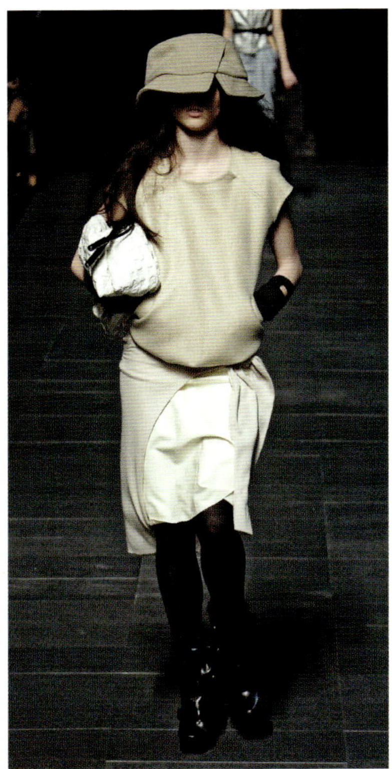

Since landing her first fashion show with Christian Lacroix, in spring 2006, model Coco Rocha has been one of the industry's top faces, appearing in virtually every major fashion publication worldwide and in advertisements for Balmain, Chanel, Dolce & Gabbana, and Longchamp. The Toronto native was discovered at an Irish dance competition in 2002; after hearing about her dancing talent, Jean Paul Gaultier enlisted her to dance down the runway for his Scottish Highlands–inspired Fall/Winter 2007 show—and from there she soared straight to the top. As a passionate and vocal activist for models' rights, Rocha was instrumental in pushing through a 2013 New York labor law that protects models under the age of eighteen and has served as brand manager for Nomad Mgmt modeling agency since 2016. Here she talks about a few of her favorite bags and reveals her own handbag tips.

What was the first bag you fell in love with?

My mom worked as a flight attendant my whole life and would frequently bring me bags back from Asia and overseas. Let's just say they weren't always "originals," but I remember the girls in middle school would be so jealous as they would see me walking by with my supposedly "designer bags." I started working as a high fashion model while still in high school. I'd spend weekends working in New York or Paris and then fly back for school on Monday. It was after becoming a model that I saw the vast difference between real, beautifully constructed designer pieces and their imitation knockoffs. By my junior year I was wearing the real thing around school, but by then I'm sure the other girls just assumed they were fakes. What normal high school girl takes a $3,000 purse to school?

What bag means the most to you?

My first Louis Vuitton bag was given to me by Marc Jacobs himself for being his fit model in Fall 2006 and walking in the show. It was a very special time in my life and my career, and I remember blurting out to the team how excited I was to finally own a *real* Louis Vuitton. The casting director laughed and said to never admit that again.

When it comes to getting dressed—bag first or outfit first?

I always choose my outfit first unless I just got a new bag, and then absolutely I will dress around a bag!

What are your handbag style tips?

Don't buy a bag because it's trendy or the cool girl is wearing it. Buy a bag because you love it and you want to make it part of your life. You want a bag that works for years and makes a statement without being outdated in a few months.

Describe one moment of handbag envy.

I absolutely loved Alexander Wang's 2015 spring bags. They have this sport element that I based my clothing line Co + Co around. Obsessed!

ABOVE:
Coco Rocha on the Louis Vuitton runway, Fall 2006.

OPPOSITE:
Coco with a bag of her own design in collaboration with Botkier, Holiday 2015.

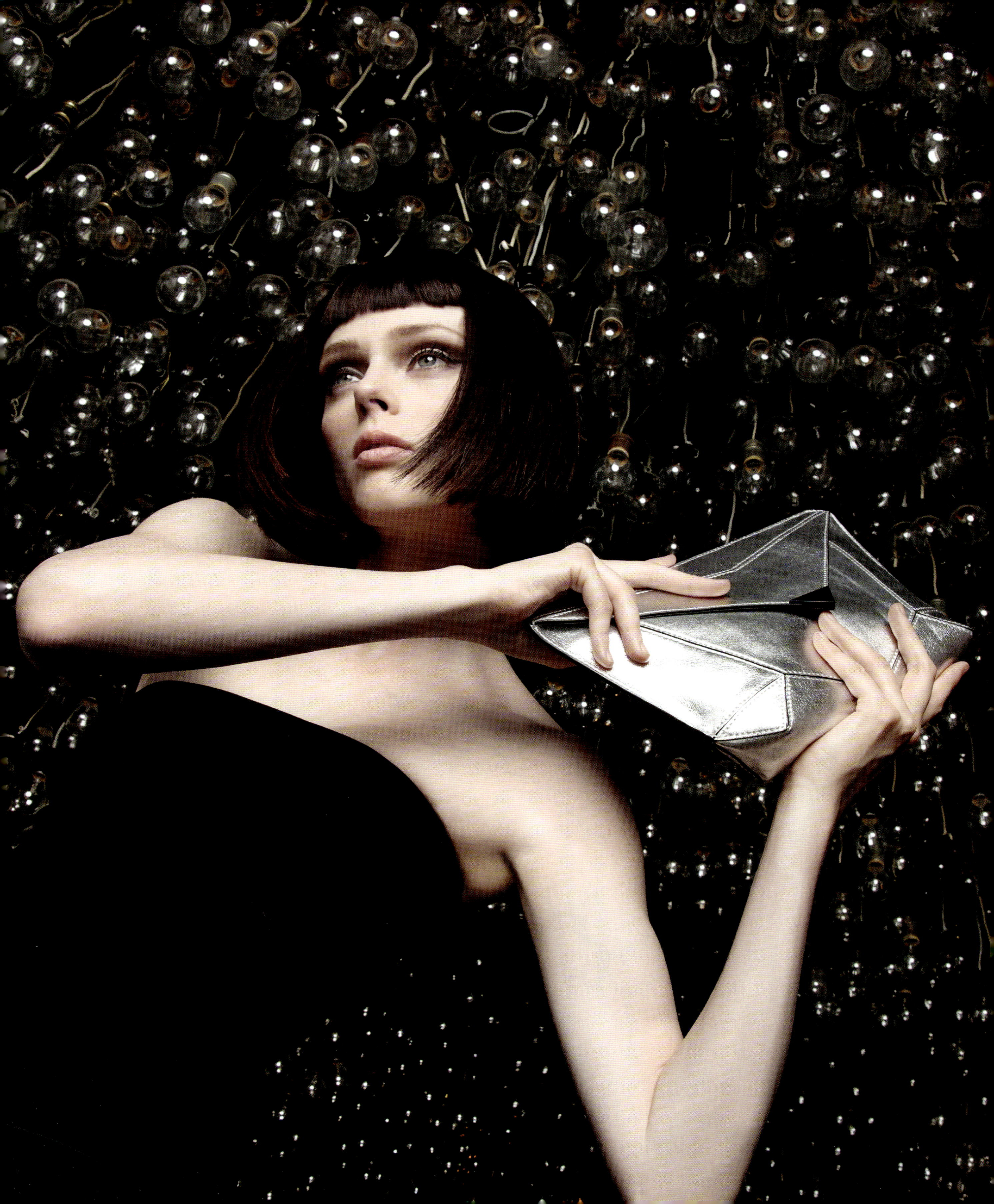

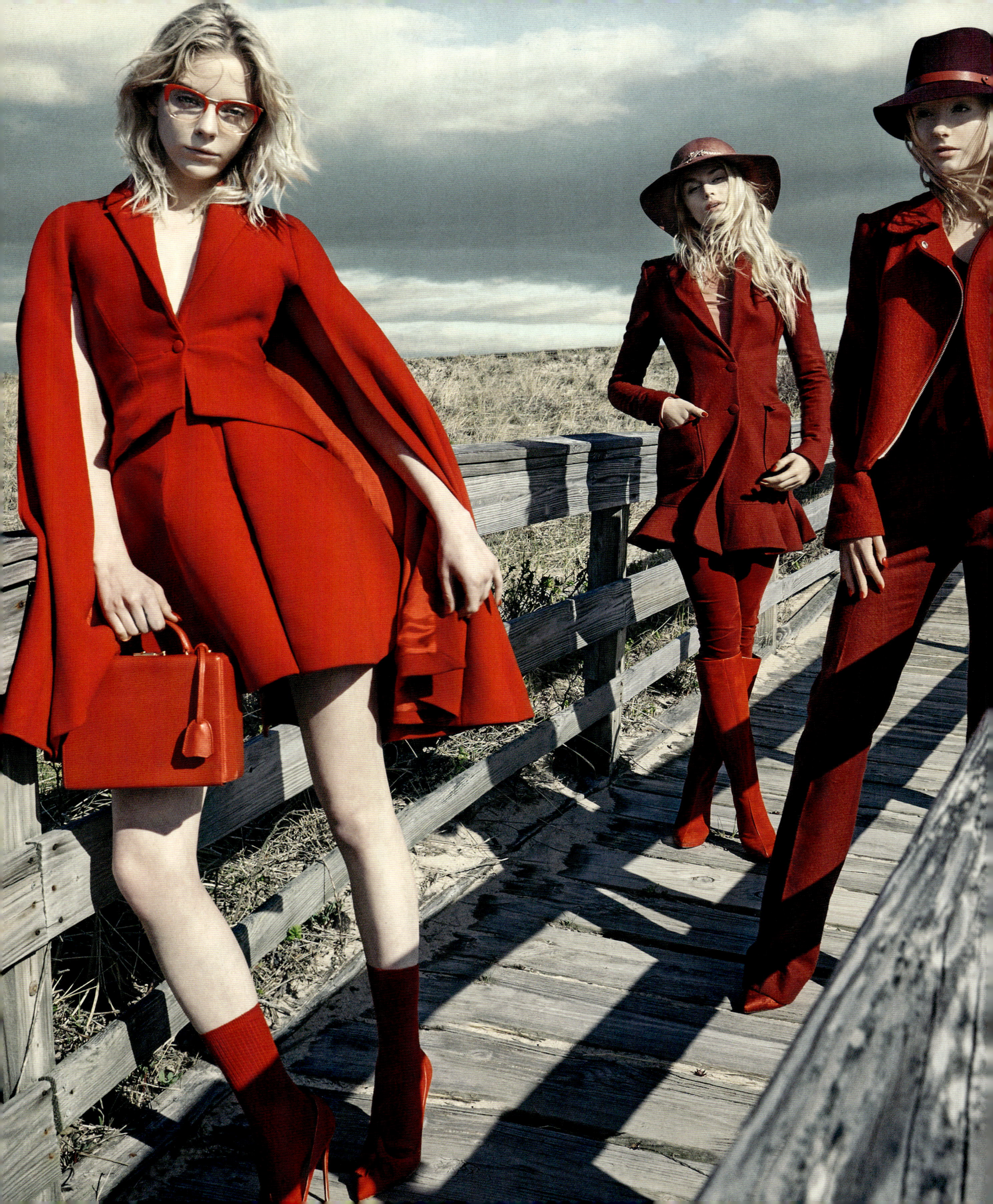

Mark Cross

GRACE BOX, 2012

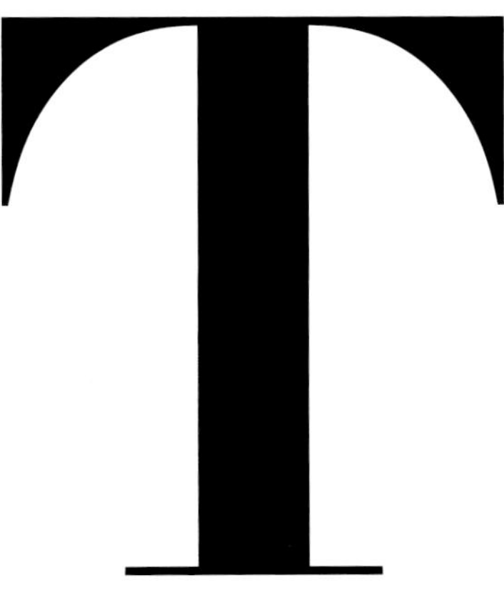

he American luxury firm Mark Cross, founded in 1845 in Boston as a purveyor of leather equestrian goods, had its Hollywood debut in 1954 in Alfred Hitchcock's film *Rear Window.* There's a scene in which Grace Kelly, as Lisa Fremont, arrives at her boyfriend's apartment carrying a boxy black overnight case by Mark Cross. No mention is made of the bag, but as she enters the room, a stunning vision of sophisticated polish in pearls and a veiled hat, she places it on a table next to James Stewart, who's playing her beau, L. B. "Jeff" Jefferies, broken-legged and in a wheelchair. The camera follows them as they converse about the man who lives across the courtyard—they suspect he has murdered his wife—and the bag is right there in the foreground—slim and spare, with a top handle and gold hardware.

The scene ends up revolving around that Mark Cross bag, which was created especially for the movie. Kelly picks it up and puts it down, all the while musing out loud about how handbags can demonstrate a woman's predictability. Minutes later, she whispers that she's staying the night. "I won't be able to give you any pajamas," replies Stewart.

Kelly closes the blinds and opens her case while sitting on his lap so he can see a negligee and slippers spill out—we catch a glimpse of the bag's detailed interior, the red lining and the mirror. "Preview of coming attractions," she purrs and retreats to the bedroom to change. Pretty hot stuff for the 1950s and a fantastic showcase for the bag, which, in an early example of product placement, gets named twice.

There's plenty more glamour behind this accessories firm, one of America's oldest. It was owned by the family of Gerald Murphy, who, with his wife, Sara, became part of the expatriate circle of wealthy artists and writers who settled in France in the 1920s. They were allegedly the inspiration for the jet-set figures Nicole and Dick Diver in F. Scott Fitzgerald's *Tender Is the Night* (1934).

After all these years, the company continues to mine its rich history, even though it's changed hands, closed, and relaunched numerous times. While the style seen in *Rear Window* was a one-off, a version was put into production in the late 1980s and early 1990s, then updated in 2012 and named the Grace Box—the epitome of the brand's understated American sensibility. In 2015, at the request of a collector, an exact replica of the film prop, the Grace Overnight Case, was introduced. The Scottie, named after Zelda and F. Scott Fitzgerald's daughter, was launched in 2012; like the other styles in the company's stable, the design is boxy, clean, classic, and practical yet chic.

"The glamour and roots of Mark Cross personify luxury to me," New York designer Derek Lam, who teamed up with the house on a collection in 2014, told *Vogue* that year. "And I think where American heritage exists, it should be celebrated."

OPPOSITE:
Grace Box bag, Mark Cross, *Elle Singapore*, August 2015.

PAGE 158:
Grace Kelly with a Mark Cross overnight case in stills from *Rear Window*, 1954.

PAGE 159:
Grace Box bag, Mark Cross, Paris, October 2014.

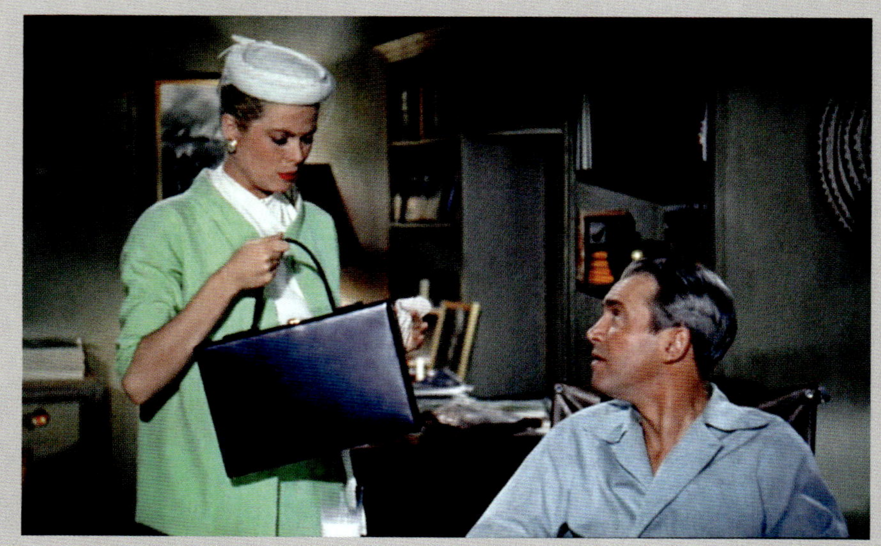

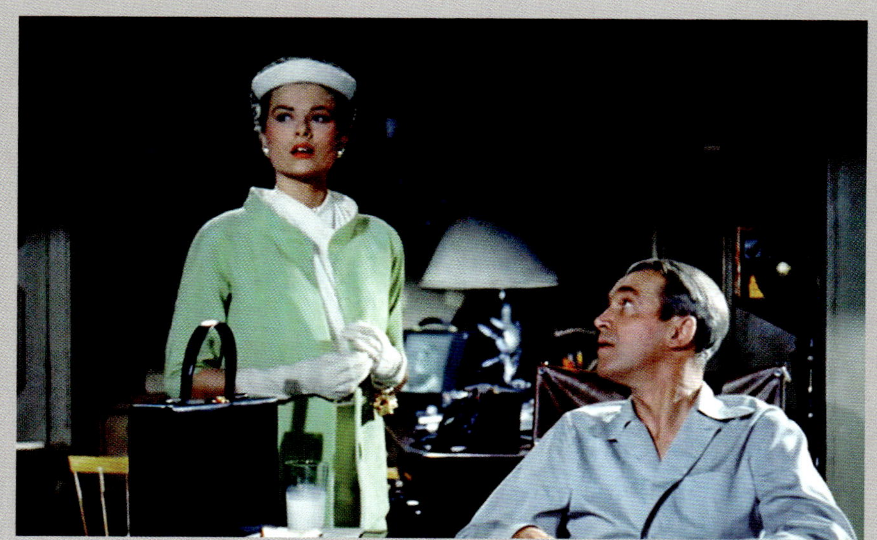

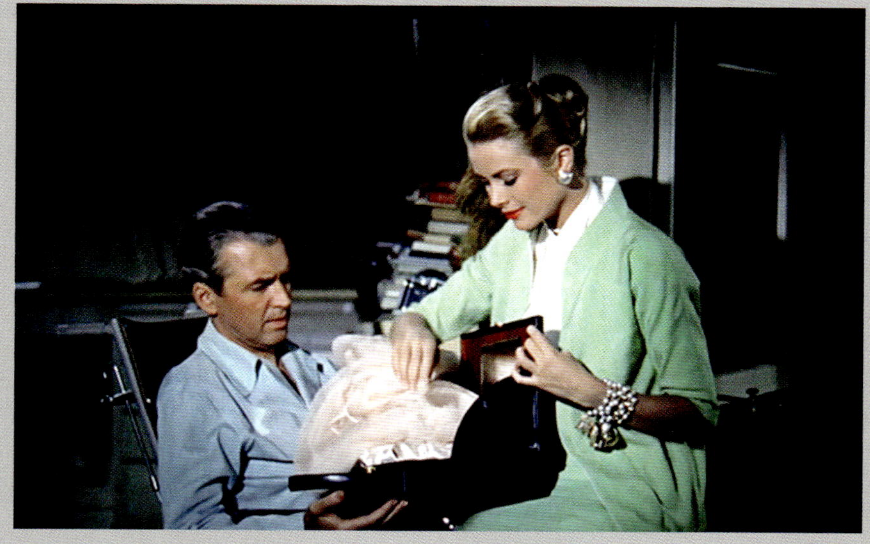

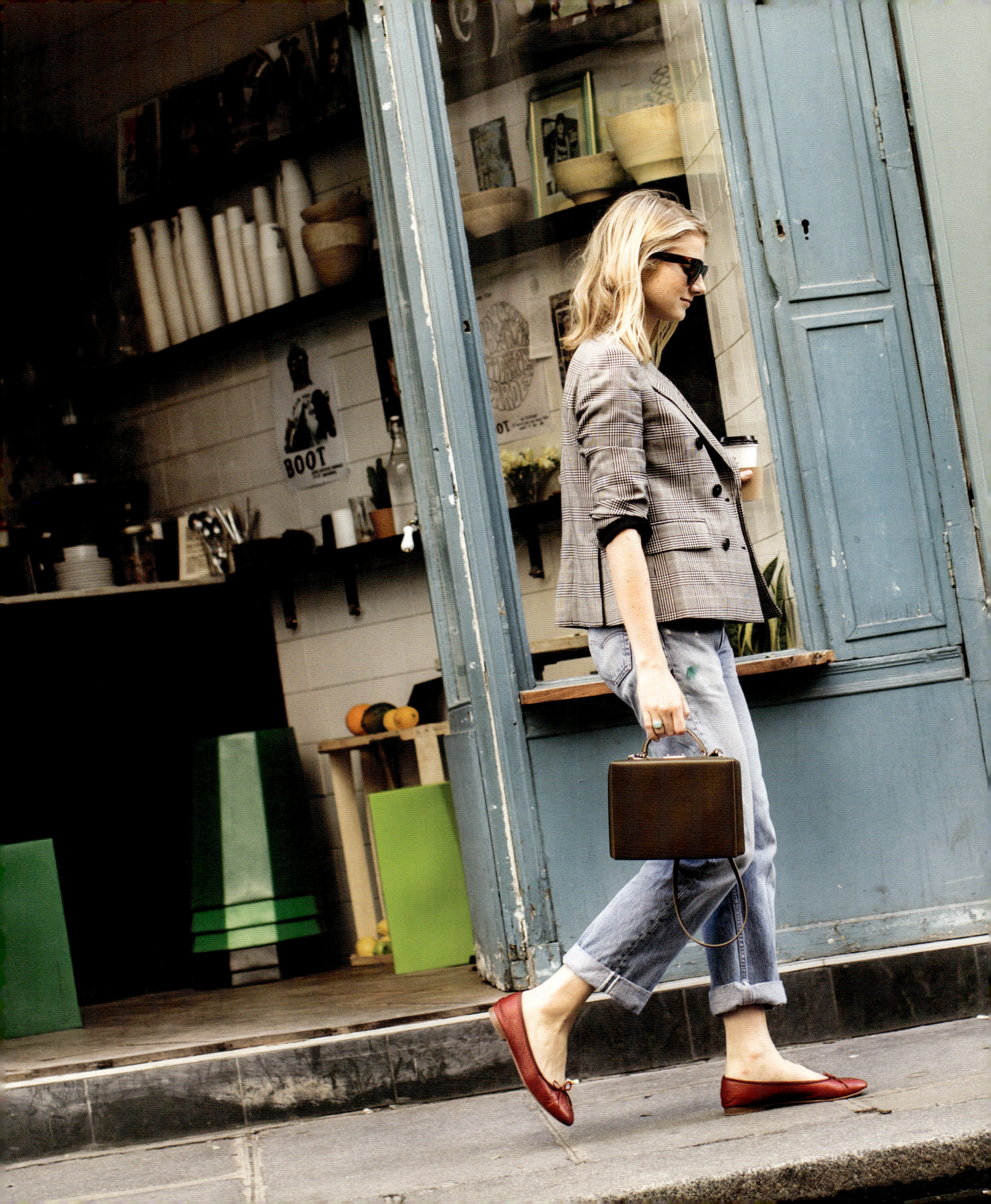
BOOT

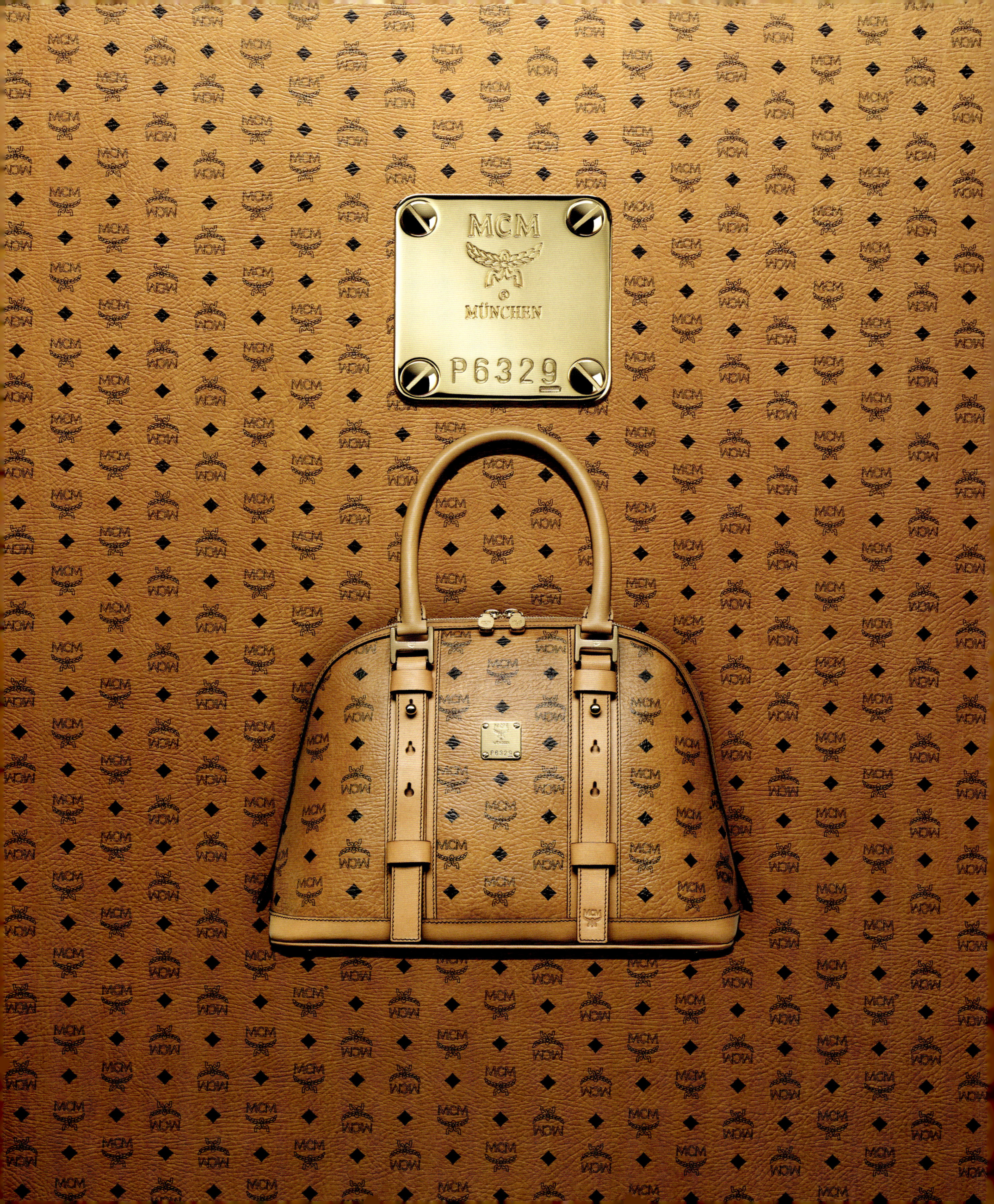
MCM
MÜNCHEN
P6329

MCM Worldwide

STARK, LATE 1970S

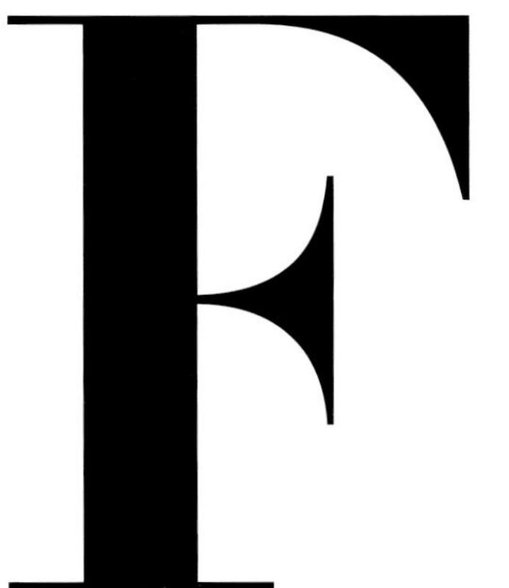

Founded by Michael Cromer in 1976, the German brand MCM Worldwide hit its stride in the freewheeling heyday of the 1980s. Its omnipresent fabric, the all-logo pattern Cognac Visetos, became a signifier for a lifestyle of flash and flamboyance. Diana Ross took their suitcases on tour. The moneyed denizens of the television show *Dynasty* traveled with trunks dotted with the MCM logo. Even the acronym, which stood for Michael Cromer München and for the Roman numerals for 1900—the year of the birth of the modern age—was jokingly termed "more cash money."

Cromer was an equally oversized figure. He played with a German youth rugby team, opened a discotheque in 1962, and made a guest appearance as an actor in the 1972 Italian miniseries *The Adventures of Pinocchio* starring Gina Lollobrigida. He came up with the idea for MCM when he saw a fellow actor with matching suitcases arriving at their hotel: "The other man was apparently accorded such fawning respect by the bell-hops that Cromer underwent an instant conversion from possessor of scruffy holdalls to manufacturer of luxury luggage," reported the *Sunday Times* in 1996.

The MCM collection expanded beyond trunks, carry-ons, and suitcases. There were MCM-logo alarm clocks, coffee cups, tennis rackets, and even dog leashes and backgammon sets. The cult item, however, was the Stark backpack, which every cool kid seemed to have. It was a simple schoolyard style covered in that iconic Cognac Visetos monogram.

But, like the market, the MCM moment ended, and 1990s minimalism came into vogue. The brand and its type of heady ostentation were over, save for a pocket in South Korea where it continued to resonate. Cromer was out of the picture.

Then, in 2005, South Korea's Sungjoo Group, led by retail magnate Sung-Joo Kim, acquired the worldwide rights and set about relaunching the brand. Kim definitely had the know-how and muscle for the job: named one of *Wall Street Journal*'s "Top 50 Women to Watch" in 2004 and *Asiaweek*'s "Seven Most Powerful Women in Asia," she had previously launched Gucci, Marks & Spencer, Sonia Rykiel, and Yves Saint Laurent in the Korean market.

Kim set about hiring a new director, Michael Michalsky; opening new stores; and putting the bags in the hands of Justin Bieber, Lydia Hearst, Heidi Klum, Rihanna, and the street-style set—not to mention the influential K-pop stars of Korea. MCM bags got screen time on *Gossip Girl*. Kim and Michalsky tweaked the original formula, doing away with the signature cognac, punching up the palette with bright colors, and reframing the MCM to mean "Mode Creation Munich." But the allover logos remained. "I'm a kid of the 1980s," explained Michalsky to *Women's Wear Daily* in 2006. "I've always loved monograms and in accessories especially, people are interested in logos, which have been there a long time. They want something with history, whether it's good or bad."

OPPOSITE:
Bowler bag, MCM, Fall 2009.

PAGES 162–163:
Stark backpack, MCM, London, February 2014.

"If the 1980s had a sound, it was a vertiginous swoon—as one person after another toppled over with envy at the sight of someone's killer handbag."

—CATHY HORYN, *Vogue*, October 1995

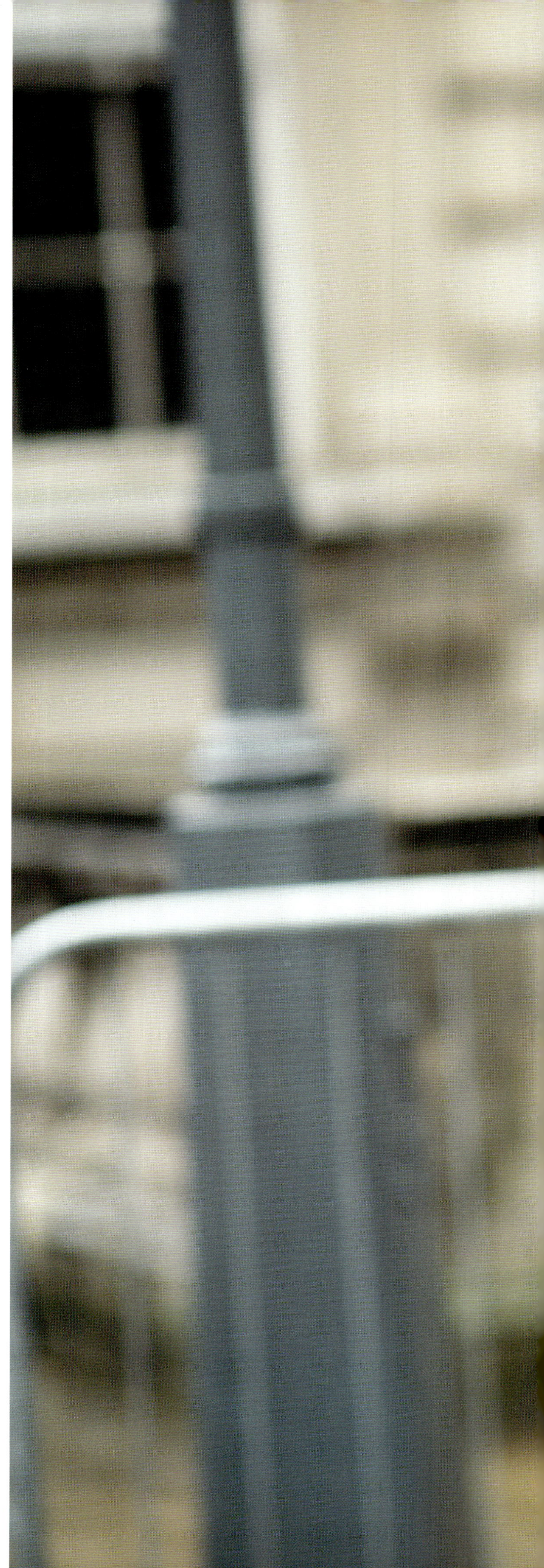

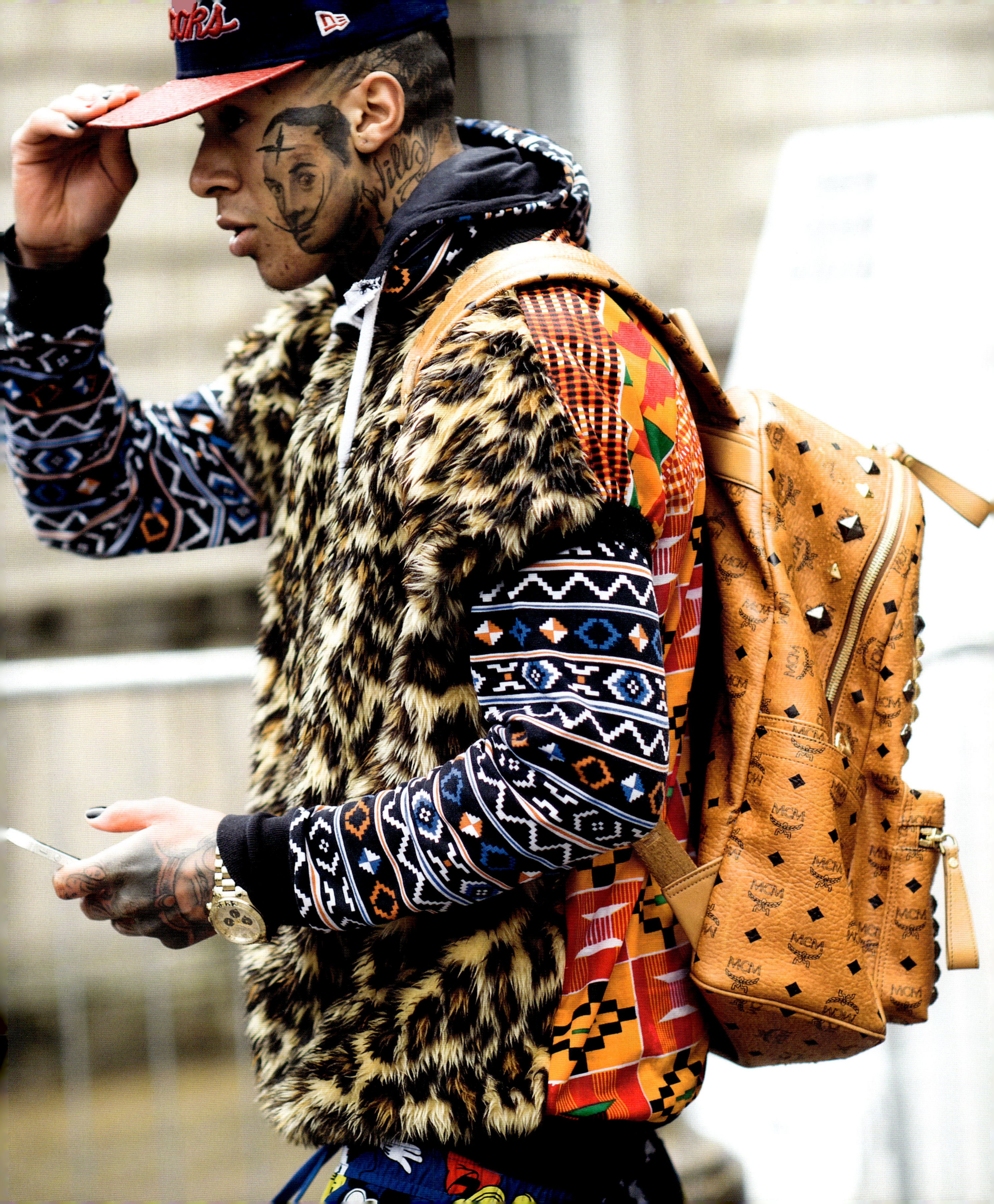
MCM

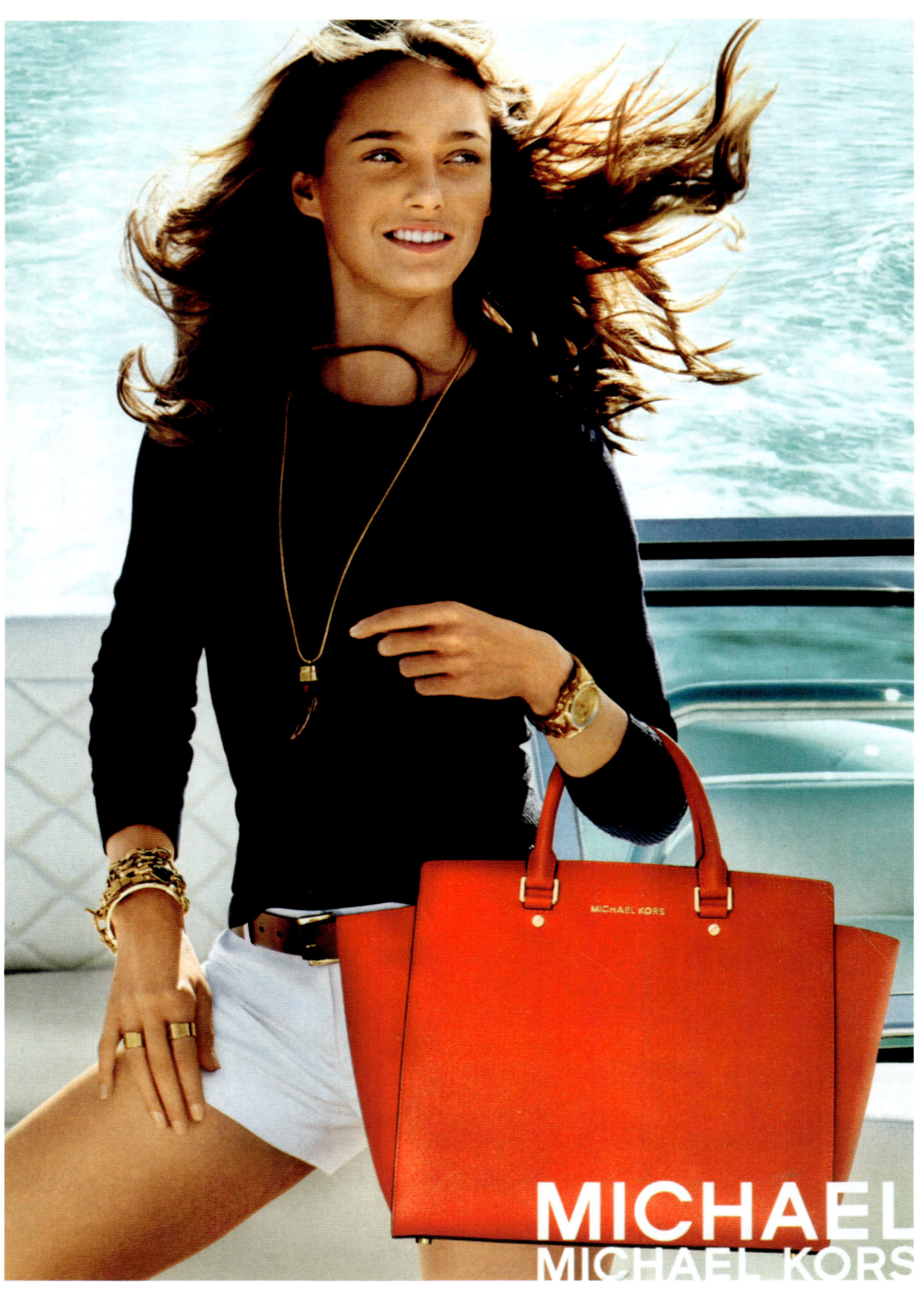
MICHAEL KORS
MICHAEL
MICHAEL KORS

Michael Kors

JET SET, 2011

SELMA, 2013

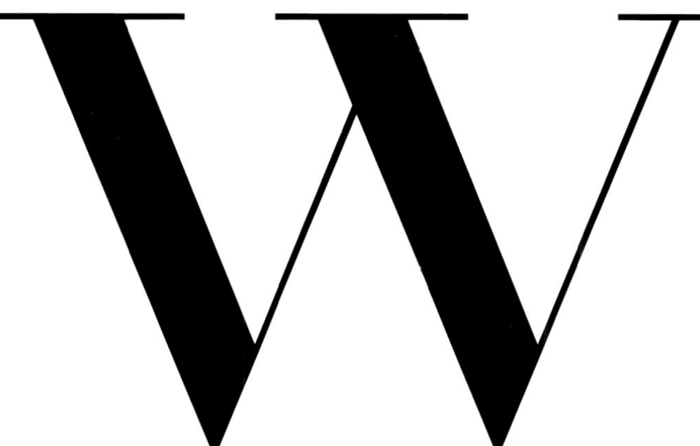

When Michael Kors first went to mainland China in 2014, he mounted a fashion show extravaganza in Shanghai in a thirty-thousand-square-foot airplane hangar complete with a private jet parked in the middle. The "Jet Set Experience," attended by Hollywood celebrities, was set against large-screen projections of such *beau monde* destinations as Capri and St. Moritz.

A lot of designers reference travel and far-flung destinations as part of their brand identity, but no one has adopted the jet-set lifestyle quite like Kors. Everything in his world hinges on "jet set"—from that epic Shanghai outing to his blog *Travel Diaries* ("Ready, Jet Set, Go!") to his ubiquitous Jet Set tote, with its slim straps and dangling logo charm.

For a company that's predicated on an image of moneyed society and the leisure life, the price tags are on the more accessible side of the luxury spectrum. As Kors told the *Times* in 2014, we either are jet set "or we want to be." And the people who want to be far outnumber those who are. For them, that elegant and clean-contoured zip-top design—flaunting textured leather, gold buckle details, and a gold logo pendant with the initials MK—becomes a projection of a lifestyle of sun-kissed mornings on the beach in Santorini, lunches in London, and nights in Saint-Tropez. "Those bags have perpetuated a deft takeover of the accessories scene; advancing from the realms of no-one's-that-bothered to all-out ubiquity in a year," announced the *Times* in 2016. The Jet Set has since given way to other popular tote styles such as the Selma (Spring 2013), with slight wings on the sides, and the boxier Mercer (Fall 2016).

Kors's success is in democratizing luxury. His appearance on the reality television show *Project Runway* made him a celebrity. In 2013 the *Observer* named Kors one of the most influential New Yorkers of the past twenty-five years and *Time* included him on its list of the one hundred most influential people in the world. "Michael takes the wonderful heritage of American sportswear into the future," designer Zac Posen told *Time* that year, "translating it internationally for every woman and man who wants to be a part of the American Dream."

OPPOSITE:
Selma bag, Michael Kors, Spring 2014.

"The idea of design integrity and quality isn't based strictly on the idea of a high price tag. That's disappeared, that's old fashioned."

—MICHAEL KORS, *South China Morning Post*, May 16, 2014

SOCIAL SWAN

AIMEE SONG

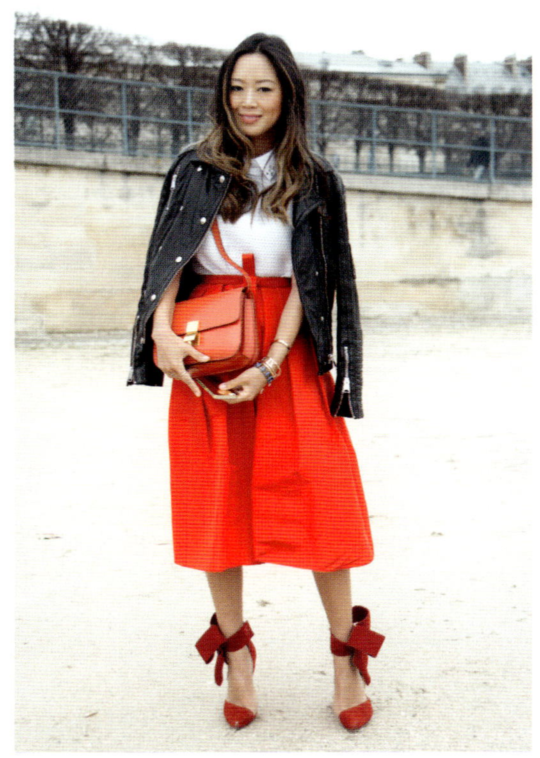

ABOVE:
Aimee Song with a Céline Box bag, Paris, 2014.

Los Angeles native Aimee Song is the powerhouse blogger behind Song of Style. In 2016, she was named one of Forbes' 30 Under 30; that same year, she published her first book, *Capture Your Style: Transform Your Instagram Photos, Showcase Your Life, and Build the Ultimate Platform*. She's partnered with numerous labels and is consistently named on the industry's lists of top fashion influencers. Here she opens up about handbag loves, past and present.

What was your first handbag?
I discovered luxury handbags when I was around eleven. That's when I saw my first Chanel bag—at the boutique on Rodeo Drive. I was with my mom, and a small quilted bag caught my eye. I wasn't as into fashion as I am now, but I remember recognizing instantly that was a pretty bag. My mom bought it—not for me, but for herself—but because it was a mini, she would let me carry it.

Where is the bag now?
I don't know. I lost it and all the contents inside one day in San Francisco. It was so cold that I must've been distracted because when the leather strap broke, I didn't notice. It was really old by that point—but it had been so durable for ten years. So I understand why people invest in luxury bags.

Do you rotate bags?
I carry the same bag a lot. The main reason is because, when I'm investing in a bag, I want to make sure it goes with a lot of things. When you're making an investment, whether it's $200 or $2,000, you want to make sure you're getting your money's worth. I love carrying a bag over and over again and wearing it different ways. Also, I'm lazy—I don't want to take the contents out of the bag.

Luxury bags are . . .
Better investments than stocks! For someone like me, who's not wealthy, buying a luxury bag is a peek into the design world. You can't wear a couture piece that often, but you can wear a bag many times. Buying a designer's bag makes you feel like you're part of the brand. You still feel like you got something.

What bags are you loving right now?
I'm obsessed with the Petite Malle from Nicolas Ghesquière for Louis Vuitton. I think Nicolas is a genius. He brought a freshness and a coolness to Vuitton while still keeping the integrity of the heritage of the brand. I also love Gucci and Chloé.

HANDBAGS TO REMEMBER

ANDREA LINETT

Creative director and brand consultant Andrea Linett began her career at the indie teen magazine *Sassy* before going on to *Harper's Bazaar* and *Lucky*, where she served as founding creative director. She has also worked as eBay's first creative director, helping to build its fashion presence, and as Michael Kors's VP global creative director. In 2014 *Fast Company* added her to its list of "Most Creative People in Business 1000." Linett is the founder of the personal style blog *iwanttobeher.com*, which spun off a similarly titled memoir in 2012. She is also the author of the style guide *The Cool Factor* (2016) and the coauthor of *The Lucky Shopping Manual: Building and Improving Your Wardrobe Piece by Piece* (2003) and *The Lucky Guide to Mastering Any Style: How to Wear Iconic Looks and Make Them Your Own* (2008). Here she shares memories and shopping tips.

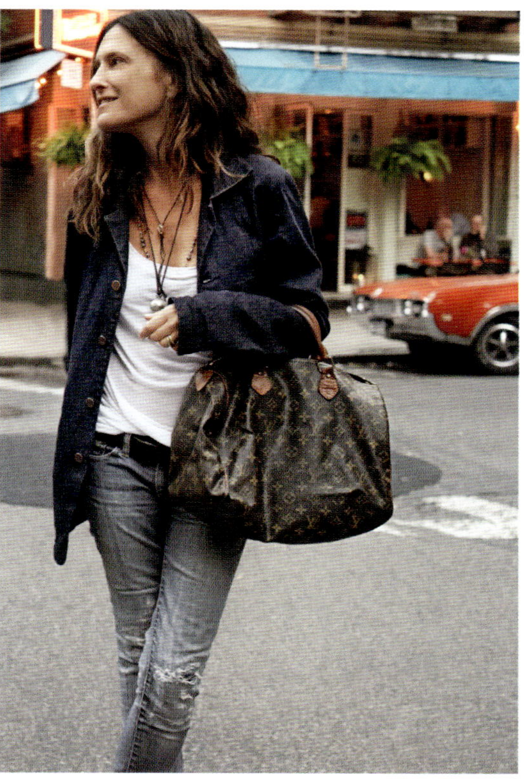

What was the first bag you fell in love with?

I seem to remember my mom's cool white mod bag in the late 1960s that has to have been the style inspiration for that first Marc Jacobs It Bag in the late 1990s.

How do you keep things organized in your bag?

I put smaller things in the inside zipper pocket and my Matthew Swope clutch and then everything else falls into the black hole.

What is one thing about handbags that only a true handbag lover would understand?

They have the power to change your look and attitude like nothing else.

When shopping for a bag . . .

Look for a good inside pocket and good or no hardware. Bad hardware can ruin a perfectly great bag.

Describe one moment of handbag envy.

I saw a super cool—I'm guessing French—girl walking around Soho. She had messy hair and was in all black and was carrying a perfectly beat-up old brown Kelly bag that I decided had been her grandma's and she was rocking it her way. I think about that girl/bag a lot!

If you could save one bag in your wardrobe from a fire . . .

My mom's old dark brown saddlebag from the 1960s. So cool and irreplaceable.

ABOVE:
Andrea Linett with a Louis Vuitton Speedy, New York City, 2014.

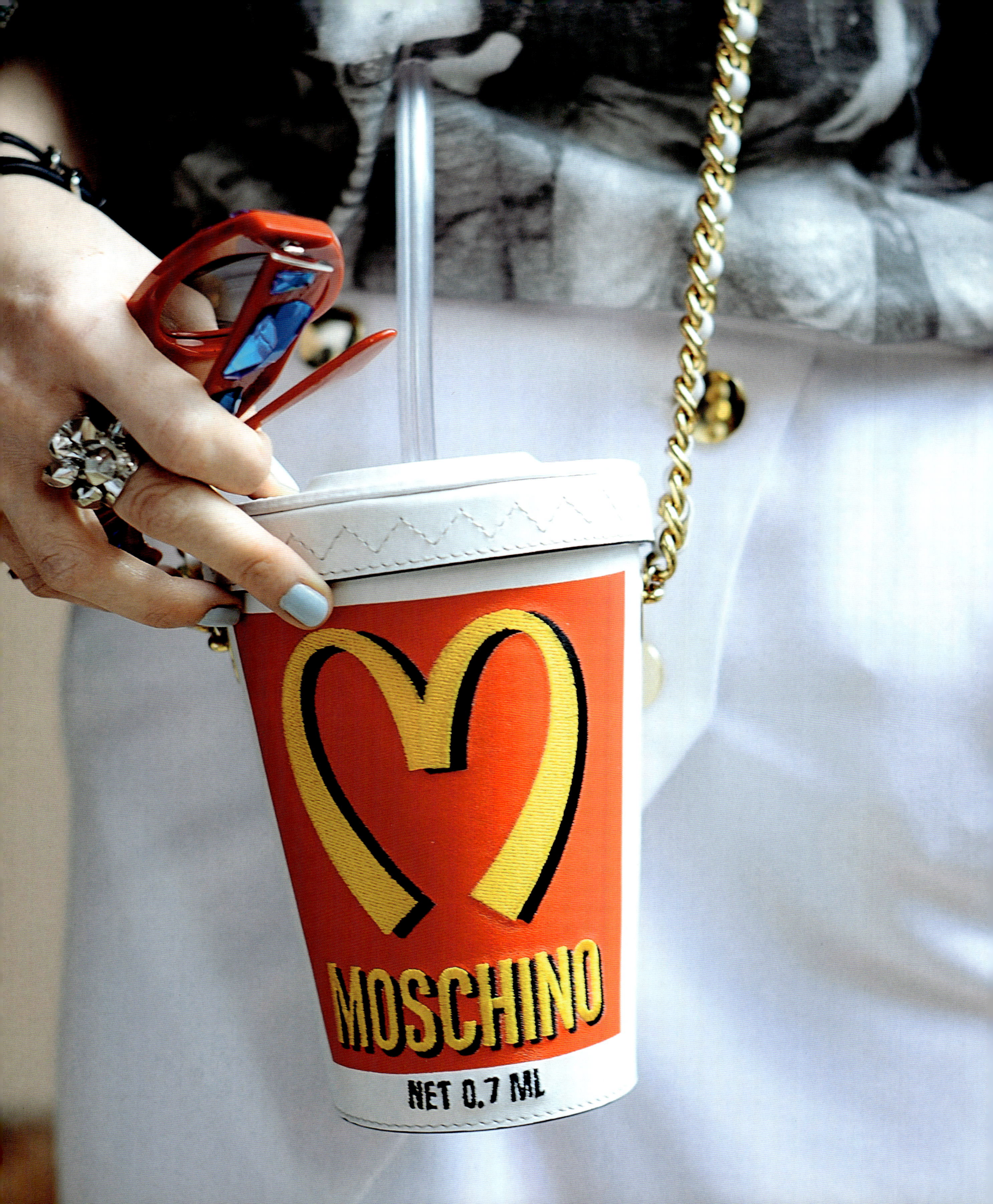
MOSCHINO
NET 0.7 ML

Jeremy Scott for Moschino

GOLDEN ARCHES, 2014

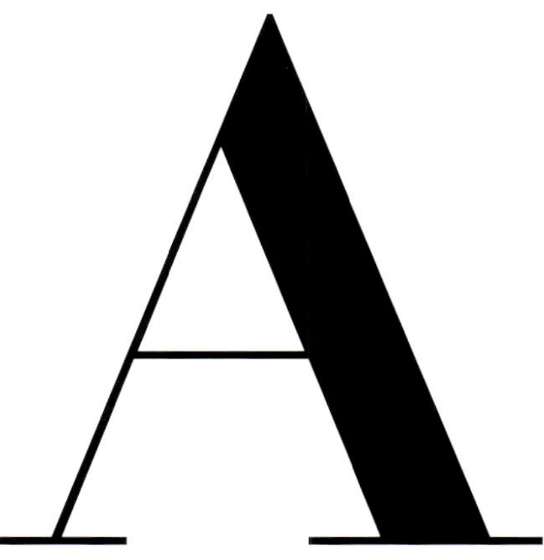

A former illustrator for Gianni Versace, Franco Moschino launched his line in 1983, at the height of the fashion industry's fling with status. He took logos and signature items and subverted them, riffing off Chanel jackets and Burberry raincoats. There was the jacket with the words "Waist of Money" embroidered in gold around its middle; a white button-down, with extra-long arms that wrapped around the body, which had "For Fashion Victims Only" emblazoned on the back. "'His debunking of the fashion industry was quite remarkable, because it came at exactly the right time," Lisa Armstrong, then associate editor of *British Vogue*, told the *Sunday Times* in 1994. "During the 1980s, fashion designers began taking themselves far too seriously, and he deflated them all." At the court of fashion, Moschino was the jester—he was on the sidelines, poking fun, but still very much a part of the system.

When Moschino died in 1994 of complications from AIDS, his longtime assistant Rossella Jardini took over and continued with his witty pop-meets-surrealist take for two decades, until she handed over the reins to Jeremy Scott in 2014. Scott's fashion is similar to Moschino's in its postmodern borrowing, tongue-in-cheek rebellion, and staging of runway shows that are more about an idea and entertainment than establishing a trend. Like Moschino, Scott has a penchant for using teddy bears in his designs and spoofing Chanel. He also loves a good double entendre.

For his debut collection at Moschino, Scott offered a commentary on consumer culture with a junk food–themed show, complete with Hershey's Kisses gowns and McDonald's Happy Meal handbags. There were Chanel-like tweed skirt suits in ketchup red and French-fry-bright mustardy yellow. One model carried a quilted handbag with gold chains that had the McDonald's arches reimagined as a heart. The collection was Scott's play on fast fashion: the merging of high and low, couture and street.

The McDonald's theme resonated with Scott on a personal level, too. In *Jeremy Scott* (2014) he recalled when the first McDonald's arrived in his hometown, Lowry City, Missouri, putting it "finally on the map." As art dealer Jeffrey Deitch observed in the foreword to the book, "The Missouri farm boy has recycled one of the most all-American icons to create a sensation for one of the most iconic European fashion brands—and become an icon all his own along the way."

OPPOSITE:
Golden Arches bag, Moschino, Milan, September 2014.

PAGES 170–171:
Various Golden Arches bags, Moschino, *Vogue Japan*, October 2014.

> "I think of myself as an artist. I'm an artist who uses fashion as a medium."
>
> —JEREMY SCOTT, *Jeremy Scott*, 2014

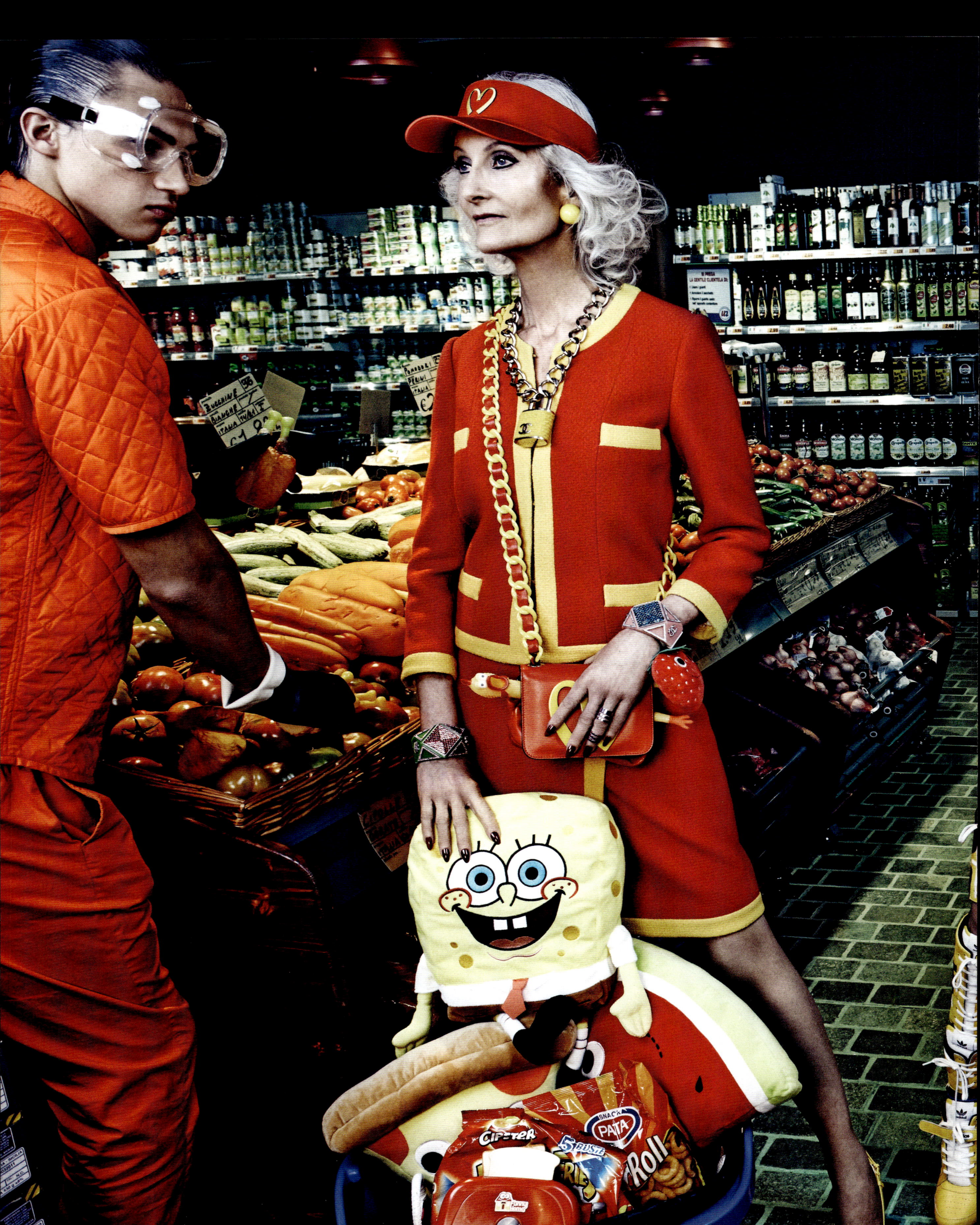

CIPSTER
SNACK
PATA
5 BUSTE
Roll

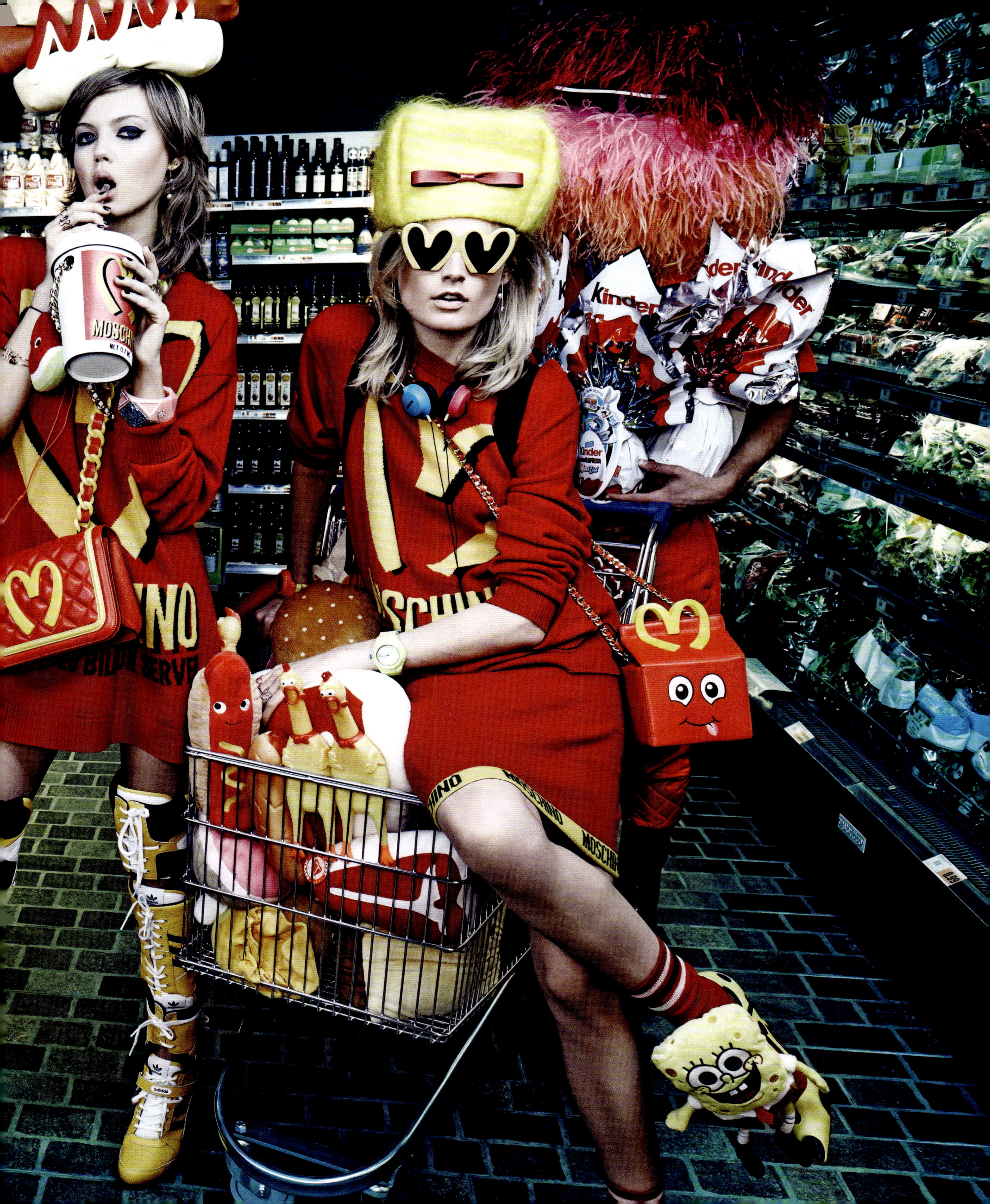
kinder

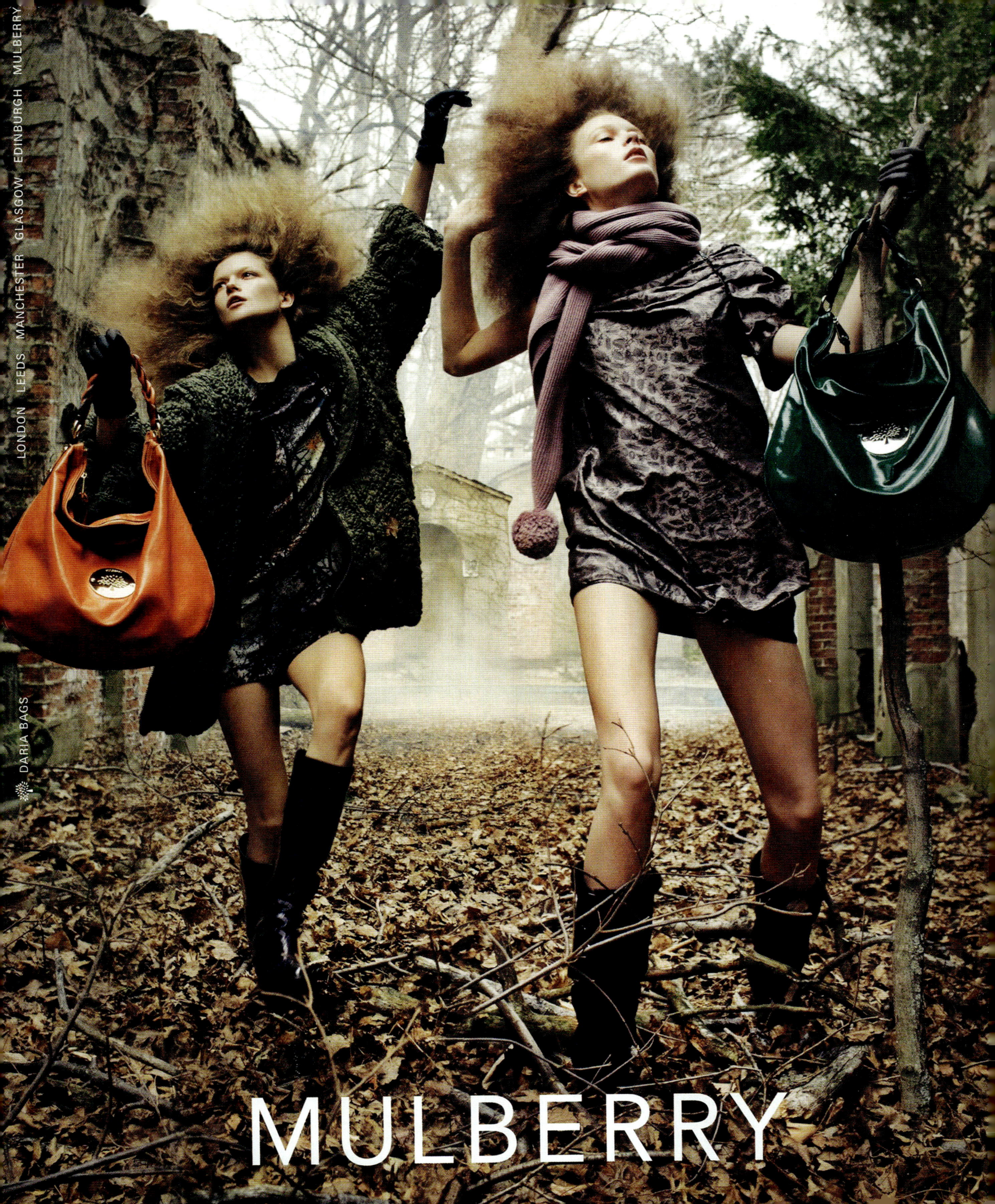
LONDON LEEDS MANCHESTER GLASGOW EDINBURGH MULBERRY
DARIA BAGS
MULBERRY

Mulberry

GISELE AND BAYSWATER, 2002

ROXANNE, 2004

ALEXA, 2010

DEL REY, 2012

CARA, 2014

OPPOSITE:
Daria hobo bags, Mulberry, Fall 2009.

PAGES 174–175:
Cara Delevingne with her eponymous Mulberry bag, Fall 2013.

PAGE 176:
Alexa bag on top of vintage luggage, Mulberry, 2011.

PAGE 177:
Alexa Chung carrying her eponymous Mulberry bag, London, September 2009.

Few handbag companies have built a brand on a synergistic relationship with celebrity quite like Mulberry. Founded in 1971 by Roger Saul, Mulberry began as a small line of leather chokers and belts in Somerset, England, and didn't really become a luxury contender until Singapore mogul Christina Ong began a serious rebranding push. Mulberry soon became a lightning rod for top accessory design talent—Nicholas Knightly, Stuart Vevers, Emma Hill, and Johnny Coca—and produced a succession of It Bags: Gisele, Bayswater, Roxanne, Alexa, Del Rey, and Cara. They all draw from Mulberry's distinctly English heritage and feature wonderful leathers that have character and feel lived in; they are precisely the kind of bags you can carry to knock around the city.

Most of the bags bear women's names. "A lot of brands adopted women's names, such as Mulberry's Roxanne, that made customers adopt a best-friend relationship with their bags," explained Laura Davidson, accessories buyer for Selfridges in London, to *Women's Wear Daily* in 2006. The Gisele, done in collaboration with Luella Bartley, was named after Brazilian model Gisele Bündchen, who wore the bag on the runway. The Del Rey was named after singer Lana Del Rey; Alexa, one of the brand's biggest moneymakers, after British personality and television presenter Alexa Chung; Cara, after English model and actress Cara Delevingne. "We're not tea and crumpets and the Queen-British," Hill told the *Telegraph* in 2012. "We're bonkers and crazy and craft." There's a sense of anti-establishment rebellion to Mulberry, and that sensibility goes straight back to its hippie founder: Saul became a spelt farmer in Glastonbury.

"The handbag is a rare delight, it's like Aladdin's cave—all sorts of things are hidden there, that females like to save."

—BRIDGID PATRICK, from *Bags & Purses: The Story of Chic and Practicality* by Ida Tomshinsky, 2016

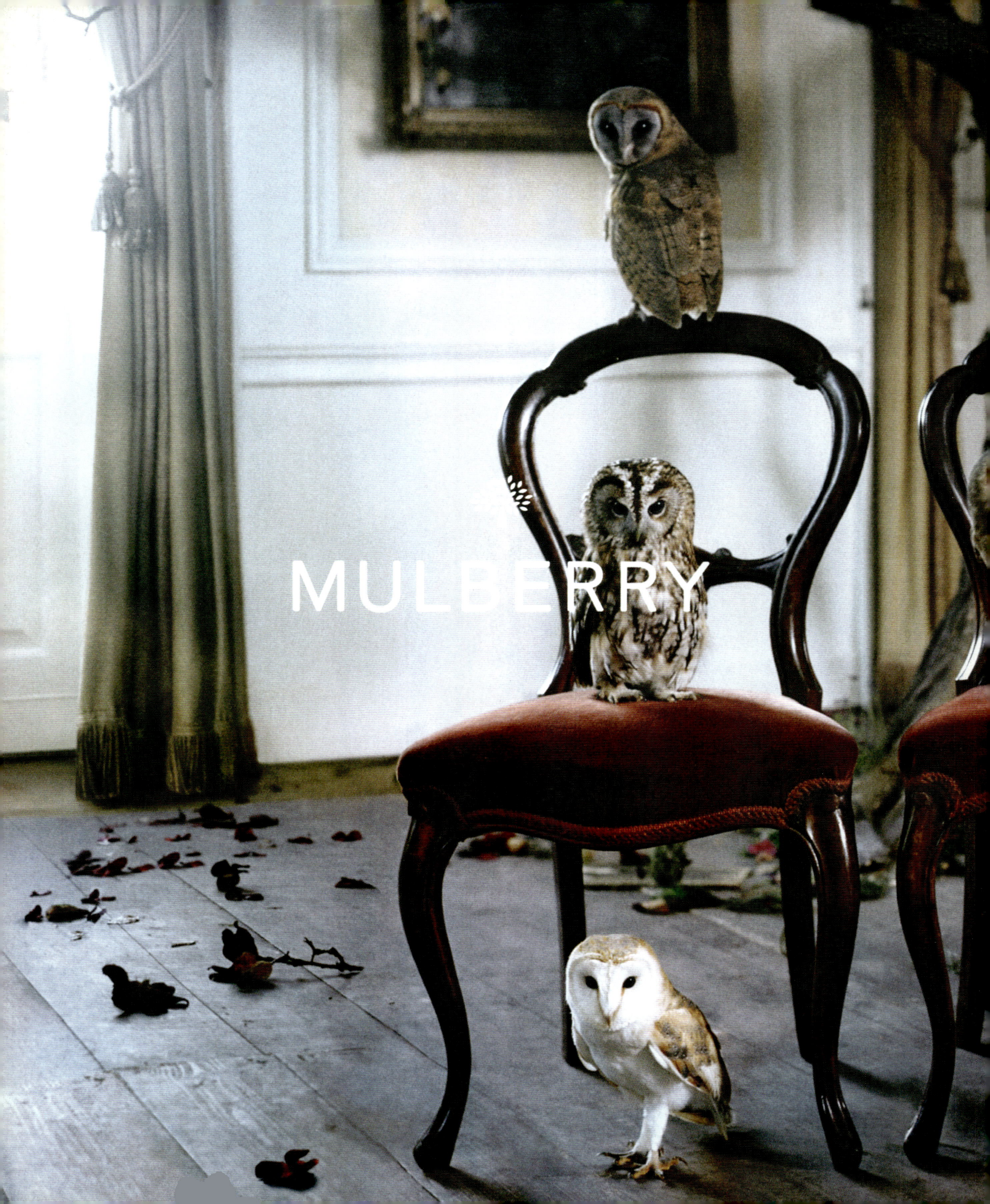
MULBERRY

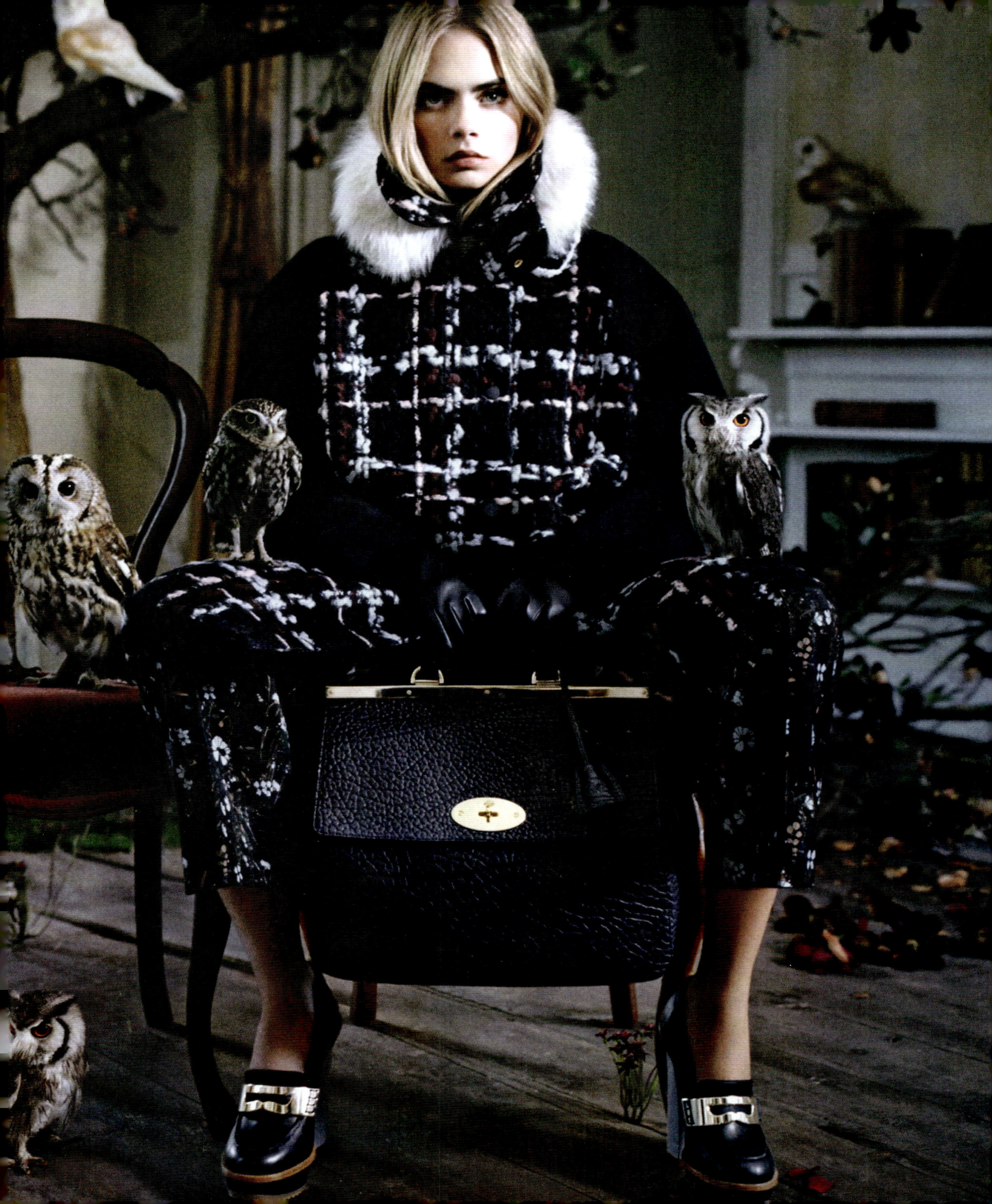

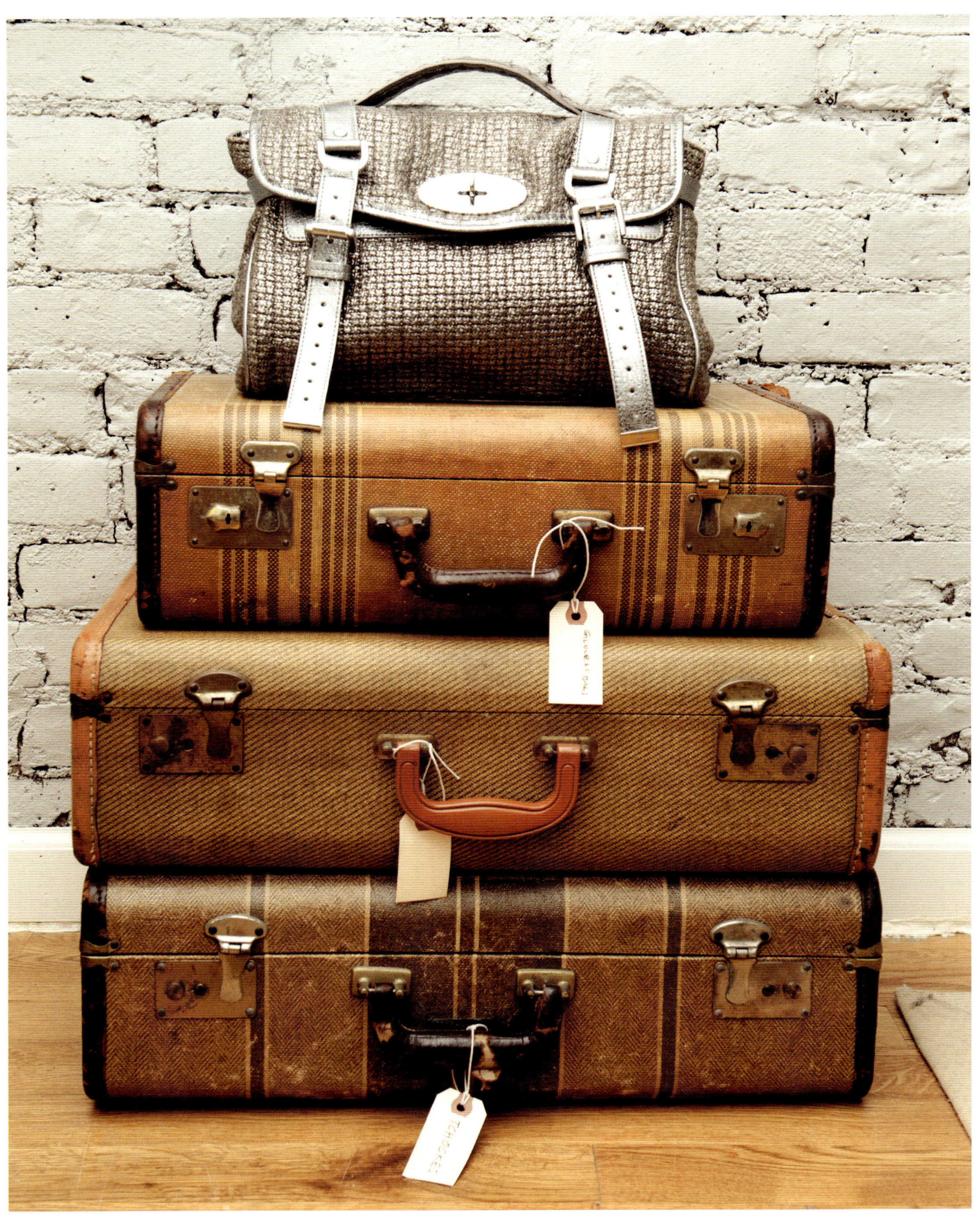

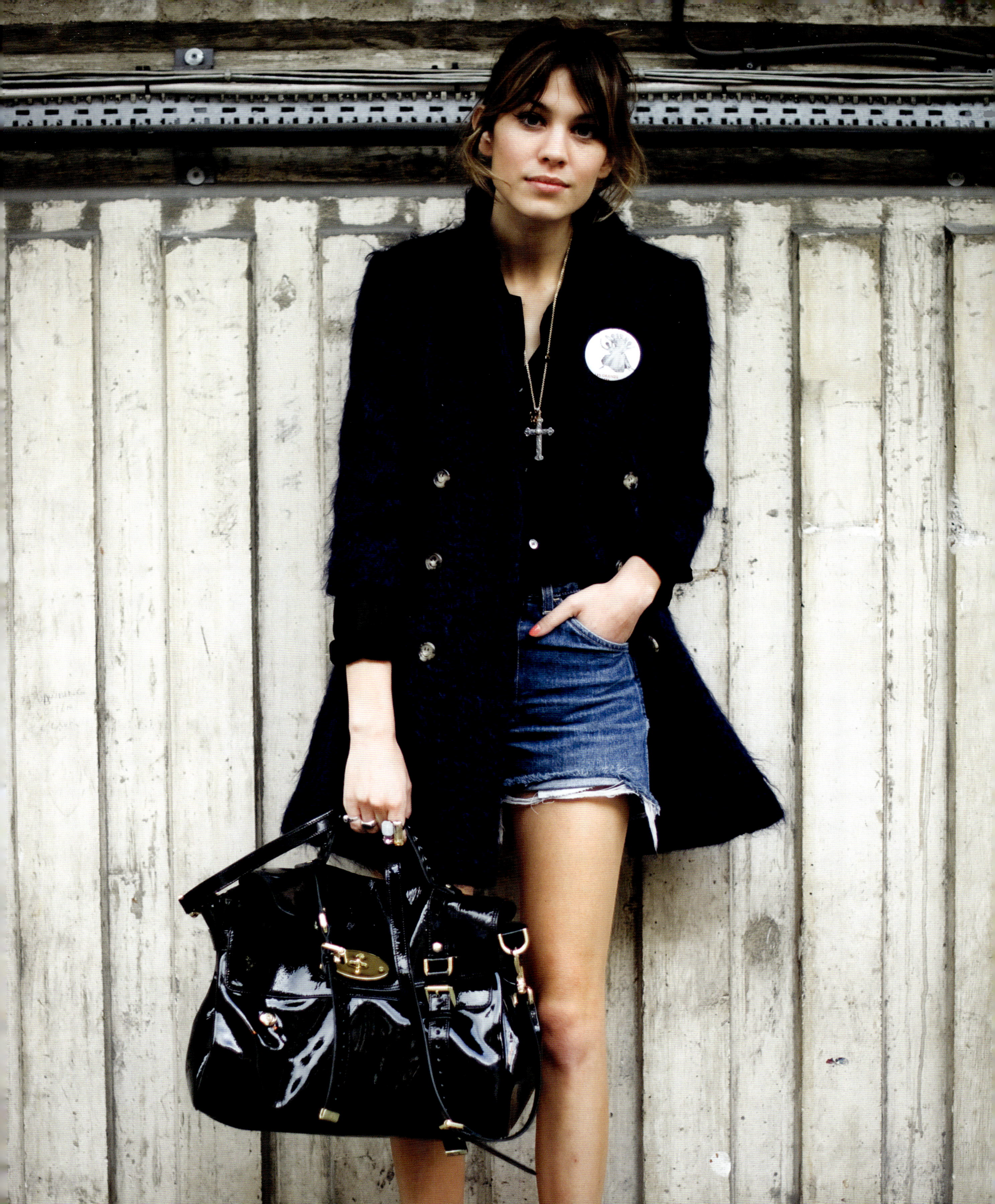

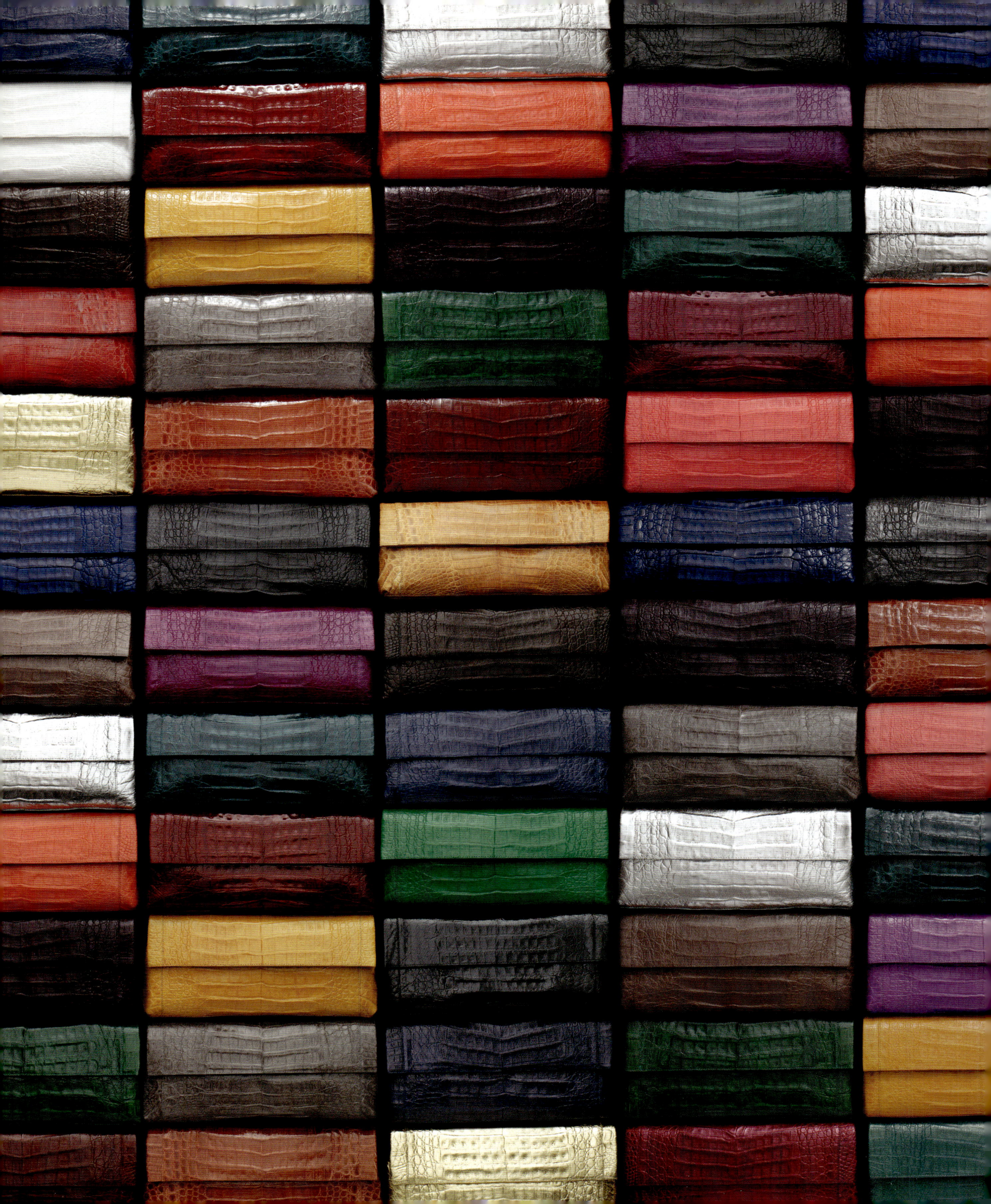

Nancy Gonzalez

ENVELOPE CLUTCH, 1998

LEAF TOTE, 2005

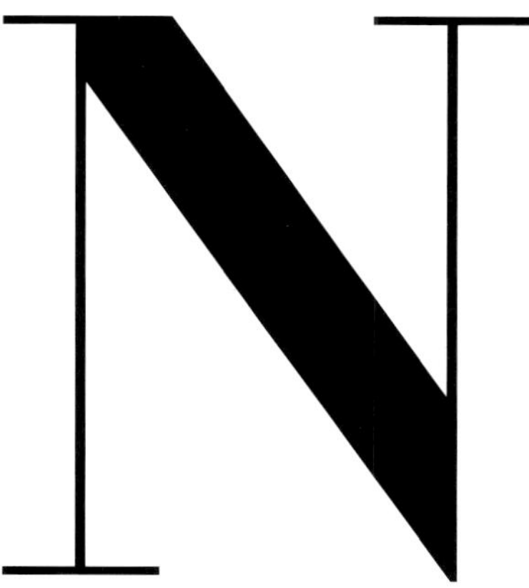

Nancy Gonzalez's bags don't have an identifying signature—a logo, a motif, a pattern, or even a distinctive shape—like those by other designers. Improbably for this day and age, they don't even have identifying hardware. Gonzalez's designs are free of brand fingerprints, save for the luxury materials from which they're crafted.

In 1988 Gonzalez began selling her designs with a line of belts in her native Colombia under the label Encueros de Colombia. She then expanded to bags and entered the market in the United States a decade later. She dyes and treats her exotics in a sublime way—for example, punching up her signature crocodile skins in vibrant, beautifully saturated colors like deep fuchsia and peacock green, experimenting with laser cutting for three-dimensional floral accents, and creating strands and weaving them together for a wicker-like effect. Her signature crocodile chain links are made of titanium covered in the precious skin. "I believe the highest form of luxury is having options," Gonzalez said in Pamela Golbin's *Nancy Gonzalez* (2013). Her line strikes a chic counterpoint between verve and a restrained and ladylike sense of design or, as she told *Women's Wear Daily* in 2006, "a cross between fantasy and classic." Among the more popular styles: the Gotham Clutch, a cocktail-hour favorite, and the roomy Leaf Tote. She also launched a shoe collection in 2016 that is proving to be as popular as her bags.

While Gonzalez hasn't cornered the market on exotics—you'll find plenty of other skin lovers in this book—she does have the advantage of owning the entire production line, right down to the crocodile farms and tanneries. For the customer, that means that her handbags cost a fraction of the others.

"I started because I was looking for something that I really love," Gonzalez told the *Miami Herald* in 2012. "It was not a business orientation or the idea of having my own company. It was more for me, inside."

OPPOSITE:
Assorted Envelope crocodile clutches, Nancy Gonzalez, Fall 2009.

> "I like the idea that women buy my bags just for themselves—it doesn't matter if no one else understands it. To me, this is the largest luxury."
>
> —NANCY GONZALEZ, *South China Morning Post*, February 8, 2013

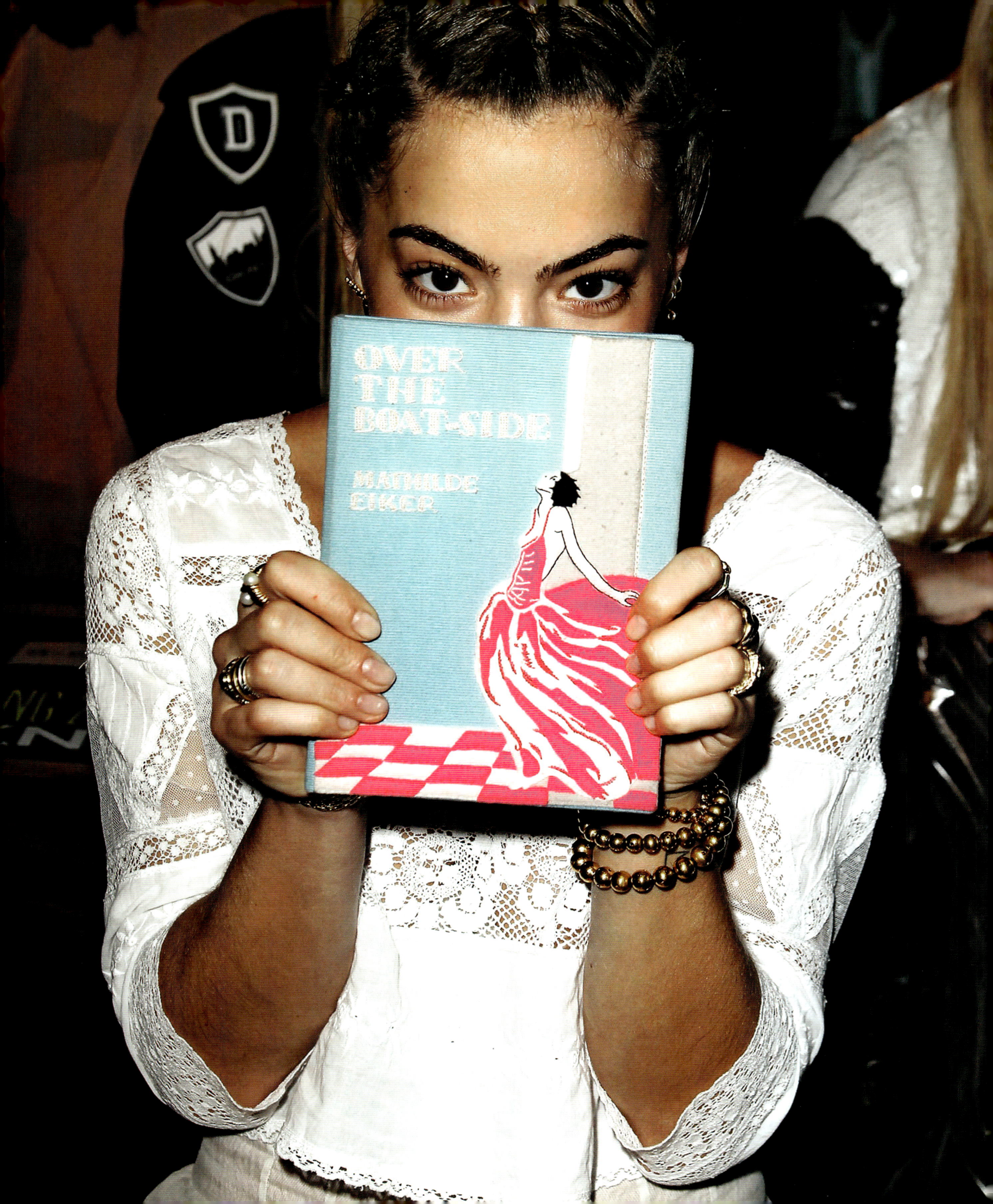
OVER
THE
BOAT-SIDE
MATHILDE
EIKER

Olympia Le-Tan

BOOK CLUTCH, 2010

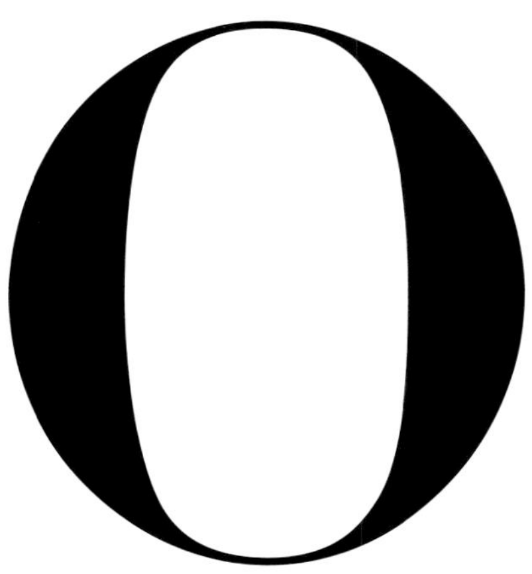

Olympia Le-Tan's charming collection of "book" bags—small, rectangular minaudières hand-embroidered to resemble book jackets—debuted in 2010 with reproductions of first-edition covers for *Lolita*, *Moby-Dick*, *1984*, *The Catcher in the Rye*, and other classics. For her initial collections, Le-Tan hand-embroidered each "cover" herself, using basic stitches she learned as a child from her grandmother. Today, she has a professional team of embroiderers at her Paris studio doing the work and personally trains each one to keep the same style of stitch in order to preserve the bag's authentic tactility.

The bags are constructed with an architectural base around which the embroidered felt "cover" is wrapped. In May 2013, after model Miranda Kerr was spotted in New York City carrying Le-Tan's *The Last Tycoon* clutch, the *Sun* printed a do-it-yourself guide on how to make a Le-Tan bag in seven easy steps. The headline preceding the instructions read: "Tome Made: Trendy Bags Cost £1,000 . . . Our Guide Gives Book Look for £23." Apparently, all you need is a hardcover book, cardboard, gold spray paint, glue, scissors, a pin, and a paper clip. Le-Tan noted that the article was one of her favorite press clippings about her work. "I've always been obsessed with books," explained Le-Tan, who majored in Italian literature, to the *Independent* in 2013. "I grew up in a house where the walls were all books. My father has a very big collection of old books and I was always attracted by the nice graphic covers." Her father is famed illustrator Pierre Le-Tan, the hand behind innumerable *New Yorker* covers. The elder Le-Tan did her logo, which is also the monogrammed wall fabric at her Paris store. Peek inside her bags, and you'll find linings designed by him, too.

It's easy to see why her minaudières quickly found fans—including Natalie Portman and Tilda Swinton—and became collector's items. Few luxury bags resonate on this Proustian level, tapping into a nostalgic nerve, whether you favor Fitzgerald or Salinger, fantasize about tumbling down a rabbit hole, or have nightmares about waking up as a cockroach. Le-Tan includes artwork as well. In 2016, for instance, she released bags utilizing the work of René Magritte and Keith Haring. "I personally think books are cool," Le-Tan told the *Independent*, "so if it helps make other people think books are cool, then . . . cool!"

OPPOSITE:
Over the Boat-Side book clutch, New York City, September 2014.

PAGE 182, TOP, LEFT:
The Catcher in the Rye book clutch, Los Angeles, February 2014.

PAGE 182, TOP, RIGHT:
Little Miss Busy book clutch, London, September 2016.

PAGE 182, BOTTOM:
Alice in Wonderland book clutch, Los Angeles, March 2016.

PAGE 183:
Kiss Kiss book clutch, London, July 2015.

All clutches by Olympia Le-Tan.

> "There are books of which the backs and covers are by far the best parts."
>
> —CHARLES DICKENS, *Oliver Twist*, 1838

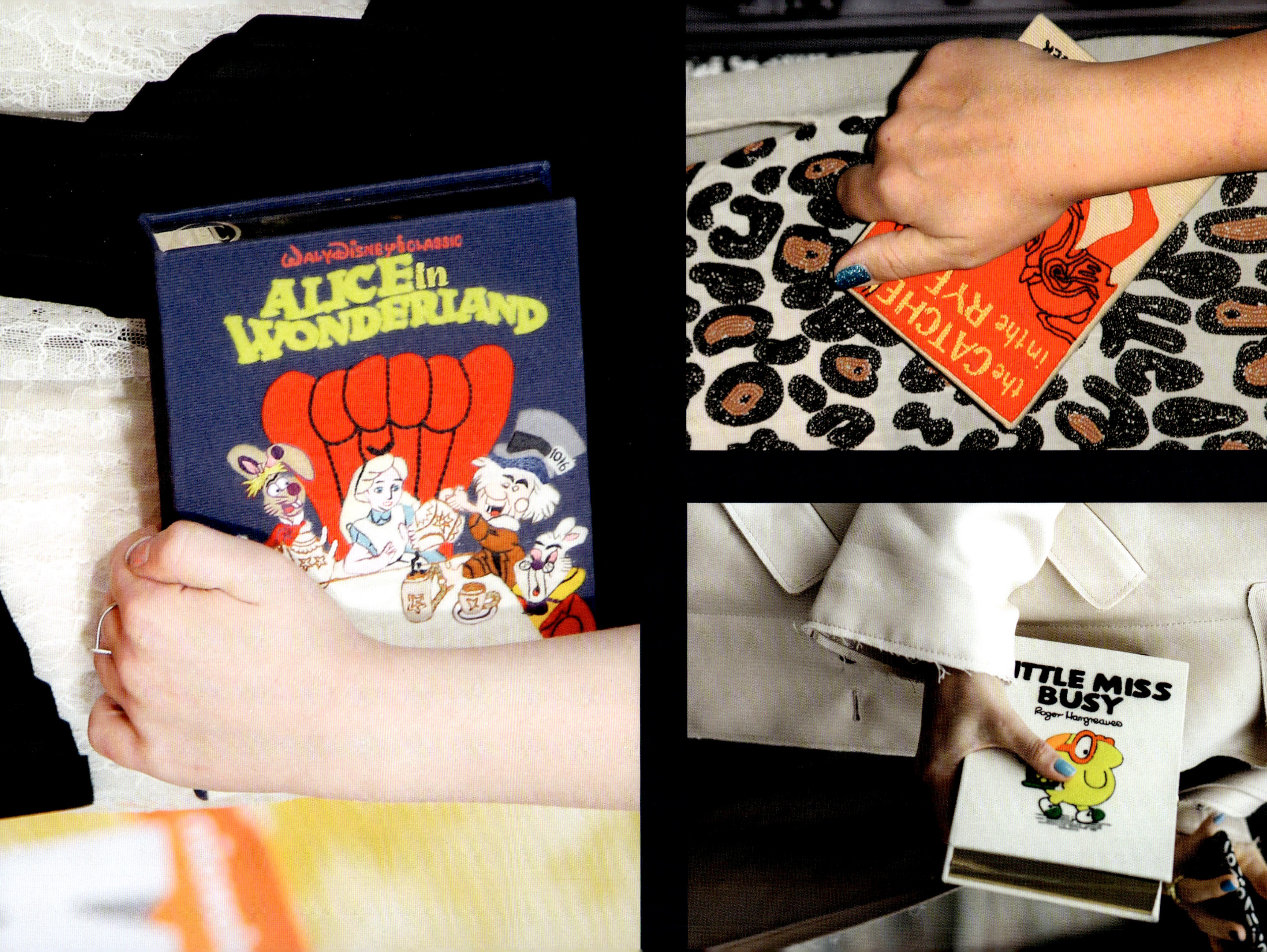
Walt Disney's Classic
ALICE in
WONDERLAND
1016
the CATCHE
in the RYE
ITTLE MISS
BUSY
Roger Hargreaves

ROALD DAHL

Kiss

Kiss

Eleven fine new stories by the author of SOMEONE LIKE YOU

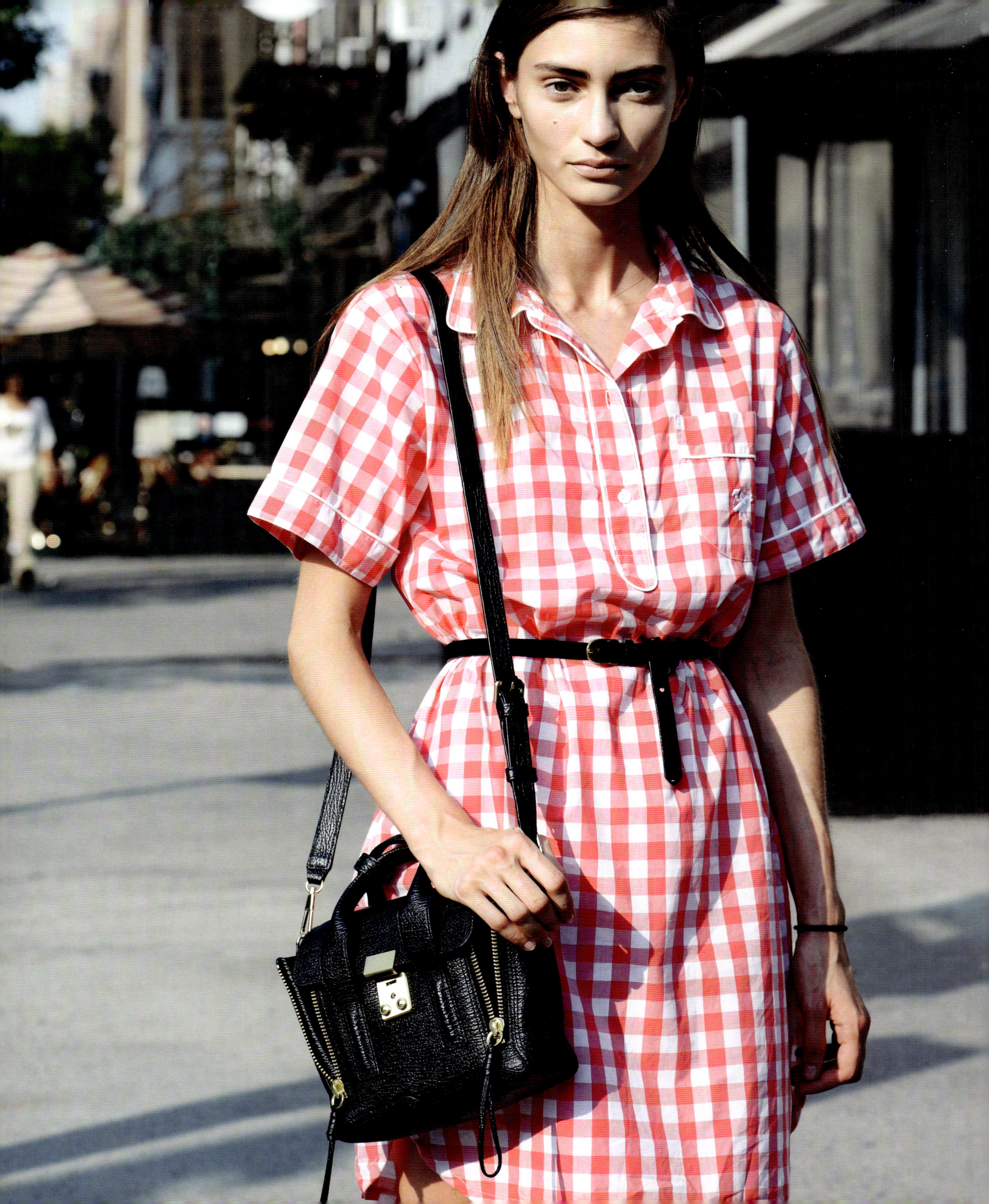

Phillip Lim

PASHLI, 2011

31 HOUR, 2012

Designer Phillip Lim warmly embraces the practical, functional aspect of the fashion equation, and it's been critical to his success. Since launching 3.1 with business partner Wen Zhou in 2005—both were thirty-one at the time, hence the name—he's catapulted to the top of the established designers with his intuition for, and command of, easy, unfussy clothes that women simply want to wear. His approach to accessories is the same.

An entirely utilitarian bag, Lim's knockout Pashli satchel launched with the Fall 2011 collection, "Girls on Bikes," and was inspired by the idea of a cool girl biking around the city. This is the bag Lim imagined accompanying her from morning meetings to dinner and drinks. Crafted from shark-embossed calfskin, the style features distinctive hardware and practical double-zips that allow the silhouette to expand for a more casual look, reflecting a day-to-night versatility.

Its more streamlined cousin, the 31 Hour tote, launched in spring 2012, is less structured, almost squishy, with a zipped-top fold-over lip. Inspired by Russian nesting dolls, it has a matching portfolio case that fits inside the bag and a small cosmetic pouch that fits inside the case; both double as clutches. The name references the brand itself as well as the thirty-one-hour lifestyle of the Phillip Lim girl, who's constantly connected and on the go.

Both bags were blockbusters, covetable for the cool street-wise designs at affordable prices. Years after their debut, as retailer after retailer can attest, the bags continue to be bestsellers. "[Our bags] are quiet, simple and functional, but don't forsake design," Lim told *Women's Wear Daily* in 2012. "I just want a bag that will work with our consumer and let her get through the day. It's not the most expensive, it's not the least expensive, it's not the most luxurious, but it's luxurious enough. It's a modern choice for that modern person."

OPPOSITE:
Pashli bag, 3.1 Phillip Lim, New York City, September 2013.

"Designing accessories is like sculpting: How to make something supple yet rigid, and inject it with desirability."

—PHILLIP LIM, *The Business Times Singapore*, January 4, 2014

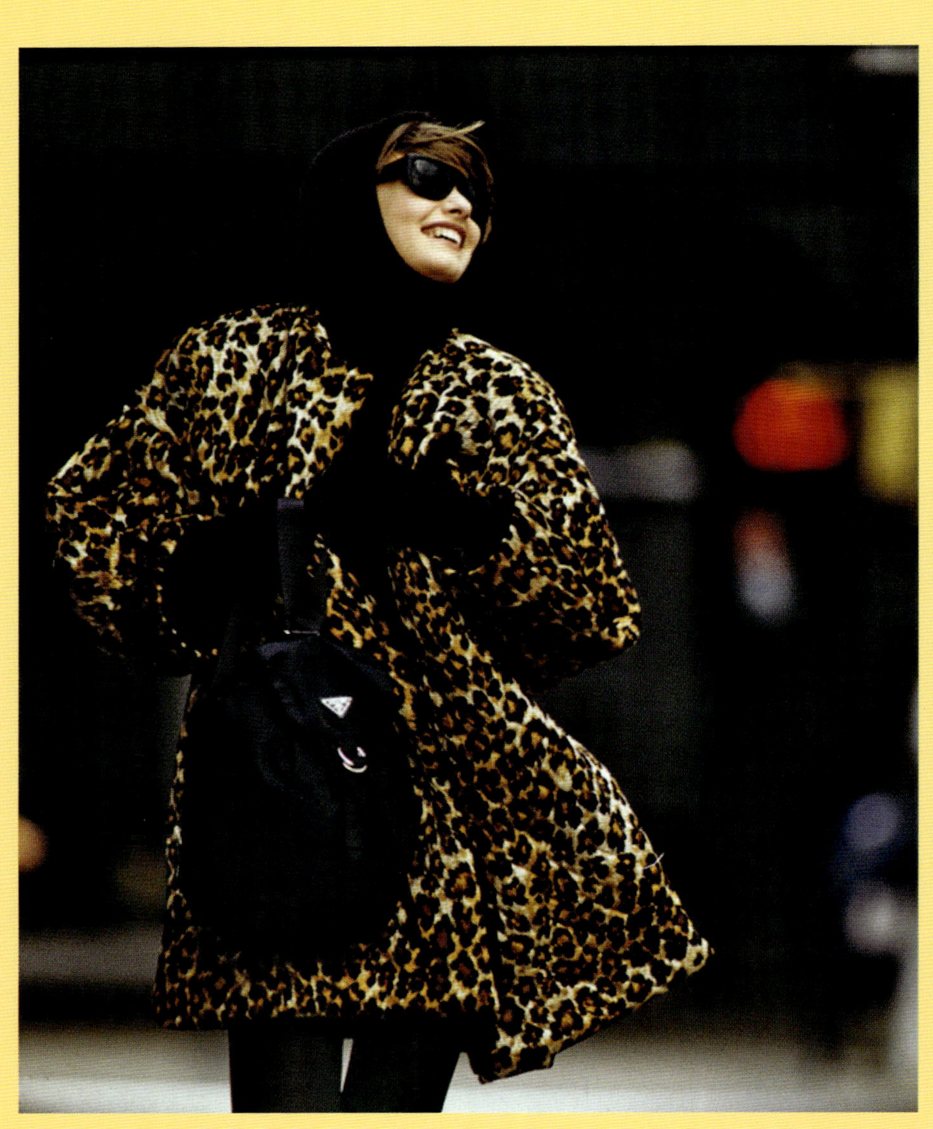

Prada

NYLON BACKPACK, 1984

In 1913 Mario Prada opened the Prada leather shop in Milan's glass-vaulted Galleria Vittorio Emanuele II shopping arcade. Six years later, he became an official supplier to the Italian royal family and aristocratic patrons soon followed. The 1920s and 1930s—when luxury travel was on the rise—was a flush time for the company, which was famous for well-made suitcases and steamer trunks of walrus skin fitted with tortoiseshell and ivory accessories. When Mario died in 1958, there was no real successor. His son chose instead to run his own business, and the firm descended to his daughter-in-law Luisa, who was raising three children. The Prada name waned; there was no design innovation during those years, and unlike Gucci, Prada did not have celebrity associations and was little known outside Italy.

Prada's granddaughter Miuccia, who would eventually take the firm to new heights, never intended to go into fashion. She received a doctorate in political science from the University of Milan, joined the Communist Party, and was a mime at Milan's Piccolo Teatro for several years. In the 1970s she began working at the family's leather company and, at a trade fair in 1978, met Patrizio Bertelli, who owned a leather factory in Tuscany. She gave him the exclusive license to manufacture Prada's leather goods. In 1987 they wed. Today Bertelli is as much a driving force behind the Prada empire as Miuccia. He is the business side; she, the creative. Together, they have transformed the business into a worldwide phenomenon.

In 1984, while high fashion was a dizzying spin of shoulder pads, Lacroix pouf skirts, and gold chains, Miuccia Prada released a black nylon backpack. Wholly utilitarian, made from the same material that the military uses for tents and parachutes, and even sewn on the same machines used for the Italian army's gear—the bag was out of step with the era's decadence and appetite for luxury. It didn't really become an object of desire until the 1990s, when the collections of Calvin Klein, Helmut Lang, and Jil Sander ushered in a return to minimalism. Prada's anti-status backpack quickly became emblematic of the trend.

"I come from a background of leather, and I thought it was really boring and old. I like industrial things, and I found a very special fabric that was both technological and beautiful," recalled Prada. "It took six or seven years to convince anyone to work with it, because they couldn't stitch it, but then the workmanship turned out to be very good. The nylon bags were more expensive than the leather bags. That was the beginning of what was interesting for me," she told the *Los Angeles Times* in 2004.

Prada is one of the few designers—Marc Jacobs is another—who has the creative force and influence to be able to change themes from season to season, and therein lies her genius. For handbag lovers, it means a medley of unique hits whose common thread is Prada's ability to realign our notions of desire and beauty. We're hit with the familiar and the unexpected at the same time—and in this case, vaulting humble nylon to lustworthy heights.

OPPOSITE:
Nylon backpack, Prada, *Vogue*, August 1989.

PAGE 188:
Nylon backpack, Prada, 1984.

PAGE 189:
Various nylon bags, Prada, Resort 2008.

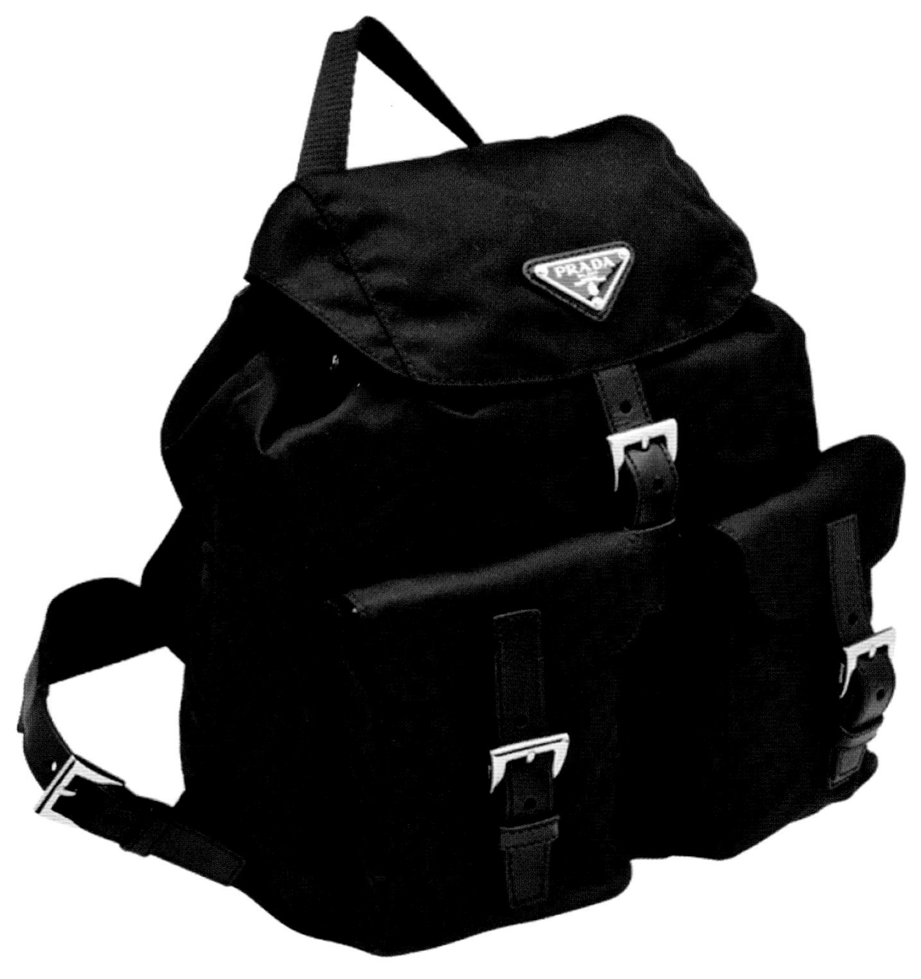

"I was a feminist in the '60s and can you imagine? The worst I could have done was to be in fashion."

—MIUCCIA PRADA, *Newsweek*, May 7, 2012

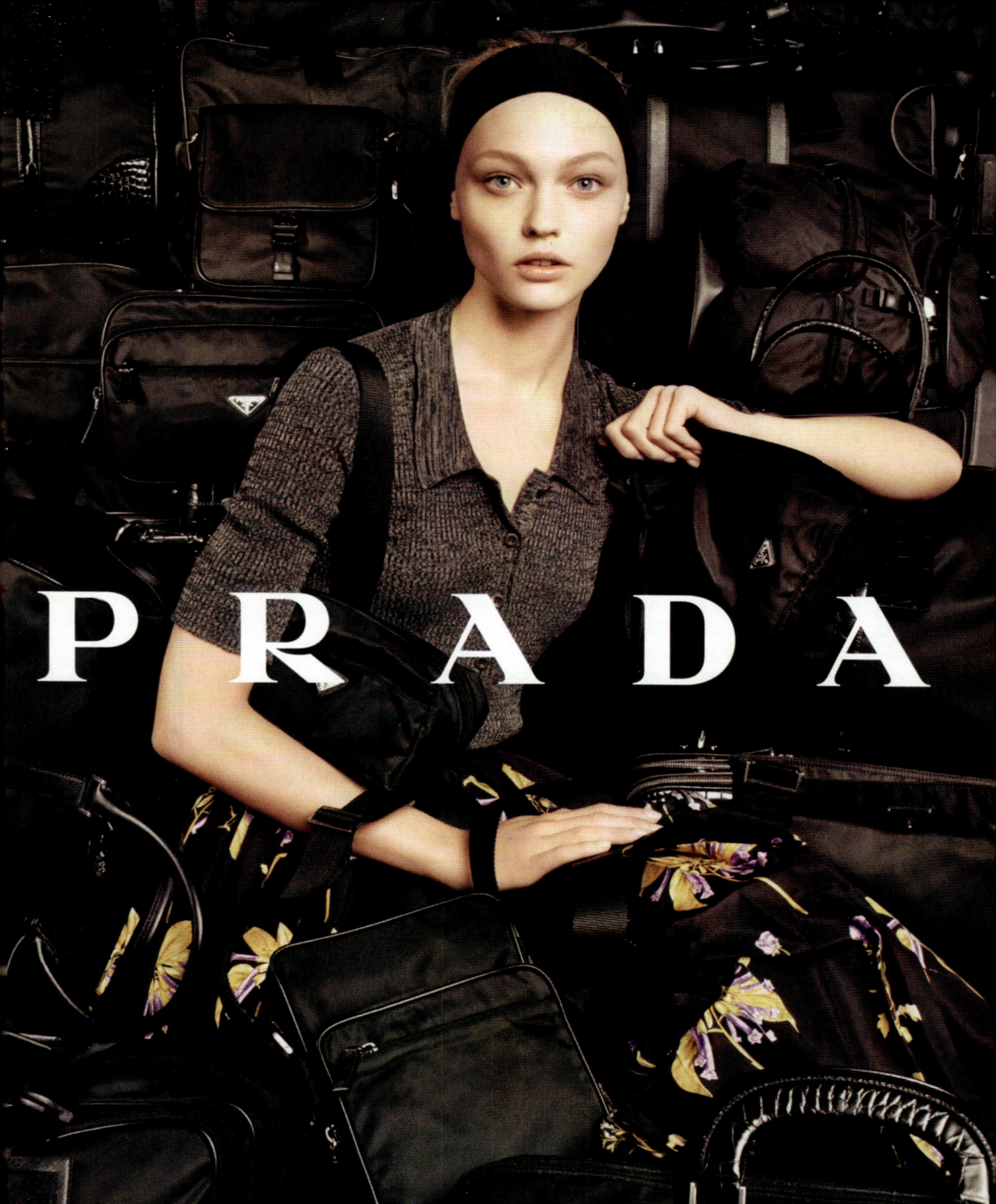
PRADA

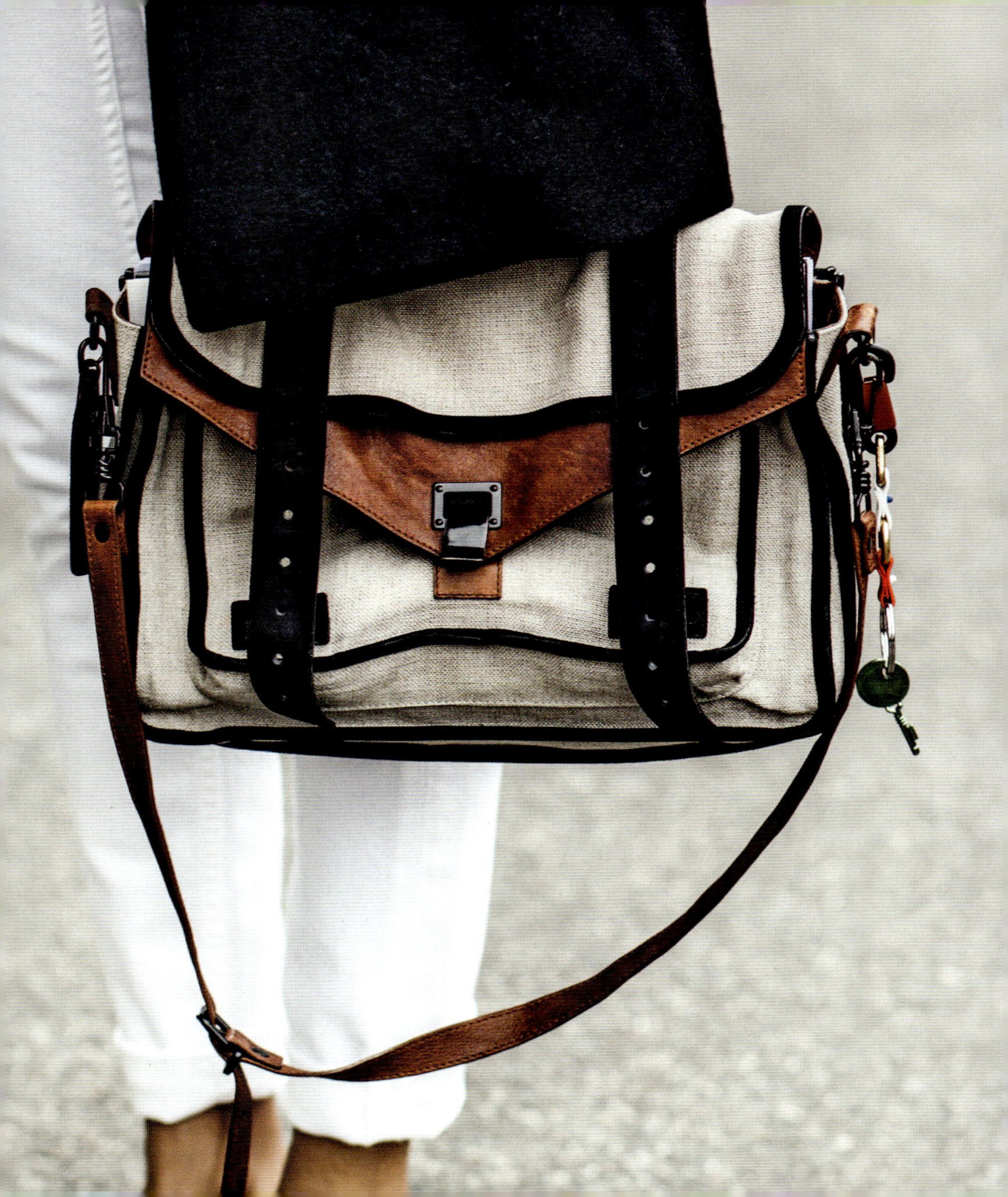

Proenza Schouler

PS1, 2008

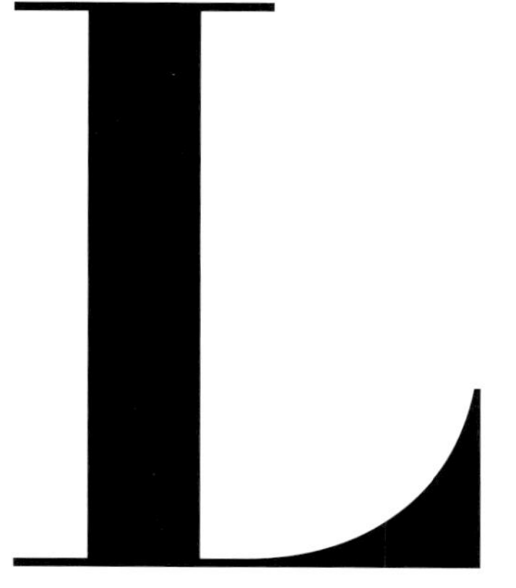

Lazaro Hernandez and Jack McCollough met while studying at Parsons School of Design. In 2002 the college gave them permission to collaborate on their senior thesis, and the result was the first collection for Proenza Schouler, named after their mothers' maiden names. Barneys New York picked up the entire collection.

The PS1—part of the firm's first handbag line, launched in 2008—cemented the duo's status as designers with both commercial and creative appeal. The PS1 is an impeccably designed vintage-style schoolboy satchel with utilitarian straps and buckles. The leather is supple and butter soft; while the hardware treatments are minimal, there is a beautifully polished subtle S-shaped metal clasp in the center that draws attention—not unlike the curved sculptures by Richard Serra that McCollough and Hernandez love to reference in their designs. The name is a nod to New York City, the place where the brand was born, and also references the naming system of its public schools. At a time when old-guard designer handbags dominated the scene, the PS1's slouchy schoolboy aesthetic stood out—and in a chic step-to-the-beat-of-a-different-drummer way.

Instead of targeting the runway for launch, they gave prototypes to their close female friends for a test run in New York, asking them to keep mum about their provenance. Holding back on the bag's debut was an excellent strategy, as everyone wanted what they couldn't get, increasing its covetability. When the bag debuted, it was an instant classic. "When you show a bag [that way] it kind of becomes old news the next season, and we wanted to do this classic item," explained McCollough to *Women's Wear Daily* in 2013.

The two have since launched other handbag collections—like the bag on the opposite page—that all use the PS1 as the foundation for their design. "Once you have a family and new codes, it's really easy to build upon that, because there is a world now," McCollough explained to *Women's Wear Daily* in 2016. "It's the beginning, creating that idea is the tricky part."

OPPOSITE:
PS1 bag, Proenza Schouler, Paris, 2013.

> "Our teachers at school hated us. We were the worst students. We got into fights with them. That kind of spirit stays with us today."
>
> —LAZARO HERNANDEZ, harpersbazaar.com, April 6, 2015

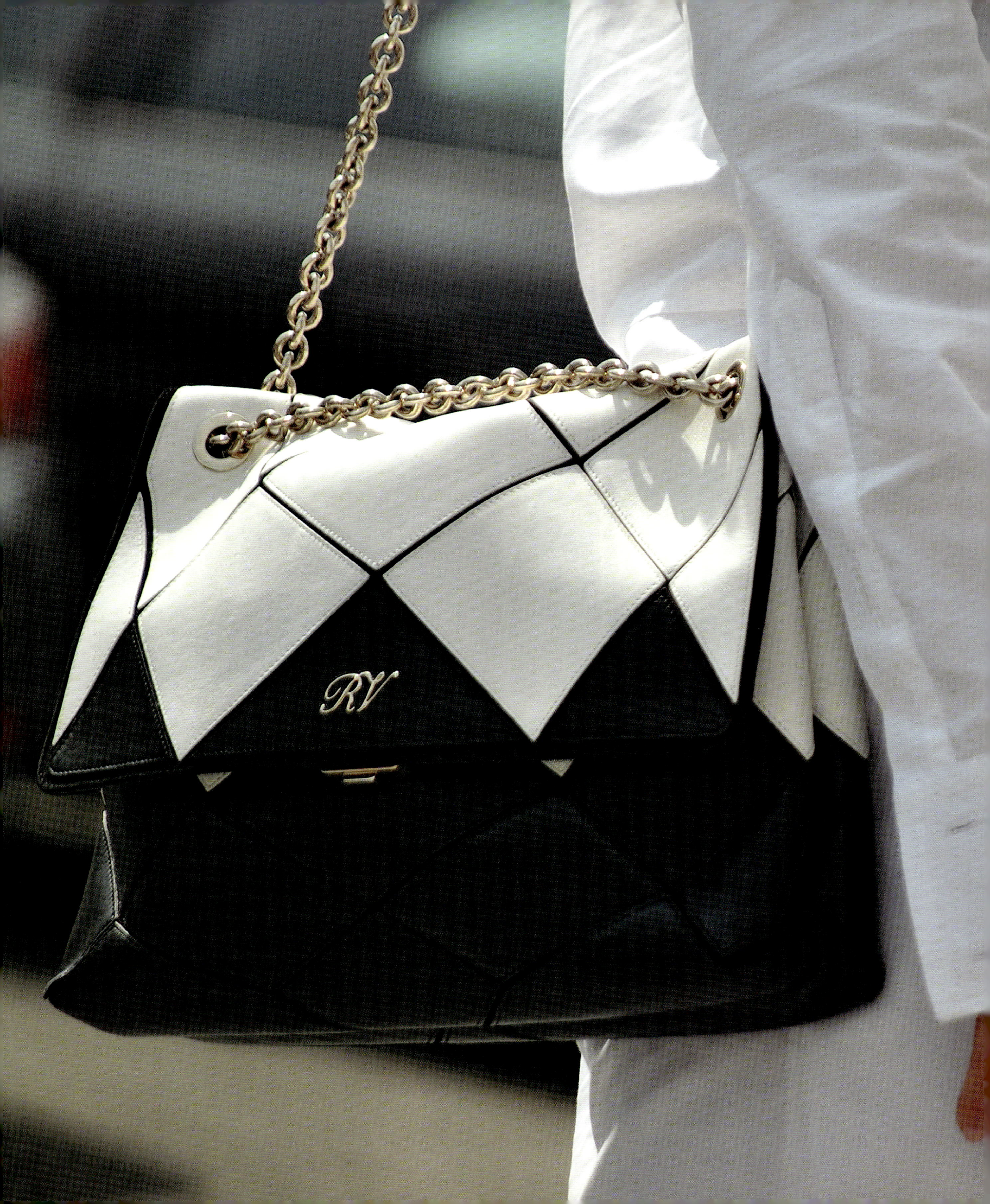
RV

Bruno Frisoni for Roger Vivier

PRISMICK, 2012

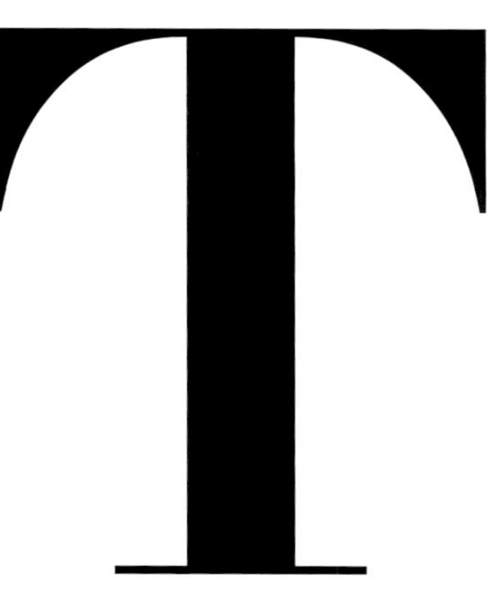

he celebrated history of Roger Vivier begins with the shoemaker founder himself, who's credited with inventing the modern stiletto. The house, founded in 1937, has had many illustrious clients, including Brigitte Bardot, Marlene Dietrich, Audrey Hepburn, and Elizabeth Taylor. In Luis Buñuel's classic *Belle de Jour* (1967), Catherine Deneuve leads a double life in a pair of black patent Roger Vivier pumps topped with a massive gold buckle. That shoe has remained iconic, even after Vivier died in 1998 and fashion magnate Diego Della Valle of Tod's took over the firm, installing Bruno Frisoni as creative director and model Inès de la Fressange as ambassador.

The futuristic-looking Prismick, introduced in 2012, was based on the faceted 2008 Navette clutch. There are multiple versions—flap clutches, totes, bucket bags—all with the identifying gemstone-cut graphics; some styles rework the lines as quilting patterns for an appearance that's bold yet ladylike. All that geometric precision, the equivalent of seeing a bag through a prism, is an ode to Vivier's love of collage and his brilliance with elegant, nimble construction—exemplified in the way he curved the heel just so to create his trademark sexy Virgule shoe, named after the French word for "comma," which was developed with aeronautical engineers.

The Prismick is a similar combination of imagination and innovation. Its assembly is a highly intricate process that can be done only by hand and results in a modern, streamlined silhouette. Put simply, artisans begin by measuring and cutting each geometric facet of the gemlike bag. Then they carefully piece and sew it together based on its pattern, almost like putting together a jigsaw puzzle. The Prismick has been offered in suede, python, and napa in a variety of colors, from single- and two-tone to more kaleidoscopic patterns. There's another level of ingenuity here, too. Frisoni's Prismick series has demonstrated that the designer could create a new iconography for the house while honoring its founder's love of collage. While Vivier's iconic buckle is still front and center on many a bag, Frisoni has created a new cult classic.

OPPOSITE:
Prismick bag, Roger Vivier, Paris, 2013.

PAGE 195:
Roger Vivier poster by Antoine + Manuel, 2009.

"By all means match the color of your bag and shoes if you are under thirty. After that, prepare to age ten years."

—INÈS DE LA FRESSANGE, *Parisian Chic: A Style Guide*, 2011

rogerVivier

ROGER VIVIER
PARIS

VIVIER

PARIS

ROGER
VIVIER
PARIS

Vivier

VIVIER PARIS

rogerVivier
PARIS

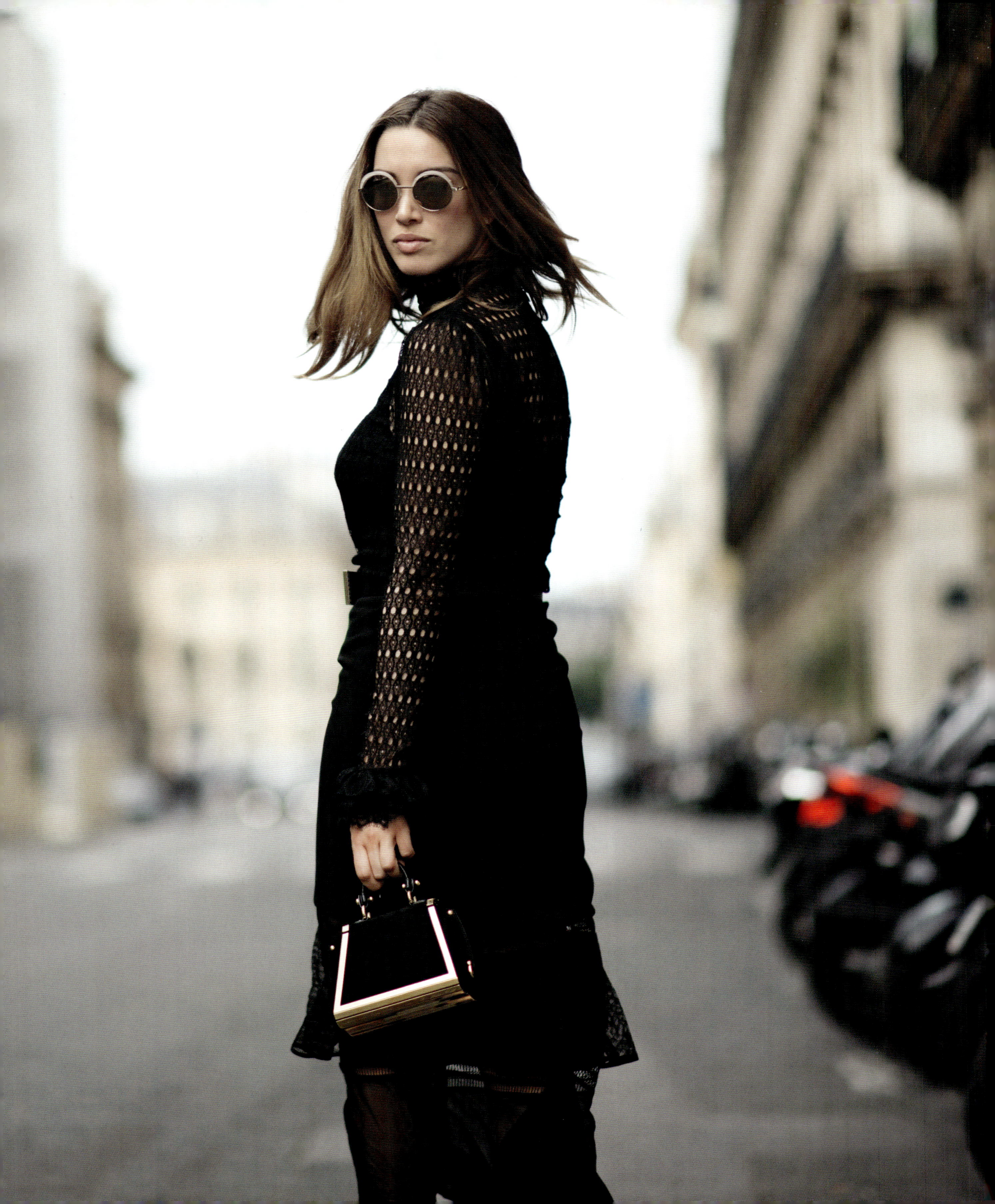

Salvatore Ferragamo

GANCIO TOP-HANDLE BAG, 1990
FIAMMA, 2014

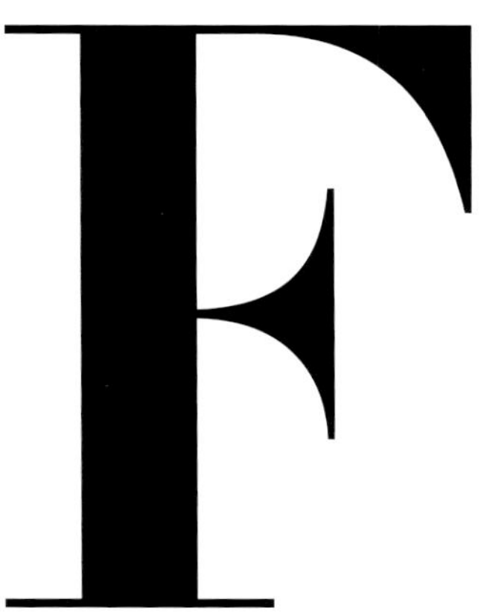

erragamo is one of Italy's famous family-run firms, and Salvatore Ferragamo's tale is legendary. Born in Bonito, the eleventh of fourteen children, he knew he wanted to become a shoemaker from an early age. At nine, he made his sister's First Communion shoes. At eleven, he was apprenticed to a shoemaker in Naples. By the time he was sixteen, he had joined his brothers in the United States to learn more about the business.

In 1914 Ferragamo worked at a shoe factory in Boston and five years later moved to Santa Barbara, an emerging center for the film industry. His first job there was to make cowboy boots for the American Film Manufacturing Company, also known as Flying "A" Studios. When moviemaking moved to Hollywood, so did Ferragamo, who opened a shop on Hollywood Boulevard in Beverly Hills. He continued to make shoes for movies such as Cecil B. DeMille's *The Ten Commandments* (1956) and garnered a clientele of loyal Hollywood stars, including Marlene Dietrich, Greta Garbo, Mary Pickford, and Gloria Swanson.

As his reputation grew, so did his orders, with department stores Saks Fifth Avenue and I. Magnin knocking on his door. But unable to find enough skilled artisans, Ferragamo returned to Italy in 1927. The following year the company Salvatore Ferragamo was officially launched in Florence. In the ensuing decades, Ferragamo came up with one footwear innovation after another, such as metal shanks for arch support and invisible sole stitching, and experimented with novel shoe materials like plaited raffia, crochet, wicker, straw, fish skins, cork, and candy wrappers—materials he turned to when leather was scarce during World War II.

The company didn't really enter the handbag scene until 1965, five years after his death, when his daughter Fiamma, who had trained with him in the atelier, launched a line for the house. Among her early styles was the Salvatore, a big doctor's bag with zippered side pockets that was inspired by a bag her father used to carry his footwear prototypes.

But it wasn't until 1990 that Ferragamo made a real impact with a hit bag. Previously, Fiamma's attentions were set on innovating the footwear business, proving to buyers and clients she was a worthy successor to her father. In 1978, for instance, she designed the Vara shoe, topped with a flattened grosgrain bow—a detail now seen on handbags as well. In 1990 Fiamma created the now-iconic Gancio, originally called the Gancino, a trapezoidal ladylike satchel that was crafted from myriad materials—wicker, plaited calfskin, Plexiglas, and crocodile, among others—and is emblematic of the brand's polished elegance. Its defining feature is the horseshoe-like Gancino logo. According to *Salvatore Ferragamo—Evolving Legend, 1928–2008* (2009), the design was inspired by the wrought iron gates of the Palazzo Spini Feroni, Florence, where the Ferragamo offices are based. Since then Ferragamo has created such popular bags as the Lotty and the Sofia, named after Sophia Loren, born Sofia Villani Scicolone. The Fiamma, a rounded top-handle design with a lock closure, is named in honor of Fiamma, who passed away in 1998.

OPPOSITE:
Mini Sofia bag, Salvatore Ferragamo, Paris, July 2016.

PAGES 198–199:
Gancio top-handle bags have been made from a wide range of materials over the years, including—but not limited to—wicker, wood, various plastics, brushed and dyed steel, and exotic skins.

PAGE 200:
Black leather and straw-fringe tote, Salvatore Ferragamo, date unknown.

PAGE 201:
Audrey Hepburn with Salvatore Ferragamo and his wife Wanda, Italy, August 1954.

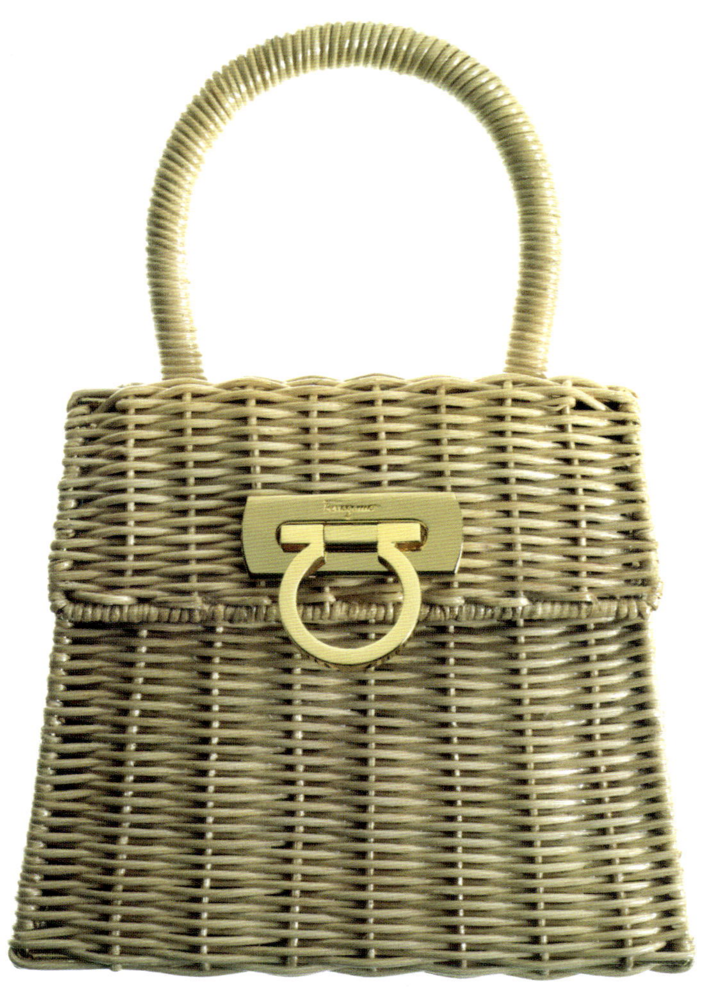

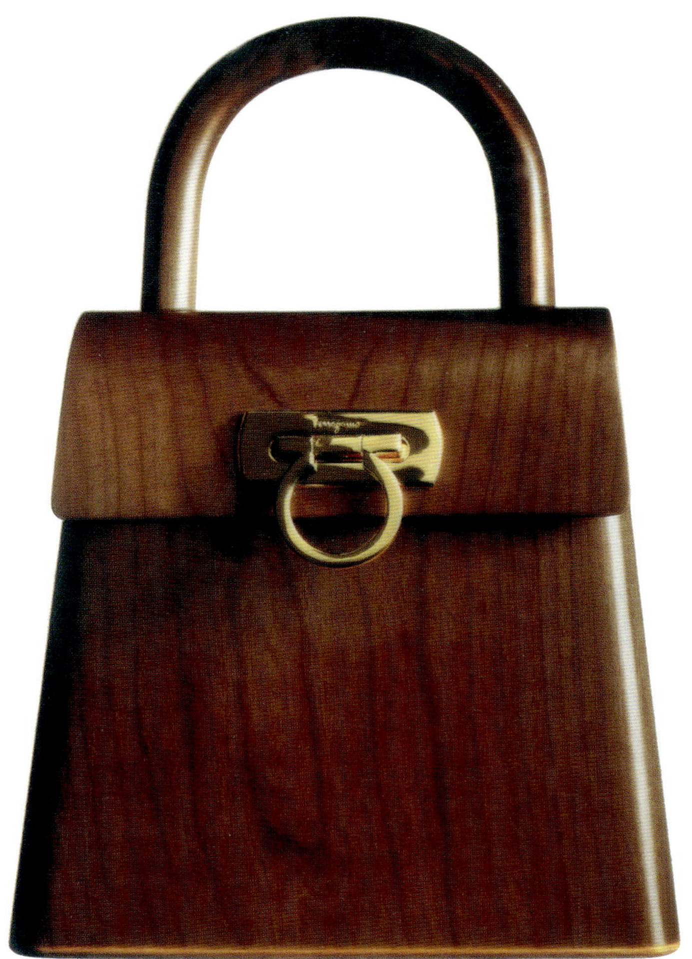

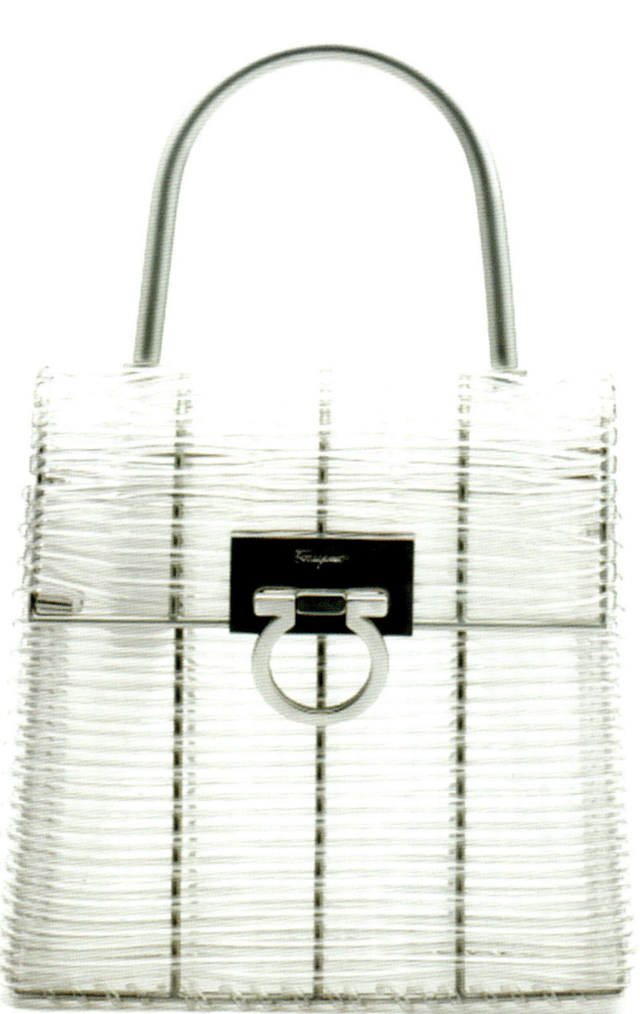

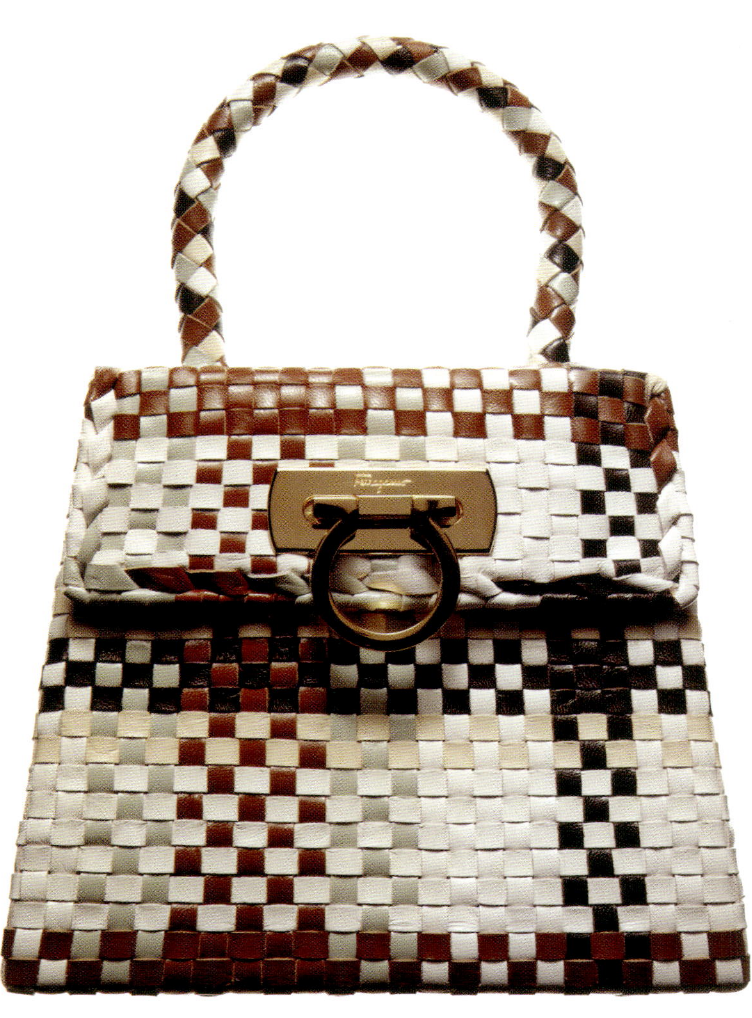

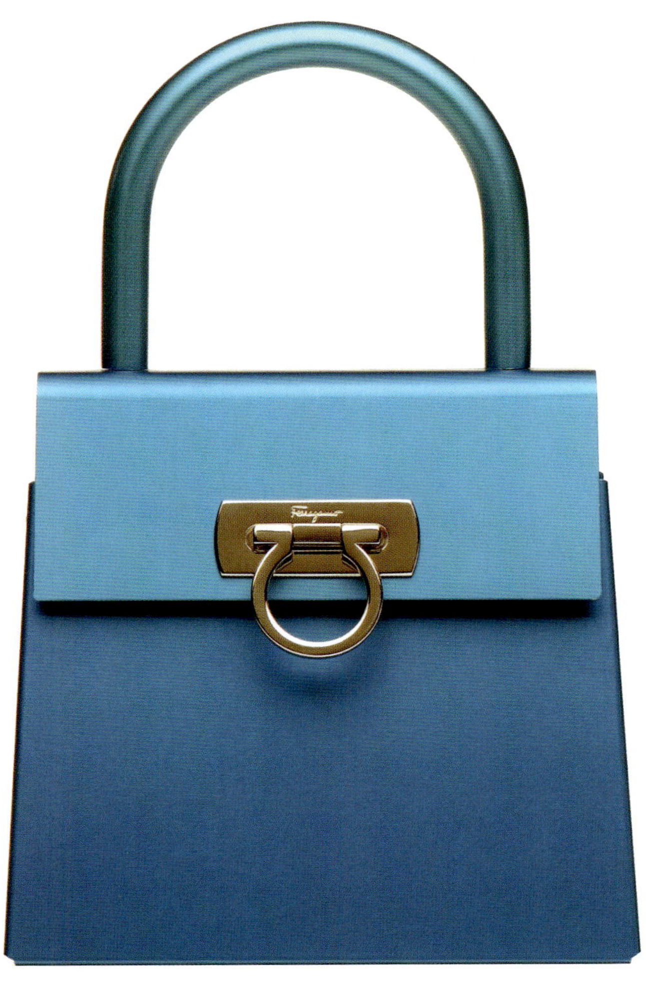

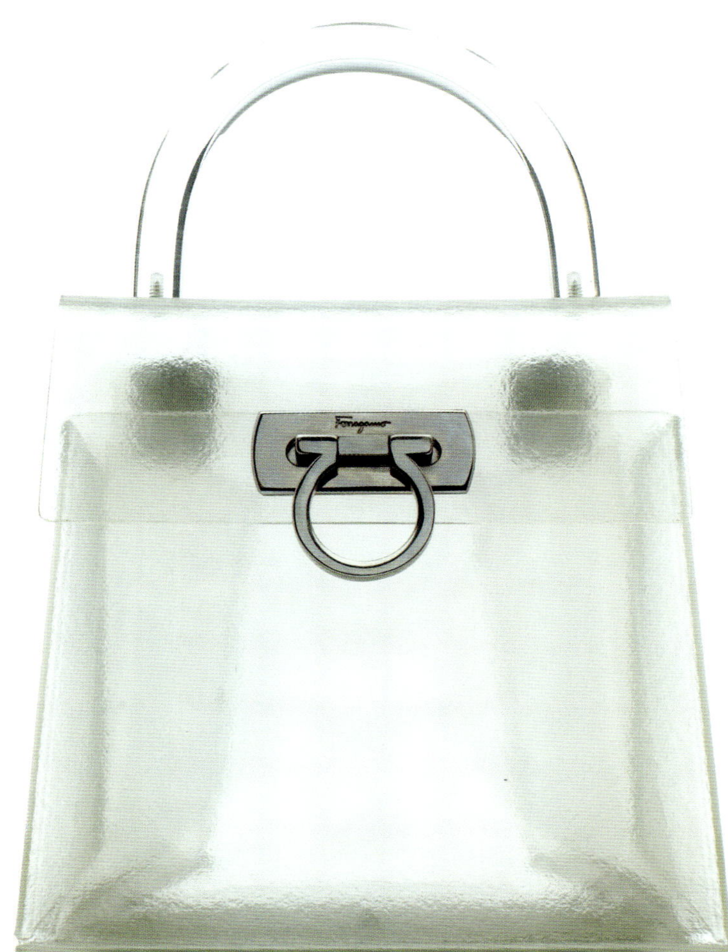

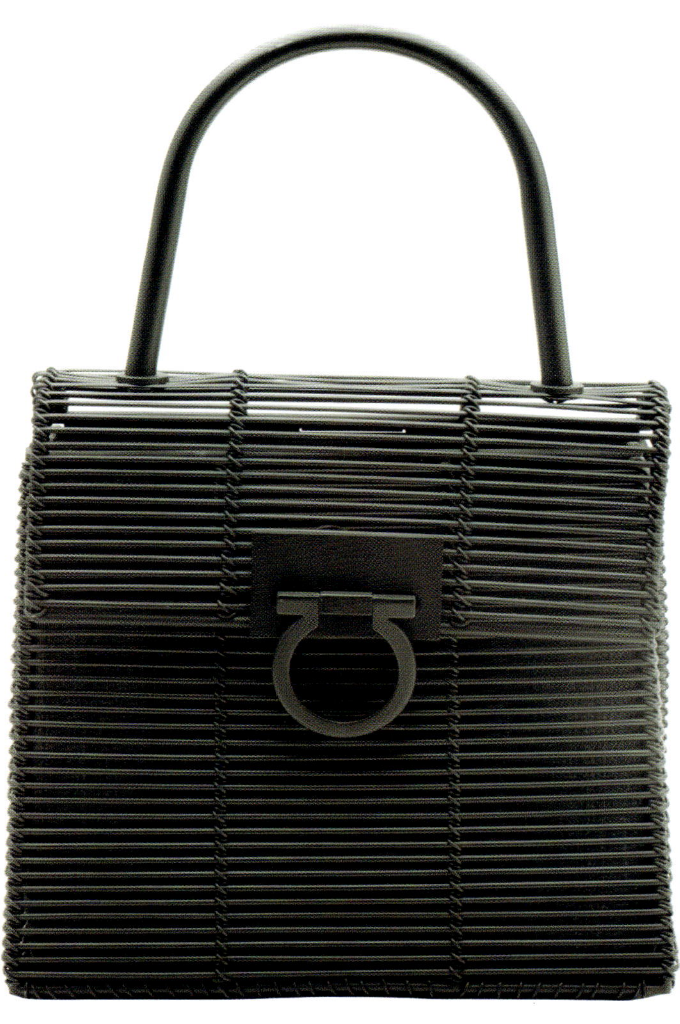

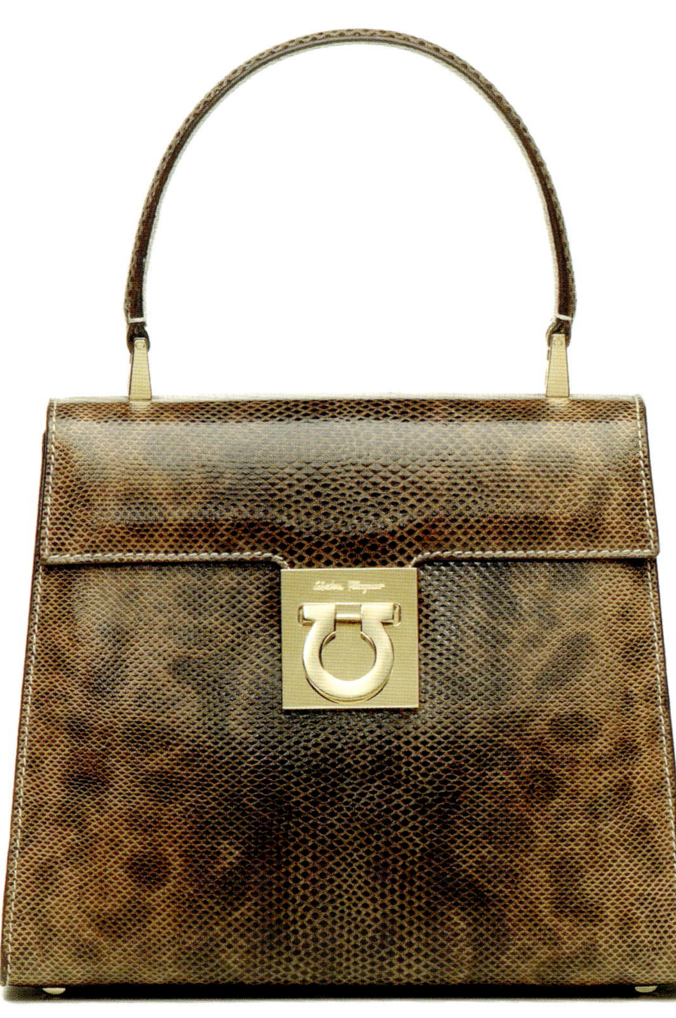

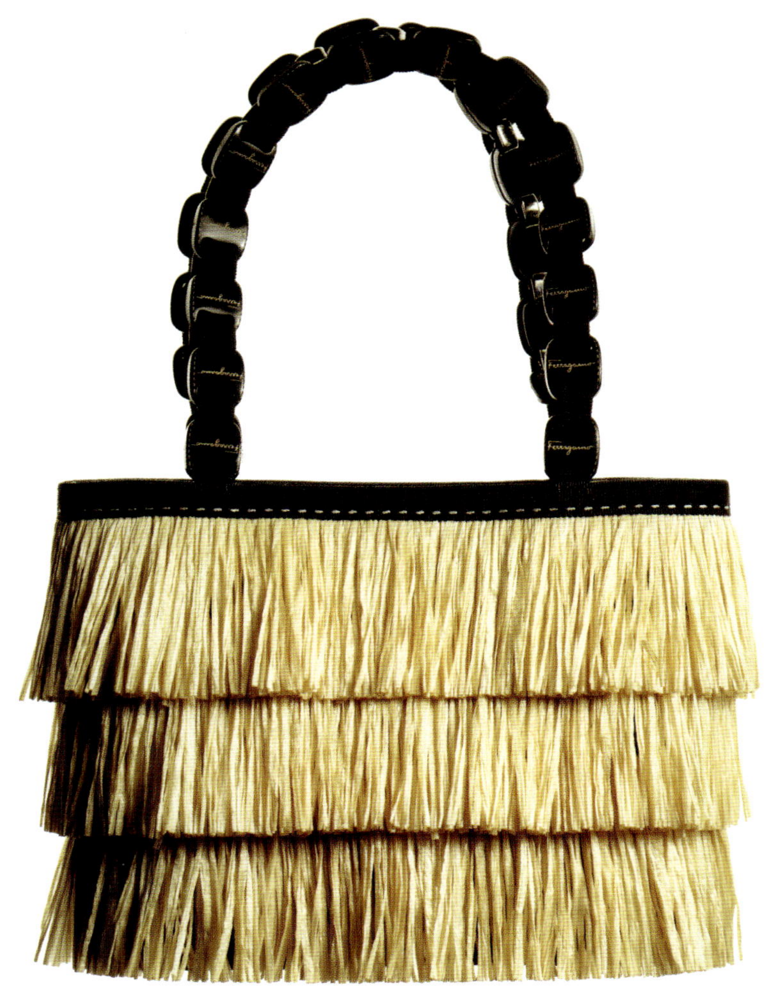

“If designers must wait for their customers to become conscious of new styles, who, then, determines fashion? The answer is: new fashion begins in the mind of the designer.”

—SALVATORE FERRAGAMO, *Shoemaker of Dreams*, 1985

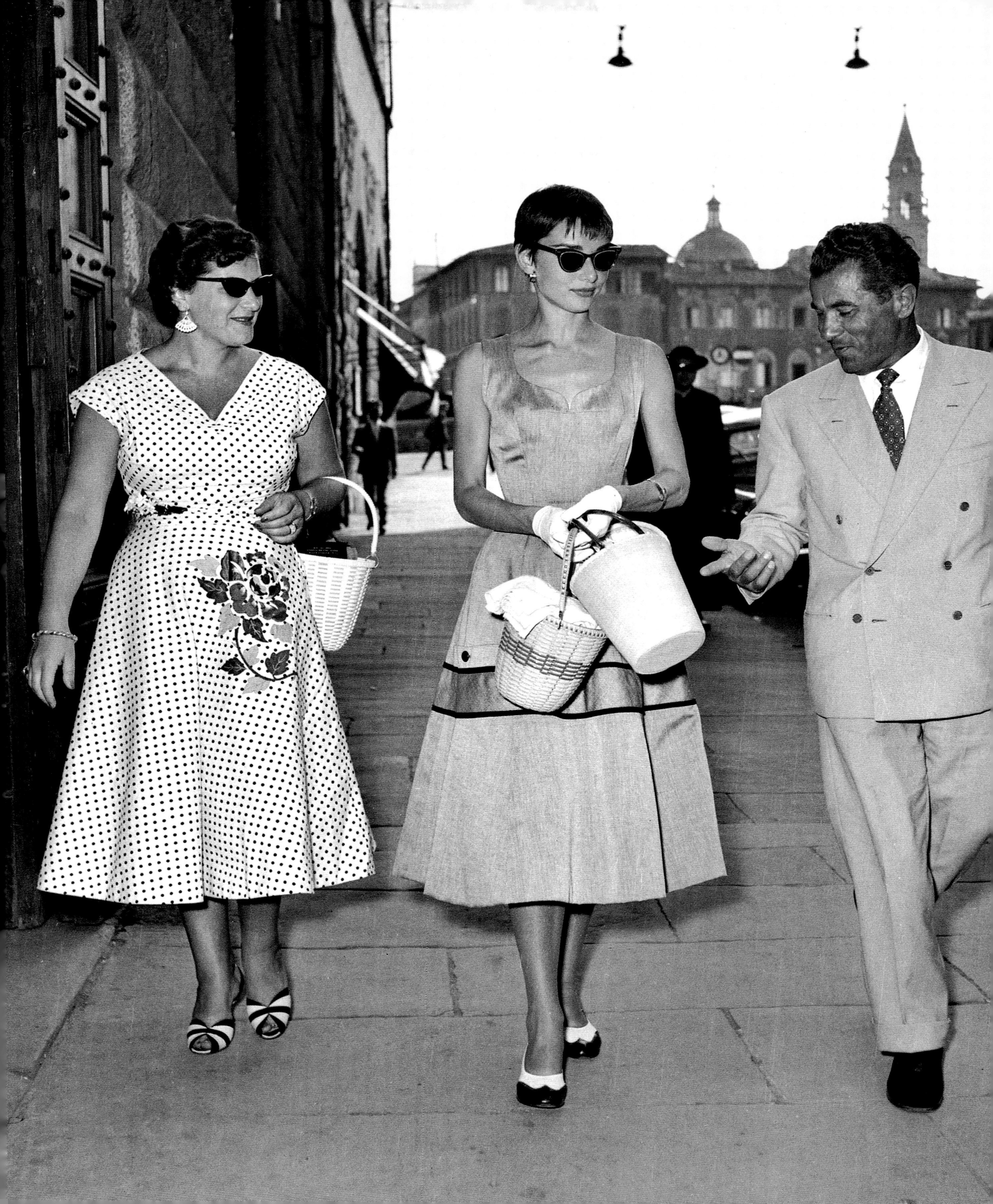

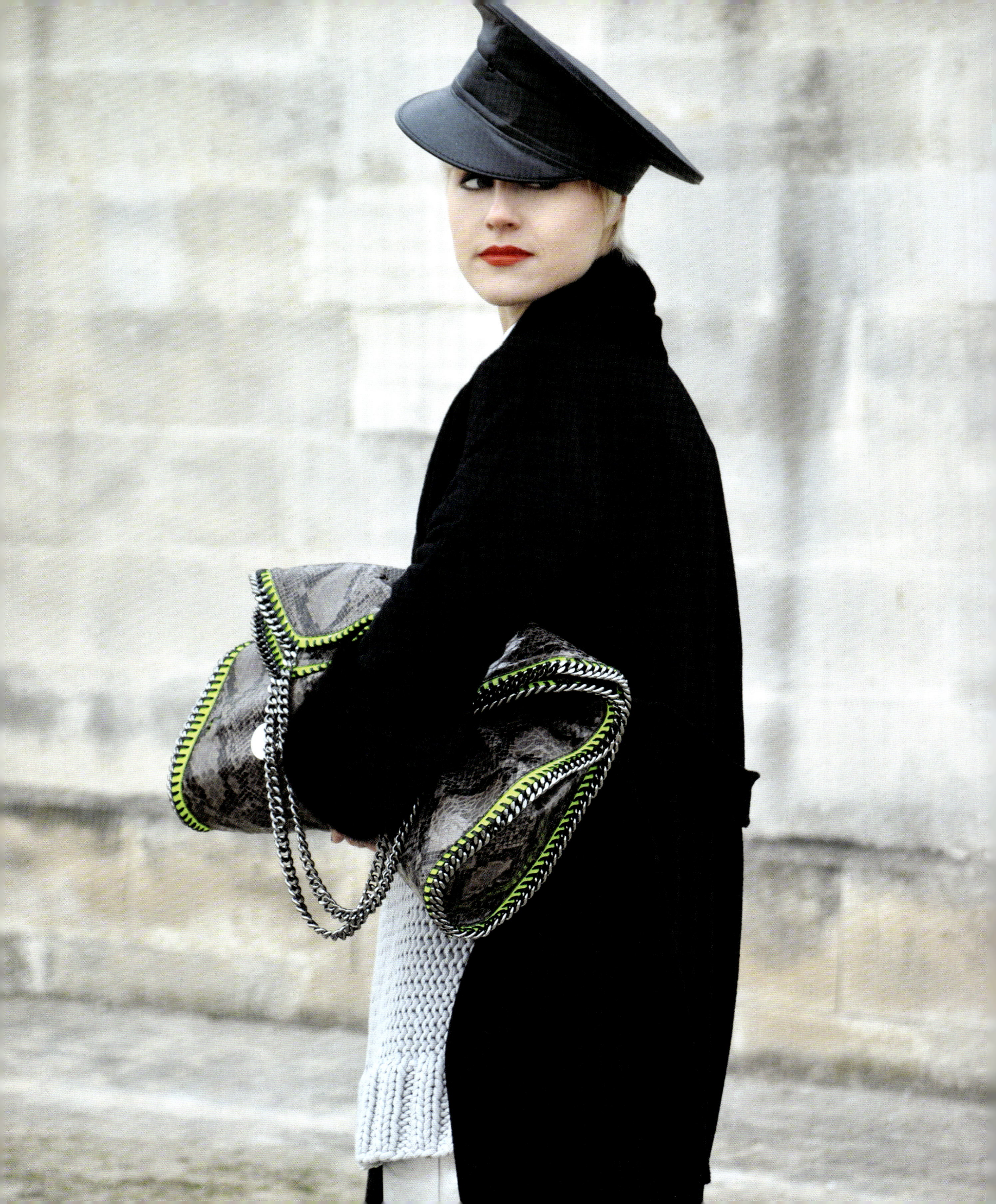

Stella McCartney

FALABELLA, 2009

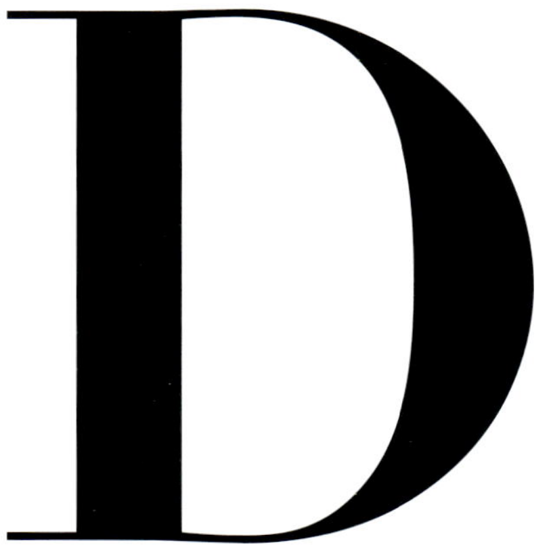ecades ago, if you told anyone it was possible to build a successful handbag business without leather, you would have been laughed out of the room. But that was before vegan Stella McCartney became a force in the fashion industry, using her influence to pave the way for an animal-friendly yet covetable collection, the Falabella.

The designer's environmentally conscious values are deeply ingrained, as her famous parents, legendary Beatle Paul McCartney and photographer Linda McCartney, were committed vegetarians and advocates for animal rights. McCartney is equally passionate and has channeled her lifelong personal beliefs into a company mission. "From day one, I was never going to compromise or be hypocritical," she explained to the *South China Morning Post* in 2013. "I don't eat animals for ethical reasons; why would I kill them to make a handbag?"

Sticking to cruelty-free animal products is a hard enough proposition in ready-to-wear, but it's almost impossible in accessories, which hinge so heavily on leather. McCartney herself was told as much by her former CEO James Seuss. "It's a real struggle and people can't get their heads around it," he told *Women's Wear Daily* in 2012. But she kept at it, delivering one style after another: the coated cotton-and-velvet Appaloosa bag of 2006; the Losina patent camera bag of 2007. She uses feathers only if they come from a supplier who collects them after they naturally fall from the bird—no plucking—and cruelty-free silks that are removed after the silkworm has emerged from the cocoon.

She struck gold in 2009 with the Falabella, a coated Lycra tote with a single chain link that trims the sides and forms a handle up top. There are cotton, wool, polyester, and linen versions meant to

OPPOSITE:
Falabella, Stella McCartney, 2013.

RIGHT:
Stella McCartney carrying her own Falabella, London, February 2011.

> "Being brought up on an organic farm and having a different way of looking at life comes into everything that I do."
>
> —STELLA MCCARTNEY, *Vanity Fair*, September 2012

mimic fur and python. "The funny thing, what I always find strange about the leather industry, is that actually a lot of it doesn't look like leather anyway," said McCartney to *Women's Wear Daily* in 2012. "There are a lot of treatments you can do and apply to a base. Most people just apply that to a leather base and we apply it to another base."

The Falabella tapped into the market at the perfect time, when "sustainability" and "eco-consciousness" were no longer buzzwords but a sought-after reality by companies and customers worldwide. In spring 2009, for instance, the *International Herald Tribune* organized the Sustainable Luxury Conference in New Delhi; that fall, *Vogue Italia* sponsored Citta dell'arte Fashion: Bio Ethical Sustainable Trend, a conference that brought the fashion, publishing, and manufacturing industries together in Biella, Italy, for a fashion show and panel discussion on the topic. Plus, no one does eco-style like McCartney; her innovative use of non-leather materials still delivers on great design.

McCartney's approach to design and manufacturing forced women—and the industry at large—to rethink luxury. She even convinced the holding company Kering, which has a stake in her firm, to publish an environmental profit-and-loss statement for all its brands. For the Spring 2013 Falabella collection, McCartney incorporated wool collected from sheep on her farm in the Cotswolds. The Itsy Bitsy Falabella, which features fluffy patterned piles, was named after two of her sheep: Itsy and Bitsy.

RIGHT: Paul McCartney and Linda McCartney with daughters *(from left)* Heather, Stella, and Mary in Rye, East Sussex, April 1976.

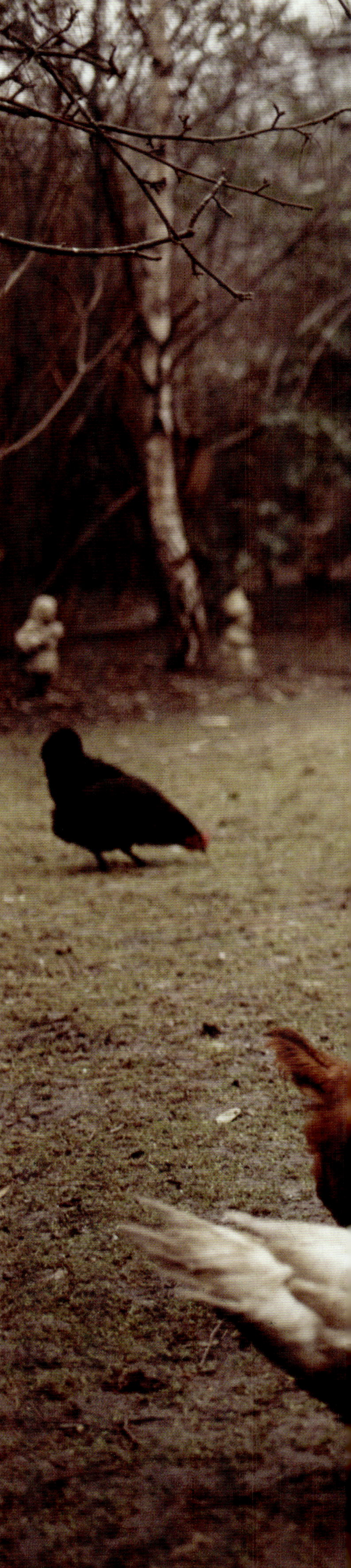

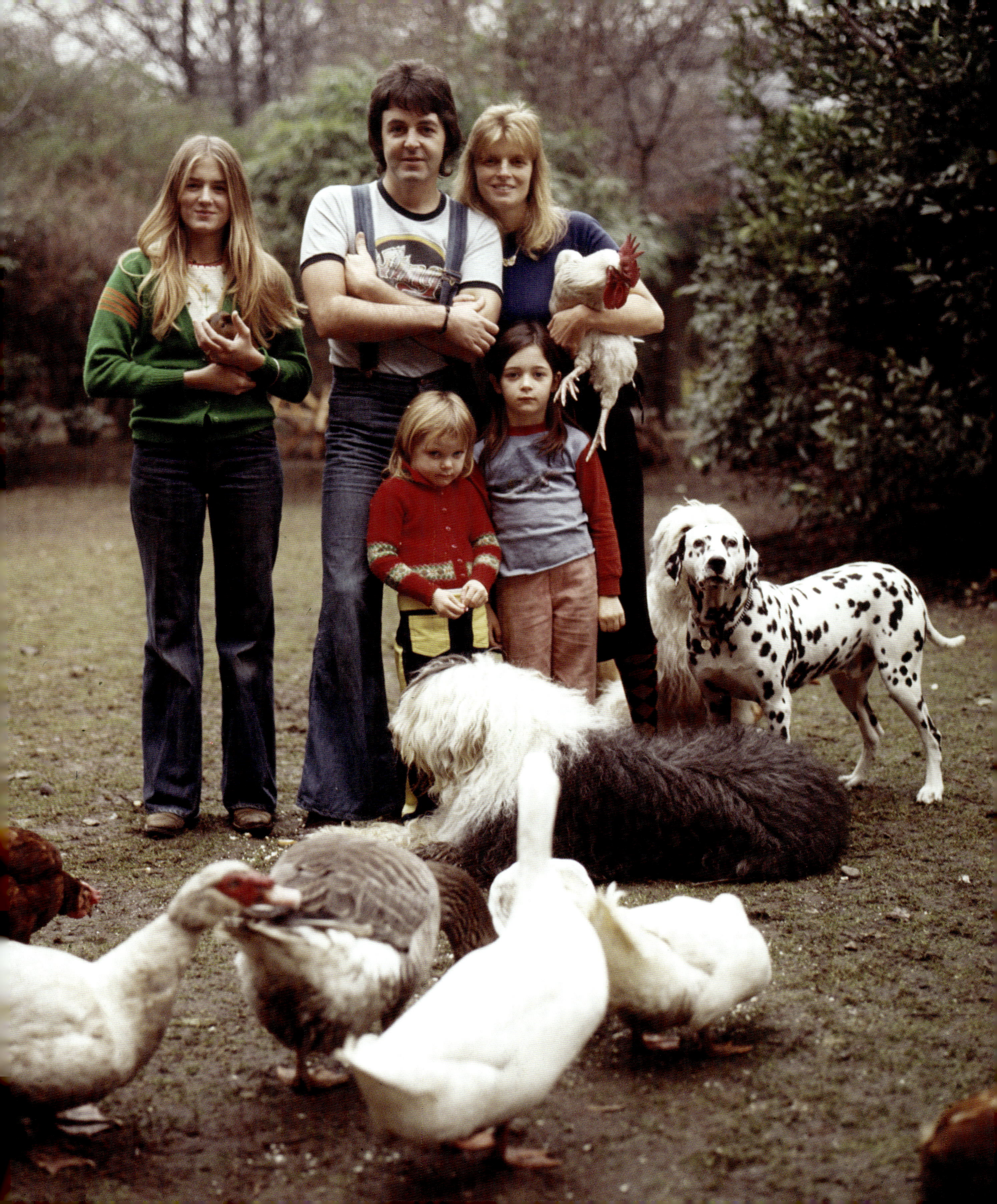

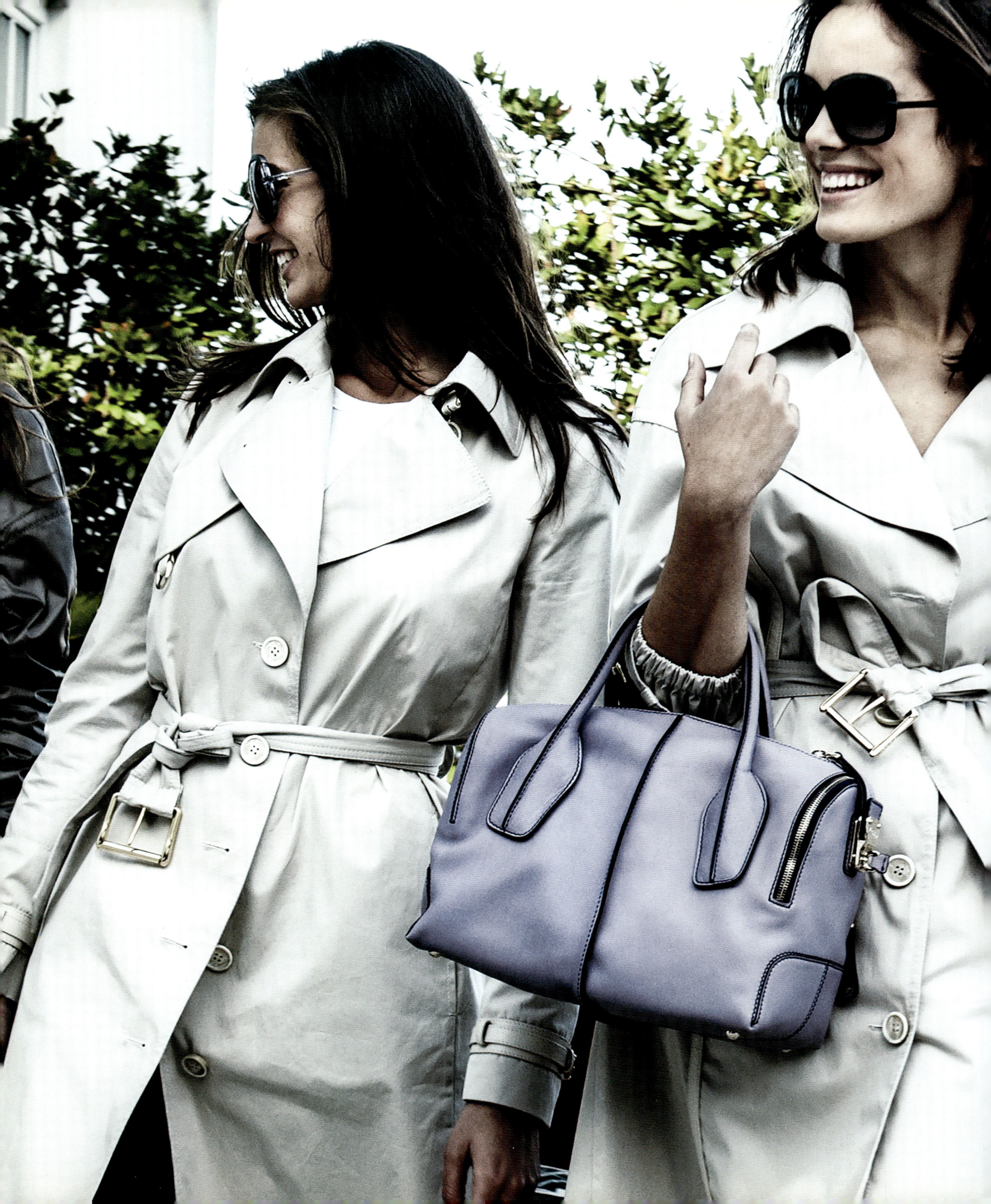

Tod's

D BAG, 1997

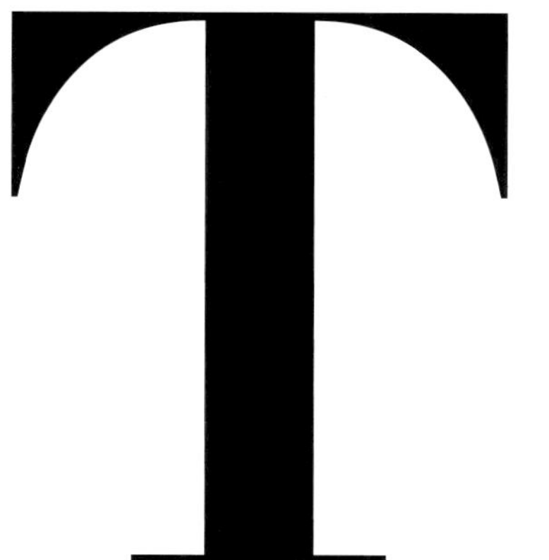
od's story begins with Filippo Della Valle, a cobbler from Casette d'Ete in the Italian region of Le Marche, a famed center of shoemaking. His son Dorino turned the family trade into a thriving shoe business in the 1920s with a factory that created private-label footwear for clients in Europe and the United States, including Bergdorf Goodman, Neiman Marcus, and Saks Fifth Avenue. But it wasn't until the third generation, with Dorino's son Diego Della Valle, that Tod's began to resemble the brand recognized the world over today.

In 1978 Diego renamed the firm with the decidedly non-Italian moniker J. P. Tod's, which he pulled from a Boston phone book. He wanted a name that would be easily pronounceable worldwide, including Japan. The initials eventually faded—the exact date is lost in the history books, though customers did notice. A 2004 *New Yorker* article noted, "Tod's still receives letters from concerned Japanese customers, wondering whether Mr. J. P. has died."

The brand represents an embrace of leisure luxury lifestyle—equal parts Italian jet set and sporty American casual chic. The iconic Tod's Gommino driving shoe, introduced by Diego in 1979—which features 133 tiny pebbles on the sole and catapulted the company to fame once Gianni Agnelli, the Fiat magnate and influential fashion plate, began wearing them—symbolizes that. In 1997, when the company launched its first line of handbags, it reinforced that theme, too, with a number of styles featuring the signature Gommino nubs as a design detail.

Tod's most famous style is its most classic: the D Bag, a simple and sturdy leather tote with intricate hand-stitching and hand-painted edge detailing. It's crafted using the same techniques adopted by traditional saddle makers. Each bag is finished with small steel nibs at the bottom, recalling the brand's signature Gommino shoe. A beautifully understated and sophisticated design, the D bag was named after Princess Diana, who was seen carrying the tote around London as well as on her philanthropic travels such as her visit to the Shaukat Khanum Memorial Cancer Hospital and Research Centre in Pakistan. In 2015 Della Valle added another classic that, like the D, marries Italian craftsmanship with American sportiness: the Wave, a softly structured bag with a rounded band. The rubber pebbles appear prominently as a design detail, once again evoking a sense of luxury and leisure.

OPPOSITE: D bag, Tod's, Fall 2009.

PAGES 208–209: Tod's advertisements, Fall 2001.

"Luxury is possible to buy. Good taste is not."

—DIEGO DELLA VALLE, *Forbes*, 2011

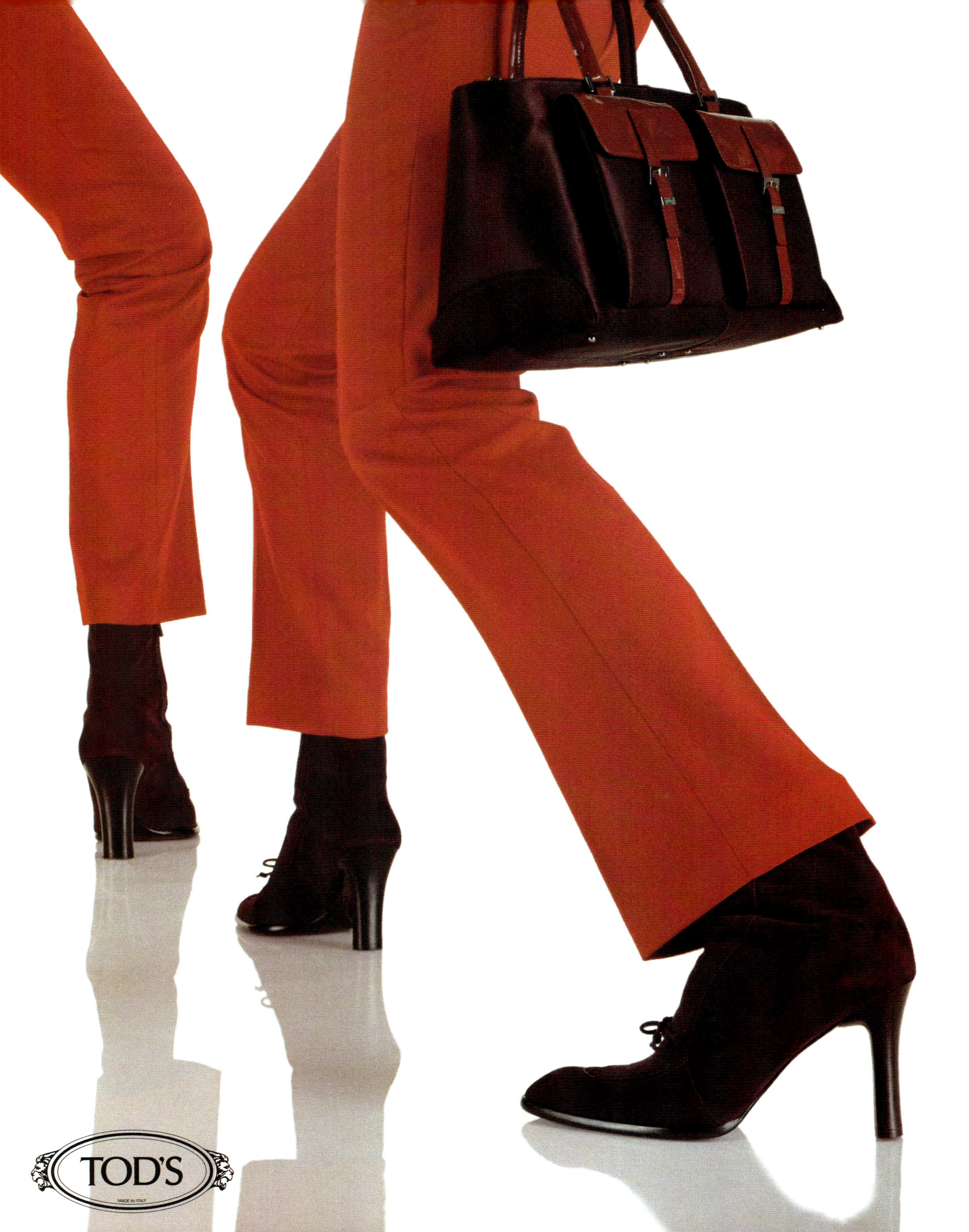
TOD'S
MADE IN ITALY

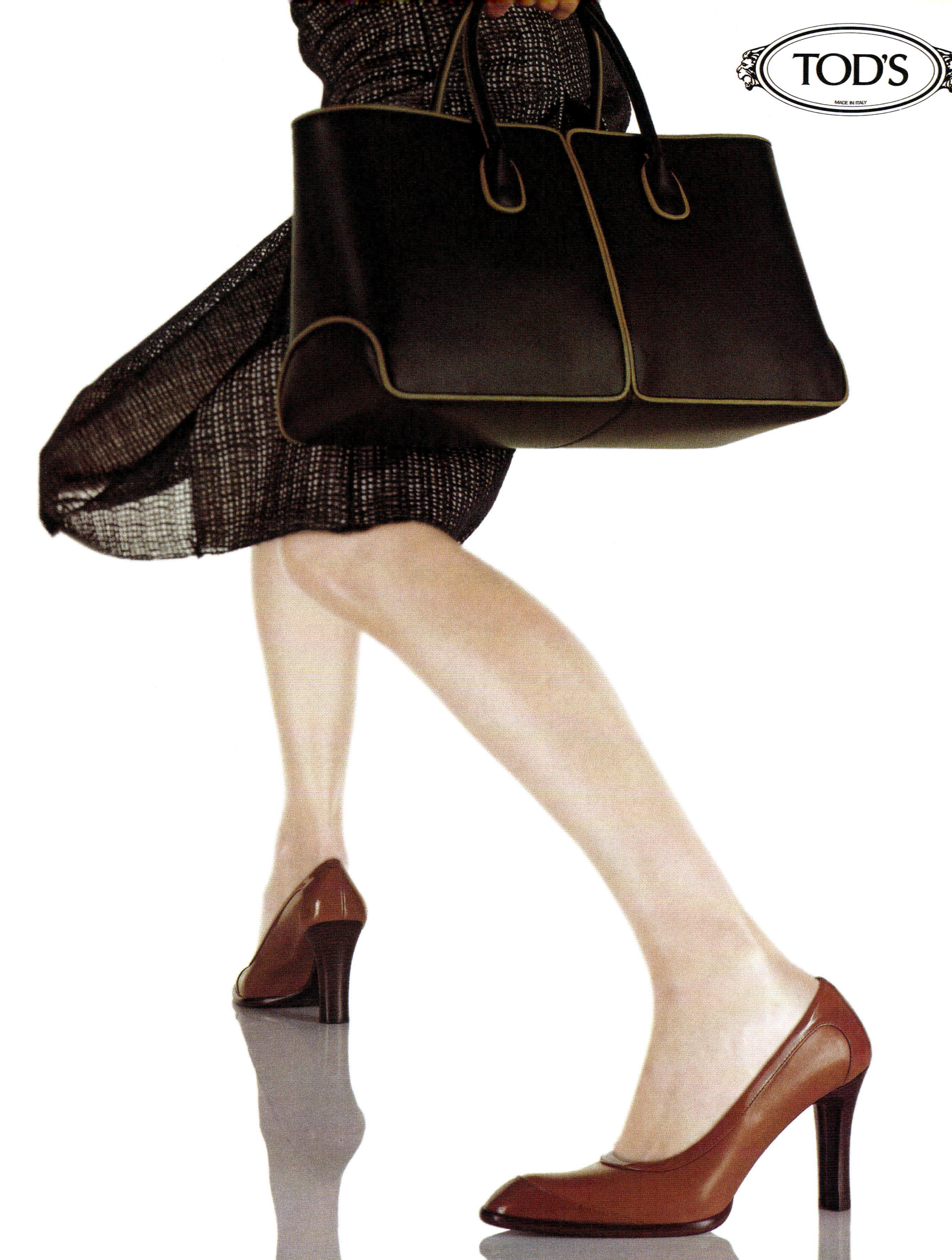
TOD'S
MADE IN ITALY

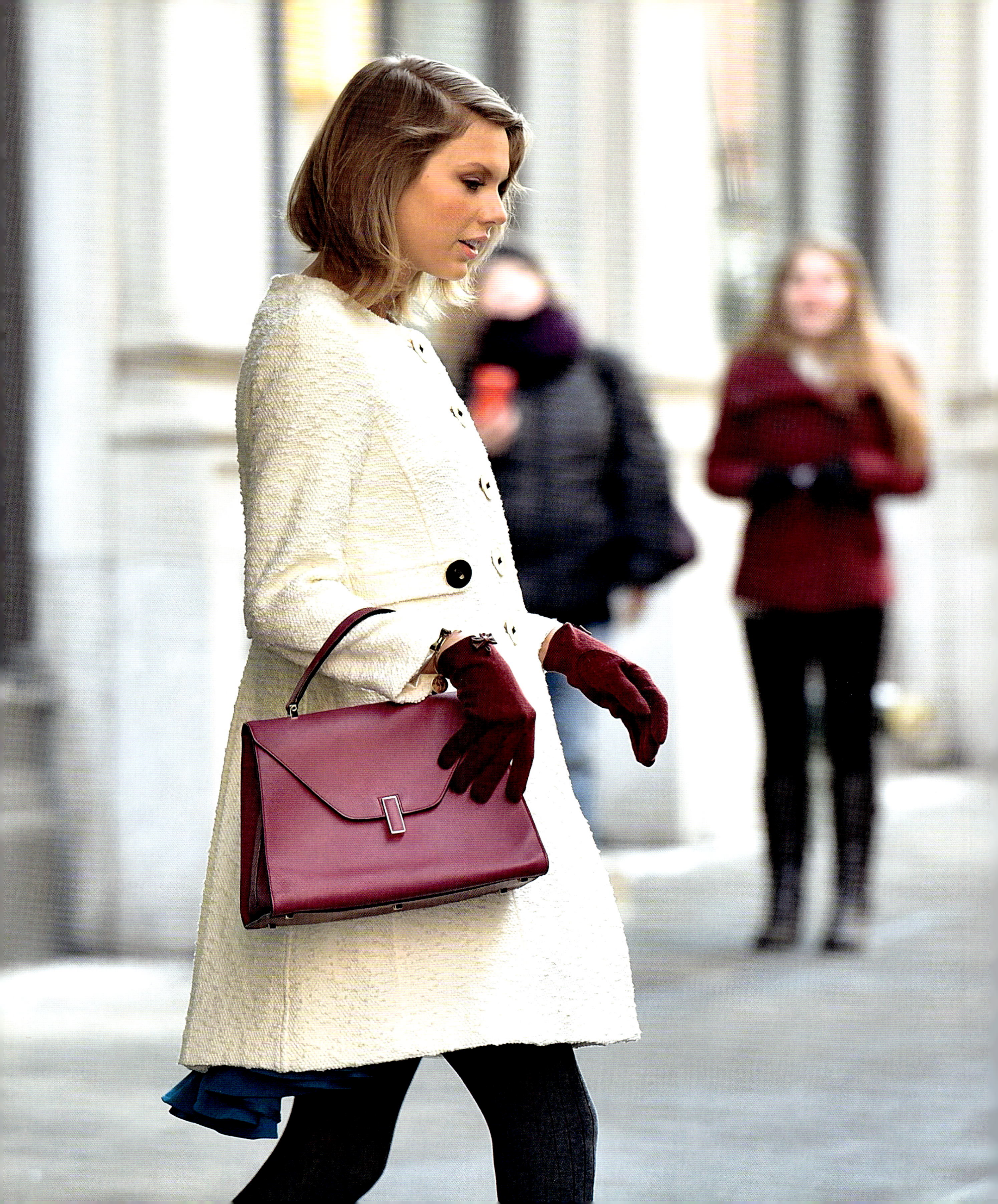

THE SILENT TYPES

In the world of luxury handbags, it's possible to fly under the radar yet boast high-profile fans such as Maria Callas, Grace Kelly, and Jacqueline Kennedy Onassis. A brand can claim design awards and have an iconic overnight case picked up by New York's Museum of Modern Art and Milan's La Triennale for their permanent collections but still have a name that's a mystery to the majority of consumers.

Three such firms are Delvaux, Valextra, and Moynat, founded as part of the big luxury luggage boom that accompanied the rise of the Industrial Age and advancements in travel, the automobile and the train in particular. What many of these silent types have in common is a heritage—at times forgotten until a modern-day relaunch—an obsessive focus on craftsmanship, and its by-product: a very steep price tag. These handbags require you to come up close and, when you do, you'll see that the leathers, stitching, details, and design are crafted to perfection.

Founded by Charles Delvaux in 1829, Delvaux is the oldest of these luxury leather firms. Throughout the centuries, the Belgian company has experienced ups and downs. In 1883 it was awarded the title of royal warrant holder for the court of Belgium. Yet by the early 1900s the company was in decline. A 1933 takeover by agricultural engineer Franz Schwennicke revived the firm with a major expansion in handbags. The most popular design was the 1958 Le Brillant, a structured top-handle satchel that featured the Delvaux's first logo: a D-shaped buckle.

Familiarity with the firm was largely limited to Belgium until 2011, when Delvaux was acquired by Fung Brands Limited and entered the international market. The high level of craftsmanship remains: each bag is handmade, from the stitches to the leather cutting and shaving, by at least three artisans. The process takes roughly ten hours. "From the beginning, I didn't want to pretend to reinvent," artistic director Christina Zeller told the *South China Morning Post* in 2014. "It was clear that we all, including the owners, wanted to build on what had been done already."

In 1937 in Milan, Giovanni Fontana founded Valextra, a luggage manufacturer specializing in fine leathers and exotic skins—the label is a combination of *valigia*, the Italian word for "suitcase," and "extra." The extra takes the form of extra effort. Consider this bespoke example: a fourteen-piece luggage set, requested by a former Kuwaiti emir, created entirely from hippopotamus hide.

But for all those history highlights, the brand is happy to remain outside the mainstream, away from the clamor of the new and the next. Valextra bags have none of the familiar brand reinforcements such as logos, hardware, and accents. From the 1951 Punch tote to the 1960s Carita hobo, they have only hand-lacquered piping that outlines the contours and silhouette. "We believe in an introverted luxury rather than an extroverted one," explained former CEO Massimo Suppancig to *W* in 2004.

Moynat's renaissance dates to 2011. LVMH's chairman and CEO, Bernard Arnault, is responsible for waking up this sleeping beauty, which, founded in 1849, had folded in 1976. Unlike Louis Vuitton, whose contemporary turnaround was much splashier—big-name designers at the helm, much-publicized collaborations—the relaunch of Moynat was a muted affair, and that, says businessman Arnaud de Lummen, who sold Arnault the rights to the company, was a smart move. As de Lummen told *Women's Wear Daily* in 2012, it reinforces the idea that the storied brand never went away. "You start with roots and a history," he explained. "When you relaunch, you already have a story to tell. After a few years, people completely forget that the brand was dormant. People think it's always been there."

And, like France's other great leather houses, Moynat has an enviable heritage, including countless medals at world's fairs and international exhibitions. Started by Pauline Moynat and brothers Octavie and François Coulembier, it's a pioneer in the luggage world: Moynat invented the waterproof trunk, the lightweight wicker-and-canvas English trunk, and its celebrated Limousine trunk, with its curved bottom that fit snugly over a car. Customers could

OPPOSITE: Taylor Swift carrying Valextra's Iside bag, New York City, February 2015.

even custom order styles to match the color of their vehicles. In fact, during its dormant years, the only people who knew the name Moynat were avid car enthusiasts.

But the name wouldn't resonate with the style-savvy set today if not for the extreme detail that goes into the making of each and every Moynat design. The leather patterns are created not by stamping or printing but by using marquetry, an ages-old technique in which the individual pieces of leather are hand-cut and assembled. The Réjane, a structured satchel with pure, uncluttered lines, takes one artisan twenty hours to make; it was originally designed for nineteenth-century French actress Gabrielle Réjane. "One thing you cannot copy is heritage—and that's a difference," creative director Ramesh Nair told *Women's Wear Daily* in 2015. The Limousine is back, too, now as a briefcase that is concave on one side.

England, meanwhile, has its own purveyors of introverted luxury steeped in history. Smythson, for example, dates to 1887, though it didn't enter the handbag market until 2003 and its entrée was subtle. Smythson is the ne plus ultra of stationery and diaries, with three royal warrants and an impressive client list: the British royal family, Charles Dickens, Winston Churchill, Indian maharajas, Sigmund Freud, and Katharine Hepburn. Its trademarks are beautifully hand-painted notecards and gorgeous leather-bound diaries with gilt-edged featherlight blue paper. While the move into fashion may have surprised some, it made sense in light of the extraordinary quality of its leathers; in addition to factories in the United Kingdom and Italy, Smythson uses the same French tannery as Hermès.

The company made an initial attempt at handbags in 1990, but it never really took off. Six years later, when it hired Samantha Cameron—first as head of product design, then creative director, and now creative consultant—the centuries-old stationery firm was able to shake off its staid reputation. Cameron, whose husband, David, would become prime minister, introduced bold, bright leathers to the agendas and passport holders—and even a Bible with a pink leather cover—as well as a range of beautifully understated handbags, including the softly quilted Nancy, which sold out after three weeks, boxy shoulder bags, and slim clutches. "I steered away from too much hardware or any obvious logo," Cameron told the *Times* in 2007. "It's not what Smythson is about." No doubt her peers at Delvaux, Valextra, and Moynat share her sense of discretion.

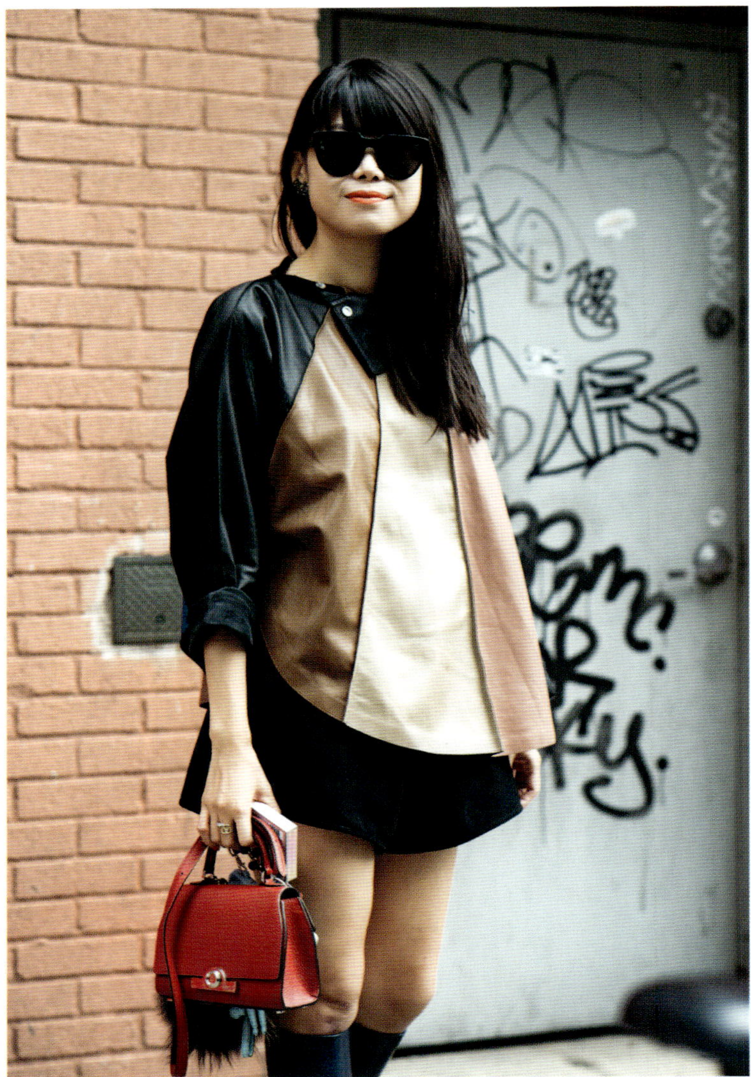

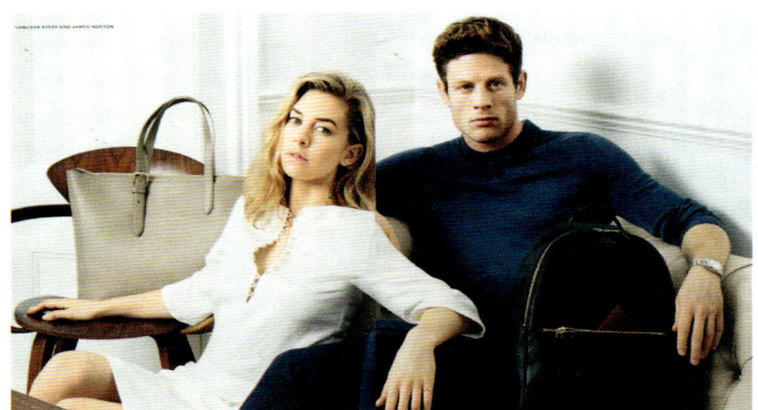

TOP: Mini Rejane, Moynat, New York City, September 2015.

ABOVE: Actors Vanessa Kirby and James Norton with the Burlington hobo bag and backpack, Smythson, Spring 2016 advertisement.

OPPOSITE: Brillant bag, Delvaux, Paris, September 2014.

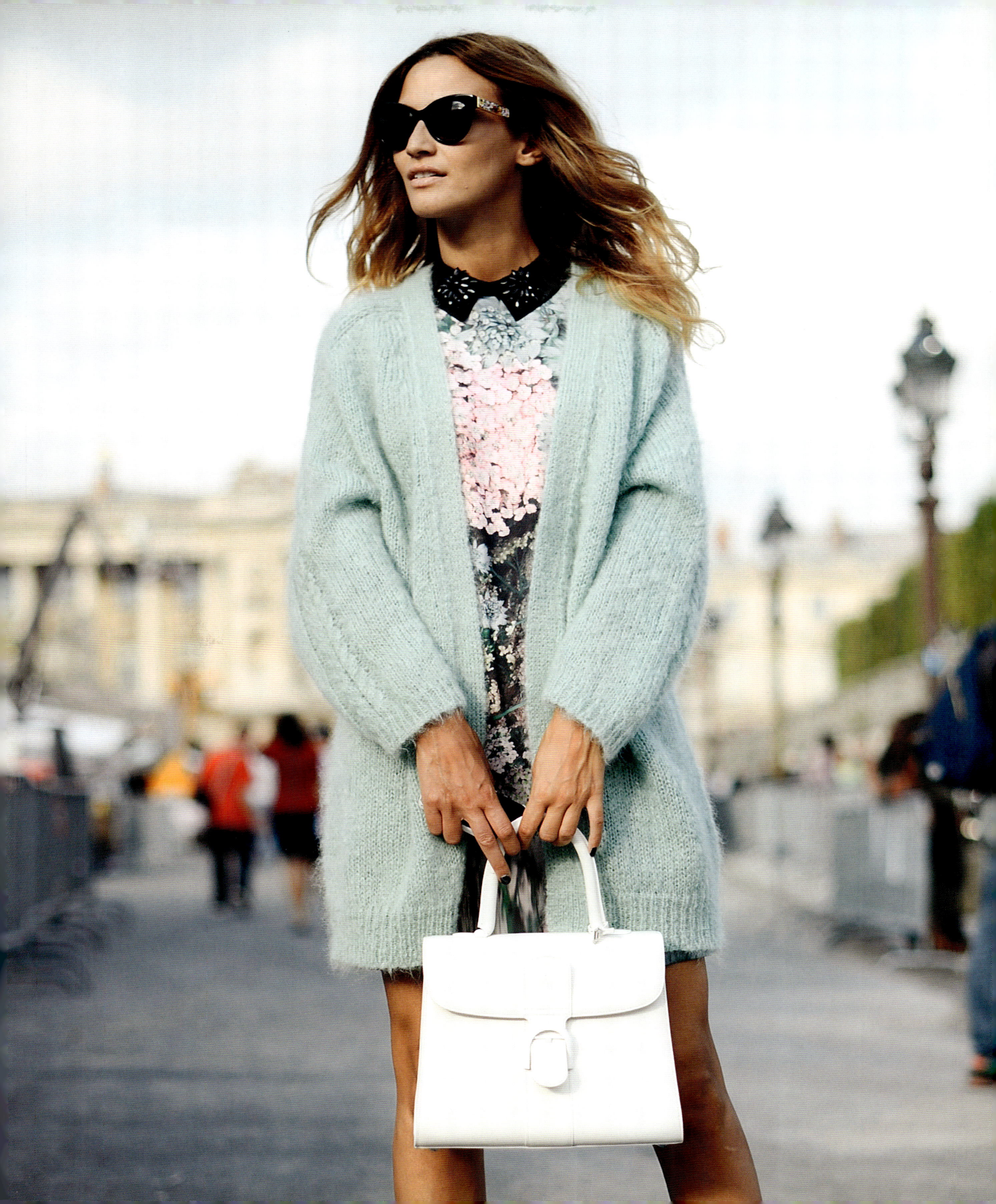

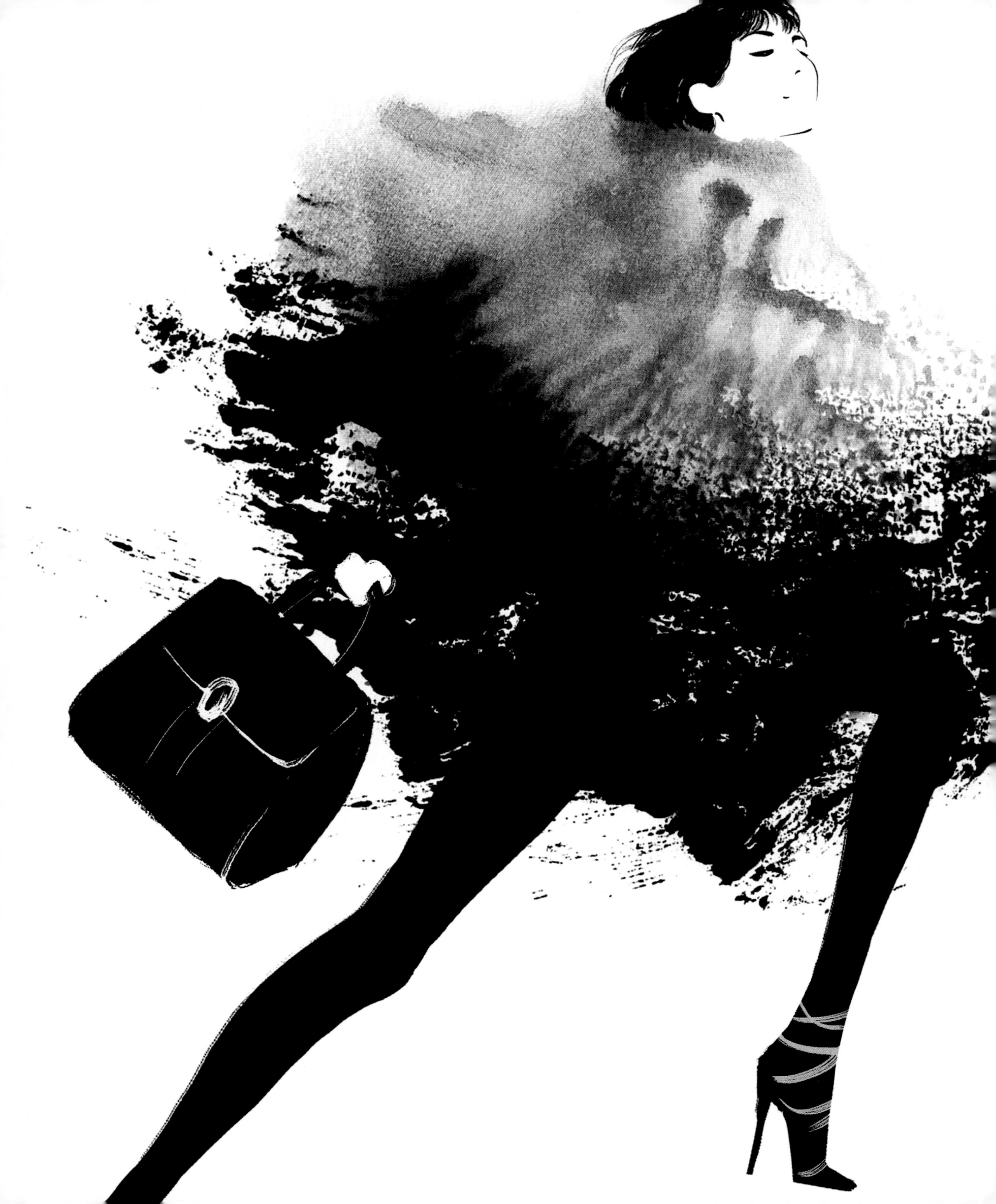

"You want a bag that can go through anything. And a little bit of softness is always lovely. If I don't have a dog, I can just pet my bag!"

—CARA DELEVINGNE, teenvogue.com, September 9, 2014

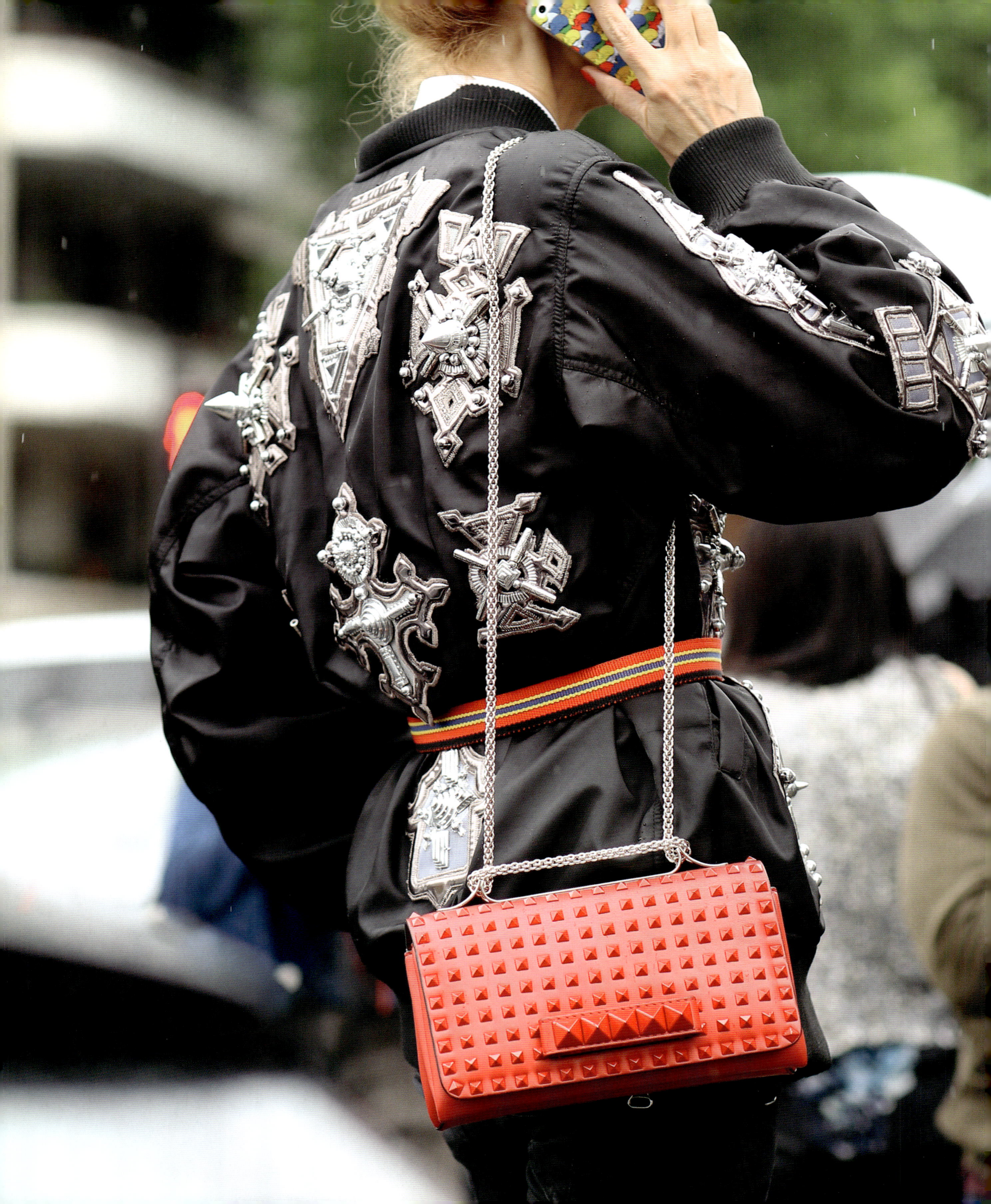

Valentino

ROCKSTUD, 2010

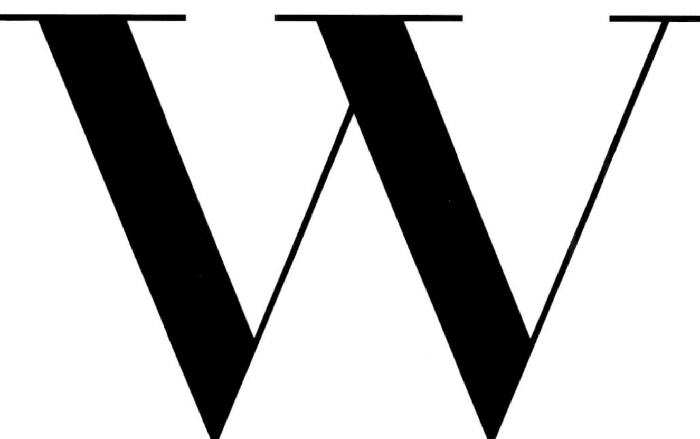

hen Valentino Garavani, who founded his eponymous house in Rome in 1960, retired in 2008, the designer duo Maria Grazia Chiuri and Pierpaolo Piccioli took over as creative directors. They had been at the house since 1999 and were well versed in the Valentino signatures, like the color red and dramatic florals—one of their early bag hits was a fanciful shopper decorated in oversized petal-like ruffles. And before that, they had spent ten years designing handbags at Fendi and were part of the team behind the Baguette. "We are like an old married couple," Chiuri remarked to *Harper's Bazaar* in 2013. Their desks at Valentino even faced each other.

In 2010 Chiuri and Piccioli launched the Rockstud collection, fusing tradition with contemporary currency: the leather is smooth, the silhouettes are structured and ladylike—a frame bag, a demure clutch—pure Valentino. Yet with square pyramid studs sparingly applied just as trim, as an outline, the bag takes on an edgier look. "You put on something very elegant, but with the studs it becomes very different," Piccioli told the *Times* in 2012. "Women are fussier today; they are not only elegant or only rock, so when you use both together, the elegance with the rockness of the studs, the result is very similar to modern women." While metals studs as detailing are common enough, Chiuri and Piccioli transformed the square pyramid stud into a Valentino signature, used across the collection. There's even a line of studded unisex clothing called Rockstud Unlimited. Explaining their take on the punk staple, Chiuri told *New York Magazine* in 2015, "Everybody paints the same Madonna, but there is a big difference between Caravaggio and somebody else."

In 2016 Chiuri became artistic director of Christian Dior, leaving Piccioli as the sole creative director of Valentino. It was the first time either had worked without the other in twenty-six years. One of Piccioli's first independent projects was the launch of the Rockstud Spike bag, a quilted ladylike design prettily dotted with stud detailing. To celebrate, Piccioli teamed up with photographer and director Terry Richardson and created a video diary of the handbag in New York City, casting a motley group of people straight off the street—a move inspired by the blog and book *Humans of New York*. "It is not the accessory that defines the persona," Piccioli explained to *Women's Wear Daily* in 2016, "but it is the object that allows the persona to express one's character, attitude and diversity."

OPPOSITE:
Rockstud bag, Valentino, Paris, June 2014.

PAGES 218–219:
Models in Valentino Red, The *New York Times Magazine*, July 2007.

"Fashion is not so complex. It is about making a woman beautiful."

—VALENTINO GARAVANI, *The New Yorker*, September 26, 2005

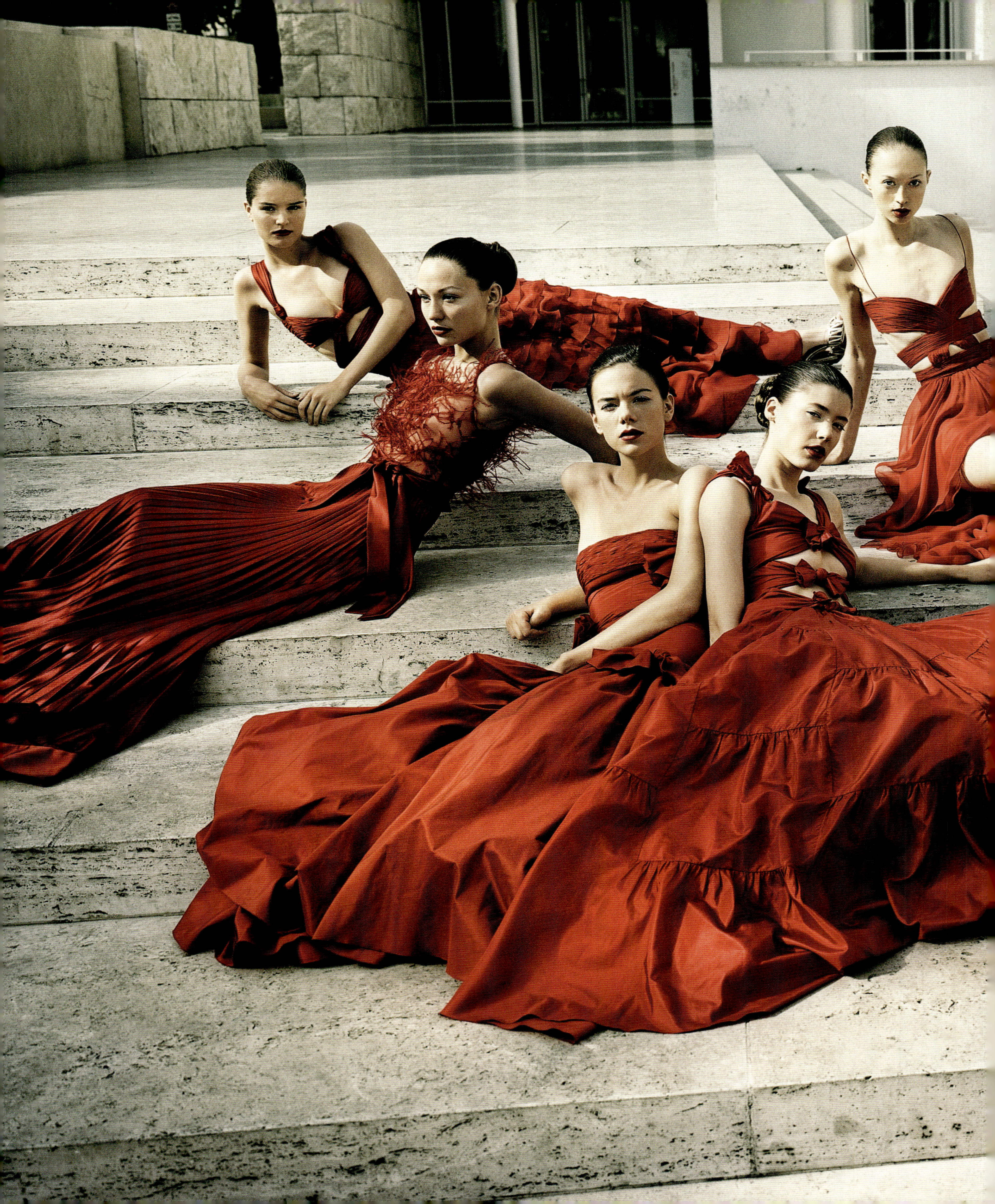

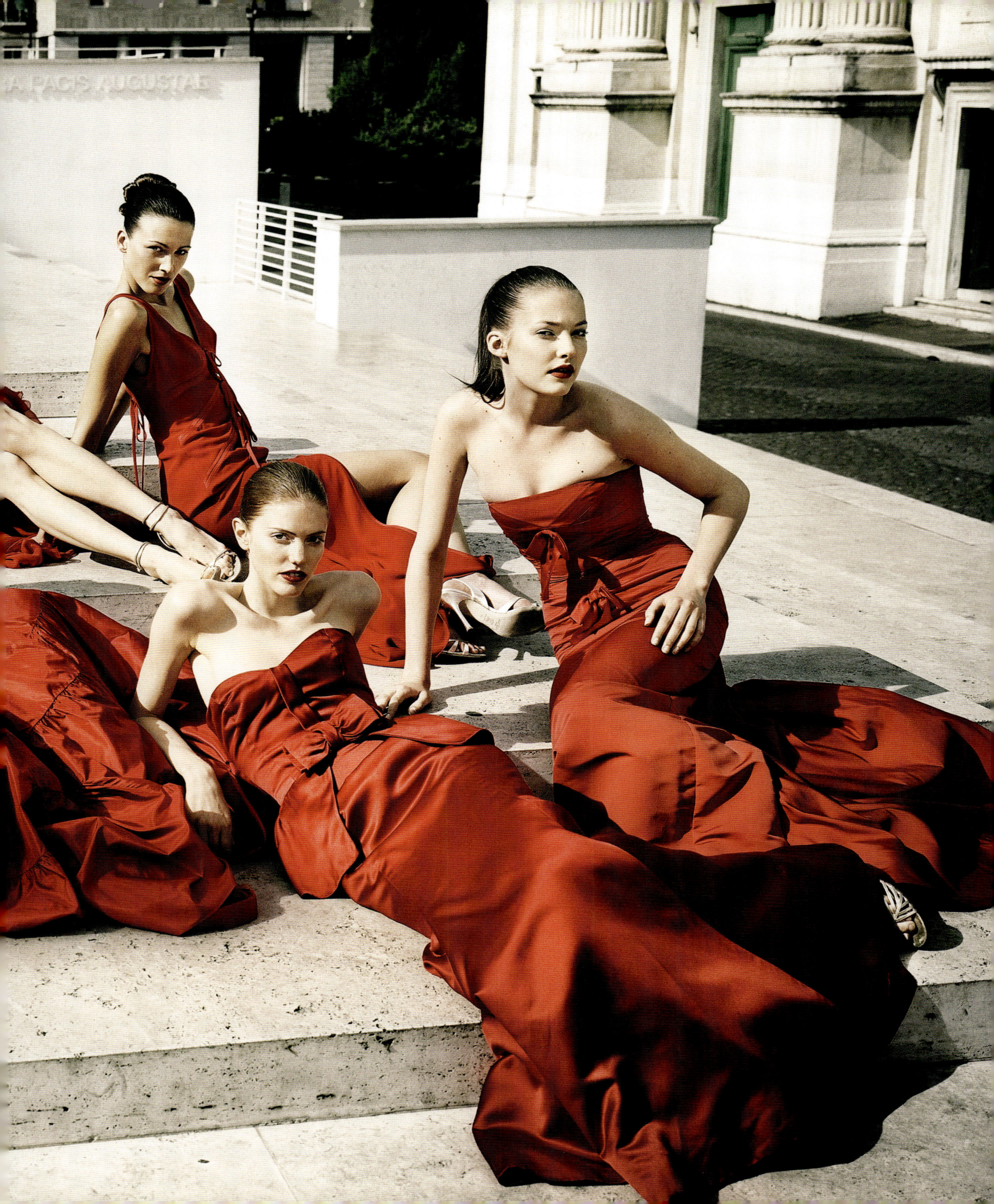
PACIS AUGUSTAE

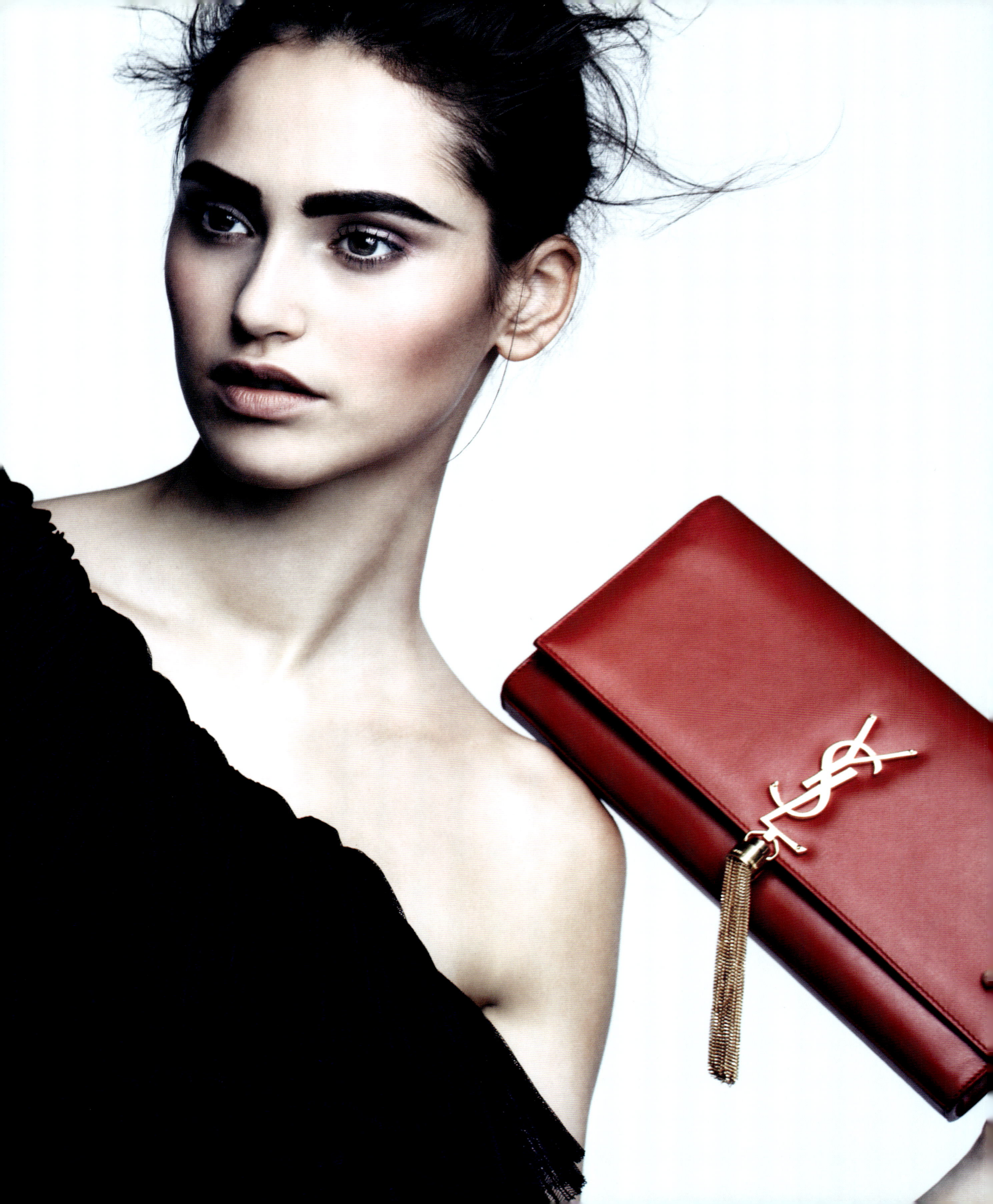
YSL

Yves Saint Laurent

MUSE, 2005

MONOGRAM, 2013

SAC DE JOUR, 2013

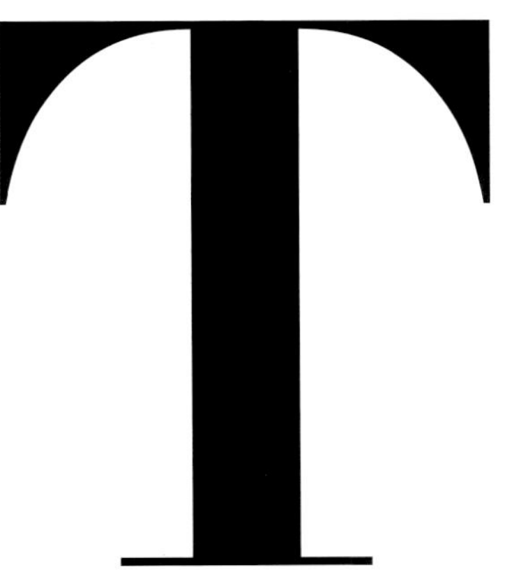he signature logo of the house of Yves Saint Laurent was created in 1961 by artist Adolphe Jean-Marie Mouron, also known as "Cassandre," who intertwined serif and sans-serif letters to elegant effect. That monogram is "as synonymous with—as significant to—20th-century style as T. S. Eliot's is with literature," wrote journalist Olivia Barker in *USA Today* in 2008.

Curiously enough, the early hit handbags did not feature the famous logo. The Muse—a sleek, oversized take on the traditional bowling bag—has a subtle Y-shaped panel stitched on the side instead. The Muse Two, which appeared three years later, in 2008, is a chic, utilitarian rectangular satchel with a front flap and a circular gold closure. Speaking to the *New York Times* that year, creative director Stefano Pilati explained the repurposing of the bag's name despite the very different styles: "Customers seem to like to ask for bags by name, but I don't really like to name my bags—they are not children or pets."

In 2012 Hedi Slimane became creative director, ushering in a sea change for the company. He revamped the stores, chose to work from his hometown of Los Angeles rather than move to the firm's Paris headquarters, and restored the long-forgotten blocklike Helvetica logo, introduced by Monsieur Saint Laurent himself for the ready-to-wear Rive Gauche line launched in 1966. The revival logo appeared on one of Slimane's debut handbags, the Sac de Jour, a seductively spare and modern style reminiscent of the Hermès Birkin, with practical compartment dividers and expandable, pleated sides. The Sac exuded a cool allure, and the brand surged in popularity: Joan Jett and Courtney Love sat front and center at the runway shows, Joni Mitchell and Marilyn Manson starred in ad campaigns, and countless hip-hop artists invoked it in song.

Despite widespread public misconception, Slimane did not do away with the original Mouron logo. It continued to be used with fragrances and accessories such as the Monogram bag. While the style comes in numerous versions—from a ladylike crossbody with chevron quilting to a glamorous gold-tassel clutch—the highlight is the original YSL logo prominently displayed on the front, both a status marker and beautiful design element. With its rock-and-roll edginess, the Monogram has given the storied logo a renewed sense of currency for a new generation. Slimane left the company in 2016, yet Saint Laurent continues to be a cult favorite, bridging the worlds of high fashion, pop culture, and music.

OPPOSITE: Monogram bag, Yves Saint Laurent, *Marie Claire France*, Spring/Summer, 2014.

PAGE 222: Monogram bag, Yves Saint Laurent, Fall 2014.

PAGE 223: Monogram bag, Yves Saint Laurent, New York City, 2015.

"My YSL bag deserves a seat all of its own."

—SARAH HOLDEN, *Daily Mail*, July 16, 2007

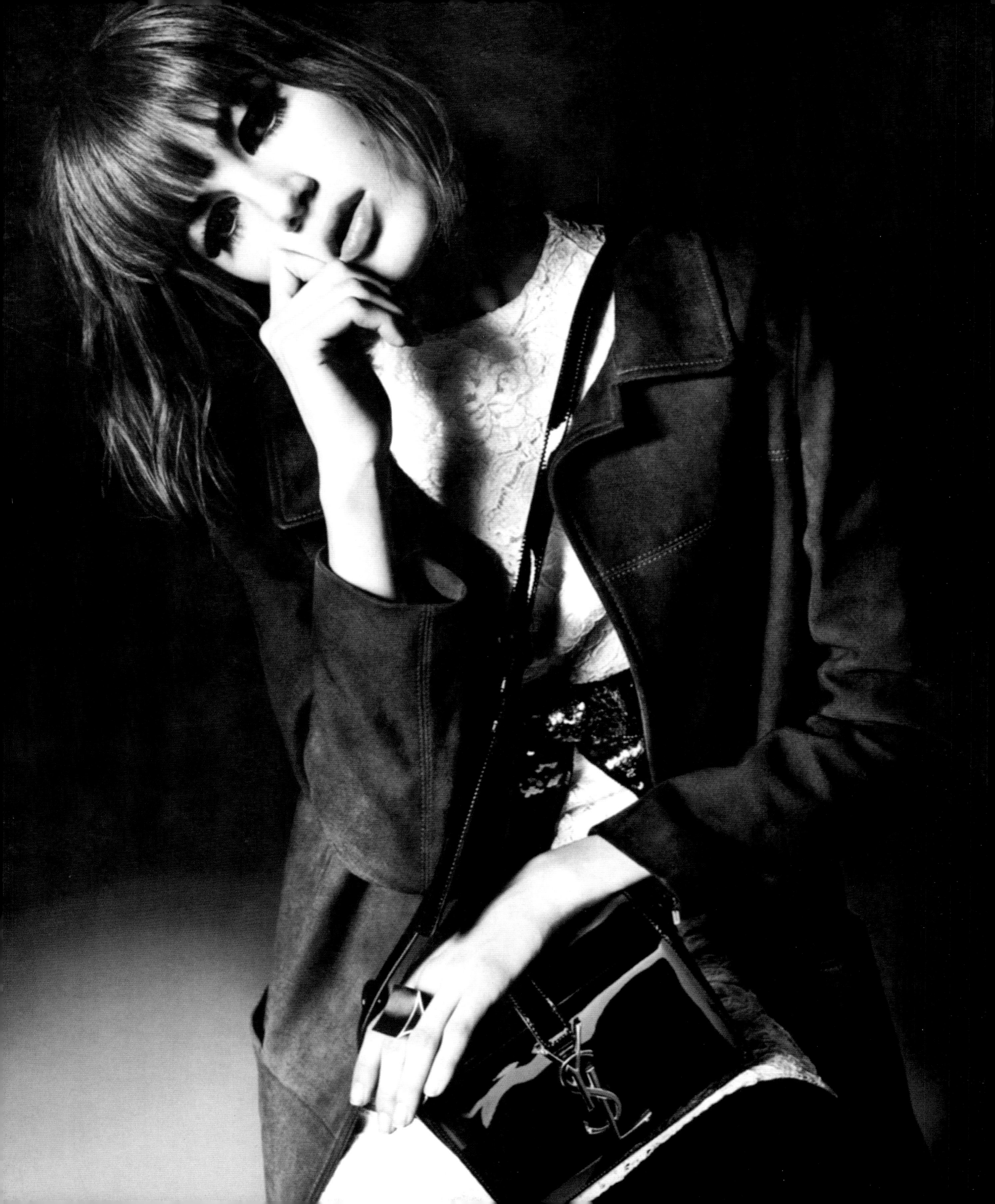

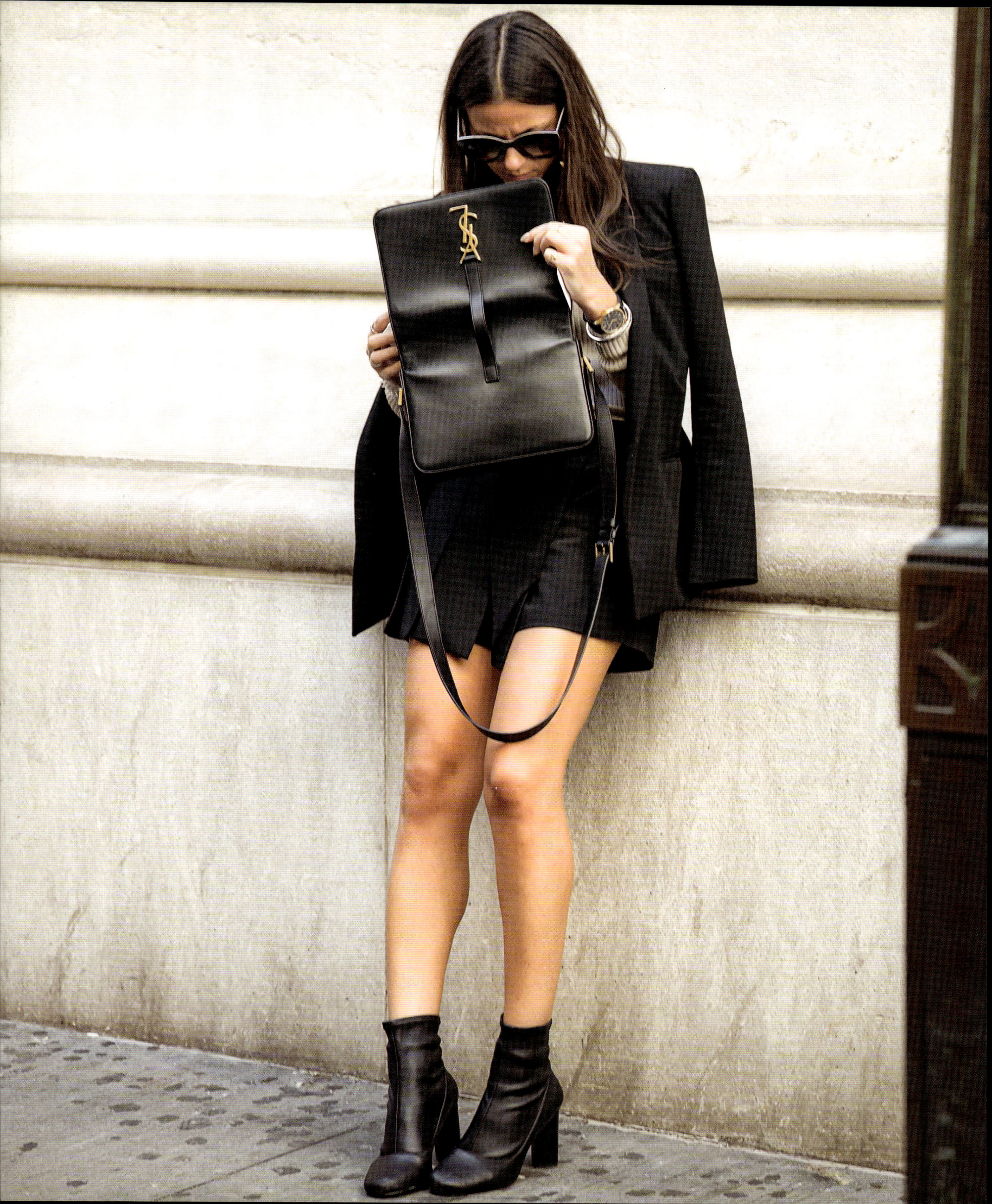

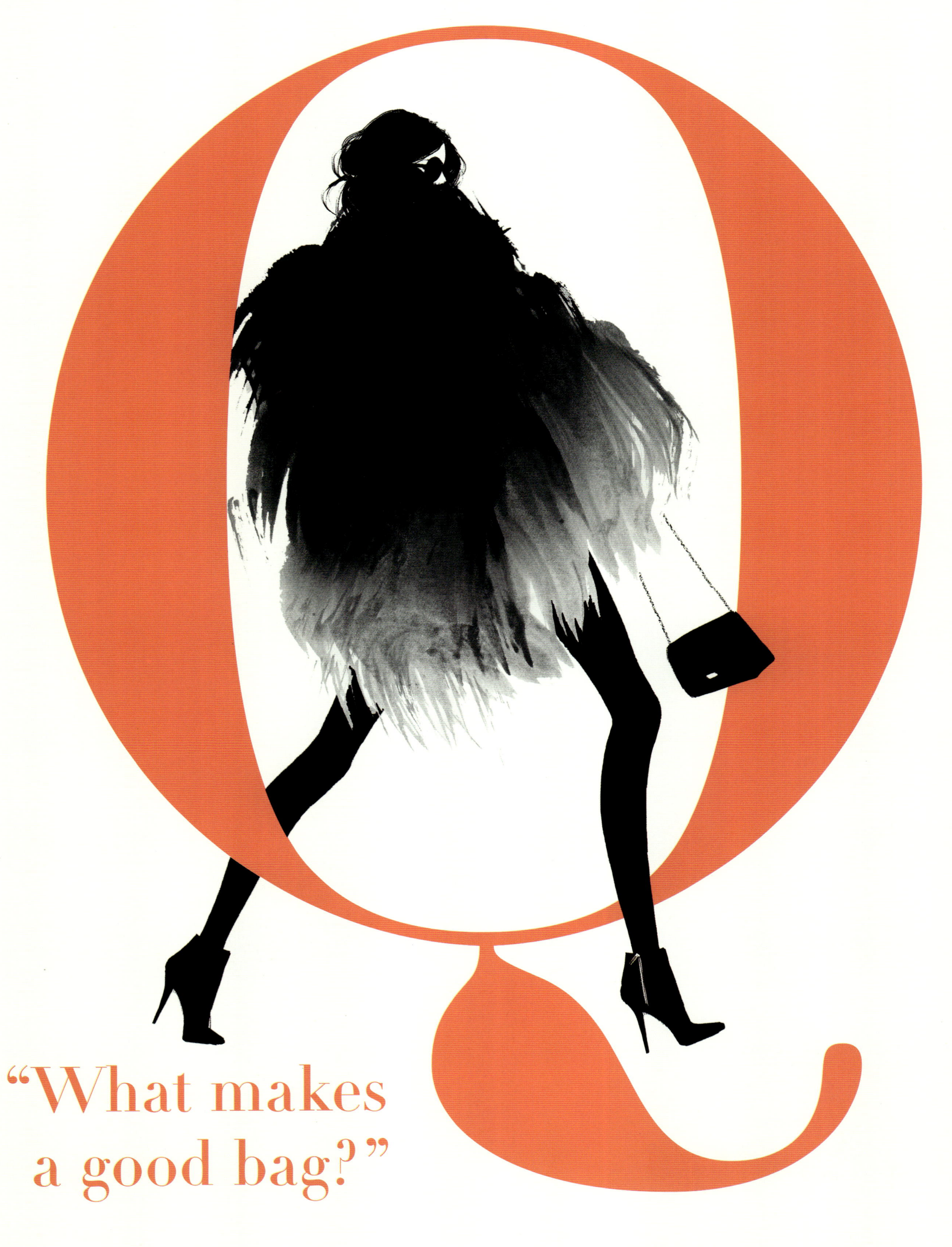

“What makes a good bag?”

"You gotta have it or you'll die!"

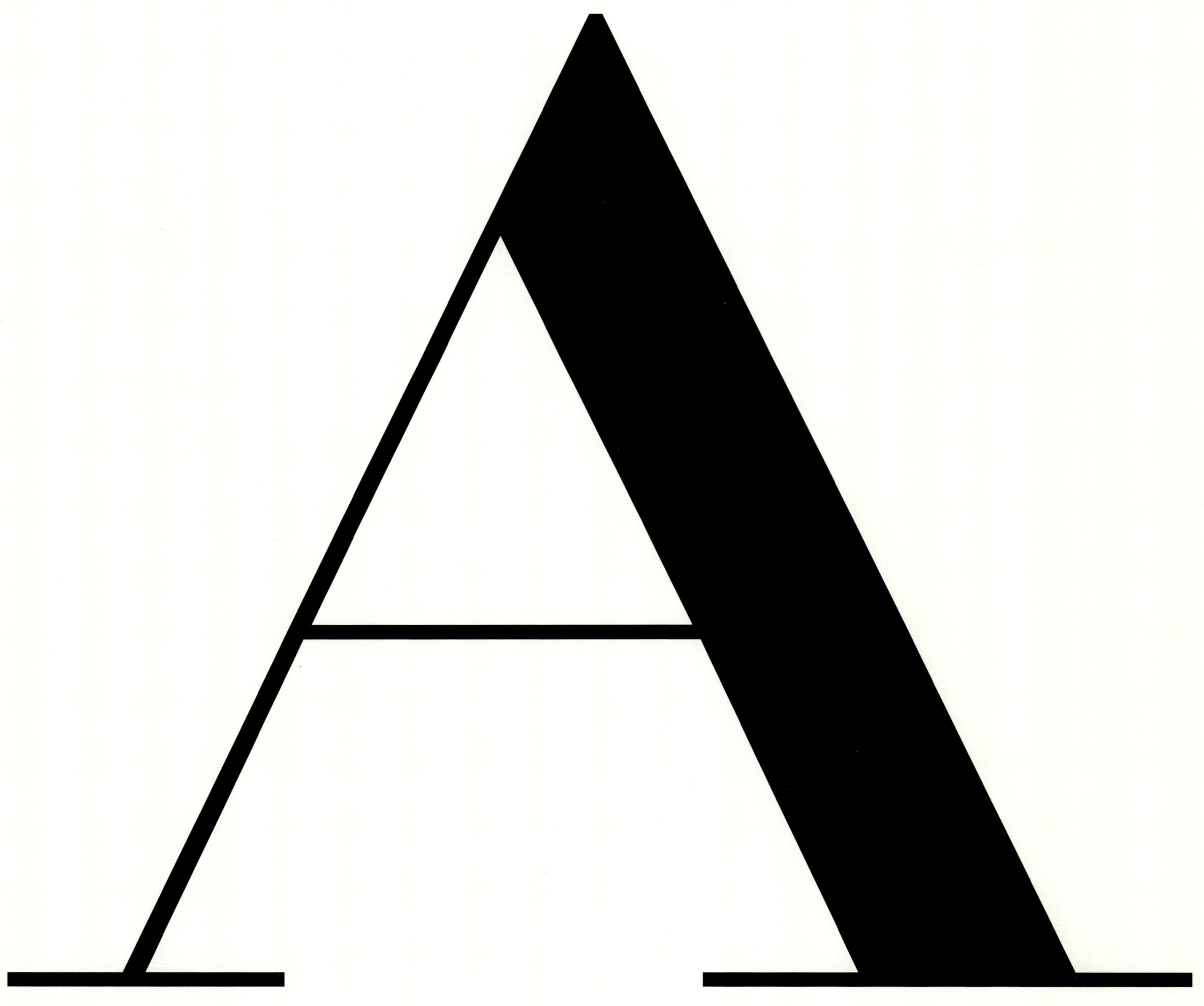

—TOM FORD, from *Purse Pizzazz* by Marie Browning, 2005

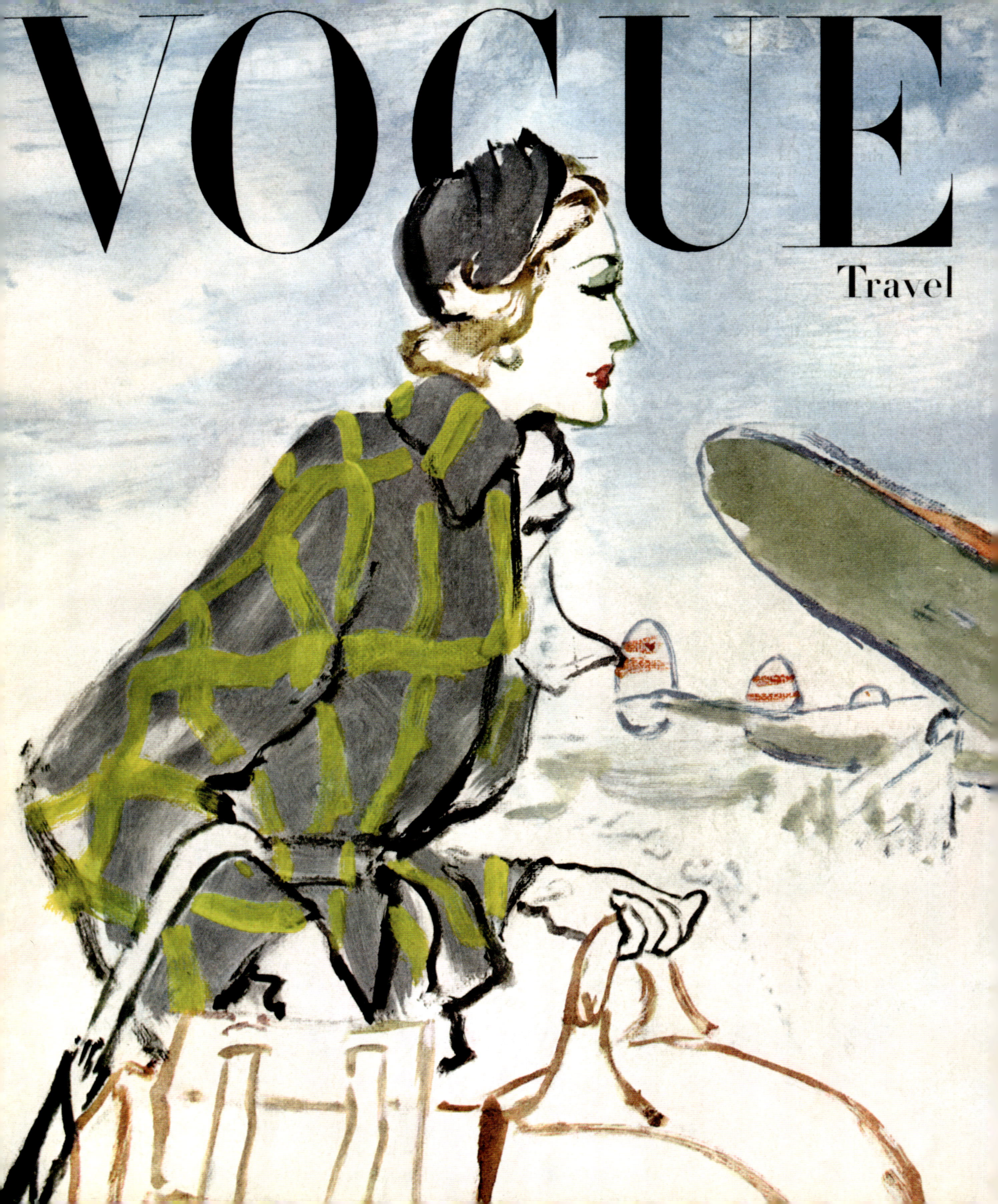
VOGUE
Travel

ACKNOWLEDGMENTS

I want to thank my husband, Dean, for believing in me from the very beginning, when handbags were just a twinkle of a dream; my children, Sloane, Saige, and Olive, for inspiring and supporting me in this passionate journey while mommy was "making" and "obsessing over bags"; my parents, Joseph and Maria, for being so proud and supportive even when I made mistakes; and my sister, Nicole, for working with me in the early days and lending her talent. My family has been my rock.

I am grateful to my friends who have encouraged my entrepreneurial spirit, my amazing creative sisterhood—you know who you are.

I also want to thank my Botkier family, who have given me their best over the years. We learned together, and my appreciation goes beyond words. Thanks, too, to my colleagues, whose energy and shared interest in the bag business have taught me so much over the years: Beca Alexander, Kyle Anderson, Karen Giberson, Julie Gilhart, Steven Kolb and the Council of Fashion Designers of America, Aroom Han, Brooke Jaffe, John Manolucci, Roxanne Robinson, Kel Rowe, Aimee Song, and all the retail buyers who have supported my work. I'd also like to thank the team that helped me put together this book, including my agent, Nancy Chanin; writer Venessa Lau; photography editor Rebecca Karamehmedovic; my editor, Elizabeth Viscott Sullivan, and the rest of the team at HarperCollins: Lynne Yeamans, Susan Kosko, Dani Segelbaum, Pamela Barr, and Shubhani Sarkar.

OPPOSITE: *Vogue* cover, illustrated by Carl Oscar August Erickson, January 1947.

SELECT BIBLIOGRAPHY

Alger, Horatio. *Adrift in New York*. New York: Street & Smith, 1904.

Allen-Mills, Tony. "When Will I Be Famous?" *Sunday Times*, March 24, 1996.

Annis, Elisa. "Pattern, the Subtle Way to Brand." *New York Times*, March 5, 2013.

Armstrong, Lisa. "Spain's Got Talent." *Telegraph*, May 23, 2012.

Asome, Carolyn. "The Fashion Editors' New It Bag." *Times*, January 14, 2015.

Atkinson, Nathalie. "Tiffany's Got a Brand New Bag." *National Post*, October 15, 2011.

Aucouturier, Marie. *Longchamp*. Paris: Éditions de la Martinière, 2008.

Azhar, Rohaizatul. "Furla for All." *Straits Times*, June 28, 2013.

Ball, Deborah. "Gucci Revives YSL's Faded Glory." *Globe and Mail*, September 22, 2006.

Baran, Michelle, and Eric Newman. "Getting Coached." *Footwear News*, April 24, 2006.

Barker, Olivia. "Yves Saint Laurent's Work, Life Were Iconic." *USA Today*, June 2, 2008.

Baudot, François. *Alaïa*. New York: Assouline Publishing, 2006.

Bergman, Randi. "Altuzarra in Toronto!" http://fashionmagazine.com/fashion/altuzarra-exclusive-interview/. Accessed April 23, 2016.

Bertoli, Rosa. "Anatomy of a Rebrand." http://www.wallpaper.com/design/anatomy-of-a-rebrand-we-dissect-loewes-new-identity-designed-by-mm-paris. Accessed October 10, 2016.

Binkley, Christina. "Record Price for Hermès Birkin Bag." *Wall Street Journal*, April 13, 2016.

Bita, Natasha. "Bags of Class and Panache." *Australian*, November 18, 2005.

Blanchard, Tamsin. "Radical Fashion." *Observer Magazine*, October 7, 2001, 23.

Blasberg, Derek. "Valentino's New Reign." *Harper's Bazaar*, May 2013.

Blumenthal, Erica M. "A Street-Style Trick That Works IRL and More." *New York Times*, January 29, 2015.

Bolton, Andrew. *Alexander McQueen: Savage Beauty*. New York: Metropolitan Museum of Art, 2011.

Bonsor, Sacha. "Bags of Talent." *Harper's Bazaar UK*, November 2013, 108.

Bott, Danièle. *Chanel: Collections and Creations*. London: Thames & Hudson, 2007.

Bowles, Hamish. "The Phoebe Files." *Vogue*, March 2013, 580.

Braunstein, Peter. "Head Coach." *W*, November 2001, 230.

Brown, Jessica Price. "Designer Bags to Suffer in Wake of Consumer Slowdown." *Drapers*, March 11, 2008.

Browning, Marie. *Purse Pizzazz*. New York: Sterling Publishing Co., 2005.

Brubach, Holly. "The French Connection." *W*, March 2015, 318.

Buck, Joan Juliet. "Body Genius." *Vogue*, November 1985, 190–95.

Bullock, Maggie. "Balenciaga's First Fragrance in 55 Years." http://www.elle.com/fashion /a10925/balenciagas-first-fragrance-in-55-years-416242/. Accessed October 4, 2016.

Bumiller, Elisabeth. "In Her Clutches." *Washington Post*, January 20, 1995.

"The Cabat." http://www.bottegaveneta.com/us/collection/the-cabat_grd876. http://www.bottegaveneta.com/us/collection/the-cabat_grd876. Accessed April 23, 2016.

Calaway, Libby. "Get 'Em While You're Hot." *New York Post*, July 29, 2002.

Carreon, Blue. "The House That Loafers Built." http://www.forbes.com/sites/bluecarreon/2011/06/20/the-house-that-loafers-built/#1a88824e7c5c. Accessed October 10, 2016.

Carter, Lee. "His Wildest Dreams." http://www.wmagazine.com/fashion/2015/09/karl-lagerfeld-fendi-fur/photos/. Accessed October 10, 2016.

Cartner-Morley, Jess. "Boy Done Good," *Guardian*, September 19, 2005.

——. "How Workout Leggings Set the Pace in Fashion." *Guardian*, February 15, 2016.

——. "The Marc of Luxury." *Guardian*, March 2, 2002.

Cavendish, Lucy. "Le Pull of Fame." *Sunday Telegraph*, November 9, 2008.

Chabbott, Sophia. "Nancy Gonzalez Sticks to Her Inner Skin." *Women's Wear Daily*, August 7, 2006.

———. "Stepping Up at Coach." *Women's Wear Daily*, February 5, 2007.

Charles-Roux, Edmonde. *The World of Coco Chanel: Friends, Fashion, Fame.* London: Thames & Hudson, 2005.

Chenoune, Farid. *Carried Away: All About Bags*. New York: The Vendome Press, 2005.

Chernikoff, Leah. "Barneys' Amanda Brooks and Simon Doonan on The Row's New $39,000 Bag and the Return of the Backpack." http://fashionista.com/2011/07/barneys-amanda-brooks-and-simon-doonan-on-the-rows-new-39000-bag-and-the-return-of-the-backpack. Accessed April 23, 2016.

Chrisafis, Angelique. "Hermès and Jane Birkin Resolve Spat Over Crocodile Handbags." *Guardian*, September 12, 2015.

Colapinto, John. "Just Have Less." *New Yorker*, January 3, 2011, 32.

Colavita, Courtney. "The Branding of Italy." *Daily News Record*, March 24, 2003.

———. "The Celebrity Connection." *Women's Wear Daily*, June 5, 2006.

Coles, Joanna. "Fashion's Philosopher." *Marie Claire*, March 2011, 160–62.

Collins, Amy Fine. "Alaïa's Sweet Bondage." *Vanity Fair,* September 2012, 333.

Compton, Nick. "Bottega Veneta: The Dream Weavers' Tale." *Telegraph*, March 1, 2014.

Conti, Samantha. "Prada takes L.A." *Los Angeles Magazine*, September 1, 1998, 72–74.

Cooper, Anderson. *Anderson Cooper 360°*. CNN, October 6, 2011.

Corcoran, Monica. "From 'It' to Obit." http://articles.latimes.com/2008/jan/20/image/ig-rage20. Accessed April 23, 2016.

Cordle, Ina Paiva. "Nancy Gonzalez Has Made an Empire Out of Exotic Skin Handbags." *Miami Herald*, September 26, 2012.

Craik, Laura. "Rivets and Ruffles." *Times*, November 21, 2012.

Cunningham, Bill. "The Trophy." *New York Times*, December 10, 2006.

Dahl, Roald. *Charlie and the Chocolate Factory*. New York: Alfred A. Knopf, 1964.

Daswani, Kavita. "Double Happiness." *South China Morning Post*, September 2, 2011.

Davies, Dean Mayo. "Stuart Vevers." http://www.dazeddigital.com/fashion/article/15308/1/stuart-vevers. Accessed April 23, 2016.

DeFanti, Mark, Deirdre Bird, and Helen Caldwell. "Gucci's Use of a Borrowed Corporate Heritage to Establish a Global Luxury Brand." *Competition Forum*, 2014, 45.

de la Fressange, Inès. *Parisian Chic: A Style Guide*. New York: Random House, 2011.

Delap, Leanne. "Deliver Us from Trendiness." *Globe and Mail*, December 5, 1996.

Delevingne, Cara. http://www.teenvogue.com/story/cara-delevingne-interview-mulberry-collection. Accessed March 15, 2017.

Dello Russo, Anne. "10 Front-Row Rules." http://www.annadellorusso.com/2012/09/09/10-front-row-rules/. Accessed October 11, 2006.

Dickens, Charles. *Oliver Twist*. Reprint edition. Harmondsworth: Penguin, 2003.

Dior, Christian. *The Little Dictionary of Fashion*. New York: Harry N. Abrams, 2007.

"Discover Lady Dior." http://www.dior.com/couture/en_us/womens-fashion/leather-goods/lady-dior/discover-lady-dior. Accessed May 1, 2016.

"Discover My Dior." http://www.dior.com/couture/en_us/jewellery/jewellery-collections/my-dior/discover-my-dior. Accessed May 1, 2016.

Donovan, Carrie. "Salute to Yves Saint Laurent." *New York Times*, December 4, 1983.

Drier, Melissa."MCM Seeks Return to Prominence." *Women's Wear Daily*, July 12, 2006.

D'Souza, Christa. "What a Girl Wants." *Glamour*, August 2015, 170.

Ferragamo, Salvatore. *Shoemaker of Dreams*. Florence: Giunti Publishing, 1985.

Finnigan, Kate. "A Cut Above." *Harper's Bazaar UK*, March 2015, 340–43.

———. "Meet the Woman Who Invented the It-Bag." *Sunday Telegraph*, October 11, 2015.

Fisher, Alice. "Mama's Gotta Brand New Bag." *Guardian*, July 23, 2006.

Fitzgerald, F. Scott. *The Great Gatsby*. New York: Charles Scribner's Sons, 1925.

Fogg, Marnie. *Vintage Handbags*. London: Carlton Books, 2013.

Foley, Bridget. "2013 WWD CEO Summit: Lazaro Hernandez and Jack McCollough." *Women's Wear Daily*, January 9, 2013.

———. "The Balenciaga Factor." *Women's Wear Daily*, August 15, 2011.

———. "Nicolas Ghesquière Makes Choices, Not Compromises." *Women's Wear Daily*, November 16, 2005.

Forden, Sara G. *The House of Gucci: A Sensational Story of Murder, Madness, Glamour, and Greed*. New York: William Morrow, 2001.

Foreman, Katya. "Name Game Brings Retail Results." *Women's Wear Daily*, July 10, 2006.

Friedman, Vanessa. "The Jane Birkin-Hermès Fuss Needs to Be Put in Perspective." http://www.nytimes.com/2015/07/30/fashion/the-jane-birkin-hermes-fuss-needs-to-be-put-in-perspective.html. Accessed May 23, 2016.

Fury, Alexander. "Alexander McQueen's Savage Beauty." *ES Magazine*, December 10, 2015.

———. "Chanel's 2.55 Celebrates 60 Years as the Greatest It-Bag of All Time." *Independent*, August 24, 2015.

———. "Coach at 75." *Independent*, February 15, 2016.

Gallant, Mavis. *A Fairly Good Time: With Green Water, Green Sky*. New York: NYRB Classics, 2016.

Ganeriwal, Neha. "Tod's Tradition Pays." *Shoes & Accessories*, June 2010.

Garratt, Sheryl. "Keeping It Real." *Daily Telegraph*, June 7, 2008.

Gaudoin, Tina. "Anya Hindmarch: Handbag Queen." *Wall Street Journal*, February 7, 2013.

Gautier, Jérôme. *Dior: New Looks*. New York: Harper Design, 2015.

———. *Chanel: The Vocabulary of Style*. New Haven: Yale University Press, 2011.

Geyer, Christina. "The Blogger Who Has It in the Bag." *Dallas Morning News*, March 30, 2014.

Givhan, Robin. "The Curator Wears Prada." *Newsweek*, May 7, 2012, 45.

———. "Sweetening the Purse." *Washington Post*, September 3, 2007.

Golbin, Pamela. *Couture Confessions*. New York: Rizzoli Ex Libris, 2016.

———. *Louis Vuitton/Marc Jacobs*. New York: Rizzoli, 2012.

———. *Valentino: Themes and Variations*. New York: Rizzoli, 2008.

Goldberg, Shoshana. "The Fashion Bingers." *Daily Mail*, July 16, 2007.

Goldstein, Lori. *Lori Goldstein: Style Is Instinct*. New York: Harper Design, 2013.

Grant, Linda. "Cheap at Twice the Price." *Guardian*, January 29, 2008.

Guinness, Daphne. "The Conceit of Luxury." *Sydney Morning Herald*, September 6, 2007.

Hagerty, Barbara G. *Handbags: A Peek Inside a Woman's Most Trusted Accessory*. Philadelphia: Running Press Book, 2002.

Hambro, Nathalie. *The Art of the Handbag: A Contemporary Collection*. London: NMH, 1998.

Haramis, Nicolas. "An American in Shanghai." *New York Times*, October 19, 2014.

Harilela Divia. "Hide and Chic." *South China Morning Post*, February 8, 2013.

———. "Ready, Jet Set, Go." *South China Morning Post*, May 16, 2014.

———. "Tote Recall." *South China Morning Post*, March 10, 2014.

Hartman, Eviana. "Anya Hindmarch." *New York Times*, November 16, 2014.

Healy, Orla. *Coach*. New York: Assouline, 2002.

Hirschberg, Lynn. "The Man Who Loves Women." *W*, May 2013, 156.

———. "The Tastemaker." *New York Times*, August 31, 2008.

Hirshlag, Jennifer. "Mulberry Blooms with Stateside Stores." *Women's Wear Daily*, November 27, 2006.

"History Lesson," *Women's Wear Daily*, February 23, 2011.

Hodnett, Cindy W. "Natuzzi Urges Action on Worker Exploitation in Italy." *Furniture Today*, March 31, 2014.

Holgate, Mark. "Not Just Kids." *Vogue*, February 2011, 190.

———. "Totes Amaze." *Vogue*, July 2014, 62.

Hooper, John. "Europe Immigrant Communities Under Pressure." *Guardian*, November 18, 2010.

Horwell, Veronica. "Taking High Heels to New Heights." *Guardian*, October 14, 1998.

Horyn, Cathy. "How Nicolas Got His Groove Back." *New York Times*, August 28, 2005.

———. "In Paris, Only the Moat Was Missing." *New York Times*, July 9, 2006.

———. "Silent Treatment." *Vogue*, October 1995, 146.

Howell, Georgina. "The Titan of Tight." *Vogue*, March 1990, 456–59.

Ilari, Alessandra. "Bolognese Sauce." *W*, March 2005, 252. .

———. "The Furla Formula." *Women's Wear Daily*, February 21, 2007

———. "Valextra's Second Act." *W*, March 2004, 236–37.

"Interview with Fashion Powerhouse: Marc Jacobs." *New Zealand Herald*, July 12, 2012.

Iredale, Jessica. "3.1 + 10." *Women's Wear Daily*, September 2, 2015.

———. "The First Couple." *Women's Wear Daily*, February 4, 2013.

———. "Good Things Come to Some Who Wait." *Women's Wear Daily*, July 19, 2007.

———. "Logorrhea." *Women's Wear Daily: The 100th Anniversary Issue*, November 1, 2010.

———. "Stella McCartney and the Art of Nonleather Goods." *Women's Wear Daily*, November 28, 2012.

Iturbe, Mercedes. *Walking Dreams: Salvatore Ferragamo, 1898–1960*. Spain: Editorial RM, 2006.

Jackson, Benjamin. "In Conversation: Joseph Altuzarra and Tomoko Ogura." http://thewindow.barneys.com/altuzarra-handbags-2015. Accessed April 23, 2016.

Jacobs, Laura. "From Hermès to Eternity." *Vanity Fair*, September 2007, 376.

———. "Life According to Lulu." *Vanity Fair*, January 2006, 72.

———. "Stella Performance." *Vanity Fair*, September 2012, 330.

Jacobs, Marc. @themarcjacobs Instagram post. April 23, 2016. https://www.instagram.com/p/4iFNEOGJCd/.

James, Noah. "Leather for Status." *Globe and Mail*, December 20, 1983.

Jenkins, Christopher. "Origins: Furla." *South China Morning Post*, September 5, 2007.

Johnson, Anna. *Handbags: The Power of the Purse*. New York: Workman Publishing, 2002.

———. "It Bags." *Sun Herald*, December 7, 2003.

Jones, Dylan. "Cheerful, but Never Cheap." *Sunday Times*, September 25, 1994.

Kaiser, Amanda. "Michael Kors Sweeps into Mainland China." *Women's Wear Daily*, May 8, 2014.

———. "Miu Miu Comes into Its Own." *Women's Wear Daily*, March 3, 2006.

———."Stepping Back: Ferragamo's History Runs from Rural Italy through the Sets of Hollywood to a Worldwide Luxury Empire." *Women's Wear Daily*, September 25, 2006.

Kandil, Caitlin Yoshiko. "The Bag Lady of Park Avenue." *Moment*, January 2012, 26–34.

Kane, Colleen. "Why a $223,000 Hermès Birkin Bag Might Actually Be a Good Investment." http://fortune.com/2015/06/23/hermes-birkin-investment/. Accessed April 23, 2016.

Kane, Florence. "My Secret Identity." *Vogue*, November 2008, 190.

Karimzadeh, Marc. "Accessory Designer of the Year: Marc Jacobs for Marc Jacobs." *Women's Wear Daily*, May 30, 2006.

———. "The Coach Creative." *Women's Wear Daily*, September 26, 2011.

Kemp, Charlotte."The £80 Folding It Bag That's Conquered the World." *Daily Mail*, November 5, 2015.

Kerwin, Jessica. "King Louis." *W*, August 1, 2004, 178.

"Kim Kardashian's App Is Getting Hooked Up with Accessories." *Hollywood Reporter*, September 29, 2015.

Kwaak, Jeyup, "Are Your Prada, Vuitton Bags Made in China?" *Korea Times*, August 1, 2011.

La Ferla, Ruth. "Accessories Designers Come into the Spotlight." *New York Times*, March 5, 2015.

Lake, Stephanie. *Bonnie Cashin: Chic Is Where You Find It*. New York: Rizzoli, 2016.

Lankarani, Nazanin. "Breathing New Life into an Old Brand." *International Herald Tribune*, November 19, 2009.

Larocca, Amy. "53 Minutes with . . . Pierpaolo Piccioli and Maria Grazia Chiuri." *New York Magazine*, November 30, 2015.

———. "Marc Jacobs Exposes the Latest It Bag." *Harper's Bazaar*, January 2009, 126.

———. "The Spades' New Bag." *New York Magazine*, February 22, 2010.

Lau, Venessa. "Alexander Wang Gets His Shop On." *Women's Wear Daily*, February 12, 2011.

———. "The Brilliantly Uncool Mr. Elbaz." *Women's Wear Daily*, November 1, 2010.

———. "Heir Force One." *W*, March 2009, 198.

———. "Kid Rocks." *W*, September 2009, 168.

———. "The Lovely Bones." *Women's Wear Daily*, November 17, 2011.

———. "The New Players." *Women's Wear Daily*, January 3, 2005.

———. "Pop! Goes Dior." *Women's Wear Daily*, November 30, 2011.

———. "Summer Camp." *W*, July 2008, 72.

———. "Wang's New Groove." *Women's Wear Daily*, August 6, 2008.

Leitch, Luke. "How Jane's Birkin Bag Idea Took Off." *Telegraph*, March 6, 2012.

———. "Meet Ms Mulberry, CBE." *Telegraph*, June 20, 2012.

Le-Tan, Olympia. *Olympia Le-Tan*. New York: Rizzoli, 2016.

Levy, Ariel. "Brand-New Bag." *New Yorker*, April 25, 2011, 30.

———. "Enchanted: The Transformation of Marc Jacobs." *New Yorker*, September 2008, 91–98.

Lidbury, Olivia. "Stella McCartney Gets Sheepish with Latest Handbag Design." *Telegraph*, February 20, 2013.

Lockwood, Lisa. "Growth Spurt." *Women's Wear Daily*, February 4, 2013.

Macalister-Smith, Tilly. "Allez Alaïa!" *Harper's Bazaar UK*, October 2013, 132–34.

Madsen, Axel. *Chanel: A Woman of Her Own*. New York: Henry Holt and Company, 1990.

Maier, Tomas. *Bottega Veneta*. New York: Rizzoli, 2012.

Mair, Avril. "Simply Perfect." *Harper's Bazaar UK*, June 2015, 178–81.

Marcus, Bennett. "Alber Elbaz on the Relentless Pace of Fashion." http://nymag.com/thecut/2015/10/alber-elbaz-on-the-relentless-pace-of-fashion.html. Accessed April 23, 2016.

Marriott, Hannah. "Jane Birkin Handbags Hermès—But Can She Get Her Name Back?" *Guardian*, July 29, 2015.

———. "The World in a Bag: The Rise of MCM." *Guardian*, August 14, 2014.

Martin, J. J. "Tomas Maier: Dreamweaver." *Harper's Bazaar*, February 2008, 234.

———. "What's Hot Now." *Harper's Bazaar*, October 2008, 330.

Martin, Wednesday. *Primates of Park Avenue: A Memoir*. New York: Simon & Schuster, 2015.

McCarthy, Fiona. "The Bag Lady." *Wish Magazine*, March 4, 2011, 42.

McCarthy, Lauren. "The Drag on Bags." *Women's Wear Daily*, August 19, 2015.

McHugh, Fionnuala. "Boats, Bags and a Bash." *South China Morning Post*, September 10, 1995.

MCM: Cognac Visetos Collection. New York: Assouline, 2010.

McNicoll, Tracy. "The Good Life." *Newsweek*, December 19, 2005, 62.

"Men Behind the Monogram." *Sydney Morning Herald*, March 15, 2012.

Menkes, Suzy. "Building a Brand, a Bag at a Time." *New York Times*, November 17, 2013.

Mistry, Meenal. "A Bag Called 'It.'" *W*, September 2005, 323.

Moin, David. "Bergdorf Expands the World of Bottega Veneta." *Women's Wear Daily*, April 14, 2009.

"Money Bags." *Press*, February 16, 2006.

Moodie, Martin. "Sung-Joo Kim Plans Great Asian Powerhouse." *Moodie Report*, October–November 2006, 238–45.

Moore, Booth. "Handbags Carry the Day." *Los Angeles Times*, November 15, 2015.

———. "Mrs. Prada's Epicenter Shakes up L.A." *Los Angeles Times*, July 14, 2004.

Mouzat, Virginie, and Colombe Pringle. *Roger Vivier*. New York: Rizzoli, 2013.

Mower, Sarah. "Attention, Shoppers." *Vogue*, May 2007, 121.

———. *Chloé: Attitudes*. New York: Rizzoli, 2013.

———. "Spring 2006 Ready to Wear: Givenchy." http://www.vogue.com/fashion-shows/spring-2006-ready-to-wear/givenchy. Accessed April 23, 2016.

Murphy, Anna. "Chanel Visio." *Sunday Telegraph*, September 7, 2008.

Murphy, Robert. "Hermès Heritage." *Harper's Bazaar*, February 2013, 210.

———. "Q&A Sonia Rykiel." *Women's Wear Daily*, October 1, 2008.

Nelson, Karin. "Happy Bags Happy Girls." http://www.wmagazine.com/people/insiders/2015/03/mansur-gavriel-bag-designers/. Accessed October 4, 2016.

———. "The New Guard." *W*, April 2013, 128.

———. "Snake Charmer." *W*, July 2011, 30.

Nemy, Enid. *Judith Leiber: The Artful Handbag*. New York: Harry N. Abrams, 1995.

Ong, Cat. "It's All in the Bag." *Straits Times*, October 4, 1998.

Pasols, Paul-Gérard. *Louis Vuitton: The Birth of Modern Luxury*. New York: Harry N. Abrams, 2005.

Paton, Elizabeth. "Can a Creative Star Turn Mulberry Around?" *New York Times*, February 22, 2016.

Pesce, Nicole Lyn, and Eloise Parker. "A City Gone Mad," *Daily News*, July 19, 2007.

"A Phone Call from Vogue . . . and the Start of a Fashion Transformation." *Sunday Mirror*, August 16, 1998.

Pilger, Zoe. "Alexander McQueen: Savage Beauty Review." *Independent*, March 13, 2015.

Pogoda, Dianne M. "Leather Road." *Women's Wear Daily*, September 26, 2011.

Posen, Zac. "The 2013 Time 100." *Time*, April 18, 2013.

"A Promenade through Time." *Women's Wear Daily*, September 25, 2006.

Powell, Jeff. "Chloé's Clare Waight Keller on Resort Trends, Paris and the Brand-New Everston." https://blogs.nordstrom.com/ fashion/chloe-everston-resort-collection-designer-handbag/. Accessed October 4, 2016.

Pulver, Andrew. "Tom Ford: A Single Man and His Address Book." *Guardian*, January 28, 2010.

Pungkanon, Kupluthai. "It's in the Bag." *Nation*, November 20, 2014.

Rawsthorn, Alice. "The Change Agent." *W*, March 2011, 230.

Reardon, Kate. "The Queen of Cozy Cool." *Vanity Fair*, September 2009, 208.

Rennolds Milbank, Caroline. *The Couture Accessory*. New York: Harry N. Abrams, 2002.

Ricci, Stefania, et al. *Salvatore Ferragamo: Evolving Legend, 1928–2008*. Milan: Skira; and London: Thames & Hudson, 2009.

Richards, Katie. "Chanel's 60-Year-Old Bag Is Still a Paragon of Over-the-Shoulder Fashion." *Adweek*, November 30, 2015.

Roberts, Alison. "The It Bag Is Dead." *Evening Standard*, October 6, 2008.

Roberts, Andrew. "Power Player." *W*, March 2009, 196.

Ross, Deborah. "What Is It with Women and Handbags?" *Spectator*, August 29, 2009, 18.

Royce-Greensill, Sarah. "Guicci's Alessandro Michele and the rebirth of the logo." *The Telegraph*, May 10, 2016.

Rubenstein, Hal. *100 Unforgettable Dresses*. New York: Harper Design, 2011.

Rushton, Susie. "In the Bag." *Independent*, February 15, 2005.

———. "Making His Marc." *Independent*, February 12, 2005.

Ryan, Suzanne C. "For Designer Kate Spade, Success Is in the Bag." *Boston Globe*, July 14, 1999.

Rykiel, Sonia. "Sonia Rykiel on Living with Parkinson's." *Harper's Bazaar UK*, August 2012, 49–50.

Scott, Jeremy. *Jeremy Scott*. New York: Rizzoli, 2014.

Seah, Lionel. "Sacs and the City." *Straits Times*, September 19, 2002.

Searbrook, John. "Shoe Dreams." *New Yorker*, May 10, 2004.

Shaw, Bernard. "Interview with Margaret Thatcher." http://www.cnn.com/WORLD/9706/30/thatcher.transcript/. Accessed April 23, 2016.

Sherman, Lauren. "Beyond the 'It' Bag." http://www.businessoffashion.com/articles/intelligence/beyond-the-it-bag. Accessed April 23, 2016.

Silver, Cameron. "Tomas Maier: Dreamweaver." *Harper's Bazaar*, February 2008.

Sinclair, Charlotte. *Vogue on Christian Dior*. New York: Harry N. Abrams, 2015.

Slater, Sasha. "Rise Up." *Harper's Bazaar*, November 2013, 111–12.

Smith, Ray A. "Double Vision." *Australian*, July 26, 2014.

Smith, Virginia. "Last Look." *Vogue*, June 2010, 194.

Socha, Miles. "Back to Their Roots: 'Heritage' Key Focus for Fashion Brands." *Women's Wear Daily*, February 2, 2010.

———. "Dior, Harrods Collaborate on Extravaganza." *Women's Wear Daily*, March 12, 2013.

———. "The Fashion Dean." *Women's Wear Daily*, March 2, 2016.

———. "Fashion's Brand Reviver." *Women's Wear Daily*, May 2, 2012.

———. "Givenchy's Riccardo Tisci Looks Ahead." *Women's Wear Daily*, May 25, 2016.

———. "The Little Engine That Could." *Women's Wear Daily*, April 29, 2015.

———. "Luxury Gets Hyper." *Women's Wear Daily*, August 15, 2011.

Solca, Luca. "The Truth About Handbags." http://www.businessoffashion.com/articles/opinion/the-truth-about-handbags. Accessed April 23, 2016.

Soo, Candy. "Bottega Veneta." *South China Morning Post*, July 4, 2007.

Sowray, Bibby. "One to Watch: Mansur Gavriel." *Telegraph*, September 5, 2013.

———. "Saint Laurent's Sac De Jour Becomes the Bag du Jour." *Telegraph*, October 17, 2013.

———. "Who Would Pay $55,000 for a Rucksack?" *Telegraph*, July 5, 2013.

Specter, Michael. "The Kingdom: In the Court of Valentino." *New Yorker*, September 26, 2005, 124.

Spencer, Mimi. "The Year Our Handbag Habit Got Out of Control." *Observer*, December 2, 2007.

Steele, Valerie, and Laird Borrelli. *Handbags: A Lexicon of Style*. New York: Rizzoli, 1999.

Steigrad, Alexandra. "Krakoff Exiting Coach to Focus on Own Line." *Women's Wear Daily*, April 24, 2013.

Strugatz, Rachel. "Charting the New 'Modern Luxury.'" *Women's Wear Daily*, October 29, 2012.

Sullivan, Courtney J. "Ouch! My Bag Is Killing Me." *New York Times*, December 7, 2006.

Sussman, Jeffrey. *No Mere Bagatelles*. New York: Judith Leiber LLC, 2009.

Thomas, Dana. *Deluxe: How Luxury Lost Its Luster*. Reprint edition. London: Penguin Books, 2008.

———. "Made in China on the Sly." *International Herald Tribune*, November 24, 2007.

———. "What Hubert de Givenchy Can Teach You About Fashion." *Harper's Bazaar*, June 2005, 168.

Thurman, Judith. "Dressed to Thrill." *New Yorker*, May 16, 2011, 116.
Tomshinsky, Ida. *Bags & Purses: The Story of Chic and Practicality*. Bloomington: Xlibris, 2016.
Topolski, Julia, and Marc Karimzadeh. "Crystal Persuasion." *W*, September 2003, 274.
"Tradition, Customization Key to Goyard Success." *Daily Yomiuri*, March 13, 2009.
"Travel Diaries." http://destinationkors.michaelkors.com/jet-set/travel-diaries/. Accessed April 23, 2016.
Turra, Alessandra. "V Is for Versatile." *Women's Wear Daily*, October 15, 2012.
van der Post, Lucia. "A Clasp Act." *Times*, August 10, 2007.
Vernon, Polly. "Mister Money Bags." *Times*, July 5, 2014.
Walden, Celia. "The It Bag Is Dead." *Daily Telegraph*, May 5, 2011.
Walker, Harriet. "Olympia Le-Tan and the World's Coolest Book Club." *Independent*, February 11, 2013.
White Sidell, Misty. "Proenza Schouler Reassesses Handbag Line, Unveils Updated Version of PS1." *Women's Wear Daily*, June 6, 2016.
Wilcox, Claire. *A Century of Bags*. London: Quarto, 1997.
Wilsinson, Tracy. "Slaving in the Lap of Luxury." *Los Angeles Times*, February 20, 2008.
Wilson, Anamaria. "Flying Coach." *W*, December 2005, 118.
Wilson, Bee. "Fierce, Feathered and Fragile." *Guardian*, March 7, 2015.
Wilson, Eric. "Instincts as Sharp as Ever." *New York Times*, October 7, 2009.
Witchel, Alex. "Handbags That Make Headlines." *New York Times*, May 1, 1996.
Yaeger, Lynn. "Carried Away." *Atlantic Monthly*, April 1, 2007.
Yip, May. "The Pragmatist." *Business Times Singapore*, January 4, 2014.
Zargani, Luisa. "Debut of Pierpaolo Piccioli as Valentino's Sole Creative Director with Rockstud Spike Bag." *Women's Wear Daily*, September 8, 2016.
———. "Scott's Vision for Moschino." *Women's Wear Daily*, February 19, 2014.
Zhang, Jing. "Stella Standing." *South China Morning Post*, August 4, 2013.

PHOTOGRAPHY AND ILLUSTRATION CREDITS

Advertising Archives: 38, 70, 80, 126, 164, 172, 174–175, 222.

AKG: 195: © Les Arts Décoratifs, Paris/ Jean Tholance/akg-images.

Alamy: 40-41: The Advertising Archives/ Alamy Stock Photo; 81: Daily Mail/ Rex/Alamy Stock Photo; 110, right: Photo 12/Alamy Stock Photo; 151: Robert Vos/ EPA/Alamy Stock Photo; 212, bottom: The Advertising Archives/Alamy Stock Photo.

Archivio Foto Locchi: 201.

Art & Commerce: 55 and 118–119: Regan Cameron/Art & Commerce.

Art Partner: 160: Anthony Cotsifas/Art Partner.

Associated Press: 144, top: Rex Features/ AP Images.

Bauer Griffin: 125: Jack Ludlam/ bauergriffinonline.com.

Blau Blut Edition: 22–23: The Urban Spotter/Blaublut-Edition.com; 128–129: Frenchy Style/Blaublut-Edition.com; 190: Sandra Semburg/Blaublut-Edition.com; 212, top: Carola de Armas/Blaublut-Edition.com.

Botkier: 10: Monica Botkier; 155: Sophie Elgort for Coco Rocha x Botkier.

Bridgeman Images: 52: Archives Charmet/Bridgeman Images; 73: Berard, Christian (1902–49)/ Bibliothèque des Arts Décoratifs, Paris, France/Archives Charmet/Bridgeman Images; 76: © The Advertising Archives/ Bridgeman Images; 77: Bridgeman Images; 90: Gruau, René (1909–2004)/ Archives Charmet/Bridgeman Images; 100, right: Bridgeman Images; 108: Collection Gregoire/Bridgeman Images; 111: Bridgeman Images.

Calero, Anita: 178: © Anita Calero/ Supervision NY.

Cole, Jo: 30.

Condé Nast: 28: Christopher Coppola/ Condé Nast Collection; 83: Tim Hout/ Condé Nast Collection.

Everett Collection: 18; 53: Advertising Archive/Courtesy Everett Collection; 100, left: Mirrorpix/Courtesy Everett Collection; 110, left: Everett Collection.

FirstView: 140, 154.

Feurer, Hans: 186.

Gagosian Gallery: 146: © Richard Prince. Courtesy the artist and Gagosian.

Gaslight Advertising Archives: 58, 59, 64, 68, 88, 91, 136, 137 (4), 138, 139, 189, 208, 209.

Getty Image: 17: Michael Tran/ FilmMagic/Getty Images; 19: Catwalking/ Getty Images; 32 (2): Guy Marineau/Condé Nast/Getty Images; 33: David Roemer/ Figarophoto/Contour by Getty Images; 48: Christian Vierig/Getty Images; 54, top: Santi Visalli Inc./Getty Images; 54, bottom: Bettmann/Getty Images; 57: Willy Rizzo/Paris Match/Getty Images; 72: Tim Graham/Getty Images; 94: Melodie Jeng/Getty Images; 96: Alo Ceballos/FilmMagic/Getty Images; 97: Ernesto Ruscio/Getty Images; 101: Henry Clarke/Condé Nast/Getty Images; 102: Bettmann/Getty Images; 103: Ron Galella/Getty Images; 104–105: Christian Vierig/Getty Images; 109: Howard Sochurek/The LIFE Picture Collection/Getty Images; 132: Bert Stern/ Condé Nast/Getty Images; 143, top: Glenn Koenig/Los Angeles Times/Getty Images; 145, top: Robert Francois/AFP/Getty Images; 147, top: Stephane Cardinale/ Corbis/Getty Images; 150, top: Loomis Dean/The LIFE Picture Collection/ Getty Images; 166: Kirstin Sinclair/Getty

Images; 168: Vanni Bassetti/Getty Images; 196: Timur Emek/Getty Images; 204-205: David Montgomery/Getty Images; 210: James Devaney/GC Images/Getty Images; 213: Vanni Bassetti/Getty Images; 226: Carl Oscar August Erickson/Condé Nast via Getty Images.

Goldstein, Lori: 112, 114–115, 116, 117: Bramble Trionfo, courtesy of The Thick; 113: Jason Frank Rotherberg.

Holland, Sophy: 156.

Leone, Paolo: 206.

Lloyd-Evans, Jason: 122–123.

Mary Evans Picture Library: 133: © Illustrated London News Ltd/Mary Evans.

Neal Peters Collection: 78–79.

Paramount Pictures: 158 (3).

Schneider, Luke: 62.

Shutterstock: 150, bottom: Nick Harvey/REX/Shutterstock; 177: Wayne Tippetts/REX/Shutterstock; 180: Schwab/StarPix/REX/Shutterstock; 182, top left: Jim Smeal/BEI/REX/Shutterstock; 182, top right: SIPA/REX/Shutterstock; 182, bottom: Lauren/Variety/REX/Shutterstock; 183: Anna Sandul/REX/Shutterstock; 203: Beretta/Sims/REX/Shutterstock.

The Licensing Project: 220: Jacob Sadrak + Carrol Cruz/Thelicensingproject.com; 223: Ian Bartlett/TheLicensingProject.com.

Trunk Archive: 16: The Coveteur/Trunk Archive; 20: Adam Katz Sinding/Trunk Archive; 24–25: Kevin Tachman/Trunk Archive; 26–27: Tommy Ton/Trunk Archive; 34: RM/Trunk Archive; 36–37: The Coveteur/Trunk Archive; 42 and 43: Kevin Tachman/Trunk Archive; 44 and 46–47: Phil Oh/Trunk Archive; 49: Tommy Ton/Trunk Archive; 50: RM/Trunk Archive; 60–61: Phil Oh/Trunk Archive; 66-67: Tommy Ton/Trunk Archive; 74–75: The Coveteur/Trunk Archive; 82: RM/Trunk Archive; 84, 86-87: Trunk Archive; 98: David Burton/Trunk Archive; 106: Kenneth Willardt/Trunk Archive; 134–135: Giampaolo Sgura/Trunk Archive; 148: Melanie Galea TheStreetMuse/Trunk Archive; 152, 159: Garance Doré/Trunk Archive; 162–163: Adam Katz Sinding/Trunk Archive; 170–171: Giampaolo Sgura/Trunk Archive; 176: The Coveteur/Trunk Archive: 184: Tommy Ton/Trunk Archive; 192 and 202: Melanie Galea TheStreetMuse/Trunk Archive; 216: Lee Oliveira/Trunk Archive; 218–219: Jason Schmidt/Trunk Archive.

Van den Hoek, Judith: front and back cover, 6, 15, 93, 130, 214, 224.

Waring, Michael: 167.

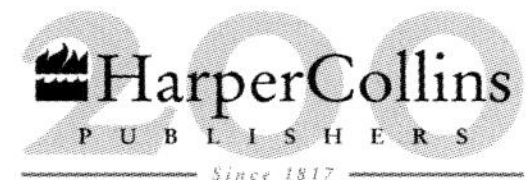

HANDBAGS: A LOVE STORY

First published in 2017 by
Harper Design
An Imprint of HarperCollins*Publishers*
195 Broadway
New York, NY 10007
Tel: (212) 207-7000
Fax: (855) 746-6023
harperdesign@harpercollins.com
www.hc.com

Distributed throughout the world by
HarperCollins*Publishers*
195 Broadway
New York, NY 10007

ISBN 978-0-06-242835-6
Library of Congress Control Number: 2015939516

Printed in China
First Printing, 2017

Cover illustrations by Judith van den Hoek

Art Direction by Lynne Yeamans
Cover and book design by Shubhani Sarkar

ABOUT THE AUTHOR

Monica Botkier is the founder and creative director of Botkier. She launched her business in 2003 by creating an affordable designer bag, Trigger, which started a cult following. Her accessories and bags have been spotted on some of the most recognized women in the world and featured in the pages of *ELLE*, *Harper's Bazaar*, *InStyle*, *Marie Claire*, and *Vogue*. A member of the Council of Fashion Designers of America, she lives in Brooklyn, New York, with her husband and three children.